Polkabilly

AMERICAN MUSICSPHERES

Series Editor
Mark Slobin

Fiddler on the Move
Exploring the Klezmer World
Mark Slobin

The Lord's Song in a Strange Land
Music and Identity in Contemporary Jewish Worship
Jeffrey A. Summit

Lydia Mendoza's Life in Music
Yolanda Broyles-González

Four Parts, No Waiting
A Social History of American Barbershop Harmony
Gage Averill

Louisiana Hayride
Radio and Roots Music Along the Red River
Tracey E. W. Laird

Balkan Fascination
Creating an Alternative Music Culture in America
Mirjana Lausevic

Polkabilly
How the Goose Island Ramblers Redefined American Folk Music
James P. Leary

Cajun Breakdown
The Emergence of an American-Made Music
Ryan André Brasseau

POLKABILLY

How the Goose Island Ramblers Redefined

American Folk Music

James P. Leary

New York
OXFORD
UNIVERSITY PRESS

2006

OXFORD

UNIVERSITY PRESS

Oxford University Press, Inc., publishes works that further
Oxford University's objective of excellence
in research, scholarship, and education.

Oxford   New York
Auckland   Cape Town   Dar es Salaam   Hong Kong   Karachi
Kuala Lumpur   Madrid   Melbourne   Mexico City   Nairobi
New Delhi   Shanghai   Taipei   Toronto

With offices in
Argentina   Austria   Brazil   Chile   Czech Republic   France   Greece
Guatemala   Hungary   Italy   Japan   Poland   Portugal   Singapore
South Korea   Switzerland   Thailand   Turkey   Ukraine   Vietnam

First published as an Oxford
University Press paperback 2010

Published by Oxford University Press, Inc.
198 Madison Avenue, New York, New York 10016

www.oup.com

Library of Congress Cataloging-in-Publication Data
Leary, James P.
Polkabilly: how the Goose Island Ramblers redefined American
folk music / James P. Leary.
p. cm. – (American Musicspheres)
Includes bibliographical references (p.) and index.
ISBN 978-01-9975696-4
1. Goose Island Ramblers. 2. Polkabilly music–history and criticism.
I. Title. II. Series.
ML421.G66L43 2006
781.62'130775—dc22   2005023081

The audio files on the referenced Campanion CD are available
online at www.oup.com/us/polkability

Printed in the United States of America
on acid-free paper

Preface

> The syncretic and emergent qualities of American folk culture, influenced by complex interethnic relationships and popular culture, are often excluded from public presentation.
>
> —Baron and Spitzer 1992

The phrases "American folk music" and "Goose Island Ramblers" are hardly synonymous in Americans' thoughts and speech. And yet I have come to think of them as inextricable. Nor does the term "polkabilly" trip off of many tongues. And yet I am convinced that it should. What links these words? What do they mean? Why have their connections and significance been largely unnoticed? Why should we care?

Notions of what is "American" or, conversely, "un-American" have been debated from the nation's origins through the present. Concepts of "folk," particularly when applied to music, likewise have sparked controversy as often as consensus. Meanwhile, distinctive regional styles of music, however enduring and pervasive, have sometimes escaped widespread recognition until christened with a succinct, compelling name (blues, jazz, salsa, zydeco, hillbilly, polka) and promoted by entrepreneurs, practitioners, scholars, and other advocates.

In December 1997, I served with a dozen folklorists and ethnomusicologists on a panel convened by the Folk Arts Program of the National Endowment for the Arts to decide which traditional artists—nominees from all over the United States—would be honored as national treasures—as 1998's recipients of prestigious National Heritage fellowships. Gathered in a room for three days, we discussed the lives, viewed the works, heard the sounds, and assessed the worth of several hundred traditional craftspersons, storytellers, dancers, and musicians—especially musicians. In the end, the 11 awardees included 7 musicians or musical groups: the Aspara Ensemble, exponents of Cambodian court music from the greater Washington, D.C., area; Eddie Blazonczyk, a Polish-American polka band leader from Chicago; the Tejano conjunto accordionist Tony De La Rosa; the Epstein Brothers, klezmer musicians raised in the Jewish neighborhoods of Brooklyn and Manhattan's Lower East Side; a Greek Byzantine chanter, Harilaos Papapostolou, from Potomac, Maryland; the African-American blues and gospel guitarist and singer Roebuck "Pops" Staples from Chicago by way of the Mississippi Delta; and the Kansas City swing fiddler Claude Williams. In previous years, including three when I'd served on the panel, fellowships were awarded to a mariachi musician, an Armenian oud player, and a Lao singer, all from California; a Finnish accordionist from the Upper Peninsula of Michigan; southern Appalachian fiddlers, banjo players, guitarists, and ballad singers; Cajun and zydeco musicians from Louisiana; an Apache fiddler from Arizona; an Irish flautist from the Bronx; and many more.

Participants in each panel unfailingly invested their discussions of a dazzling array of genres and individuals with remarkable expertise. Again and again, they were able to situate and evaluate the significance of this musician or that style within the larger fabric of American cultural life. The Goose Island Ramblers, however, mystified them. Here were three men from south-central Wisconsin, togged out variously in cowboy hats and Viking horns, playing a shifting array of instruments (guitar, mandolin, fiddle, eight-string fiddle, one-string electric toilet plunger, harmonica, Jew's harp, jug, piano accordion, and bandonion), singing in Norwegian, German, Polish, English, and "broken English," while favoring a repertoire that shuffled, bent, and fused British and Irish fiddle tunes, ballads, and sentimental songs with Hawaiian marches, Swiss yodels, and the polkas, waltzes, schottisches, and mazurkas of Central and Northern Europe. Panelists were baffled, several blurting, "What kind of music is this?" or "I don't know how to evaluate this." The Goose Island Ramblers defied their categories and eluded their experiences.

Neither thoroughgoing performers within an old time Anglo-American country music tradition, nor single-minded proponents of a particular ethnic American genre, the Goose Island Ramblers clearly inhabited and sustained a hybrid, or syncretic, or creolized musical territory. Bewildering to my colleagues, the Ramblers' "soundscape," to borrow Mark Slobin's useful phrase, was one in which I'd been immersed for most of my life.

I was born in 1950 and raised in the small northwestern Wisconsin city of Rice Lake. Like most in my community, I heard various forms of popular music from afar during the 1950s and 1960s via radio, television, and commercial recordings. Yet I also encountered other sounds in homes; on the school playground; in churches, halls, and taverns; and through broadcasts of locally generated programs. Perched on a hill west of town, WJMC radio allotted air time to the Erik Berg Band's blending of Scandinavian dance melodies with late nineteenth-century pop tunes, to the Polish Barn Dance's mixed Slavic-hillbilly repertoire, and to occasional yodeling by Schweitzers like John Giezendanner from nearby Barron. Sixty miles to the south, in Eau Claire, the Rhythm Playboys from Osseo had a weekly show on WEAU-TV that combined honky tonk songs with Scandinavian and German dance pieces. Similar shows, fusing various strains of "country" music with Scandinavian, German, Czech, Slovenian, and Polish tunes, beamed our way from KSTP in St. Paul, WCCO in Minneapolis, and, if the weather was right, WDSM in Duluth. Around my town and the surrounding countryside, I encountered schoolmates singing bawdy, blasphemous comic songs in mock "Scandihoovian"- and "Dutchman"-inflected English. Small combos with an accordion, drums, and perhaps a guitar or fiddle entertained for wedding dances at the Moose Club, in the ski lodge at Mount Hardscrabble in the Blue Hills to the east, or at rural watering holes like Sokup's Tavern and Virgil's Bunny Bar. Otto Rindlisbacher, proprietor of the Buckhorn Bar and Café on Rice Lake's Main Street festooned his walls with "the world's largest assortment of odd lumberjack musical instruments." The son of Swiss immigrants, he was not only adept at playing alpine ländlers on the button accordion, but also masterful with both the nine-string *hardingfele*, or Hardanger fiddle, of Norwegian immigrants and the conventional four-string fiddle on which he deftly bowed the jigs, reels, and "crooked tunes" of Irish, French, metís, and Ojibwe lumbercamp musicians.

Adventurous players in the Rice Lake of my boyhood days, like the Goose Island Ramblers 250 miles to the south, drew on a broad span of locally performed, ethnically grounded musical traditions, then combined those influences with several genres whirling their way through mass media to fashion an eclectic yet regionally understandable style. However discernible to experienced insiders, that style nonetheless has lacked both larger recognition within American culture and a distinctive name.

Perhaps because I had not yet fully grasped these truths on that December day in Washington, I was momentarily as baffled by my colleagues' ignorance as they were by the Ramblers' music. Had I been quicker, I might have pointed out that observers a century before were similarly perplexed and astonished by the nameless New Orleans sonic melange that came to be known as jazz. Had I been much, much quicker, I might have pointed out that the musical stream navigated by the Goose Island Ramblers has been around as long as jazz, but for complicated reasons bound up partly with accident and partly with constructions of race, ethnicity, region, and national identity, America's folklorists, ethnomusicologists, and kindred tastemakers have elevated some folk musical forms while denigrating or ignoring others.

I wasn't quick. But in missing my moment, I was moved eventually to write this book.

My tasks, consequently, are to win recognition for the music of my hometown, of the Goose Island Ramblers, of America's Upper Midwest— by sketching its broad history, its particular embrace by exemplary performers, its relationship to ideological currents—and to dub that music polkabilly.

Hence I seek, through successive chapters, to establish the Upper Midwest as a region characterized by a creolized culture that has resisted the assimilative forces of a WASP-dominated mainstream while fostering polkabilly sounds; to examine the formative musical experiences of each of the Goose Island Ramblers' members, particularly as they resonate with the experiences of their fellow regional musicians; to analyze the group's live sets, recorded performances, and varied audiences within the regional con-

Figure P.1. Cotton dishtowel with polkabilly band, from the author's childhood home, Rice Lake, Wisconsin, c. 1955.

text of the Upper Midwest; and to reassess the nature of American folk and vernacular music to include performers like the Goose Island Ramblers and regions like the Upper Midwest.

This study draws on more than 25 years of field research and scholarship devoted to the region's music, as well as on a decade of intermittent work with the Goose Island Ramblers.

Throughout that long span, whether working directly with regional musicians or encountering them along the way, I have had support from the

Figure P.2. Postcard of Otto Rindlisbacher in his "museum bar," the
Buckhorn, 1950s. Author's collection.

American Folklife Center at the Library of Congress, the Folk Arts Program of the National Endowment for the Arts, the Office of Folklife Programs at the Smithsonian Institution, the Illinois Humanities Council, the Michigan Traditional Arts Program at Michigan State University, the Minnesota Arts Board, the Minnesota Historical Society, the Wisconsin Arts Board, the Wisconsin Folk Museum, the Wisconsin Historical Society, the Wisconsin Humanities Council, Folklore Village Farm, Up North Films, Northland College, and the University of Wisconsin's Center for the Study of Upper Midwestern Cultures, Folklore Program, and Mills Music Library. Within those organizations, a dedicated contingent of musically oriented folklorists, ethnomusicologists, filmmakers, and archivists has been especially helpful, including Judith Gray, Bucky Halker, Joe Hickerson, Cathy Kerst, Geri Laudati, Michael Loukinen, Doug Miller, Phil Nusbaum, Nicki Saylor, John Solon, Laurie Sommers, Nick Spitzer, Steve Sundell, and Tom Vennum.

Roby Cogswell, the long-time state folklorist for his native Tennessee, coined the term "polkabilly" on hearing a Goose Island Ramblers recording for the first time. I wish I'd thought of it first. An array of independent scholars generously shared hard-won insights and hard-to-find source materials: Bob Andresen, Julane Beetham, John Berquist, Paul Gifford, LeRoy Larson, Gus Meade, Dick Spottswood, Oren and Toni Tikkanen, Paul Tyler, Nick Vrooman, and Christoph Wagner. Many Goose Island Ramblers fans, Bill Lagerroos especially, offered reminiscences regarding the band's performances in the 1960s and 1970s. The incomparable investigations of polka music and immigrant songs by University of Wisconsin, Milwaukee, historian Victor Greene were constant inspirations. Closer to home, in the Madison area, I was very lucky indeed to learn from Richard March, Phil Martin, and Bill Malone. I first heard of the Goose Island Ramblers from Richard March in 1973 and first met them through Phil Martin a decade later. Richard, with whom I had the pleasure of producing Wisconsin public radio shows featuring the group, has remained a font of knowledge on all Upper Midwestern folk musical matters. Thanks to Phil Martin and the philanthropy of Bill Graham, I was able not only to conduct extensive interviews with the Ramblers in 1990 but also to benefit from earlier field research Phil had undertaken with the superb documentary photographer and photographic researcher Lewis Koch. Bill C. Malone's insights into the Goose Island Ramblers' relationship to country music, offered while we took in several of the band's performances, were as delightful as they were valuable.

Margaret McEntire, while a folklore student at the University of Wisconsin, helped me to track down numerous accounts of polkabilly music in local histories and reminiscences. Students in my American folk and vernacular music course also offered a critical sounding board for my observations about American folk music and the Goose Island Ramblers, while demonstrating unbridled enthusiasm for the group's music. Onno Brouwer of the University of Wisconsin's Cartography Lab made a pair of fine maps charting both the Goose Island Ramblers' range and the regional presence of polkabilly scenes. Nicki Saylor, archivist at the Center for the Study of Upper Midwestern Cultures, made digital scans of maps and photographs.

Janet Gilmore, intrepid partner and fellow folklorist, along with our kids, Bella and Finn, have enjoyed the Ramblers as much as I and has supported my research in every phase.

Were it not for Mark Slobin, however, this book would never have been written. As editor of the American Musicspheres series in which this volume appears, he proposed that I contribute something about the Midwest. Then he waited and waited, coaxing and cajoling, critiquing and encouraging, until at last I was finished. Thanks, Mark! Kim Robinson, Norm Hirschy, and Suzanne Ryan, music editors at Oxford University Press, were unfailingly helpful, pleasant, and professional. Stacey Hamilton, the book's production editor, and her fine staff worked ably and swiftly to ensure stylistic consistency and factual accuracy. Kip Lornell, Neil Rosenberg, and a pair of anonymous readers of both the prospectus from which this book grew and the final manuscript offered kind words and many valuable suggestions—most of which I have tried to incorporate.

Finally, I cannot thank the Goose Island Ramblers enough. The late Windy Whitford, George Gilbertsen, and Bruce Bollerud, along with their wives and families, cheerfully endured my many questions and requests. Bruce and George both read the manuscript thoroughly, providing numerous corrections, clarifications, and additions. While these editorial efforts are largely hidden, the Ramblers' eloquent words and telling experiences are, as they should be, the heart and soul of this study.

Contents

Polkabilly

1

Polkabilly
Old Time Music in the Upper Midwest

No field collector can of course investigate all the United States, or even a
succession of regions, in one lifetime. But fieldwork done in depth in a
relatively limited area can illuminate the entire American scene.

—Dorson 1952

Image and Authority

My name it is nothing, my age it means less,
The country I come from is called the Midwest.

—Dylan 1963 M

So sang Bob Dylan, guitar-playing nouveau New Yorker, having shed his
identity as Robert Zimmerman from the accordion-obsessed mining town
of Hibbing, Minnesota. From his cosmopolitan vantage, in a faux-folk,
American Gothic, neoprimitive mode, Dylan evoked an anonymous Midwestern everyman, a plainspoken, God-fearing voice from America's corn-
fed heartland.[1]

Ohio, Indiana, Illinois, Michigan, Wisconsin, Minnesota, Iowa, Missouri—
perhaps extending into the Dakotas, Nebraska, and Kansas.

The Midwest. The Middle West.

Like middle-aged, middlebrow, middle of the road, middle class, and
middle American, the words suggest, at best, reliable stolidity, at worst,
dull mediocrity. Scholars, media producers, and artists painting the region's face within America's family portrait have often shared Dylan's
broad brush. Lacking the antiquity of the East, the tragedy of the South,
or the destiny of the West, the Midwest is most often conceived of as an en-
duringly average region in the American imagination: a vast flat land to fly
over where, despite rusty factories and troubled farms, small towns and
neighborhoods persist and family values remain intact.

The Midwest's distinctive folk music, however, and especially that of the
Upper Midwest, contests such homogenized, largely condescending, occasionally romantic visions. Indeed Dylan's conjuring of America's regional
middle has more to do with outsiders' stereotypes than with insiders' self-

3

conceptions, more to do with the constraints of language than with less restricted reality. Consider insider Bob Andresen's observations:

> In the Upper Midwest the various immigrant groups who brought their music from Europe began to exchange songs and tunes. The music of one ethnic group would often be picked up by other ethnic groups. And all of this music began to mix with American popular music and with American country music. When we had live radio shows in such places as Duluth, Fargo, and Minneapolis, the programs featured a mix of old time ethnic music and regional country music. (*Northland Hoedown* 1984 M)

So said Bob Andresen, a voice of clarity, truth, and deceptive simplicity. The occasion was a special two-hour version of his normally half-hour "Northland Hoedown" program, complete with an array of performers and broadcast live over KUMD radio from a packed Duluth, Minnesota, auditorium.

Aficionados of American folk music might well imagine similar retrospective observations, with substitutions of people and places, emanating over the airwaves from Atlanta, Georgia, where the exuberant hillbilly fiddling of Gid Tanner and his Skillet Lickers and the bottleneck blues guitar wizardry of Blind Willie McTell once prevailed; or from the trans-Mississippi cotton country of Memphis, Tennessee, and Helena, Arkansas, home to so many pioneering blues, jug band, gospel, and rockabilly artists; or from Lafayette, Louisiana, in the damp rice and cattle country spawning Cajun and zydeco sounds; or from the cities of central Texas where Blind Lemon Jefferson, Leadbelly, Narciso Martinez, Valerio Longoria, Bob Wills, and Ernest Tubb made their respective reputations as proponents of emerging blues, conjunto, western swing, and honky tonk genres. In contrast, the cities of Duluth, Fargo, and Minneapolis invoked by Andresen are seldom associated with American folk music, except by a few who remember that Robert Zimmerman lived in two of them before departing for New York to become Bob Dylan. Similarly, what Andresen describes as the Upper Midwest's "various immigrant groups who brought their music from Europe" are ignored at best, or at worst regarded as sausage-chomping accordion squeezers garbed in short pants and puffy shirts.

But why have some people and places come to be revered as thoroughgoing American folk musical exponents and hearths, while others are ignored or disparaged?

Can it be that the Upper Midwestern music Andresen circumscribes is too recent, too varied, too fluid? To be sure, as modifiers of "music," the words Andresen chooses—"ethnic," "regional country," "old time" (and, one might add "roots," "traditional," and "folk")—all connote long-standing, even mystical, and organic relationships between people and places. Yet such seemingly bounded, immutable associations are invariably belied by the combinatory and dynamic practices of musical performers in everyday life. In American places especially, indigenous, enslaved, and immigrant peoples and their descendants have not only contended and intermingled locally for centuries, but also been influenced by a succession of popular musical strains. To consider grand notions of American folk music realistically, then, is to recognize that complex musical changes and exchanges are not the exception but the rule. Aptly characterized by folklorist Alan Lomax as "folk music with overdrive," the bluegrass sound of Bill Monroe—to sketch one example among many—emerged in the wake of World War II out of the convoluted interplay of Anglo-American and African-American sacred and secular performances. These performances were further creatively infused by Monroe, a rural Kentuckian who had once toiled in a northern Indiana oil refinery, with both a heartbreaking nostalgia for lost backwoods worlds and a hard-headed, jumped-up, modern fervor anticipating rockabilly.[2]

Perhaps the fact that we know a great deal about the particular cross-fertilization and evolution of some local and regional musics—e.g., bluegrass, western swing, country, blues, gospel, Cajun, zydeco, and conjunto—while other nonetheless widespread, vital, and compelling genres merit scant recognition has less to do with those who participate in neglected musical scenes than it does with those who name, promote, study, and consume what gets called American folk music. As I will argue more fully in chapter 6, the study of American folk and vernacular music, until very recently, has focused largely on the Anglo-Celtic and African-American traditions of performers in the East, the South, and the West. This intellectual preoccupation with a British-derived mainstream tempered by the frontier and powerfully affected by African-American "others" has been interwoven with the ideology of a consensus approach to American history. Traditional performers outside of the aforementioned cultural groups and geographical regions have been either ignored or scrutinized as isolated practitioners of discrete ethnic repertoires (e.g., Cajun, Chicano, Ojibwe, Polish) who nonetheless battle continuously against their own and, especially, their audiences' assimilation to the media-disseminated strains of American popular music. We know little, consequently, about performers whose repertoires are highly eclectic, who combine both local and popular traditions, and who are based in regions not canonized as folk music hearths by prior scholars.[3]

Andresen's Mix

Robert F. "Bob" Andresen was one such performer. His astute reflections on the music of the Upper Midwest resulted from lifelong experience.[4] Born in 1937 in Minneapolis, Bob Andresen was raised on a farm near Outing in northern Minnesota's Cass County. His dad, Bjarne, played accordion for local house parties, barn dances, and resort doings, emphasizing a mixture of old country dance tunes (the schottische *"Gamle Ole Mattis"/*

Figure 1.1. Robert "Bob" Andresen, polkabilly musician, scholar, and producer of the "Northland Hoedown" on Duluth's KUMD radio, mid-1980s. Mills Music Library Collection, University of Wisconsin.

Old Ole Mattis), singing cowboy pieces ("Moonlight on the Colorado"), and dialect songs ("Ole Olson, the Hobo from Norway"). Bjarne's parents, likewise performers, had emigrated from southern Norway to Minnesota in the early 1900s. Thorvald Andresen (originally Andreassen) favored an array of Norwegian songs and hymns, while his wife backed him on guitar. Young Bob Andresen absorbed bits of his grandparents' repertoire, while learning to play accordion from his dad.

Back in the 1940s and early 1950s, the airwaves teemed with live music, and Andresen was captivated by the regional mix of ethnic polka and northern country sounds from Fargo, Duluth, Minneapolis, and beyond. One of his favorites was Famous Tim Lashua, a French Canadian from the logging town of Rhinelander, Wisconsin, who played guitar and sang on Duluth and Eau Claire radio stations KDAL and WEAU.

> I can remember getting off the school bus and Famous [Lashua] had a show in the afternoon. We had goats then. I'd give water to the goats and hay, and tune in something like Don Messer and the Islanders from Canada. Then Saturday nights, it was just full of live shows. Not only local things, but far away: WLS ["Barn Dance" from Chicago] and WSM ["Grand Ole Opry"] from Nashville. . . . But the local shows were really interesting. Out of WDAY Fargo every noon came the Co-op Shoppers, a group named for a farm co-op. And they had accordion and fiddle and yodelers and everything. (Andresen 1994 I)

The Norwegian and rural American stylings of "Slim Jim" (Ernest Iverson of Broten, Minnesota) over WDGY from Minneapolis were a special favorite with dialect songs like "Ay Yust Don't Give a Hoot" and "The Vistling, Drifting Snow."[5]

In 1954, Bob moved to Minnesota's twin cities, Minneapolis and St. Paul, for a brief stretch at the University of Minnesota, followed by a succession of factory and office jobs. Eventually he became an apprentice sign painter, finished art school, and made his living as a graphic artist. During those first years away from home, he concentrated on guitar, while dabbling with other stringed instruments: steel guitar, mandolin, and banjo. His musical cohorts were other rural Minnesotans who had come to town. Working a tremolo bar to ethereal perfection, he picked hymns like "Near the Cross" and *"Den Store Hvite Flokk"* (Behold a Host of Radiant White) on electric guitar for old folks on the porch of his rooming house. Some evenings found him in taverns jamming with metís fiddlers from the Turtle Mountains of North Dakota or with Finnish singers like Harold and Niilo Oja from Kettle River. By the end of the 1950s, Andresen was playing twin cities' tavern jobs with groups like the Hoedowners and the Woodchoppers that emphasized rustic roots.

Bob married JoAnn Alberg in 1964 and moved to Duluth in 1965. Adjacent to Superior, Wisconsin, and a harbor city at the southwestern end of Lake Superior, Duluth was home to a diverse array of musical performers: Croatians, Poles, Slovenians, Finns, Norwegians, Swedes, Ojibwes, French, and metís sustaining and combining Balkan tamburitza music, polkas, waltzes, Old World hymns, Canadian fiddle tunes, American country songs, pop standards, and rockabilly with gleeful abandon. In 1970, Bob and JoAnn joined with her brother and sister-in-law, Dale and Dorie Alberg, to form the Wildwoods, a four-piece band that played in local taverns and halls until 1981.

A decade later, Bob and JoAnn's sons Gary and Tim converted a reel tape recording from the group's live gigs into a cassette. Adorned with a photo of the four musicians in matching patterned shirts and surrounded by their instruments—accordion, fiddle, electric and bass guitars, banjo, drums, and saxophone—the cassette's cover touted "35 Great Hits!" while adding, in a parody of late-night television pitches for Box Car Willie or Zamphir, "not sold in stores." Certainly the group's repertoire, a distillation of their collective experience, defied the commercial categories of music marketers. Here were the "May Waltz" (*Mai Vals*) of Norwegian immigrant bandleader Thorstein Skarning, the "Stove Poker Waltz" (*Spis Kroks Vals*) of Swedish-American comic singer Charles Widden, "Life in the Finnish Woods" (*Livet i Finnskogarna*) beloved by Finns and Swedes alike, the German drinking song "In Heaven There Is No Beer" (*Im Himmel Geb'ts kein Bier*), the Polish "Old Time Mazurka," the Slovenian favorite *"Moja Baba Je Piana"* (My Wife Is Drunk) popularized by Frankie Yankovic, Fred Rose's country classic "Blue Eyes Crying in the Rain" somewhat altered by the local Croatian tamburitza cover version (*Suze Liju Plave Oči*), Anglo-American fiddle tunes like "Cumberland Gap" and "Ragtime Annie," minstrelsy's "Golden Slippers," the parlor anthem "Home Sweet Home," honky tonk favorites like "Don't Be Angry" and "Chained to a Memory," the lounge classic "Harbor Lights," Chuck Berry's "Memphis," Creedence Clearwater Revival's roots rock standard "Proud Mary," and a good deal more.[6]

In the 1970s, as Alex Haley's *Roots*, the nation's bicentennial, civil rights activism, and an array of other factors contributed to the "new ethnicity" movement among European Americans, Bob Andresen began to conduct research on his region's traditional music, while seeking out older performers. One was Otto Rindlisbacher (1895–1975) of Rice Lake, Wisconsin. The son of Swiss immigrant musicians, Rindlisbacher was not only adept at Swiss music on the fiddle and button accordion, but also played second piano accordion for the Norwegian immigrant accordionist Thorstein Skarning; made and played Norwegian Hardanger fiddles; formed a Hawaiian band in the 1920s to play on Minneapolis radio; mastered lumber-camp Anglo-Celtic, French, and metís fiddle tunes; and ran the Buckhorn Bar and Café, a haven for old time musicians.[7] Leonard Finseth (1911–1993), a Mondovi, Wisconsin, farmer, factory worker, and fiddler, was a periodic visitor to the Buckhorn where he swapped Norwegian and lumberjack tunes. By the mid-1970s, Bob Andresen was playing rhythm guitar for Finseth, producing several LP recordings of his tunes, and accompanying him for performances at Sons of Norway Lodges, Nordic Fest (sponsored by the Norwegian-American museum Vesterheim in Decorah, Iowa), the pan-Scandinavian "Snoose Boulevard" Festival in Minneapolis, and the Smithsonian Institution's Festival of American Folklife in Washington, D.C. (Finseth 1979, 1981 M).

Chiefly a rhythm guitarist in his public performances, Andresen began experimenting at home in the 1980s with what he called "Jack Pine style" guitar picking. Sometimes also referred to as "Hardanger guitar," Andresen's arrangements combined the clean lead flatpicking techniques of such southern bluegrass guitarists as Doc Watson and Clarence White with Upper Midwestern melodies and additional guitar harmonies evoking the overtones that resonate from the five sympathetic strings beneath the bridge of a nine-stringed Norwegian Hardanger fiddle.

> It seemed just natural to try to pick out some of these tunes in a lead manner on guitar. So, I'd been doing this around home for quite a while and my sons had kind of picked up on that. My son Gary plays guitar and my other son, Tim, plays string bass. Gary and I sometimes play harmony. Sometimes we just play lines back and forth, and Penny Perry plays rhythm guitar . . . mostly Scandinavian tunes, but also some old Midwest lumberjack tunes and a couple of Slovenian tunes. Things like that. (Andresen 1994 I)

The Andresen Guitar Group performed at the Smithsonian Institution's Festival of American Folklife in 1991 and produced three cassettes from 1993 to 1994. The last, *Guitar Hymns*, was made not long before Bob Andresen died of cancer on March 10, 1995. He was 57.

North Coast Creoles

Circumspect studies of performers like Bob Andresen are distinctly lacking amid the efforts of folklorists and ethnomusicologists concerned with musical practices in North America.[8] In keeping with conventional approaches, Andresen's music might be examined primarily as ethnic music. Reduced to Norwegian and Norwegian-American elements, his music might be dissected subsequently with regard to three major phenomena: survival and retention, conservation, and syncretism. In the first instance, scholars have sought transplanted yet pristine examples of "old country" music from immigrants and their offspring. With a few exceptions, these examples, or "survivals," are found to be fading with the demise of the second generation. Conservation, an aspect of self-consciously ethnic institutions established by newcomers, involves the formal presentation of selected old country tunes (be they of folk, popular, patriotic, nationalist, or even classical origin) through music education, written music, and seasonal concert programs. Meanwhile, syncretism entails the synthesis or hybridization of Old and New World sounds into a distinct ethnic American sound (Nettl 1978). Separate though they are, these three approaches all emphasize gradual assimilation through the implicit assumptions that ethnic music disappears unless buttressed by formal organizations and that it is marginal to and must eventually be absorbed by the folk and popular musical genres of a dominant Anglo-American culture.

The workings of the foregoing trio of cultural forces might readily be found in Bob Andresen's musical repertoire and performances. Hymns and dance tunes of evident Norwegian origin and acquired from family members survived as a small part of his active playlist, with others having presumably faded either before he could learn them or because he did not favor them. From the mid-1970s to the mid-1990s, he played frequently at Scandinavian festivals, museums, fraternal lodges, and other events encouraging the conservation of an ethnic repertoire. Likewise both his Anglo-Norwegian dialect songs and Norsky bluegrass guitar picking epitomized syncretism.

Yet it would be a mistake to view the entirety of Bob Andresen's music as characterized by a dialectic between ethnic margin and American mainstream. For one thing, a preoccupation with the survival, conservation, and syncretism of his Norwegian repertoire ignores his equally strong preference for Germanic, Slavic, Finnish, Canadian, and metís songs and tunes. For another, Andresen's versions of Anglo-American music—whether fiddle tunes, post–World War II country music, or 1960s roots rock—were not sound-alike covers. Frequently rendered with an accordion, they were not merely informed but *transformed* by a regional aesthetic. In other words, mainstream tunes were absorbed by marginal sounds as much as the other way around. Considered as a whole, Bob Andresen's music embodied what he described so aptly as a "mix of old time ethnic music and regional country music"—the grassroots sound that, since the mid-nineteenth century, has evolved and echoed throughout the Upper Midwest.

Extending from the western edge of the Great Lakes to the eastern border of the Great Plains, bisected by the upper Mississippi River, the Upper Midwest has long been home to an extraordinary number of ethnic groups. Siouxan-speaking Dakota and Ho-Chunk peoples and numerous Algonquians (Menominees, Mesquakies, Odawas, Potawatomies, and especially Ojibwes) have occupied the region for centuries, with the Iroquoian Oneidas arriving as refugees in the early nineteenth century. Small numbers of English, French, Irish, and Scottish fur traders established themselves in the region in the eighteenth century, with assorted Yankees, Yorkers, Upland southerners, and Canadians arriving steadily by the 1830s. Likewise from the late 1830s until the restriction of immigration in the aftermath of World War I, there was an enormous influx of Germanic and Nordic peoples into the Upper Midwest, along with significant numbers of various Slavs and Southern Europeans, drawn to farms, small towns, lumber camps, mines, and industrial cities.

When the 1980 U.S. census gave citizens the option of indicating a particular "nationality" other than "American," within the continental United States only residents of Minnesota, North Dakota, and Wisconsin registered responses above 90 percent. Meanwhile Wisconsin and the adjoining Upper Peninsula of Michigan include the greatest variety of American Indians east of the Mississippi River. And the Upper Midwest also includes the nation's largest concentrations of such European Americans as Belgians, Czechs, Danes, Finns, Germans, Hollanders, Luxembourgers, Norwegians, Poles, Swedes, and Swiss, with significant populations of many other groups, from Armenians to Cornish, Croatians, French Canadians, Irish, Italians, Jews from many countries, Latvians, Russians, Serbs, Slovaks, Ukrainians, and Welsh.[9]

Because these varied peoples were often able either, in the case of Woodland Indians, to sustain elements of their old way of life or, in the case of newcomers, to establish a measure of what cultural geographers call "first effective settlement"—the creation and maintenance of fundamental patterns of living—white Anglo-Saxon Protestant (WASP) settlers were never able to gain complete control of the Upper Midwest's political and social institutions.[10] To be sure, the lives of newcomers and their descendants have been affected considerably by larger forces in mainstream American life, yet many in the Upper Midwest continue to think of themselves and their communities not only as American but also as Czech, German, or Ho-Chunk, as Norwegian, Polish, or Potawatomi. Indeed, the region's culture has been marked for two centuries by a high degree of cultural pluralism, by the coexistence of peoples sustaining diverse cultural practices and identities.[11]

At the same time, the Upper Midwest's long-standing pluralism has fostered equally venerable patterns of cultural blending among participants in numerous ethnic groups (Degh 1966). Distinct though they are, the region's Algonquian, Iroquoian, and Siouxan peoples for centuries have shared many common Woodland practices, nowadays most visibly evident in pan-

Indian powwows on the Great Lakes circuit (Browner 2002; *Honor the Earth Powwow* 1991 M). Likewise the Upper Midwest's non–Anglo-European peoples often settled alongside not only kindred immigrants but also those who had been their neighbors in Europe: Czechs and Germans, Germans and Poles, Swedes and Norwegians, Finns and Swedes, Italians and Slovenians, Hollanders and Luxembourgers, French and Belgians. These peoples too shared many cultural traits as a result of extended proximity in Old World and New.

In the Upper Midwest, such relatively familiar patterns of exchange across rather permeable ethnic boundaries were also paralleled by encounters in that no-man's-land between more rigidly defined cultural borders, between WASP and foreigner, European and native. The historian Richard White, considering interactions in the Great Lakes region between 1650 and 1815, characterizes the Upper Midwest as a "middle ground." Investing "middle" with connotations suggesting anything but bland humdrum, White contends:

> On the middle ground diverse peoples adjust their differences through what amounts to a process of creative, and often expedient, misunderstandings. People try to persuade others who are different from themselves by appealing to what they perceive to be the values and practices of those others. They often misinterpret and distort both the values and practices of those they deal with, but from these misunderstandings arise new meanings and through them new practices—the shared meanings and practices of the middle ground. (White 1991: x)

Frequent, highly charged, and sufficiently mysterious to inspire confusion and wonder, the process that White chronicles—attempts "to persuade others who are different from themselves by appealing to what they perceive to be the values and practices of those others"—has yet another side. While tribal leaders and the European emissaries of economic and colonial empires typically harnessed their imaginative role-playing rhetoric to religion and politics in hopes of gaining more than they gave, humbler folk sometimes did something quite different. More concerned with pleasure than with conversion, aggrandizement, or persuasion, as intent upon recognition as discovery, they often found their own values and practices residing firmly in the peculiar yet familiar practices of others.

In the 1830s, Henry Rowe Schoolcraft, an Indian agent in Sault St. Marie, Michigan, was delighted to discover the Ojibwe hero Wenabozho's resemblance to the Greek Hercules, the Nordic Loki, and an array of European tricksters and culture heroes (Schoolcraft 1839). The first to write about such tales, Schoolcraft could hardly have been the first European to hear them, and there is no doubt that other listeners reciprocated with tales of their own. A century after Schoolcraft, Victor Barnouw and fellow anthropologists documenting the cultural practices of northern Wisconsin's Lac Court Oreilles and Lac du Flambeau Ojibwes recorded numerous folktales fusing European and native motifs. The tellers, many of whom had been born in the 1860s and 1870s, had acquired stories from their parents' and grandparents' generations, prompting Barnouw to observe that "the voyageurs, fur traders, and lumberjacks evidently spent much time telling their stock of tales to Indian listeners." Woodland Indians likewise shared their stories: "Despite prejudice, warfare, and exploitation, there persisted a sort of freemasonry of folklore in which, temporarily at least, the story-teller and his audience were united" (Barnouw 1977: 225). What Bob Andresen termed "a mix," what Richard White calls the creative interactions of the "middle ground," what Victor Barnouw refers to as intercultural "free masonry," other scholars have labeled "creolization."

In their introduction to an issue of the *Journal of American Folklore* devoted to the topic, editors Robert Baron and Ann C. Cara declare, "Creolization is cultural creativity in process." Meanwhile, they astutely contend that, because of their populist, emergent, and combinatory nature, "creole forms and behaviors" have been characterized

> by outsiders as "impure." Too often, creole expressions have been viewed as manifestations of fragmentation and degeneration, thereby suffering in comparison to the supposedly fully formed, reified, historically sanctioned expressions of a colonial or "westernized" elite. In sharp contrast, creolists see creolization as creative disorder, as a poetic chaos, thereby challenging simplistic and static notions of center and periphery. The cultural and critical lens of creolization, in other words, allows us to see not simply "hybrids" of limited fluidity, but new *culture in the making*. (Baron and Cara 2003: 3–4)

Baron and Cara go on to enumerate distinctly creole musical forms ("jazz, salsa, calypso . . . the tango, the mambo, the samba"), while they and fellow contributors locate creolization in tropical climes where European traders, soldiers, missionaries, and colonizers encountered African, Arab, and East and West Indian peoples—implicitly suggesting that cultural fermentation occurs only amid extreme heat and humidity.

Surely their "cultural and critical lens" would neither fog up nor freeze if refocused to include the Upper Midwest. Here, putatively superior Anglo-American elites were never completely successful in forcing the assimilation of supposedly inferior Woodland Indian and European immigrant peoples. Here, musical interactions have long been distinguished by egalitarianism, by freewheeling accommodation and blending across complex boundaries. Here reside North Coast creoles.

All Gathered There

In his *History of Langlade County* (1922), Dessureau reports that, from 1855 to 1885, "mixed blood Menomini" in northern Wisconsin established taverns and "stop over" places along ancient trails.

[They] were typical of the western mining town, where the frontier elements held sway. Hotels and travelers' rests would spring into existence in a day . . . [with] saloons and dance houses . . . the river driver, the woodsman, the teamster, the Indian, all gathered there. (Dessureau, cited in Keesing 1939: 177)

As neighbors on farms, along lake shores and river banks, in and about small towns, in mining locations, in urban working-class neighborhoods, or as seasonal laborers in lumber camps, hop-picking fields, and cranberry bogs, Upper Midwesterners traded songs and tunes, forging a new regional style that creatively fused their cultural and linguistic similarities and differences. The grammar of their musical lingua franca drew considerably upon traditional patterns of participatory, calendrical, life-cycle, and nocturnal performances shared alike by indigenous and immigrant peoples: Woodland Indian seasonal gatherings and social dances; the Irish *ceilidh* with its insistence that all present entertain with a song, a tune, a dance, a story, or a trick; the French winter *veillée* wherein neighbors might fiddle, dance, and tell tales all night long; the Norwegian practice of *julebukking* with masked revelers roaming house to house at Christmas; the pre-Lenten, harvest, wedding, house party, and hall celebrations of European Americans generally; and the patriotic holiday revelries and fashionable "balls" established by "old stock" Americans.[12]

Examples abound of creolized music made by "all gathered there." From the 1840s through the early decades of the twentieth century, winter lumber camps flourished across the northern halves of Michigan, Wisconsin, and Minnesota. While some camps were predominantly Anglo American, or Swedish, or Finnish, or French, most included a proverbial "duke's mixture" of tongues and tastes.[13] Saturday nights were frequent occasions for collective entertainment. As the Norwegian immigrant Ola Johnson of Wisconsin Rapids put it, "There were many nationalities in camp, Yankees, Germans, Frenchmen, Irishmen, and we three Norwegians. In the evenings we had a big time" (Helgeson 1985: 270).

Born on northeastern Wisconsin's Menominee Reservation in 1938, Everett "Butch" Waupoose recalled that his great-grandfather Wanawat "only had one name. And he had eight brothers. They came from that Michigan country up there, and they brought a lot of that [fiddle music] down with them. So it finally come down to us, this generation, the fourth generation" (Waupoose 1989 I).

Wanawat worked in nineteenth-century lumber camps with French Canadians, as did his son, Dave, who married a French-Indian woman with the surname Frechette. Dave Waupoose would leave the reservation in the winter to work as a chopper in the woods. In the spring, he came home with a store of fiddle tunes. By the time Dave's son Alex (1903–1972) began working in the woods, the Menominees had their own sawmill and logging operations. Modifying his fiddle with "Indian medicine" (a deer bone for the nut, porcupine quills in the soundbox), Alex fiddled in Menominee logging camps and for reservation square dances that sometimes included calls in

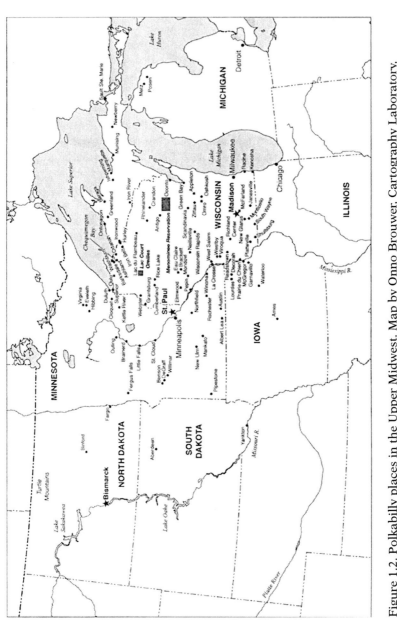

Figure 1.2. Polkabilly places in the Upper Midwest. Map by Onno Brouwer, Cartography Laboratory, University of Wisconsin.

the Menominee language. He also played couple or "round" dances for German neighbors and at larger doings that included the Fourth of July, threshing parties, and the county fair (Leary 1992: 33).

The pattern was much the same when loggers returned to farm communities, or when they never left those communities at all. Alfred Erickson's backward glance at social life in nineteenth-century Scandinavia, Wisconsin, included a mixture of Anglo-American fiddle tunes and the couple dances favored by fellow Norwegians.

> In addition to hard work . . . there was much merriment and amusement in our neighborhood—dancing, house parties, church and school cantatas, skiing, and skating. At Christmas time the holiday celebrations started on Christmas Day and continued till January third. In later days a huge roller-skating rink was built in the village and it was well patronized, not only for skating but for dancing—square dances, cotillions, Virginia reels, waltzes, and hop waltzes [sic]. (Erickson 1949: 201)

Not far away, in the German hamlet of Zittau, Ted Dorschner, Sr., a blacksmith whose early twentieth-century customers included Yankees and Norwegians, played the fiddle for dances, eventually organizing his sons into a band that, in the 1930s, favored "some polkas and waltzes, and then kind of a country type of what then was called 'hillbilly music'" (Dorschner 1988 I).

P. T. Gillett's reminiscences concerning "Fiddlers We Have Known" bespoke a similar ferment in the potato-farming country in and around Antigo, Wisconsin. Harking back to the 1870s and 1880s, he sketched the lives of some 30 fiddlers: several Irish, a "Scotch Canuck," "a Frenchman," a "real old Yankee fiddler," a handful of "Kentucks" come north to work in the woods, some Czechs or "Bohemians," and numerous Germans like the Raess Brothers, "Charlie, Jake, Herman, and Al." While each had their special repertoires, they learned from one another and likewise entertained their mixed crowd with roughly unified programs.

> The music seemed to be of the same class. Much of Irish and Scotch extraction. The round dances seemed to have come mostly from the German and Bohemian and local ¾ time songs. The music played by the southern fiddlers in the main has a different style. Many southern folk songs, "Take Me Down My Walking Cane," "Leather Breeches," and "Chicken Reel" etc. were of course the old standard tunes played by all. (Gillett 1932: 8)

String bands in Antigo and surrounding Langlade County were paralleled by and sometimes conjoined with brass and reed bands that "entertained at picnics, weddings, and played at dances" (Lukas 1983: 1).

Fred Woodford, born in 1895, was raised on a farm nine miles south of Eau Claire, Wisconsin, the grandson of a fiddling English immigrant. Fred's dad, Elmer, and an uncle were also fiddlers who played for "country dances, barn dances, house dances, whatever." Some neighbors were English, some Irish, and there were Norwegians, Poles, and especially Germans around. "The German neighbors were great on waltzes. Then they had some fast tunes that later on got to be called polkas. That was the way it was." Fred and an older brother, Guy (1890–1976), likewise took up the fiddle, while another brother, Glen, backed them on guitar. By 1910 they were playing for dances.

> Oh yes, we played square dances. And waltzes. Waltzes and two-steps we played in them days, but not foxtrots. We didn't learn to play foxtrots until we was on the road . . . in 1919. . . . We'd never played anything like that before. We'd played two-steps, waltz[es], and then there was what they called the mazurka, and we played quadrilles for square dances. We had one caller, he lived out here toward Brackett. Meyers was his name. He knew a lot of these changes, see, like the mazurka and the schottische. (Woodford 1994 I)

Those, according to Fred Woodford, were "just the tunes that were common in them days."

The factory hamlet of Barksdale along Lake Superior's Chequamegon Bay, site of a Du Pont munitions plant, was settled prior to World War I by Swedes, Norwegians, Finns, Germans, Irish, Anglo Canadians, and Hungarian and Lithuanian ex-miners by way of western Pennsylvania. Vivian Eckholm Brevak learned tunes from her Swedish father, a Finnish boarder, her Hungarian husband's relatives, and Anglo-Canadian neighbors. She and her childhood friend Netty Day Harvey, whose family hailed from the Canadian maritimes, had fond memories of house parties with "all kinds of people . . . just neighbors, all neighbors and friends that knew everybody else." In keeping with the crowd's varied composition, there were "lotta square dances. Schottisches though too, and old time waltzes and polkas . . . and the broom dance, and the circle two-step" (Leary 1983: 222; Leary 1984: 75). Reino Maki attended and also played for dances in the Barksdale area and the surrounding countryside as a teenager in the early 1920s.

> Many townships here, many schoolhouses used to have dances. I used to go to them. . . . There's many different nationalities across the river: Swedes, Norwegians, Finnlanders. So it didn't make much difference. . . . And there was talent that used to come to Washburn years ago. And we went to them places where they played lotta music.

The Maki family sometimes traveled to Iron Belt where Reino was born, on the Wisconsin-Michigan border near Hurley and Ironwood: "There was lotta music at Iron Belt. Many different nationalities" (Maki 1981 I).

Indeed in the industrialized backwoods towns and hamlets of the Lake Superior region—where farmers, miners, factory hands, merchants, dock workers, and sailors mingled—successful working musicians of whatever background acquired new songs, tunes, and styles partly out of curiosity and partly because of the shifting demands of their diverse audiences. In Ashland, Wisconsin, Bruno Synkula, a Pole, not only learned to play an accordion from an Italian, but also acquired a Swedish version of a Finnish song from a Norwegian accordionist whose repertoire included mostly German tunes (Synkula 1981I). Nearly every self-respecting veteran of home and hall parties acquired at least one tune that might appeal to each of the many different nationalities. Raised in the hinterlands southwest of Duluth, Florian Chmielewski, for example, drew upon musical versatility to launch an extended career in the Minnesota legislature.

> The road I live on is called the Polish Road; everyone on it is Polish. Just three miles to the south is the Bohemian Road and everyone on that road is Bohemian. And as you go up to Denham, it's what we call the Swedish Road and everyone on that road is Swedish. So when we come out to these dances, I pretty soon realized that I had to learn *"Helsa Dem Darhemma"* [for the Swedes] . . . and I had to learn *"Svestkova Alej"* for the Bohemians. . . . And I don't know how I ever would've been elected to office unless I'd known how to play Finnish numbers. (Chmielewski 1990 I)

Not surprisingly, Chmielewski knew and played square dances and other Anglo-American tunes as well.

Lewis Reiman's experience in the early twentieth century was much the same in Iron River, a mining town in the western Upper Peninsula of Michigan.

> Every nationality brought their native dances . . . [and] danced them with abandon in their new American homes. Schottisches, waltzes, two steps, gavottes, Irish jigs, Scottish flings, Polish Rounds and a great variety of other steps from European lands enlivened the parties and weddings of the time.

What Reiman called "American square dances" were also extremely popular and were typically "interspersed with other dances brought from abroad" at community dances in town and Grange halls (Reiman 1981: 97–98).

Nor was the musical mix appreciably different in the rolling hills and farmland of the Upper Midwest's lower reaches. The creolization of sounds and dance steps had commenced by the mid-nineteenth century in the river, mining, and farming communities on both sides of the Mississippi River where Illinois, Iowa, Minnesota, and Wisconsin flank and link with one another. In 1857 in McGregor, Iowa, a "Grande Masque Ball" was "held on New Year's Eve under the sponsorship of the German residents. . . . The easy integration of native Americans and foreigners on the Iowa frontier was demonstrated at this ball." The local newspaper editor A. P. Richardson, a Yankee, observed:

The Germans are not partial to Cotillions and "our folks" are partial to scarcely anything else. Whether the dancing was well or ill done we cannot judge; those who decide such points assure us that the Music was enrapturing and that the Polkas, Waltzes, Schottishe [*sic*], Gallopades [aka Galops], etc. etc. were faultless in execution. (Petersen 1959: 9–10)

Four years later in nearby Shullsburg, Wisconsin, Dennis O'Neil, an immigrant from Ireland's County Wexford, and his German immigrant wife took the dance floor with their "large family of handsome daughters" and the aid of an Anglo-American colonel.

On the Fourth of July of that year a ball was held in the court house at Shullsburg, mother and daughters attending. During the evening the floor was cleared for the special use of Mrs. O'Neil and her seven daughters to dance a waltz. The mother and daughters were all dressed in white and when they appeared on the floor with their partners, the mother and Col. E. C. Townsend of Shullsburg led the dance. (Murphy 1993: 15)

Perhaps Charles Mon Pleasure, born four miles from Shullsburg in 1830, led the band on that occasion

Mon Pleasure, of French heritage, played for dances intermittently on both sides of the Mississippi from the late 1840s through about 1900. His memoirs, serialized in the *Platteville Witness and Mining Times,* show that he was adept at playing minstrel pieces as well as Anglo-American fiddle tunes brought up river by settlers and traveling entertainers: "Arkansas Traveler," the breakdowns "Gray Eagle" and "Gal on a Log," such reels as "Sailor on the Shore," and a handful of jigs and rags (Meade, Spottswood, and Meade 2002: 759–761, 704, 707, 729). He also played quadrilles, "especially the lancers," as well as assorted contra dances and such Central European couple dances as redowas, mazurkas, polkas, schottisches, and waltzes. In the late 1860s, Mon Pleasure's band combined all of these elements, and his subsequent remarks indicate a keen awareness of genre bending.

We used the old-fashioned post horns and bugles, so we had the first violin, second violin, double bass, post horn, clarinet, and bugle. They were all Bohemians but myself. I guess we would look like monkeys nowadays with such a band, but it was all right in those days. (1910–1911: 93)

The group played for balls in the old fur-trading mecca of Prairie du Chien, Wisconsin, and across the Mississippi in McGregor, Iowa.[14]

A similar mix of dance tunes, instruments, and ethnicities continued to flourish a generation later throughout Wisconsin's "coulee region"—the hills and valleys extending inland from the Mississippi River. Long before he teamed with Bob Andresen, Leonard Finseth of Mondovi, a fiddler whose parents hailed from Gudbrandsdal in Norway, played for Sons of Norway and Norden Lodge dances, for fraternal groups like the Modern Woodsmen, and in homes: "Got to play in the house parties. Them days they didn't have rugs in the rooms. They'd just move the furniture . . . and have a square dance. There'd probably be a waltz or a schottische" (Finseth 1988 I; see also Martin 1985: 33).

In the 1920s, Bernard Johnson of Richland Center began playing with a succession of groups, such as the Simpson Band, the Kickapoo Troubadors, and Smelzer's Hotshots. The grandson of a fiddler whose English ancestors had lived for generations in southern Ohio before settling in southwestern Wisconsin, Johnson likewise took up the fiddle. Steeped at home in old time Upland southern pieces like "Cindy" and "Ragtime Annie," Johnson readily acquired German waltzes, Czech songs, and polkas from fellow musicians like Emil Janacek and Scandinavian tunes like "*Stegen Vals*" (Stepladder Waltz) from dancers.

> We played in Westby and Viroqua and Reedstown. And I have played a time or two in LaCrosse. Yeah, we was in Norwegian territory up there. One time I was up there playing, we was playing in a Rod and Gun Club in Westby. A fellow came up and wanted me to play the "Stepladder Waltz," and I said, "I don't know it." "Well," he said, "You don't know it?" I said, "No." "Well," he said, "I'll give you a record when you get ready to go home. If you take that record, you can learn to play it." So he did. He gave me the record, and I took it home and played it. And I learned to play it. And when we went back there the next time, I played it on the fiddle for him. (Johnson 1989 I)

Experiences like those of Bernard Johnson, Leonard Finseth, Charles Mon Pleasure, A. P. Richardson, Dennis O'Neil, Lewis Reiman, Florian Chmielewski, Bruno Synkula, Reino Maki, Netty Day Harvey, Vivian Eckholm Brevak, Fred Woodford, P. T. Gillett, Ted Dorschner, Alfred Erickson, Dave and Alex Waupoose, and Wanawat might be compounded endlessly with those of other musicians, dancers, and communities throughout the Upper Midwest.[15]

Traveling Troupes Meet Home Talent

In the late nineteenth and early twentieth centuries, the Upper Midwest's interrelated, overlapping local musical scenes and creolized styles were both stimulated and validated by the regular appearances of strange and familiar touring musicians working dance-hall, vaudeville, and Chautauqua circuits. Nearly every little community had a hall or so-called opera house where not only home talent but also traveling troupes drew enthusiastic crowds (Slout 1972: 2–7). Tent shows and county fairs flourished too in fair weather, attracting performers from afar.

African Americans often played on river boats plying the upper Mississippi, or took on extended jobs in river towns, bringing the ragtime, blues, and incipient jazz sounds that had emerged downstream in St. Louis and Memphis. As early as the late 1860s, at the time that fiddler Charles Mon Pleasure had a quadrille band in Prairie du Chien composed mostly of Bohemians, "Jim Williams, a negro [*sic*], had a band across the [Mississippi] river at South McGregor [Iowa]. He sometimes played in Prairie du Chien and I would play at South McGregor." Mon Pleasure not only learned to play tunes to which dancers shuffled instead of jigging, but he also composed a piece he called "Kansas City Rag" (Mon Pleasure 1910–1911: 93, 107). And traveling minstrel shows and jubilee singers were active both along the upper Mississippi and in the hinterlands. As a lumber-mill town on the Red Cedar River and a burgeoning agricultural trading center, Rice Lake, Wisconsin, boasted an imposing opera house where, as the *Rice Lake Chronotype* indicated on April 10 and May 1, 1896, such groups as the Plantation Minstrels and Slayton's Jubilee Singers barnstormed onto the stage. During that era, Ashland—a mill town, Great Lakes port, and rail hub—similarly hosted companies like Great Barlow's Minstrels and the Dixie Jubilee Singers. On May 7, 1902, the *Ashland Daily Press* proclaimed: "Saturday evening a minstrel show will play at the opera house, a good house for that company is not questioned." That such extraregional, professional performances were not lost on audiences is evident in a January 12, 1904, account from the *Ashland Daily Press* concerning a "Home Talent Minstrel Night" in the hall of St. Agnes's Catholic Church. While roughly 1,000 gathered, "Hilda Bloomquist recited a Negro piece," and others enacted a "tambo and bones blackface minstrel show" complete with "coon songs which were all hits."

That Ashland "home talent" show also included an "Italian and Bear Act" by local Croatian immigrant Will Garnich and his Italian-American friend John Allo, wherein the "Dago maka de beara clima the pole to the telegraph." Local antics of this sort were inspired, predictably, by the proliferation of traveling European ethnic acts on Upper Midwestern stages. As early as 1839, the Tyrolese Family Rainer, a singing and yodeling vocal group from Austria, embarked on an American tour, spawning imitative "mountain" singing troupes in the nation's hinterlands and paving the way for succeeding forays by Austrian, Bavarian, and Swiss yodelers (Nathan 1946). Considering the often dominant presence of Germanic peoples in the Upper Midwest, it is hardly surprising that similar entertainers found receptive audiences throughout the region.

In 1904, Iowan Keith Vawter initiated the circuit, or "tent Chautauqua," movement that flourished until the onset of the Great Depression, conjoining moralizing Christian lecturers with rustic comedy and musical entertainment (Harrison 1958: 16; Tapia 1997: 1). While some of the musical groups on Vawter's Midwestern circuit included the Kaffir African Boys, assorted blackface minstrel troupes, and various African-American jubilee singers, such ensembles as Fiechtl's Yodelers, the Tyrolean Alpine Singers and Yodelers, and Rudolph's Swiss Singers and Players—"in national costume . . . using the unique instruments of their native land"—were just as common (Harrison 1958: 97, 108; MacLaren 1938: 96, 140, 216; Tapia 1997: 43, 99, 173). From the 1880s through the 1930s, the steady influx of Swiss and German artisans required by Wisconsin's cheese-making industry also fostered opportunities for sojourning musicians like the Swiss Family Frauenfelder, the Moser Brothers, the Jolly Rigi Boys, the Scheidigger Seven, and many more (Leary 1991a: 29–30; Wagner 2002). In the 1920s, the Mosers relied on a Swiss immigrant insurance agent to book their tour through a network of Swiss-American clubs and newspapers. Wisconsin was a favorite stop, with the heavily Swiss city of Monroe serving as a base from which they traveled to New Glarus, Mount Horeb, Dodgeville, and other communities with Swiss concentrations. Attired in short pants, black velvet jackets embroidered with an edelweiss, and the leather beanies of cheese makers, the Mosers often performed with a painted alpine backdrop. As Rudy Burkhalter, a Moser accompanist, recalled:

> We had a printed program. We had probably nine or ten numbers, then an intermission, then another nine or ten numbers. We'd usually start out with a march, an opening march that had a little yodel at the tail end of it. Then some Swiss music of the more somber type. Then, as we went along, we changed to happy songs, funny ones. (Leary 1991a: 46)

The Mosers also tried their hand at jazz and hillbilly tunes. Customarily they were invited to stay at people's homes, where "we played dance music until 2, 3 o'clock in the morning—when we finally got out on the farm there would be 50–60 cars in a lot around there" (Leary 1991a: 43–46). Thanks in part to the camaraderie of these after-hours sessions, Rudy Burkhalter eventually left the Mosers to settle in Madison, found an accordion school, play for Swiss events, and perform with German, Irish, Italian, and Norwegian musicians in a succession of bands with hybrid repertoires (Leary 1991a: 54).

In the early twentieth century, German or, as they sometimes came to be termed in America, "Dutch" acts were especially common not only in major cities like Chicago and Milwaukee, but also in heavily German rural and small town environs. The Famous Boscobel Dutch Band charmed attendees of southwestern Wisconsin events like Fennimore's Big Days. The group's 1911 promotional postcard shows five members toting various brass instruments, whose costumed appearance closely matches that of the celebrated New York City "Dutch" vaudevillians Weber and Fields: healthy paunches, unkempt (probably false) chin whiskers, colorfully patched and billowing outmoded suits, ill-fitting derbies, and wooden shoes (Leary 2004b: 22–25; Wittke 1952: 225–226). In 1914, Helmut, Max, and Wilhelm Peters, who had immigrated two years before to the coal fields around Henryetta, Oklahoma, parlayed their local theater appearance into a

THE FAMOUS 10—SCHWEITZERS—10. WRJN RADIO ARTISTS

Figure 1.3. Postcard of the Famous Schweitzers, performers over WRJN radio, in a hall adorned by a painted alpine backdrop, Racine, Wisconsin, c. 1930. Author's collection.

vaudeville career that extended into the late 1930s. Billed as "Players from Germany" and a "World Famous Concertina Troupe from Germany," despite their permanent residence in the United States, the Peters Brothers played mostly in Illinois, Michigan, Minnesota, and Wisconsin (Leary 2002: 216–218). Meanwhile, the December 10, 1915, edition of Wisconsin's *Cuba City News-Herald* touted the upcoming arrival of Ben Holmes, "The Fatherland's Sweet Singer, in His Famous Musical Comedy-Drama *Happy Heinie*," featuring such new songs as "I'm a Jolly German," "My Fatherland," and "Happy Heinie." An accompanying ad included a cartoon of a grinning, corpulent fellow in too-tight formal attire, while bestowing a second title, "The Prince of German Dialect Comedians" on Holmes (Leary 2004b: 25). Holmes was described similarly as "The Prince of German Singing Comedians" in December 29, 1915, by the *Daily Northwestern* of Oshkosh prior to his appearance in that city's Grand Opera House on January 2.

Slavic entertainers were also active, particularly on the Chautauqua circuit, where both "Bohemian" (Czech) and "Jugoslav" (Bosnian, Croatian, and Serbian) performers traversed the Upper Midwest and points beyond. Born in Prague in 1875, Bohumir Kryl was an immigrant trumpet virtuoso who performed with the nationally celebrated bandmaster John Philip Sousa before forming Kryl's Bohemian Band in 1910. By 1912, Kryl was one of several barnstorming musicians to lead an advertised "World Famous Bohemian Orchestra" (Greene 1992: 78–79; Harrison 1958: 91, 99–100; Tapia 1997: 62–63). While such aggregations were exotic in, for example, Henderson, Kentucky, where howling dogs unleashed by mischievous boys once obliterated a Kryl solo, Bohemian visitors were far more familiar in the Upper Midwest, where Czech communities and fraternal organ-

Figure 1.4. The Famous Boscobel Dutch Band—togged out in the frumpy clothes, chin whiskers, padded stomachs, and wooden shoes of comic "stage Dutch" performers—posing here at a festival in nearby Fennimore, 1911. Mills Music Library Collection, University of Wisconsin.

izations often supported local Bohemian bands and held dances open to all comers. When the Big Chautauqua Special, advertising musical "Bohemians fresh from Bohemia," opened in tiny Suttons Bay, Michigan, on August 7, 1917, the enthusiastic crowd consisted of "lumbermen, fishermen, storekeepers, farmers, teachers; Norwegians and Swedes and Bohemians, a few Frenchies and Chippeway Indians—two hundred in all."[16]

The Adriatic Tamburica Band, the Croatian Tamburica Orchestra, the Elias Serenaders, the Jugoslav Tamburica Orchestra, the Sloga Orchestra, and the Zvonimir Orchestra all played some combination of Chautauqua and vaudeville circuits in the early twentieth century (Harrison 1958: 245; MacLaren 1938: 144; March 1983: 211–217; Tapia 1997: 128, 172). Dragutin Ilijaš, who changed his name to Charles Elias, was born in Slavonia in 1886 and immigrated to Milwaukee in 1903. Elias formed tamburitza ensembles in that city, as well as in the Iron Range town of Virginia, Minnesota, prior to his death in 1937. Featuring a repertoire of folksongs and couple dance tunes, Elias often played in Upper Midwestern communities with South Slavic immigrant populations and local tamburitza bands. His band leading, teaching, compositions, and arrangements, succeeded by the efforts of his son and musical heir, Charles Elias, Jr., spawned tamburitza bands in Wisconsin, Minnesota, and northern Illinois that persist to the present (March 1983: 215–216). Possessing a repertoire of songs and tunes interwoven with Old World polka music traditions, tamburitza bands prize rapid, virtuoso picking and rely on a family of lute-like stringed instruments. Not surprisingly, by the 1930s, tamburitza-inflected polka-hillbilly fusions emerged all over the Upper Midwest.

Nordic traveling performers were likewise active throughout the region's farming, logging, and mining communities. They too inspired local imitation, while fostering further musical cross-pollination. John Rosendahl, an immigrant fiddler and banjoist, played a Finnish-American circuit that extended from Fitchburg, Massachusetts, and New York City westward to the Lake Superior region; Rock Springs, Wyoming; and the Pacific Northwest—with an occasional trip back to Finland in between (Leary 1990b). Hjalmar Peterson, a Swedish immigrant known as Olle i Skratthult (Ole from Laughtersville), offered a formal program of comic skits and songs, followed by a dance. As a Swedish *bondkomiker*, or peasant comedian, Skratthult donned "squeaky boots, overcoat, long scarf, peasant cap with a big flower, and a blacked out tooth under [a] straw colored wig" (Harvey and Hulan 1982: 6). In this hick get-up, playing, spouting jokes, and singing in a pronounced rural dialect, Skratthult made a deep impression on local audience members like Fritz and Carl Swanson, who attended one of his Ashland performances just after World War I. For decades thereafter, with Fritz on accordion and Carl on banjo, the latter would sing Skratthult's trademark number, "Nikolina," "clown around," and "pull all kinds of foolishness" (Leary 1983: 223). Skratthult's "Nikolina" was eventually sung in broken-English "Scandihoovian" by the Iverson Brothers, who wore cowboy hats, billed themselves as Slim Jim and the Vagabond Kid, and combined Nordic, hillbilly, and cowboy songs (Greene 1992: 151–152). Fellow Norwegian-American Thorstein Skarning, who had recorded accordion solos in Norway before coming to Rice Lake, Wisconsin, worked a succession of Norwegian halls. In 1917, as the December 20 edition of Madison's *Capital Times* reported, Skarning's "Accordeon [*sic*] Concert Pleases" a large gathering of "local music lovers," most of them "Norwegian born," in nearby Stoughton. A month later, on January 17, central Wisconsin's *Grand Rapids Tribune* touted the upcoming "Notable Concert" at Daly's Theatre by "Thorstein Skarning, World-Noted Accordion Virtuoso." Like Skratthult, he typically followed each concert with an extended dance. Wisconsin Swiss musicians Otto and Iva Rindlisbacher often played with Skarning, interjecting alpine elements into both his formal program and subsequent dance. Rindlisbacher was also adept at lumbercamp fiddling, a genre that, as we shall see, would eventually exert a powerful affect on Skarning's traveling shows.

Indeed, while the prolonged forays of black jubilee and blackface minstrel performers offered exotic yet thoroughly American grist for the Upper Midwest's musical mill, the visits of musicians steeped in familiar European folk and vernacular traditions reinforced ongoing practices and inspired future emulation. What's more, many touring performers, even those billed as arriving directly from Europe, were often already or soon to become Upper Midwestern residents. And like the local amateurs they influenced, barnstorming professionals were typically affected by their adopted region's sonic ferment. A chaotic, creative, compelling, creolized musical force was alive and about.

Figure 1.5. Hjalmar Peterson, Swedish immigrant vaudevillian, in his Olle i Skratthult (Ole from Laughtersville) get-up, Minneapolis, c. 1925. Note the typical *bondkomiker* (peasant comedian) look: pudding-bowl haircut, cheap workman's cap adorned with an oversized flower, rustic woolen scarf, old-country greatcoat with metal buttons, artificially blackened tooth, and goofy grin. Minnesota Historical Society (negative 97994).

From Old Time Music to Polkabilly

By the 1920s, a fairly standard regional instrumentation had emerged, albeit still with considerable variation. Typical bands consisted of a fiddle and some sort of "squeezebox" (either a button accordion, a piano accordion, or a German concertina) as the basic unit.[17] For larger aggregations—depending on local preferences and the availability of musicians—either a string bass (aka a "bull fiddle") or a tuba (often called a "brass bass" or a "bass horn") offered "bottom"; a piano, a four-string banjo, or a standard guitar, either separately or in combination, might chunk out chords; wind instruments sometimes provided melody, harmony, and fills; while a drummer tapped steady beats (Leary 1984).

In the 1920s and 1930s, increasing numbers of ambitious Upper Midwestern musicians also began to expand their audiences and increase their incomes by emulating their vaudeville predecessors and peers. Radio, the telephone, better roads, reliable cars, and sound recordings enabled bands to reach listeners from afar, arrange for paying jobs, travel on a dance-hall circuit, and supplement their income by selling records. Leighton "Skipper" Berg, for example, won fans beyond his home in Albert Lea, Minnesota, when his Viking Accordion Band began performing over a succession of radio stations, beginning with WMT in Waterloo, Iowa. Despite its name, the band was neither dominated by accordions nor limited to a Scandinavian repertoire; rather, they played "country and modern songs," as well as Berg's "specialty . . . the ethnic folk songs in Norse, Bohemian,

Figure 1.6. Pee Wee King, polkabilly pioneer and member of the Country Music Hall of Fame, in Louisville, c. 1937. Mills Music Library Collection, University of Wisconsin.

German and Italian." Listeners responded, and the seven members of Berg's band crammed into "an old Hudson sedan with a rack on the top for the small instruments covered with a waterproof canvas cover and the drum and bass horn fastened on the running board." Their territory eventually included the southern half of Minnesota, the eastern Dakotas, northern Iowa, and western Wisconsin: "we branched out to play open-air boweries, country-side dance pavilions . . . small village and township halls, ethnic Lodge halls, etc." Likewise the Viking Accordion Band recorded nearly 70 78rpm recordings from 1933 to 1941 for such labels as Banner, Champion, Columbia, Conqueror, Decca, Melotone, Okeh, and Perfect (Berg and Berg 1992: 7, 111, 17, 68–69; Spottswood 1990: 2679–2681).[18]

In 1929, 15-year-old Frank Julius Anthony Kuczynski—a concertina and accordion player from Milwaukee's Polish working-class south side—began his transformation into the nationally known country and western musician Pee Wee King by forming a band that played "pop and novelty" tunes, "Italian and German and Polish music," and eventually country music. The group's first gigs were local, "in a variety of places, from formal dances in clubs to fish fries and picnics and taverns." An initial broadcast over Milwaukee's WTMJ led to their becoming regulars on that station's "Badger State Barn Dance" by 1933, resulting in "dates all around Milwaukee and southern Wisconsin and over as far west as Madison and up to Oshkosh, Appleton, and Green Bay" (Hall 1996: 25–29).

Whether traveling to perform or playing closer to home, whether known through radio and records or simply for their prowess in house parties and halls, the Upper Midwestern musicians favoring a creolized, regional repertoire likewise found a common name for their collective genre: "old time music." The term began to surface in the early 1920s in the speech of musicians and their audiences, in newspaper ads and stories, and on the posters and business cards of assorted bands. Elizabeth Peterson Miller, for example, was the daughter of an immigrant Norwegian fiddler, Ole Peterson, who had settled on a farm near South Wayne, Wisconsin, around 1900. In the 1920s, Elizabeth joined a sister and three brothers to form the Peterson Family Band. The Petersons entertained at "barn dances and house parties." Regarding their music, Elizabeth's daughter, Shirley DeNure, reckoned: "They played old time music, but like waltzes, polkas, circle two-steps, and schottisches. They called it old time music" (Berget 2001: 13). Guy Wood, elder brother of the aforementioned Fred Woodford, shortened his surname in that era and formed a band, Guy Wood and His Cornhuskers, that billed itself as the "Midwest's Leading Old Time Novelty Band" (Corenthal 1991: 252). And places like Monticello, Wisconsin's Karlen Hall periodically sponsored an "Old Time Musical Contest and Dance," with cash prizes awarded "to the best Old Time" yodelers, singers, and jiggers; waltz, schottische, and two-step dancers; fiddlers, harmonica blowers, accordionists, and bandonion players (Luchsinger 1991).[19]

Prompted by the utility of having a shared phrase for a ubiquitous phenomenon, and clearly an acknowledgment of the genre's venerable roots, old time music also owes at least part of its currency to its Norwegian-American equivalent, *gammaldans*, roughly translated as "old dance music." Referring to such couple dances as the polka, the waltz, and the schottische, *gammaldans* tunes and steps—already prevalent in the old country before Norwegians began successive waves of emigration—steadily replaced the highly localized and intricate Norwegian *bygdedans* (regional dance) forms at Upper Midwestern house party and hall dances. To be sure, some energetic newcomers might parade their skills with the running *springar*, or amaze with the high kicks of the *halling*, but more sedate and easily acquired dances claimed New World allegiance just as surely as the conventional four-string or "flat fiddle" gradually superseded the raised bridge, sympathetic strings, and characteristic drones of the nine-string Norwegian Hardanger fiddle, or *hardingfele*.[20]

Yet even the presence of Norwegians throughout the Upper Midwest cannot account for the rapid spread and staying power of the term old time music in and beyond the 1920s. Rather, that designation emerged chiefly to distinguish dance bands whose repertoires tended to be familiar, rooted, and agrarian from those whose sounds were new, exotic, and urban. The same cars, roads, telephones, radios, and records that enabled Skipper Berg to sally forth from Albert Lea and that allowed Guy Wood to traverse the entire Midwest from his Eau Claire base brought sounds from New York, New Orleans, Chicago, and beyond into the Upper Midwest's hinterlands. Sometimes labeled "jazz," sometimes dubbed "modern," the music from afar contrasted sharply with the music near at hand. Simply put, since one was modern, the other must be old time.

The Upper Midwest's old time music was also affected in the 1920s and 1930s by distinct yet parallel and overlapping strains of old time music

Figure 1.7. Postcard of Guy Wood (b. Woodford) and His Cornhuskers, Eau Claire, Wisconsin, 1934. Guy is on the right with his fiddle, fitted out like his bandmates, with overalls and fake facial hair. Note the juxtaposition of "old time" and "modern" at the top and bottom. Mills Music Library Collection, University of Wisconsin.

from beyond the region. In that era, the Anglo-American string band sounds of the East, the West, and especially the South were likewise dubbed old time by musicians, audiences, and promoters—with the additional epithet "hillbilly" compounding antiquity with rusticity (Green 1965). In 1926, the industrialist Henry Ford endorsed the term old time music with his money and warped ideology. Captivated by both racist notions of the evolutionary superiority of Anglo Saxons and romantic conceptions of a pristine preindustrial America, Ford regarded the popular music of his day as the debased, mongrel concoction of African Americans and Jews.[21] The purportedly wild and suggestive force of jazz and the alleged foreign quality of Tin Pan Alley music, Ford imagined, were sure to diminish the moral purity of Western civilization if left unchecked. His antidote was Anglo-American old time music that featured the fiddle in particular. Southern old time fiddle contests, consciously launched as an effort to revive a venerable tradition regarded as fading, had been flourishing since the 1890s (Blaustein 1975). New Englanders troubled by the effects of industrialization on rural life generally and music particularly had likewise championed the sustenance of old time music and musicians since at least 1895 (Bronner 1987: 189). In 1926, relying on his nationwide network of automobile dealers, Henry Ford sponsored a flurry of old time fiddlers contests that were particularly well received in the Upper Midwest.

In my hometown of Rice Lake, Wisconsin, the Sampson-Stinn Motor Company hosted a dance on New Year's Day 1926, wherein participants listened to Henry Ford's Old Time Dance Orchestra on the radio, then danced to local fiddler Steve Hawkins and his piano-playing daughter. On March 24, as winter gave way to spring, Otto Rindlisbacher presided over a contest that included farmers and lumberjacks of varied Anglo, indigenous, and "foreign" pedigrees. Some were British (Manor, Tallman, Ritter, Miller, Stafford, Reed); others were Irish (Collins, Haughian), French Canadian (Brunette, Crotteau, Gabriel, LaBrie), and Ojibwe French (Guibord). There were also Norwegians (Moe, Severson), Germans (Immerfall, Reckenthaler, Gaulke), and Czechs (Bretl, Jelinek, and Wilda). And while the performances included such Anglo-Celtic standards as "Sailor's Hornpipe" and "Rocky Road to Dublin," the fiddlers, unconstrained by the prejudices of Henry Ford, offered German, Scandinavian, Slavic, and metís tunes and even "a little bit of jazz" to an enthusiastic throng (Leary 1983: 226).

The pattern was much the same throughout the Upper Midwest in the winter and spring of 1926. Besides Rice Lake, old time fiddlers contests were held in Eau Claire, Janesville, Kenosha, LaCrosse, Madison, Milwaukee, Omro, and Racine, Wisconsin; and in Albert Lea, Appleton, Austin, Benson, Brainerd, DeGraff, Duluth, Fergus Falls, Little Falls, Mankato, Minneapolis, Pipestone, Rochester, St. Cloud, Virginia, and Willmer, Minnesota. Anglo-Celtic fiddlers and tunes were abundant, but in many areas they were outnumbered or absent altogether as Germans, Slavs, and especially Scandinavians held sway. A *Milwaukee Sentinel* headline proclaimed, "Foreign Born Can Fiddle Too" (January 14, 1926). And in Minneapolis, Karl "King Tut" Schwanenberg won the "Northwest Championship" by playing a medley that—in true Upper Midwestern old time fashion—mingled his German roots with a sentimental Irish air with pieces from the American South's minstrel show and fiddling repertoire: "*Ach Du Lieber Augustine*," "Where, Oh Where Has My Little Dog Gone" (a "Dutch" dialect song that borrows its tune from "*Zum Lauterbach Hab Ich Mein Strumpf Gelorn*"), "Where the River Shannon Flows," "Dixie," and "Arkansas Traveler" (*Minneapolis Morning Tribune* February 6, 1926).[22]

Although initially sponsored by Ford, old time fiddlers contests took on a life of their own in the Upper Midwest, proliferating, competing, figuring in promotional materials, and solidifying old time music as the consensus designation for the region's culturally mixed sound. Not to be outdone by Minnesota's Karl Schwanenberg, Elmwood, Wisconsin's Ab Thompson won a rival regional contest and billed himself as "The Champion Old Time Fiddler of the Northwest." His dance band's business card went a step further by boasting an ability to play both the "Oldest and Up-to-Date Dance Music" consisting of "Quadrilles, Two Steps, One Steps, Schottisches, Hamburgers, Waltzes, Fox Trots" (Wiff 1986: 51–52).

Old time music, sometimes spelled in a consciously archaic fashion as "olde tyme," persists in the early twenty-first century as the foremost agreed-upon term for the creolized sound that has emerged and evolved in the Upper Midwest since the mid-nineteenth century. The region's musicians not only have continued to play but also to characterize their style as "old time music with a lot of drive," to host radio programs dubbed the "Old Tyme Dance Party," to refer to their music as old time in regional trade

Figure 1.8. Contestants in a Henry Ford–sponsored Old Time Fiddlers Contest pose outside of Otto Rindlisbacher's Buckhorn (a café and billiard parlor during Prohibition), Rice Lake, Wisconsin, 1926. Author's collection.

publications, to organize jamborees of old time fiddlers and accordionists, and a good deal more. Yet they have not won national recognition of their generic self-designation.[23]

In the late 1950s, influential folk music revival groups like the New Lost City Ramblers of New York City found inspiration in the music of Anglo-American southern string bands whose commercial recordings, made mostly in the 1920s, seemed more authentic to them than the updated, urbanized, amplified "country" music of the time. They and like-minded "citybillies" sought out not only the recordings of early performers but the performers themselves, creating an old time music revival that was centered mostly on the music of the South. By the early 1960s, New Lost City Rambler Mike Seeger and Newport Folk Festival organizer Ralph Rinzler were producing influential recordings like *Old Time Music at Clarence Ashley's* on the Folkways label (1963). And over the next decade, folk revival publications like the *Devil's Box, Sing Out!* and the *Old Time Herald* invoked, debated, and defined old time music as a phenomenon rooted chiefly in the culture of the Anglo-American South.[24]

There were dissenters, to be sure, foremost among them Simon J. Bronner, whose *Old-Time Music Makers of New York State* established the long-standing presence of a species of old time music in New England and upstate New York. In that region:

> Old-time music combined Anglo-Celtic fiddle tunes, square dance numbers, play-party tunes, Victorian parlor songs, native American and

British ballads, sacred songs, and minstrel songs. It was "old-time" because it symbolized old-time rural values for an era after World War I when everything seemed modern. (Bronner 1987: xiii)

While Bronner's generalizations regarding the rustic, yearning, wholesome connotations of old time surely resonate with Upper Midwestern sensibilities, his enumeration of musical specifics strikes a different note entirely. My own efforts to establish the distinctive Anglo, European, and American Indian attributes of old time music as practiced from the western Great Lakes to the edge of the Great Plains—first set down in my 1984 essay "Old Time Music in Northern Wisconsin," which forms the germ of this chapter—seem to have had little effect. Shortly after the publication of that essay, I was contacted by square dance and contra dance enthusiasts who, I suspect, had merely noted the title in some bibliography. Even the usually careful Simon Bronner mistakenly represented my work as making the case for Anglo-American dominance, as a "chronicle of old-time music carried along the Yorker path of migration to the Midwest" (Bronner 1987: 191).

What their music is called, the sources of its many strands, how well or even if it is known to outsiders perhaps matters little to those Upper Midwesterners who have sustained their distinctive version of old time music for more than a century and a half. They know what it is, they know what they like to call it, and they will keep on playing it. Yet such issues matter to me, and they ought to matter to anyone the least bit interested in understanding the richness of American folk music and how it has actually evolved in the culturally diverse United States. Since, as a broadly acknowledged term with cachet among folk music scholars and enthusiasts alike, old time music has been claimed as the exclusive property of Anglo Americans, and since naming is knowing, I am proposing an alternative designation for the Upper Midwest's creolized sound, a term that invokes what Bob Andresen so deftly described as a "mix" of "music from Europe" and "American country music," a term that aptly fuses two remarkable American roots traditions as they collide and coalesce in the middle of the country: "polkabilly."

Hidden in Plain Hearing

Polkabilly, quite obviously, compounds "polka" with "billy." The former is both the name of a dance and a designation for an American musical genre. Originating around 1830 in a Germanized Czech region bordering on Poland, the polka is a couple dance in 2/4 time that, like the Austrian waltz, became an international sensation in the mid-nineteenth century. Its popularity coincided with the invention and diffusion of the accordion, the standardization of brass and reed "band" instruments, and the migrations of European peoples to North America generally and to the Upper Midwest in particular. Polka dancing flourished in the region as immigrants of

Germanic, Nordic, and Slavic heritage sustained and shared their particular variations not only of the polka but also of many other musical styles and dance forms. By the 1930s, the word polka had entered public and music industry parlance nationally in reference to a range of ethnically derived American musical and dance traditions that all included some version of the polka (Greene 1992; Keil 1992; Leary 1996, 1998).

Billy, an Anglo-American designation for a boy or a man, has been appended to "hill" since at least the late nineteenth century, with "hillbilly" derisively casting American southerners especially as vulgar, ignorant rustics (Cassidy 1985: 238; Cassidy and Hall 1991: 1010). Disdaining its negative use by condescending outsiders, rural people have nonetheless sometimes played the hick to bamboozle parochial urbanites and entertain knowing fellow country folk; and they have embraced the word hillbilly for its positive connotations of carefree and natural simplicity. In the mid-1920s southern old time music came to be known alternatively as hillbilly music when groups like Al Hopkins's Hill Billies and George Daniells's Hill Billies, needing evocative names for their incipient careers as recording artists, chose "a funny and a fighting term" that neatly captured their playful, defiant, anachronistic yet sophisticated regional stance within the larger context of American life and music (Daniel 1983; Green 1965, 1983: 231; Harkins 2004). In the 1950s, innovative Anglo-American performers like Elvis Presley, Carl Perkins, Jerry Lee Lewis, and a host of others launched "rockabilly" music: a fusion of hillbilly sounds with African-American gospel, blues, and boogie woogie that jumped "billy" from the backwoods to jangle on Beale Street with "rock," which, as a dual metaphor for having sex and a good time, had suffused black songs since at least the 1920s (Morrison 1996: 2–3).

Polkabilly's limited status as a generic term commenced about 1991 after I produced a cassette by the Goose Island Ramblers, *Midwest Ramblin'*, epitomizing the Upper Midwest's creolized take on old time music. Later, reacting to my liner notes characterizing the music as "a hillbilly Norwegian polka tour of a region's musical traditions," Roby Cogswell, a folklorist from Tennessee, dubbed what he heard "polkabilly." When he casually dropped the word into a conversation we had months later, I wondered why someone hadn't thought of it years before.

Certainly several Upper Midwesterners had come close. In the 1930s, the immigrant accordionist Thorstein Skarning, an established performer along the Wisconsin-Minnesota border, renamed Skarning's Entertainers as Skarning and His Norwegian Hillbillies, while he and his bandmates traded the peasant finery and fjord backdrops of their old stage show for overalls and cornstalks. In 1937, the band broadcast thrice weekly on WDGY radio in Minneapolis (Greene 1992: 150; see also Martin 1994: 88; Nusbaum, 1989: 5; *Stranded in the U.S.A.* 2004: 23 M). The Swiss Hillbillies struck a similar polkabilly pose on eight 78rpm recordings made in Chicago for the Decca label in 1939 (Spottswood 1990: 150). Likewise in the 1930s, musicians in Chicago and the hinterlands established several "Polish Barn Dance" programs on radio, where groups like the Polish Mountaineers and the Polish

Figure 1.9. Thorstein Skarning, with baton, poses with farm animals and fellow performers, probably in Minneapolis, 1938. Note "Norwegian Hill Billies" on the drumhead. Minnesota Historical Society (negative 37975).

Barn Dance Band combined steel guitars, fiddles, and accordions with singing in Polish, English, and comically blended dialects.[25]

Although never nominally acknowledged, a distinctive polkabilly sound contributed to broadcasts from one of the Midwest's most powerful radio stations, WLS, where fiddle and accordion bands were common, particularly on programs like the wildly popular "Barn Dance" each Saturday night from the mid-1920s through the early 1950s. Although based in Chicago, WLS was nonetheless aligned with *Prairie Farmer* magazine and cultivated a rural audience through agricultural and weather reports, gardening and homemaking programs, and live music. Overwhelmingly old time and overtly Anglo American in character, WLS music programs nonetheless included Christine the Little Swiss Miss Yodeler, the Little German Band, Ukrainian choirs, and the Scandihoovian dialect singer Olaf the Swede from the late 1920s through the 1940s.[26] Meanwhile, fiddler Rube Tronson, leader of WLS regulars the Texas Cowboys, was actually a Norwegian from Wisconsin, likewise the home state of three other nominal Texas Cowboys: guitarists Red Blanchard from Pittsville and Lester Polfuss (Les Paul) from Waukesha and Rhinelander's French-Canadian fiddler Leizime Brusoe (*American Fiddle Tunes* 2000 M; O'Donnell 2003: 15; Patterson 1975: 13). Not surprisingly, the Texas Cowboys' combined string band instruments with clarinet, accordion, and drums to perform a polkabilly repertoire. And even such influential southern and western WLS performers as Louise Massey and the Westerners, who had grown up in Texas and New Mexico, Texan Gene Autry, and Patsy Montana (Ruby Blevins) of Arkansas incorporated Upper Midwestern polkabilly elements into their repertoires.

When Louise Massey and the Westerners joined the "Barn Dance" in September 1933, the band included newly hired accordionist Larry Wellington, who added polka, waltz, and schottische instrumentals to the group's repertoire of western songs, "old-time breakdowns," and sacred songs: "Army Rookie Polka," "Beer and Skittles," "Honeysuckle Schottische," "New Roswell Schottische," "Old Rose Waltz," "Rochester Schottische," "Squeeze Box Polka," "Starlight Schottische," "Varsovienna," "Waltz Time Melody," and "Ye Olde Rye Waltz" (Massey 2000 M; Russell 2004: 608–613). In the spring of 1934, Frank Kuczynski, soon to be better known as Pee Wee King, was playing with his band for the "Polish-American Hour" on WRJN in Racine, Wisconsin, when Joe Frank, manager of the singing cowboy Gene Autry, heard him on the radio. Frank, Autry, and members of his Range Riders band were traveling to perform in Milwaukee when their car was sideswiped, causing it to crash and slightly injure three musicians. A desperate Joe Frank called WRJN and managed to persuade Kuczynski and his sidemen to fill in for just one night. But Frank and Autry "liked having an accordion in the band because it added a different sound to the music." Since Lent had begun, Pee Wee's band had no looming jobs in heavily Catholic and Lutheran southwest Wisconsin, so he went on the road in Iowa and Illinois with Gene Autry for two weeks (Hall 1996: 30–31). The accordion was a fixture ever after in Autry's cowboy bands.[27] Recorded in 1935, Patsy Montana's best-known composition, "I Want to Be a Cowboy's Sweetheart," is what she called "a nice polka tune," and she attributed its initial success to the enthusiastic response of a "lot of polka people in Michigan and Wisconsin" (*Yodel: Straight from the Soul* 1996 M). From 1956 to 1960, Montana's long-time backup band, the Prairie Ramblers, a quartet of western Kentucky string band musicians, even teamed with singer Carolyn DeZurik and accordionist Stan Wolowic to form the Polka Chips, performing for the television series "It's Polka Time," as well as "for countless Polish and Slavic weddings, anniversaries, and celebrations" (Samuelson n.d.; Wolfe 1982: 56–60). The group's transition was perhaps eased by the participation of Carolyn DeZurik, wife of the Prairie Ramblers' Ralph "Rusty" Gill and half of the yodeling DeZurik Sisters of WLS "Barn Dance" fame. Carolyn and Mary Jane DeZurik were part of a musical Polish-American family from Little Falls, Minnesota, where their father fiddled for dances (*American Yodeling, 1911–1946* 1998 M; Plantenga 2004: 229; Retka 2004 I).

Indeed, an array of polkabilly sounds—mixing continental European and Anglo-American dance forms, accordion and fiddle, and English and "foreign" tongues—has long flourished beyond the Upper Midwest, especially in places where polka and hillbilly musicians have encountered one another in rural and industrialized backwoods regions. Perhaps the earliest proto-polkabilly sounds were made in the hills and valleys of western Pennsylvania, eastern Ohio, and West Virginia, where English, Irish, and German settlers began to mingle in the eighteenth century (Bayard 1945: xii, xx; Milnes 1999: 7, 14, 149–152). Fiddlers with obvious German surnames, like Clark Kessinger—born in West Virginia's Kanawha County in 1896 and the descendant of a fiddling great-grandfather—likely heard German tunes, along with Anglo-Celtic pieces, while growing up. Promoted by Rounder Records in 1972 as "the greatest old time fiddler around today," Kessinger recorded 82 tunes from 1928 to 1930, most of which were issued on the Brunswick label (Kessinger 1972 M). While the jigs, reels, minstrel tunes, and rags exemplifying the South's prevailing Anglo-African-American folk musical fusion predominate, more than a quarter of the Kessinger recordings—a schottische, 5 polkas, 5 marches, and 11 waltzes—hint broadly at non-Anglo-European influences (Russell 2004: 479–481). Indeed, two of the tunes, "Under the Double Eagle" (*Unter der Doppel Adler*) and "Lauterbach Waltz" (*Zum Lauterbach Hab Ich Mein Strumpf Gelorn*) are unarguably German. Echoing northwestern Wisconsin's Fred Woodford, who discovered that his "German neighbors were great on waltzes," Kessinger confessed to the Rounder Collective, "I like the waltzes the best" (Kessinger 1972 M). As Ivan Tribe, chronicler of country music in West Virginia, put it: "Although an outstanding breakdown fiddler, Clark Kessinger was probably unexcelled in his ability to play the slower and more difficult waltzes and marches with almost unequaled dexterity" (1984: 34).

The coming of Hungarian, Italian, and Slavic late nineteenth-century immigrants to the western Pennsylvania/West Virginia mining country added to the musical ferment, with some of their children crafting a full-fledged polkabilly sound by the 1930s. Doc Williams, born Andrew J. Smik, Jr., in 1914, grew up in western Pennsylvania, where his Slovak immigrant father played both Eastern European and American tunes. In the mid-1930s guitarist Williams formed the Border Riders with his brother Milo (aka Cy) and accordionist Marion Martin to perform on the "World's Original WWVA Jamboree" out of Wheeling, West Virginia. Country music historian Ivan Tribe characterized the band as having a "distinct sound" mixing

> straightforward country music with a strong dash of Eastern European influence. In regions like northern West Virginia, Pennsylvania, and eastern Ohio, which sustained a large immigrant populace, this blending of styles proved to be a definite asset. While the Border Riders were neither the first nor the only band to accomplish this musical amalgam, they probably did it best. (Tribe 1984: 47–48)

Italian-American accordionists, mandolinists, and bandleaders like Fred Gardini, Gay Franzi, Vincent Gamelli, and John Bava, all of whom were active on Wheeling, West Virginia's "WWVA Jamboree," also contributed to West Virginia's "musical amalgam" (Tribe 1984: 45, 63, 95, 134–135).

Polkabilly resounds as well in scattered areas across the Great Plains, extending from Texas to the Canadian prairie provinces, where assorted

Germans, Scandinavians, and Slavs have settled alongside American Indian, Anglo-Celtic, Hispanic, African-American, and French peoples. George W. Lyon's *Community Music in Alberta,* for example, bespeaks a ferment paralleling that of America's Upper Midwest:

> Canadian folk music is often identified with the old time musics of Quebec, Ontario, and the Maritimes, each of which has its own flavor. The music of the prairies has been a well-kept secret; indeed many folklorists have doubted the existence of indigenous folk culture on the prairies. Western Canada is a large region, and it was populated by many groups, each of whom brought their own ingredients. To the British root stock was grafted the Norwegian *hoppwaltz,* the Ukrainian *kolomayka,* and the *polkas* of many nations. (Lyon 1999: xvii)

By the late nineteenth century, musical exchanges were equally common in south and central Texas involving Anglo-American, Tejano, African-American, German, and Czech musicians mixing breakdowns, canciones, blues, polkas, waltzes, string bands, and squeezeboxes.

Adolph Hofner, born in Lavaca County, Texas, in 1916 of German and Czech parents, was raised around noted polka bands like the Patek Family of Shiner. But the country yodeling of Jimmie Rodgers, the whine of Hawaiian steel guitars, the pop crooning of Bing Crosby, and the newborn western swing of Milton Brown and the Musical Brownies were also inspirations (Hofner 1980 M). In the 1930s, after a stint with Jimmie Revard's western swing band, the singing guitarist Hofner and his steel-playing brother Emil formed their own band, going professional with a sound that had been nurtured for decades in house parties and country dance halls: "I was about the first guy to put a country music sound to German and Czech music and to this day it follows me" (*Texas-Czech, Bohemian, & Moravian Bands* 1993 M; see also Greene 1992: 148–149).

As the Czech-American chronicler Clinton Machann astutely observed, the European peasants who established farms, ranches, and small towns in Texas found a particular affinity with "Anglo rural folk music." And as their traditional, pastoral lives began to be affected by "a new, industrial, urban age," they likewise were attracted to western swing and honky tonk music, which "deal precisely with important problems such as alcoholism, infidelity, and rootlessness" (Machann 1983: 6). Besides Adolph Hofner, such Texas Czech and German musicians as Jimmy Brosch, the Czech Harvesters, the Ellinger Combo, the Hi-Toppers, Ray Krenek, Lee Roy Matocha, Joe Patek, the Red Ravens, the Vrazels, and more have sustained polkabilly sounds (Machann and Mendl 1983; *Texas Bohemia* 1994 M).

Despite their longevity and prevalence, the German and Czech polkabilly performers of Texas have received scant recognition in standard writings on western swing and honky tonk music.[28] The abundant annotated compact disk reissues of these genres, except Chris Strachwitz's work with Adolph Hofner, likewise either ignore polkabillies entirely or remark upon them with a combination of incredulity and barely concealed hilarity.

For example, the back cover copy on Thomas Meinecke's CD reissue of polkabilly performances by "Texas Bohemian-Moravian-German Bands" beckons curious listeners with lurid capitalization: "WELCOME TO THE INCREDIBLY STRANGE WORLD OF TEXAS BOHEMIA" (*Slow Music* 1996 M). *Roots and Rhythm,* the nation's leading mail order catalog for "roots music," subsequently placed Meinecke's CD in its "Ethnic & World Music" category rather than in "Country, Bluegrass & Old Timey," informing listeners that it was a "very strange album featuring recordings from the 60s, 70s, and 80s of Bohemian, Moravian, and German bands from Texas performing country and pop songs" (Scott 2003: 29). While Meinecke's come-on and the *Roots and Rhythm* review were directed at aficionados of American old time country music, Robert Klymasz had employed the same rhetoric of mysterious exoticism 20 years before in the title of an essay—"Sounds You Never Heard Before"—intended to enlighten folklorists and ethnomusicologists regarding Ukrainian polkabillies in Manitoba and Alberta (Klymasz 1972). Perhaps it is worth remembering that the "discovery" of the blues, currently the most exalted genre in America's roots music canon, coaxed similar exclamations from its eventual popularizing "father," the African-American bandleader W. C. Handy. After happening upon a blues performer in 1903 at a train station in Tutwiler, Mississippi, Handy characterized blues as "the weirdest music I had ever heard" (Handy 1941, quoted in Palmer 1982: 44–45; see also Titon 1977: 26–27).

As old an American music as the blues, polkabilly has been hidden in plain hearing along the western and eastern flanks of country music's southern core and even in its Upper Midwestern stronghold where, perhaps because it is so ubiquitous, neither influential critic nor visionary entrepreneur has clamored for its notoriety. The time has come to recognize polkabilly's presence and ponder its significance. And since so many genres of American folk and roots music have become best known through the sounds and stories of remarkable yet representative performers, let us begin with the Goose Island Ramblers.

Polkabillies Par Excellence

Writing for the journal *Old Time Country,* Henry Koretzky commenced a review of the Goose Island Ramblers' *Midwest Ramblin'* with a question: "When the label of old-time country is applied to a group like the Goose Island Ramblers, the question that comes to mind is, which country?" (1992: 27).

Natives of south-central Wisconsin, the Goose Island Ramblers grew up—like Bob Andresen and thousands of other Upper Midwestern musicians—in a region where pluralism prevailed. Even so, the collective experiences of members K. Wendell Whitford, George Gilbertsen, and Bruce Bollerud drew upon an extraordinary array of cultural strains well established since the nineteenth century in their respective home communities: Anglo-Celtic ballads and fiddle and fife tunes; minstrel and parlor songs, both comic and sentimental; marches and novelty songs featuring Hawaiian guitar; Swiss yodeling; Norwegian, German, and various Slavic polkas, waltzes, and schottisches; and dialect songs in broken English. Their creolized, highly localized repertoire also accumulated external influences from the 1920s on through radio performers in Hawaiian, hillbilly, cowboy, and bluegrass veins; touring proponents of Bohemian and Slovenian polka styles; and the recordings of Scandinavian and Dutchman (German-American) dialect comedians. By synthesizing a wide array of both local and popular musical sounds into a distinctive regional sound, the Goose Island Ramblers commanded an audience of fellow rural and working-class Wisconsinites of varied ethnic backgrounds with shared experiences of musical diversity.

For these reasons alone, the Goose Island Ramblers are polkabillies par excellence, illuminating the roughly congruent lives and times of bands that, especially from the 1920s through the present, have synthesized an array of "foreign" and "American," folk and popular, regional and national, polka and hillbilly musical strains to entertain rural, small town, ethnically diverse, working-class audiences throughout the Upper Midwestern region of Michigan, Wisconsin, Minnesota, northern Illinois, Iowa, eastern Nebraska, and the Dakotas.

Yet because, unlike most polkabillies, they performed mostly in and around the university town of Madison for roughly a half century, the Ramblers also attracted a significant college-educated audience for some combination of scholarly, romantic, antimodern, egalitarian, and purely musical reasons. As a result, the Ramblers have been photographed, recorded, written about, and interviewed to an extent unprecedented among kindred performers. Called upon regularly to tell their stories, the group's members became exceptionally articulate, vivid, and thoughtful narrators of their own musical experiences and, by extension, of the experiences of fellow polkabillies.

Just one band among many, just three performers among thousands, the Goose Island Ramblers, through their lives and sound, their thoughts and words, nonetheless exemplify the Upper Midwest's polkabillies. And in so doing, they establish the genre's indisputable presence in American life, while challenging and redefining our notion of what constitutes American folk music.

2

"Uncle Windy" Whitford

Where It All Started

> Let's start with my birthplace, down in Albion. That's where it all started,
> it seemed like to me. . . . I can go down to the cemetery at Albion, I can
> go back four generations on either side of my family in this little cemetery
> there. They were pretty much home people. Well, of course, in the
> beginning, great-grandpa and that came from New York state. Seems
> like most of them did. Some come over from England, 'cause we still got
> relatives over there.
>
> —Whitford 1990 I[1]

Kenneth Wendell Whitford—known variously as "Wendy," "Windy," or
"Uncle Windy"—was born on February 25, 1913, in Albion, Wisconsin, to
Kenneth Whitford and Gertrude Bell Smith. He worked from 1936 to 1976
for Oscar Mayer Foods, an enormous meat-packing plant on the east side
of Madison, moving from the loading docks to operating an elevator to
toiling in the Lamb and Calf Cooler Department. But family and old time
music were his lifelong passions. He married Helen Wickboldt in 1940,
and the couple raised three sons and four daughters, all of whom learned
to play and sing. When he died on June 10, 2000, Windy Whitford had lived
all of his life in Dane County, Wisconsin, and he had been playing old time
music for more than 80 years. His musical roots, however, were much older
and deeper. The elder statesman of the Goose Island Ramblers, Windy
Whitford was descended from and surrounded by musical Yorkers of English heritage who had been living in southern Wisconsin for generations.

In 1839, three years after the establishment of the Wisconsin Territory,
Windy's maternal great-grandfather Horace Bliven left Alfred, New York,
in the Hudson River Valley, traveling along the Erie Canal, through the
Great Lakes, and then overland to the newly formed community of Milton,
Wisconsin. "Milton" invoked the English poet John Milton, since the lakes
and prairies of southern Wisconsin were "paradise regained" for newcomers
who had lost their Eden on the Hudson during economic hard times. Like
most of his fellow settlers in the early years, Horace Bliven was a staunch

Seventh Day Baptist, a follower of the seventeenth-century Rhode Island dissenter and champion of religious freedom, Roger Williams. A shoemaker who was also an adept carpenter, Horace Bliven, according to family tradition, "worked for a fellow by the name of Joe Goodrich" after his arrival in Wisconsin.

Likewise a Seventh Day Baptist, as well as a fervent abolitionist, Goodrich was the driving force behind a pair of construction projects yoked to the community's prosperity and principles: the Milton House, a hexagonal stagecoach inn fitted with nooks and crannies and underlain by tunnels that would serve as hiding places for runaway slaves on the Underground Railroad; and the Milton Academy, eventually Milton College, an educational institution committed to religious tolerance. Both were completed in 1844, but by that time Horace Bliven had moved on.

While working for Joseph Goodrich, Bliven fell in love with another employee, Charlotte Clement, a recent arrival from Dunham, Ontario. Determined to work for themselves on their own land, they married in 1843 and purchased an 80-acre farm a dozen miles northwest of Milton (Anonymous 1906: 101–102). There they joined other Seventh Day Baptists—among them friends and relatives that included Windy's paternal great-grandfather William A. Whitford—to establish the village of Albion, at once the Roman term for England and the namesake of a New York community from whence several had come (Butterfield 1880: 838–839; Cassidy 1947: 59). Ten years later, this community too established a school, Albion Academy (Adolphson 1976).

Unlike the Puritans with whom Roger Williams had broken, Albion's Seventh Day Baptists appreciated dance tunes and secular songs. Both Horace Bliven's brother Silas and his son Amos were old time fiddlers. And his daughter Eliza, born in 1860, loved to sing and dance. Sometime in the 1870s, she met Charles Squire Smith (1849–1926), of English and Scottish ancestry, who had come west to farm near Albion after the Civil War. As Windy recalled: "Grandpa came from Albany, New York. He was looking for a place where the climate was good to him. They say he had asthma." Charles Smith also brought and played the fife and the fiddle. Soon he was sawing lead on fiddle tunes, while Silas Bliven played second fiddle and called figures for community dances that doubtless included Eliza Bliven. She and Charles Smith married sometime in the late 1870s. Their daughter and only child, Gertrude Bell Smith, Windy Whitford's mother, was born in 1880. Gertrude, in turn, married Kenneth Whitford, and the couple raised six boys, of whom Kenneth Wendell "Windy" Whitford was the fourth.

Music suffused every day of Windy Whitford's long life. Some parents might prop their infant in a cradle for a family photograph. Windy's dad, who "played the bass horn, tuba" in Albion's community band, set his newborn son in the big horn's bell—perhaps alluding playfully to his wife's middle name, Bell. While young Windy enjoyed his father's brass band performances, he was utterly captivated by his mother's singing and by the songs and tunes of his maternal grandparents.

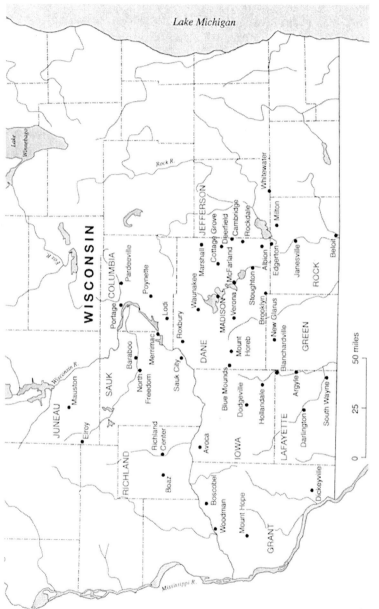

Figure 2.1. The collective musical world of the Goose Island Ramblers: Windy Whitford, George Gilbertsen, and Bruce Bollerud. Map by Onno Brouwer, Cartography Laboratory, University of Wisconsin.

I don't think I paid much attention to 'em at that time. But later on, when I got into music, everything came back from the songs my mother sang, songs that Grandpa sang. So I think that's where I got the foundation for loving country music, seeing that was the only thing, really, that I ever took a liking to.

Gertrude Bell Smith Whitford often hummed and sang while doing household tasks, especially while tending her six children. One of Windy's earliest, fondest memories was of sitting with his mother as she sang.

I don't know how old I was, must have been a year. I guess she done that to all us kids, she'd rock us in the old rocking chair and sing songs of Stephen Foster's like "My Old Kentucky Home." And "Green Fields of Virginny." I wonder if you ever heard that one? "Mid the green fields of Virginny / In the vale of Shenandoah."

In his grown-up years, Windy inherited and prized a school composition book that his mother had filled with song lyrics. Begun in 1894, during her teenage years, and updated throughout the 1890s, Gertrude Smith's notebook had "songs that were prevalent or popular" among her family and friends, including perhaps her husband, with whom she had attended Albion Academy. Poring over the pages in later years, Windy recalled: "Well Grandpa and Grandma would sing those songs, see, more than my mother. But she sang 'em."

At least five songs likely reached Albion through minstrel shows and related sheet music, pervasive media in nineteenth-century America, even in small Wisconsin towns. Blackface minstrel pieces—involving the assumption of largely invented, buffoonish personas by cork-daubed, malaprop-spouting whites who sang about chicken stealing, hoodooing, and razor walloping—were, however, completely absent from Gertrude Bell Smith Whitford's notebook. Rather she, and likely her neighbors and extended family, preferred what musicologist Nicholas Tawa calls "parlor songs on Negro-humanitarian themes" (Tawa 1980: 89) and what country music scholar Guthrie T. Meade dubbed songs about "slavery and memories of plantation life" (Meade, Spottswood, and Meade 2002: 462): "My Old Kentucky Home," "Darling Nellie Gray," "My Pretty Quadroon," "Rosalie," and "Lorena." All of them expressed a deep sympathy for the plight of African Americans, and several were closely aligned with the antislavery sentiments of Harriet Beecher Stowe whose *Uncle Tom's Cabin* (1851) must certainly have been widely read among Wisconsin's Seventh Day Baptists.[2]

"My Old Kentucky Home" (1853), best known nowadays for being sung each May at the opening of the Kentucky Derby, was composed by Stephen Foster (1826–1864). Born and raised in Pittsburgh, Foster was exposed to minstrel performers by the mid-1830s and began to write minstrel songs a decade later. In contrast to the syncopated slander of most of his fellow composers, Foster's "texts begin to take quite a different view of the black American," humanizing the characters, introducing unprecedented complaints about slavery, and decreasing the use of broad "nigger" dialect. Indeed in 1853, Pittsburgh's first stage production of *Uncle Tom's Cabin* featured several Foster songs, including "My Old Kentucky Home" (Hamm 1983: 211–215). To the Blivens, Smiths, and Whitfords, with their community's abolitionist roots, the song's poignant juxtaposition of ripening corn, blooming meadows, singing birds, and merry young folks with "hard times," weeping, old age, and separation bespoke the cruel lot of slaves. Perhaps Eliza Bliven Smith sang it to her daughter, Gertrude, as she rocked her, just as Gertrude sang Foster's composition to her children.

As a youngster, Windy Whitford certainly heard his Grandma Smith singing such songs as "My Pretty Quadroon" while doing household chores, especially while "working around the cookstove." Widely sung around the Civil War campfires of northern soldiers, "My Pretty Quadroon" (1863) concerned the despair of a slave sold down the river and separated from his sweetheart (Sons of the Pioneers 1970s M).

> My Pretty Quadroon,
> The flower that's faded too soon.
> My heart like the strings of my banjo
> Are broke for my pretty quadroon. (CD, track 4)

Windy was particularly fond of his grandmother's version of "Rosalie" or "Little Log Cabin by the Stream," dating from 1880 (Meade, Spottswood, and Meade 2002: 467), and he performed it throughout his life:

> Way down in old Kentucky, twas many years ago,
> Where we used to hunt the possum and the coon,
> The young folks they would gather round and have a merry dance
> When the fiddles and the banjos were in tune
> > Chorus:
> > Hey hang up your fiddle and the banjos on the wall,
> > Lay away your drums and tambourines.
> > Death has taken away my Rosalie,
> > The sweetest flower that bloomed,
> > From my little old log cabin by the stream.
> The stream is running just the same, the willow by its side,
> Waving o'er the grave of Rosalie.
> I sit alone beside the grave and while the hours away.
> I wonder when the saints will shelter me.
> > Repeat Chorus
> No more those merry times I'll see, the happy days of yore,
> Little darkies rolling on the green.
> Death has taken away my Rosalie, the sweetest flower that bloomed,
> From my little old log cabin by the stream.
> > Repeat Chorus

Grandpa Smith too sang such related songs as "Darling Nellie Gray," a lament composed in 1856 by Benjamin R. Hanby—an Ohio composer, teacher, minister, and abolitionist—concerning a lover sold down the river (Meade, Spottswood, and Meade 2002: 462; Tawa 1980: 89).

> There's a low green valley on the old Kentucky shore.
> There I've whiled many happy hours away
> A-sitting and a-singing by the little cottage door
> Where lived my darling Nellie Gray.
>
> Oh my poor Nellie Gray, they have taken you away
> And I'll never see my darling anymore.
> I'm sitting by the river and I'm weeping all the day,
> For you've gone from the old Kentucky shore.

"Lorena," composed like "Rosalie" in the late 1880s, was also in the family's repertoire. A "yellow gal" on "the old plantation," despite being happy while courted amid verdant nature by a fellow slave, is sold to "old Virginny," where she soon dies. Her lover finds some solace in knowing she will find peace and freedom in heaven (Meade, Spottswood, and Meade 2002: 467–468).[3]

Besides sentimental, sympathetic songs that whites composed about African Americans for minstrel stage and abolitionist parlor, Gertrude Bell Smith Whitford's notebook contained other late nineteenth-century songs that, collectively, contrasted the safety and bliss of home with the danger and sadness wrought by roving, the passage of time, inequity, and accident. Nobody dies in the Irish-American immigration song "Barney McCoy" (c. 1870s), and the tune is jaunty, yet the words are bittersweet as Barney leaves his "Nora darling" behind for a New World's promise (*Songs of Migration & Immigration* 1977 M; CD, track 5).

> That's a story about a young Irish boy that's going to leave Ireland, going to the United States, which was a great thing, I s'pose, and always has been. And his wife, or girlfriend, whichever it was, says "No, no Barney darlin', I gotta stay by mama." Stay by her mother. And he says, "Well, tomorrow morning you'll hear the signal gun. So be ready. The ship is going to be leavin', take us away." "No, no Barney darling. I got to stay by mama."

The aforementioned "Green Fields of Virginny" or "Mid the Green Fields of Virginia," composed in 1898 by Milwaukee's Charles K. Harris (1865–1930), balanced remembrance of childhood's "golden hours" in a "peaceful cottage" against an adult's realization that his home is far away and his parents gone (Meade, Spottswood, and Meade 2002: 352). The old admonished the young in "Wait till the Moonlight Falls on the Water":

> Wait till the moonlight falls on the water,
> Then take your sweetheart out for a walk.
> Mind what I say, boys,
> That's how to court her.
> Tell her you will wed her
> When the days grow short.

Meanwhile the young fretted about old age in "Will You Love Me when I'm Old?" from the early 1870s (Meade, Spottswood, and Meade 2002: 227): "a really pretty song," in Windy's estimation.

Petty morality, irredeemable loss, darker forces in family life stalked through "The Picture That Is Turned toward the Wall" from the 1890s (Meade, Spottswood, and Meade 2002: 259):

Now that always intrigued me. The girl got in the family way and her father turned her picture to the wall. That was it.

Though no tidings ever reached them
What her life or lot may be,
They sometimes think she's gone beyond recall.
There's a tender recollection
Of a face they never see
In the picture that was turned toward the wall.

Both a servant girl and a mother with babe in arms perished in "Milwaukee Fire," a ballad that began circulating shortly after the Newhall House, an "oft condemned hotel," burned, killing more than 60 people on a bitterly cold night in January 1883 (Laws 1964: 219; CD, tracks 6–7).

Twas the gray of early morning when the dreadful cry of fire
Rang out upon the cold and piercing air;
Just that little word alone is all it would require
To spread dismay and panic everywhere.

The extended Smith and Whitford family also sang "The Burning of the Granite Mill," recounting an 1874 tragedy in which more than 50 people were killed in Fall River, Massachusetts (Laws 1964: 218).

Set down in the 1890s, uniformly sentimental yet engaged with a world both glorious and dreadful, consistently emphasizing stories, the songs in Gertrude Bell Smith Whitford's notebook were the common songs of her family and community. They made a permanent impression on Windy Whitford. Referring to them a century later as "songs that you never hear" any more, he nonetheless persisted in keeping many alive through performing, recording, and, as we shall see, even writing what the critic Henry Koretzky called "original tunes" that are "hard to distinguish from the traditional ones" (Koretzky 1992: 27).

"The Great Time of the Day"

Just as ancestral voices echoed in his singing, the tunes of his Albion forebears persisted in the fiddling of Windy Whitford. Sitting in the airy kitchen of his Cottage Grove home in 1990, he acknowledged Charles Squire Smith.

Figure 2.2. K. Wendell "Windy" Whitford fiddles in the kitchen of his home in Cottage Grove, Wisconsin, 1979. Photo by Lewis Koch.

I like to say when we'd play out around, "My music teacher was born in 1849." They'd say, "Oh, you mean 1949, don't you?" And I says, "Not hardly. 1849" [CD, track 1]. . . . [Grandpa] was always humming and singing. He'd sing old time songs like Civil War songs, slave songs, just old time songs. He played the fiddle, he played the fife.

Windy Whitford's childhood home in the tiny village of Albion was just a short hike from his maternal grandparents' farm. In summers especially, when his mother was busy with the endless chores required in a household with six boys, "it seemed to be handy for Wendell to be shipped over to Grandpa's." From roughly age 5 through 12, Windy's summers followed a cherished pattern.

Life was so quiet and peaceful, it seemed like. Grandpa and I would go fishing in the afternoon. We'd go down to the crick which meandered down around behind the lot that their house was on, down through the pasture, and on down across the marsh to Edgerton. . . . he would tell me stories about trapping up and down the Hudson River when he was a boy. . . . And we'd come back. Grandma would fix supper. . . . He'd get that [fife] out and play in the evenings. You've got to appreciate or imagine what it was like in those days. No radio. No electric lights. . . . And then came the great time of the day. The twilight hour. And it seemed that that was designed just for us. Everything was peace and quiet. Grandpa'd get his fiddle out and play in the twilight. (CD, track 11)[4]

Those tunes on fife and fiddle whirling through the warm dusk, just after the wind died down, just before the whippoorwill's call, seemed an almost celestial gift to Wendell Whitford.

Many of the tunes Grandpa Smith played during those idyllic summer nights from roughly 1918 to 1926 had no names, or at least no names that Windy recalled. Indeed, old time fiddlers have often associated tunes with their key, their tempo, or the person from whom they learned the songs, rather than with fixed names. In the 1960s, as Windy Whitford played with Bruce Bollerud and George Gilbertsen as the Goose Island Ramblers, an old tune might "come out of the blue." When Bruce asked its name, Windy could only reply, "Gee, I don't know . . . but it's a tune that my Grandpa used to play. They come and go."

Windy could recall but a handful of his grandfather's tunes by name.[5] There was "Buffalo Gals," likely of eighteenth-century German origins but fused with British fiddle style in nineteenth-century America and a fixture in the minstrel repertoire (Bayard 1945: 1; Meade, Spottswood, and Meade 2002: 754–755); the plantation melody "Darling Nellie Gray"; the jubilee song "Golden Slippers" (Meade, Spottswood, and Meade 2002: 574); and an instrumental version of "The Bully of the Town"—originally a rowdy song from the African-American brothels of Saint Louis that circulated widely in minstrel shows in the 1890s (Cohen 1981: 28–29). There was the sentimental air "Flow Gently Sweet Afton," composed by the American J. E. Spilman in 1838 after lyrics by Scottish national poet Robert Burns (Tawa 1980: 9). Grandpa Smith also played the malleable "Girl I Left behind Me" (Meade, Spottswood, and Meade 2002: 152–153), popular among Civil War Soldiers and, in the version Windy recalled, associated with cowboys: "I struck the trail in '79, herd strung out behind me." The rest were a "lot of Scottish tunes as well as old American tunes."

While Windy remembered Grandpa Smith playing many tunes interchangeably "on the fife or the fiddle," that was not always the case: "it seemed like when he played the fife he played more tunes of the Scottish, music from Scotland. . . . Like bagpipe tunes, I s'pose they went hand in hand with the fife tunes." The association among the fife, Scottish tunes, and bagpipes suggests the repertoire of marches found frequently among fife-and-drum bands common in New York and Pennsylvania. As Alan Jabbour has observed:

Marching is a form of dancing, but the relationship to fiddling goes deeper: Throughout the nineteenth century many fiddlers in the United States were also fifers in local fife-and-drum corps, and there was thus a great degree of crossover between fiddling and fifing repertoires. (Jabbour 1996: 254; see also Bayard 1944, 1982)

Some of the Scottish tunes, however, as well as several "old American tunes" favored by Charles Squire Smith likely included jigs, hornpipes, reels, quadrilles, and perhaps a stray polka, waltz, or schottische. Windy did recall two Scottish dance tunes, the jig "Campbells Are Coming" and "White Cockade," a reel (Meade, Spottswood, and Meade 2002: 814, 713).

Although he chiefly heard his grandfather play at home in the evenings and always as a soloist—"Never heard anybody ever play with him"— Windy knew that Charles Smith had performed for dances years before with his wife's brother, Silas Bliven, playing second fiddle and calling figures. In the early 1930s, a half dozen years after his grandfather's death in 1926, Windy teamed up with George Matson, an old time fiddler who "played so many tunes." Many of them struck Windy as "just like some of the tunes that my Grandpa played." Among them: "Cleveland Two Step," "Kentucky Hornpipe," and "Flop-Eared Mule." And, like Grandpa Smith, George Matson fiddled in what Windy regarded as a vigorous yet "sophisticated," stately fashion.

We can neither know the full range of Charles Squire Smith's repertoire, nor just how he sounded, yet the shards Windy preserved regarding his grandfather's fiddling gain greater definition alongside several vivid accounts of fiddling Yorkers come to rural Wisconsin in the nineteenth century. Laura Ingalls Wilder was born in a log cabin near Pepin, Wisconsin, in 1867. Her father, Charles Ingalls, who hailed from Cuba, New York, was an old time fiddler with a broad repertoire. Wilder's reminiscent *Little House in the Big Woods* (1932), set in western Wisconsin in the 1870s, includes descriptions of jigging and square-dance calling, while mentioning many tunes her father played at community doings and, especially, around the family fireplace. They included the Revolutionary War ditty "Yankee Doodle"; the eighteenth-century sacred song "Rock of Ages"; the coeval aforementioned "Buffalo Gals"; the play-party favorite "Captain Jinks"; such jigs and reels as "Arkansas Traveler," "Devil's Dream," "Irish Washerwoman," "Money Musk," and "Pop Goes the Weasel"; the plantation lament "Darling Nellie Gray," as well as "Uncle Ned" and "O Susannah" by Stephen Foster; and the Scottish air "Auld Lang Syne." The sources and substance of Charles Ingalls's repertoire clearly parallel and intersect with that of Charles Smith.

Hamlin Garland (1860–1940), whose parents likewise hailed from rural New York, was born in a log cabin near West Salem, Wisconsin, and lived amid the area's coulees until 1881—the very era when Charles Smith was an active fiddler for dances. Garland's autobiographical *A Son of the Middle Border* described his first encounter with "the local professional fiddler, old Daddy Fairbanks" at a public dance:

His queer "Calls" and his "York State" accent filled us all with delight. "*Ally* man left," "Chassay *by* your partners," "Dozy-*do*" were some of the phrases he used as he played "Honest John" and "Haste to the Wedding." At times he sang his calls in a high nasal chant, "First lady lead to the *right*, deedle dum-dum—*gent* foller after—dally-deedle-do-do *three* hands round"—and everybody laughed with frank enjoyment of his words and actions. (Garland 1917: 94)

Another musician, however, made the greatest impression on Hamlin Garland. His paternal uncle David, "the handsomest, most romantic figure in all my world," was a fiddler who captivated his nephew in the 1870s much in the way that Charles Smith beguiled Wendell Whitford a half century later. Playing mostly within homes for family and relatives, David Garland "could make any room mystical with the magic of his bow." Some of his tunes were "familiar pieces," while others "had no names." Some were slow airs; the rest "were mainly dance tunes, cotillions, hornpipes—melodies which had passed from fiddler to fiddler" (Garland 1917: 54). Twenty-six years before, in his collection of short stories *Main-Traveled Roads* (1891), Garland closely modeled fiddling William McTurg after his uncle David: "He played on slowly, softly, wailing Scotch tunes and mournful Irish songs. He seemed to find in the songs of these people, and especially in a wild, sweet, low-keyed Negro song, some expression of his indefinable inner melancholy" (Garland 1891: 87). Like Daddy Fairbanks (and Charles Smith), William McTurg/David Garland also played "old tunes," including "Honest John," for set dancers, but like Charles Smith he did his most memorable work late in the evening, and perhaps late in life, when dancers had settled into their chairs to listen.[6]

Steeped in his grandfather's melodies, Windy Whitford began fiddling in 1921 at the age of eight: "I was pretty young then. One day Grandpa handed me the fiddle. He says, 'Let's see what you can do now.' So I started playing. 'Flow gently, sweet Afton, among thy green braes.' That's a song that I'd heard him play. That was the first tune that I played on the fiddle."

By 1926, the year Charles Smith died, his grandson Windy was a fair hand with a fiddle. That was also the year when Henry Ford launched a wave of old time fiddlers contests. The closest contest to Albion was in Stoughton, where fiddlers of English and Norwegian heritage prevailed. Even Charles Smith had played a few Norwegian tunes, as we shall see, and by the mid-1920s they had begun to make a profound impact on teenaged Windy Whitford.

That Was Norwegian

In the fall of 1840, Björn Anderson traveled from the Fox River Norwegian settlement in LaSalle County, Illinois, to look for land west of Lake Koshkonong in southern Wisconsin. A leader in an immigrant movement that would soon occupy much of what is now western Dane County, Anderson returned in the spring of 1841 with his wife and four children to become "the first couple that settled in the present town of Albion" (Anderson 1895: 161–162; Flom 1909: 164–165).

Anderson was raised on a farm near Stavanger, Norway, where reportedly he "was a born agitator and debater" given to "sarcastic criticisms of Norwegian laws and of the office-holding class." Rejecting the Lutheran state church, Björn Anderson "was in close sympathy" with the Society of Friends: "His life and conduct were controlled by Quaker principles" (Anderson 1895: 155). Small wonder that Anderson and fellow Norwegians, including those of Lutheran faith, lived harmoniously with the dissenting, abolition- ist, education-minded Seventh Day Baptists, who arrived at precisely the same time. Björn Anderson's son Rasmus, born on the family's Albion farm in 1856, would eventually found the nation's first Scandinavian Studies Department, at the University of Wisconsin. Before that, Rasmus Ander- son was the principal of Albion Academy from 1866 to 1869, during which time he actively increased the participation of local Norwegian students (Adolphson 1976: 50).

By 1880, one-half of the inhabitants of the town of Albion were "native born," mostly New Yorkers, while one-third were Norwegians, with the bal- ance distributed "among the English, Irish, and Germans" (Butterfield 1880: 839). And like Horace Bliven, Silas Bliven, and Charles Squire Smith, more than a few Norwegian immigrants arrived with fiddles and a fondness for dancing, which they and their descendants have sustained to the present.

The 1926 and subsequent fiddlers contests in nearby Stoughton attracted Norwegian performers from that city, from Albion, and from such other Dane County "Norsky" strongholds as McFarland, Deerfield, and Madison. They included Andrew Bosben, Even Evenson, Henry Everson, Ben Gulhaug, Ole Gutrud, Ole Haakanson, Alex Listug, George Matson, "Swede" Moseby, Adolph Sannes, Harald Smedal, and probably Clarence Reierson, who would considerably influence Windy Whitford (CD, track 11). In 1926, Hans Fykerud, an immigrant Stoughton tavern keeper, enthralled the crowd with an exhibition on the eight-string Hardanger violin. Prizes were given for the "best Norwegian selection" and also for the "best *Saeters Jenters Sondag*" (The Herd Girl's Sunday), a showpiece tune composed by the vir- tuoso Norwegian violinist Ole Bull, who had lived in Madison and enter- tained throughout the area in the late nineteenth century. In 1927, prizes were given for the best renditions of two Norwegian-American classics: the immigrant's song of home "*Kan Du Glemme Gamle Norge?*" (How Can You Forget Old Norway?) and "*Ja Vi Elsker Dette Landet*" (Truly Do We Love This Country), the Norwegian national anthem (Anonymous 1948: 6, 41; Nettl 1952: 103). Norwegian fiddlers, however, were not mere participants in token categories. Ole Gutrud captured the coveted best all-around fiddler prize in 1927, while in Madison's 1926 contest—where fiddlers were so numerous that they competed from March 8 to 13—five of the six final- ists were Norwegians: Ben Gulhaug, 77, Brooklyn; Olaf Larson, 60, Hol- landale; Andrew Bosben, 58, Deerfield; Henry Everson, 52, McFarland; and O. J. Smithback, 68, Cambridge.[7]

By his late teens, when Windy Whitford became a regular participant in the Stoughton contest, he had already encountered Norwegian fiddling through both his grandfather's renditions of Norwegian tunes and the fa- ther of a childhood playmate who, for many years, had attracted Norskies and Yorkers alike to dances in the Albion Town Hall.

Clarence [Reierson] lived on County A, just north of Albion. And he was a farmer and had an old time band that was very well received in the area, of course, before I ever come along. But when I got old enough to listen and appreciate it, boy I really always loved that—his sound and his vitality. He'd play a tune, this one that we call "Reierson's Two-Step" [CD, tracks 10–12], and he'd jig at the same time. Some called him "Fiddlesticks," but his name was Clarence Reierson.

The two-steps, jigs, and the reels for square dances that Reierson also played were hardly venerable Norwegian forms, nor was his band's instrumentation true to old country configurations: "Laurence Strandlie played guitar and Martin Hageberg played banjo with him. And his brother, Raymond Reierson, played the guitar and sang." Rather, in true old time/polkabilly fashion, Clarence Reierson combined "American" minstrel and parlor songs, with Yorker fiddle tunes, with Norwegian and Norwegian-American melodies and lyrics.

Many of his dance pieces in particular had no name: "We'd just say, that's 'Reierson's Two Step,' or that's 'Reierson's Hoppwaltz,' or that's 'Reierson's Waltz.'" Yet whatever the names and origins of his songs and tunes, Clarence Reierson delivered each with an emphatic Norwegian accent characterized by a stately tempo and rising and falling melodic embellishments, emulating a Hardanger fiddle's distinctive overtones. Windy Whitford was especially fond of one particular waltz that years later he and George Gilbertsen would feature as a twin fiddle showpiece during some of the Goose Island Ramblers' gigs.

> "Reierson's Waltz." This waltz of Reierson's is different than all the other Norwegian waltzes. It's, like George says, "If it don't say 'sidey-do,' it ain't Norwegian." [Sings] "Sidey, doodle leetle, dah de, doodle leetle, dah de, doodle leetle, dah de do." Like that. It goes around and around. It's got the old time sound that hangs into the echoes of your memories from childhood on and on and on. It never leaves you: the sound of his group playing the fiddle down there.

As a teenager, Windy Whitford played a few times with Clarence Reierson's band, getting the feel for this particular brand of old time music. He could even "talk a little Norwegian." Once, at a Sons of Norway Lodge dance, Clarence encouraged Windy to sing in the language. "He says, 'I'll say the words and then you sing 'em out.' And it was 'Kan Du Glemme Gamle Norge?'" Try as he might, however, Windy could never mold his voice to manage "the true expression like a true Norwegian." But his fingers were another matter.

Decades after Clarence Reierson's death, Windy traveled from his Cottage Grove home to play at a senior citizens' center near Albion: "I stopped at the graveyard out there. Going down on N here, that's where he's buried, right on the corner of 51 and N. I said, 'I want to dedicate my first song today to Clarence Reierson. I just got a feeling maybe he's listening to it.'"

Windy was delighted and humbled when several in attendance who had danced to Reierson's fiddle told him that they heard the old master emerge from his disciple's strings and bow.

It was Clarence Reierson who also told Windy the story of Goose Island, a name he applied to the succession of bands with which he made his finest music. As Windy explained in 1990, the Whitfords' Albion farm and those of several Norwegian neighbors abutted a marshy area known locally as Goose Island, although it was not an island at all. The term puzzled Windy until Reierson set him straight.

> This would be I s'pose like a hundred years ago—you see, what they called Goose Island was in reality a tamarack swamp. The Norwegians, when they moved into the area, moved in around it and settled their farms and started farming. And they would call that *gud land,* meaning "good land," because it was real fertile. Then the little kids would say, "goose land," he says. And by and by they got to call the area "Goose Island." (CD, track 16)

Reierson's explanation is lent credence by an observation in a history of Dane County based in part on conversations with early settlers:

> Accustomed in their native country, only to timbered land, these early [Norwegian] settlers shunned the prairie, which seemed desolate and cheerless to them, but which is now considered as the more desirable land, and settled in the edges of the [oak] openings, and along the marshes. (Anonymous 1877: 357)

Beyond the Goose Island name and a handful of memorable tunes, Clarence Reierson's bequest to Windy Whitford included the opportunity to associate with a wider network of Norwegian old time musicians, commencing with Reierson's regular guitarist, Laurence Strandlie.

In 1931, Strandlie and Whitford teamed up as part of the local Emery School District's Emery Players for a "Home Talent Night" fundraiser. Soon after, they were invited to play at Madison's Elks Club. On the way to the job, Strandlie suggested they stop to visit George Matson. Originally from nearby Deerfield's Norwegian settlement, Matson was living in Madison and had been a frequent participant in area old time fiddling contests since 1926, winning his share of prizes. As Windy recalled:

> This Laurence Strandlie, a friend of mine, showed me, "At this filling station here"—that was a Sinclair station on Williamson Street— "George Matson works nights there pumping gas. He's a state champion fiddler, old time fiddler." "Oh gee, I'd better stop and get acquainted." So I did. And he was like George Gilbertsen, he just happened to have his fiddle along with him. So we spent lot of late nights playing there when things wasn't too rushing at his station. And he was a good old time fiddler.

Soon Windy performed on the radio with Matson, and during those late night sessions and subsequent adventures, his mastery of and knowledge about old time Norwegian tunes accelerated.

It was through George Matson that Windy met Arne "Swede" Moseby, originally from Blanchardville, and learned more about the legendary Ole Gutrud. Moseby "was a Norwegian fiddler, but he was also a violinist that could play, like they say, 'long-haired music' too. He played with some big bands in the bygone years." In the early 1930s, Windy, Matson, and Swede "had a lot of fun playing together. This Swede Moseby would come over. 'Kom now Vindy,' he says, 've go down to the tavern and ve play a couple tunes and ve get a couple drinks.'" On more than one occasion, George and Swede told stories about "Ole Gutrud, the old Norwegian fiddler from down at Rockdale," who had been best all around at the 1927 Stoughton contest. One tale had a tune to go with it.

> That was the story about going to an auction at Strømmen and it rained, and Ole says, "Don't worry, I got my fiddle along with me. We'll go in the house and I'll make up this first tune and we'll call it 'Auction at Strømmen's.'" It was kind of a Norwegian tune. It was a peculiar tune too because it went in C and in D, the two keys. It's kinda contrary to regular music, because everybody thought you could go from C to G or C to F, but you don't go C to D. But that's the way this tune went that George taught me. And I had learned a lot of tunes from him. (CD, tracks 13–15)

Windy learned tunes and heard stories from other Norwegian old time fiddlers, including Henry Everson of McFarland, who at 52 was a finalist in Madison's 1926 contest.

The son of Norwegian immigrants, Henry Everson was born in 1874 in McFarland, a hotbed of fiddling Norskies. He pulled strands from a screen door as an 8-year-old to string a fiddle he'd fashioned from a cigar box, and at 12 bought his first proper fiddle. Soon he was performing for dances, and when he wasn't playing there were local fiddlers aplenty from whom to learn new tunes:

> Trace Natvig, Harris Hanson, Hans Larson, Benny Larson, Tallman Johnson, and Raymond Alsmo. . . . The parties were held in farmhouses, barns, or schoolhouses, where the rural folk would come to socialize. In the house, the parlor or the largest room would be cleared of furniture to accommodate dancing. Two or three local fiddlers would stand in the corner, playing sometimes until the sun came up. The fiddlers would pride themselves on playing the entire night without repeating a single song. (Larson 1991: 34–35)

In the early 1890s, hungry for new tunes, Henry Everson and "a few neighbors and friends . . . walked 15 miles to a dance on the Bosben farm near Deerfield, danced till 3 o'clock in the morning, then walked back home" (Larson 1991: 34). Eventually a farmer and stonemason with large, callused, yet surprisingly nimble fingers, Henry Everson fiddled into his 80s. Regarding Everson as "the oldest of the old time fiddlers" whom he knew, Windy Whitford sought the old timer out. They played together, and the youngster came away with some tunes.

Years later, when playing with the Goose Island Ramblers as the house band of a Madison tavern, Windy got to know a fellow named Knute Hervig.

Well he used to come down to Glen and Ann's to hear us play all the time. "I wish my parents could hear you folks play," he says. "Well, when they come over," my wife says, "why don't you let us know and we'll come out here and we'll play." He didn't tell us that, but his dad was an old time fiddler, but a Norwegian fiddler. And Norwegian talk—that's all he could do. He couldn't talk English at all. So when they did come over, they come out to the house and we played this afternoon—George and Bruce and I—and Knute's dad played right along with us. He really enjoyed that. Then I played some of them tunes that my Grandpa had, that I remembered from my Grandpa.

The session had coaxed out some half-forgotten melodies that Charles Squire Smith, the New York state fifer and fiddler, must have gleaned from Norwegian neighbors. When Windy put down his bow, the elder Hervig beamed in recognition: "He said, 'That was Norwegian, that was Norwegian tunes.'"

"I Want to Get Me a Guitar"

Perhaps Windy Whitford's parents dreamed that their musically precocious son would go beyond his folk roots, learn to read music, become a "serious" performer. In 1929, he told me, "the folks decided I should take piano lessons." But on July 29, "on the way to my first piano lesson, I was involved in an accident at the four corners in Albion—and wound up in the hospital." It was hot, the windows were open, and the people living across from Mercy Hospital in Edgerton had tuned in the "National Barn Dance" over Chicago's WLS radio. The "Barn Dance," begun in 1924, was a down home musical review that rivaled Nashville's "Grand Ole Opry" in popularity. Indeed it was the Midwest's dominant old time music program, with performers that included Swiss yodelers, the Little German Band, rural comedians, barbershop quartets, singing cowboys, southern string bands, and mountain balladeers.

Bradley Kincaid, "The Kentucky Mountain Boy," particularly inspired the convalescing Whitford with a repertoire that was at once exotic and familiar: "Boy, you could hear this Bradley Kincaid with his hound dog guitar. Now that really made an impression on me, these songs: tales of the mountains and the hills, songs of tragedy, songs of love, songs of mother and home. That all came to be just what I needed." A native of eastern Kentucky, Kincaid debuted on WLS in 1928 while attending YMCA College in Chicago. He played an old guitar his father had gotten in trade for a fox hound. And his songs, like the old ballads "The House Carpenter" and "Sweet Kitty Wells," were ones that he had grown up with in the mountains (Wilgus 1975: 86–94). Right away, Windy Whitford wanted to play and sing like Bradley Kincaid.

He had heard guitars before, but only occasionally; most recently in Clarence Reierson's string band and in the home of a neighbor around 1927 or 1928.

> Now over next door lived John Spencer. He was [a Civil War veteran] from Ohio and he played the fiddle. And he had a boy named Roy and he lived in Chicago most of the time. Occasionally he'd come up. Now one night, this was after Grandpa had died and Grandma and I were there at the house, it come up a storm. And this lady, John's wife, come over and she says to Grandma, "Maybe you and Wendell want to come over and spend the evening with us? 'Cause John's boy Roy is up and they're going to be playing a little bit of music." Well that was the first, it seemed like, that I had heard anybody play the guitar with a fiddle. Well that was just, I don't know how to explain it, it was so rich and so good sounding. That was great.

After hearing Bradley Kincaid sing, Windy reckoned that playing solo guitar and singing was more than great. "So when I got out of the hospital, I told my mother, 'I don't want to take no piano lessons, I want to get me a guitar and play guitar and sing these songs.'"

Before its widespread availability in the late nineteenth century through mail-order firms like Sears Roebuck and its subsequent integration into blues and hillbilly genres, the guitar was chiefly a parlor instrument favored by young women of the sort who, like Gertrude Bell Smith Whitford, might attend such schools as Albion Academy. Windy was surprised and pleased when his mother replied:

> "I used to play the guitar when I was a girl," she says, "and I got an old guitar up in the attic. We'll get it down and get some strings on it." Tuned it up and she taught me the G chord. And the first song that I sang, that she taught me, was "Red River Valley." And from that time on, it just seemed to me that I was a receptacle for old time songs. Anything I would hear I could practically remember it the first time I would hear it. I was just absorbing them. Everything just seemed to come to me natural.

Windy listened hard and often to WLS, sometimes playing along on the guitar that occupied his every spare moment, and he "learned all these songs from Bradley Kincaid."

With a few exceptions, it is difficult to know exactly which songs Windy Whitford acquired through some combination of Kincaid's radio performances, song folios, and 78s. Many "Kincaid" songs were already old when the Kentucky Mountain Boy acquired them, and nearly all were performed, recorded, and published before and after his renditions. Even so, it's clear that Windy Whitford and Bradley Kincaid appreciated many of the same songs. In his reminiscent songbook, *The Way It Was* (2000: 3), Windy recalls learning "Bury Me Out on the Prairie," "The Letter Edged in Black," "Methodist Pie," "Pearl Bryan," "When the Work's All Done Next Fall," "Billy Richardson's Last Ride," and "Wreck of [the Old] 97" from Kincaid's radio appearances. Windy also compiled a lengthy list of "old songs" during his extensive musical career to remind him of pieces he'd learned at one time or another. A dozen match titles that Bradley Kincaid recorded from 1928 to 1930: "The Butcher Boy," "Four Thousand Years Ago," "Give My Love to Nell," "I'll Be All Smiles Tonight," "The Letter Edged in Black," "Little Mohea," "Little Rosewood Casket," "Methodist Pie," "Pearl Bryan," "Streets of Laredo," "Sweet Kitty Wells," and "True and Trembling Brakeman" (Meade, Spottswood, and Meade 2002: 988; Russell 2004: 482–485). In the late 1920s and early 1930s, Windy Whitford also began to emulate Kincaid and other radio performers in other ways.

As rural, old time, mainly Anglo-American singers and musicians began to make commercial recordings, perform on the radio, produce song folios, and tour in the mid-1920s, many drew upon actual or invented connections to either the mountains of southern Appalachia or the Great Plains of America's "wild west": frontier regions that loomed especially large in versions of national history and destiny constructed by White Anglo-Saxon Protestant tastemakers. Accordingly, dignified "ancient minstrels" bearing old "Elizabethan" ballads and, more often, slovenly yet jovial "hillbillies" hailed from the mountains, singing, like Bradley Kincaid, about little cabins, gray-haired mothers, wandering boys, murdered girls, train wrecks, corn liquor, and getting religion. "Cowboys," meanwhile, populated the plains, togged out in high-crowned, wide-brimmed hats, tooled leather boots, kerchiefs, and shirts with darts and snaps, while singing about cattle drives; gun play; loneliness; the mother, home, and sweetheart they would never see again; and, of course, dying by a bullet, a fall from a horse, or beneath the hooves of stampeding longhorns right about the time they were going to draw their pay to return to mother, home, and gorgeous, pining sweetheart.[8] And, just as in the 1950s, when youngsters from Anywhere, U.S.A.—inspired by searing tunes from the radio, their hair slathered into pompadours, clad in pegged pants and jackets with padded shoulders—started guitar strumming or piano pounding in the manner of Elvis Presley or Little Richard, so also did teenage Windy Whitford emulate the mountaineer and the cowboy, performing in overalls and straw hat, or in western shirt and Stetson. He also apprenticed himself to another airwaves master.

Besides Chicago's WLS, XERA from Del Rio, Texas, carried all the way to Albion, Wisconsin. A border radio station, situated just across the line in Mexico, XERA was established in 1931 by Dr. John R. Brinkley. A former Kansas-based radio station owner and shady medical entrepreneur, Brinkley emigrated to elude federal restrictions on both the power of his signal and his practice of surgically implanting goat glands in gullible, impotent males. In the manner of early twenty-first century Clear Channel stations, Brinkley's programming combined fundamentalist preaching, right-wing politics, putative medical solutions to impotence and constipation, and old time country music (Malone 2002a: 98–100, 492–493). It was the music that affected Windy, particularly the music made by Roy Faulkner, a Kansan dubbed "The Lonesome Cowboy."

> When I would be down to my Grandma's my mother would say, "Oh you should be here in the evenings now. Monday night through the week there's a fellow from XERA in Del Rio, Texas, that they call the Lonesome Cowboy. And he sings such pretty songs. . . . Well then I got to listening to him. And I'll tell you, he was the greatest. I can't take anything away from Bradley Kincaid. Bradley was more like, folk songs, you'd say. Where he sang more songs of the true country. Like cowboy songs.

Faulkner also yodeled in the manner of Jimmie Rodgers, justly dubbed "the father of country music," who, beginning with his first recordings in 1927, fused mountain and cowboy sounds with pop music, Swiss-derived vaudeville yodeling, and a good deal more (Porterfield 1979).

By 1930, while still in his teens, Kenneth Wendell Whitford had acquired a repertoire that would serve him well for the next 70 years. Versatile with fiddle and guitar, grounded in the venerable Yorker and Norwegian repertoires of family and neighbors, armed with the new yet old timey mountain and cowboy music that was sweeping the nation, he strode out to entertain.

"We Played Fairs and Festivals"

> It just seemed like everything was waiting for me to play and sing. I'd get the calls down to the town hall. In our little town it was the focal point for PTA and school programs and community programs. And I'd always get asked to sing and play.

From 1930 to 1937, Windy played on and off with Bernard Evenson, an Albion farm kid, friend, and neighbor. By the mid-1930s, the two country boys were working and playing in the region's big city, Madison. But their start was humbler and closer to home.

> Back in those days, when there wasn't too much to do, back in Depression times, we'd get together in the fall and winter and play. He played the fiddle and guitar, and I played the fiddle and guitar. And pretty soon people was coming to get us. We were only 17 and 18, we

were pretty young, but it seemed to us like we were pretty grown up at that time. So we got a start with these people and other people that would want us to play for a house party. And house parties were [a] really fun and friendly atmosphere. People would bring sandwiches and cake and maybe a dish to pass. And they actually did roll up the rugs. Harv Cox used to call 'em "kitchen sweats." And that's about what it was. Everybody danced. They'd throw their coats in the bedroom on the bed. Little kids [got] tired and laid down and went to sleep. Those were kind of happy times.

By 1930, however, Harv Cox had moved up from kitchen sweats to playing on the radio and touring. Windy Whitford soon followed suit.

Cox (1906–1999) was born in Neillsville, in rural central Wisconsin, a self-confessed "jackpine savage" and the descendant of metís musicians. The Depression's onset found him in Janesville, a scant 17 miles south of Windy Whitford's Albion home, where there was not only a General Motors plant to boost the local economy but also a new radio station, WCLO. Seizing upon the nation's fascination with cowboys, Cox formed the Montana Cowboys and launched WCLO's first live broadcast in 1930 (Anonymous 1999: 1–2; Martin 1994: 119). Windy Whitford tuned in Cox's band as well as musicians with local connections, the Muleskinners.

Over the next few years, Whitford played with these groups and many more, on the radio and on the road.

> The Muleskinners . . . Saturday nights they'd have kind of a jamboree and invite any local talent in [to WCLO]. . . . About '31 I started going down there and setting in with their band. . . . I started playing the guitar and singing them songs. . . . Neighbor Ike, he was the drummer and the organizer of the band. Carl Mays was the lead singer. Oscar Simonson played the banjo. Tony Zabel played the accordion. And Red Nelson was fiddler. He was from my hometown too. Real good violin player. . . . So I stuck with them for a year then.

In the meantime, Windy began playing a daytime program with George Matson in Madison on the University of Wisconsin's WHA station—perhaps the first appearance by traditional musicians on public radio anywhere: "He played the fiddle, I played the guitar. He'd say, 'Sing an old time song, Windy.' And I'd sing one of the old time songs."[9] After two years of house parties, town-hall programs, and radio shows, Windy joined Harv Cox's Montana Cowboys for a summer tour in 1933 through northern Wisconsin, where he cooked "hamburger and kidney beans" for the band in addition to singing and playing guitar.

That fall, full of songs and experience, confident, and connected, Windy landed an ongoing solo job as the headliner for weekly musical evenings at Madison's Eastwood Theater. Needing a nickname that resonated with the times, he not very originally thought of XERA's Roy Faulkner. Prior to his

Figure 2.3. Harv Cox and His Montana Cowboys, before they were joined by Windy Whitford, in Janesville, Wisconsin, 1931. Goose Island Ramblers Collection, Wisconsin Historical Society (image 32829).

first performance, the "Theater News" column in Madison's *Capitol Times* proclaimed:

> Wendell Whitford, the Lonesome Cowboy from WCLO and WHA will be the feature of the Eastwood Theater amateur night program tonight. He will sing "Lamplighting Time in the Valley," "Going Back to Texas," "Bury Me beneath the Willow," "T for Texas," and "Take Me Back to Colorado" (September 1933; reprinted in Whitford 2000: 17)

Over the next three years, Windy continued to play solo jobs at the Eastwood, in duets with Bernard Evenson in area clubs, and with others. In 1934, he toured and broadcast over Poynette's WIBU with the Lonesome Cowboys, led by fiddling Jack McCann. The years 1935–1936 found him picking up the fiddle to team with Sunny Brown on guitar and accordionist Joe Weum as Mickey's Ranch Hands, regulars on WIBU who toured throughout south-central Wisconsin.

During this stretch, Windy Whitford frequently crossed paths with "big time" performers from Chicago's WLS. Since the mid-1920s, WLS had dominated the Midwestern musical scene, not only through its far-reaching broadcasts but also via road shows in theaters and dance halls throughout

Indiana, Illinois, Iowa, Nebraska, Minnesota, Wisconsin, and Michigan. Here WLS radio artists entertained and mingled with local fans and performers. And local performers who attracted the attention of the big station's personnel might also find the chance to sell a song or to tour as supporting acts under the WLS banner.[10]

Texas-born Gene Autry was arguably the station's most popular performer from 1931 to 1934 before he departed for Hollywood to become the "nation's number one singing cowboy" (Malone 2002a: 142–143). In 1933, when Autry was booked at Madison's Eastwood Theater on a night after Windy Whitford performed, the venue's manager, Bob Hutchins, insisted that the two meet.

> "Gene Autry's comin' to town. Now Windy," he says, "you stay in my apartment. Stay over. He'll be here tomorrow afternoon." I couldn't go back to Albion, that was 30 miles. So I stayed over. Gene Autry came to town. We got together and spent the afternoon together, visiting, talking. He was looking for a fiddle player to play for him, to go with his show. I didn't dare tell him I could play fiddle, because I didn't figure I could play good enough—for him. But we had some good times together, and I played him some of my songs that I had written. And then after that it got to be—if he'd play in Janesville, I'd go down to meet him—and he'd take me and introduce me to the guys in his band. . . . Just made you feel like you were one of 'em, like you were welcome.

In 1935, on a whim, Windy performed Autry's "Nobody's Darling but Mine" in a WLS-sponsored Home Talent Show competition. He won second place: $5 and an audition at the big station.

Windy's Chicago try-out went well. He met another radio hero, the Kentuckian Red Foley, and was offered work with one of the station's several traveling shows. Although tempted, he decided against the road: "I thought . . . 'I've got more better things to do.' I never did want to make it where I'd be away from home. Home and your friends, it seems like that was the sustaining part of my life."

Still, in the ensuing years, Windy Whitford was not quite satisfied. Unable to make ends meet completely with his music, he had said yes when Henry Hearst, a fan who was the loading-dock foreman at Oscar Mayer's, offered him a job. But he had also begun to imagine a band he might lead, a sound he might make, a means by which to link his Anglo-Norwegian polkabilly roots with the southern string band/singing cowboy fusion emanating from Chicago's WLS.

Then, in the late summer of 1937, at a root beer stand on Madison's east side, he heard Vern Minor, soon to be a founding member of the original Goose Island Ramblers: "I drove up and here's this fellow singing 'The First Whippoorwill Song.' It's one of Bradley Kincaid's songs. I says, 'That fellow should be playin' with me.' So it wasn't long before we were playin'."

Born in Yankton, South Dakota, Vernon Minor had moved with his family as a young boy to Madison, Wisconsin, where he grew up on the shores of Lake Monona. Dubbed "The Lake Edge Crooner," Minor had what Windy Whitford referred to as "such a nice soft voice. I was always kind of rough, it seemed to me." The two vacationed together in northern Wisconsin that fall and again the following summer, playing and singing incessantly. Their plan was to pick up a few more musicians and, through competing in another WLS-sponsored Home Talent Show, win another chance at the big time.

Whitford and Minor's first recruit was Alvin Hougan, a Norwegian farmboy from Stoughton who played string bass. Like his bandmates, Hougan was inspired by the Prairie Ramblers, fixtures on WLS who melded old time string band tunes with swing. And like Floyd "Salty" Holmes of the Prairie Ramblers, Alvin Hougan was a comic showman who, as a novelty, blew romping bass lines on the jug. Alvin Hougan quickly became "Salty" Hougan.

> Salty! . . . Just something about his personality. He'd walk out on the stage and everybody's laughing, you know. And he turns around to see what they're laughing at. "I don't want people laughing at me," he says. But he was so deadpan. . . . Sometimes Salty would get up in the cup, the form [of the bass], like a violin it comes in on the side. Salty would stand it up on a peg and he'd get it balanced just right, then he'd put his foot up in that little indenture there where it cuts it, and he'd stand up on it. Here he'd be like a monkey, and playing the bass at the same time. (CD, track 19)

Hougan also knew an array of humorous songs with rural themes that he'd been singing in a duet, Al and Don from Koshkonong, including "Hey Hey Farmer Gray (Haul Another Load Away)" and "I Worked for a Farmer."

The latter, to the tune of the late nineteenth-century popular song "Ta-Ra-Ra-Boom-Ti-Ay," was composed by the Swedish immigrant labor organizer Joe Hill as an Industrial Workers of the World (I.W.W.) or "Wobbly" anthem jovially advocating the sabotage of threshing machines unless working conditions improved (Kornbluh 1988: 16–17; Leary and March 1993: 263–264).

> Worked for a farmer threshing wheat,
> Seventeen hours on hands and feet.
> And when the moon was shining bright,
> He kept me working day and night.
> One day I am so sad to tell,
> I accidentally slipped and fell.
> I threw the pitchfork in between
> The cogwheels of the threshing machine.
> Well the cogwheels and the bolts and hay
> Went a-flying every way.
> One of the bolts of the old machine
> Hit the farmer on the bean. (CD, tracks 20–21)

As Windy put it later, "Just a farmboy's expression of what would've happened." Certainly there were Norwegian farmboys aplenty from Wisconsin who traveled seasonally to labor on Great Plains threshing crews well into the 1930s.

Howard "Stubby" Stuvatraa, another Norwegian farmboy and, like Windy, a veteran of the Stoughton fiddlers contests, rounded out the group. As Windy recalled:

> He played the mandolin and guitar, and played with the Kegonsa Four. That was a quartet of mandolin players from Stoughton that had made a good name for themselves way back in the early '30s. When I'd go down there, I wouldn't have anybody to play with me and I'd find Stubby and then he'd accompany me. And his dad played fiddle too and I learned some songs, tunes from his dad.

In October 1938, "we started our band there at the talent show from WLS," performing in "Sun Prairie and Verona and Stoughton." When the four were chosen to represent south-central Wisconsin at a WLS show in Chicago, "that was the beginning, really, of Goose Island Ramblers. We were on our way down there and I says, 'You know we don't even have a name for our group.' Well we thought, this and that, this and that, and so—'Let's call ourselves the Goose Island Ramblers,' I says." The name invoked the Prairie Ramblers, while harking back to the tamarack swamp at the edge of the Whitford homeplace and to the cultural confluence of Yorkers and Norskies. True to its name, the band combined Anglo-American fiddle tunes and ballads with a smattering of Norwegian *gammaldans* pieces.

For the next five years, through the onset of World War II, Windy Whitford, Vern Minor, Salty Hougan, and Stubby Stuvatraa stuck together: "We played fairs and festivals. We had quite a show. We had a good singing group. Now this Salty sang an awful good bass. And Vern was just a natural harmony, he could harmonize real good to me. And it just seemed like we were made for each other."

From 1939 through 1944, they were regular headliners at the annual Cottage Grove Festival just beyond Madison's southeast outskirts. "And then in '44 the guys up there said, 'We got big enough now we can hire WLS talent, but we're still going to hire you.'" Joined by Art Richards, an accordionist, the original Goose Island Ramblers more than held their own with such WLS stars as the Prairie Ramblers, cowboy singer Rex Allen, and the songsters Karl Davis and Harty Taylor of the Cumberland Ridgerunners.

Buoyed by success, Windy Whitford began to think about hitting the road and the big time.

> That following Monday morning, I don't know what possessed me, I says, "I'm going to call WLS booking down there and see if we can book through them." I called down and the guy says, "Are you the fellows that played out at the festival yesterday?" And I says, "Yeah."

Figure 2.4. The original Goose Island Ramblers, Madison, Wisconsin, 1939. (*Left to right*): Howard "Stubby" Stuvatraa, Windy Whitford, Alvin "Salty" Hougan, and Vern Minor. Goose Island Ramblers Collection, Wisconsin Historical Society (image 32832).

"You got the kid that plays the jug with you?" I says, "Yeah." He says, "I already heard about you," he says, "when do you want to start?"

Their first job was a fair in nearby Portage, substituting for the Prairie Ramblers as Patsy Montana's backup band. Windy recalled that they "went way out to Ioway, Minnesota, northern Wisconsin," including little towns like the logging hamlet of Webster, the Swedish farming strong-hold of Grantsburg, and the "Cumberland Rutabaga Festival, my wife's hometown. . . . We kept getting farther and farther from home."

Windy and his bandmates began having second thoughts. Stubby Stu-vatraa left the band about that time. Windy, meanwhile, was a family man, having married Helen Wickboldt in 1940. He had also worked a steady job at Oscar Mayer's since 1936. After a few weeks, he recalled:

My supervisor over at Oscar Mayer says, "What is really your number one job, Windy? Is it playing music or working for Oscar Mayer?" "Oh, by all means, working for Oscar Mayer." [Laughs] "Well I was begin-ning to wonder," he says. 'Cause sometimes I'd take off Wednesday, Thursday, Friday, Saturday. You know, in those days, Saturday was just like any other day. So I had to give it up.

The group's experience on the road also cost them their name. "Goose Is-land Ramblers" might have meant something in the Madison area, but that wasn't good enough for the WLS booking agent, who was convinced that audiences had to be lured with a western moniker. Like Harv Cox and his fellow Wisconsin musicians, Windy Whitford and cohorts became the Montana Cowboys.

This was not the band's first commercially motivated name change. In 1939, Windy had tried to convince Oscar Mayer to sponsor his band on local radio. Enlisting the help of announcer Ralph O'Connor, who had begun his career at Janesville's WCLO but was then with Poynette's farm-oriented WIBU, Windy made a demo recording of a 15-minute radio program: "Oscar Mayer Is on the Air." Featuring O'Connor's mellifluous voice on the credits and three commercials—each urging farmers to ship their livestock to Oscar Mayer—the show emphasized virtuosity and variety through spirited, truncated versions of eight pieces: the novelty song "Ain't No Flies on Me," minstrelsy's "Alabama Jubilee," the somber ballad "What Does the Deep Sea Say," the mariachi crossover standard "El Rancho Grande," the yodeling duet "Dear Old Sunny South," an otherwise unidentified "Norwegian Waltz," the hobo anthem "Wabash Cannonball," and a hot fiddle breakdown. Echoing the flour company affiliation of the Light Crust Doughboys, featuring Texans Bob Wills and Milton Brown, Windy proposed to Oscar Mayer that his band be called not the Goose Island Ramblers but the Goose Island Butcher Boys. Perhaps the cattle- and hog-slaughtering corporation feared the taint of poultry; perhaps "Butcher Boys" was too brutal for an organization soon to adopt the Oscar Mayer Weiner as its mascot; perhaps it was simply indifferent to the old time music aspirations of an employee. Whatever the explanation, "Oscar Mayer Is on the Air" was never broadcast; and the Butcher Boys reverted to the Ramblers.

Yet in 1944, just as the homesick, work-anchored, newly christened Montana Cowboys had reclaimed the Goose Island Ramblers identity, the band was compelled to abandon its name once more.

> In '44 we auditioned for [Madison's] WIBA. And Ken Schmidt, the program director, says, "Gee, I like your music, but I don't like that Goose Island Rambler[s] name." He says, "You change your name and you're hired." . . . I says, "Well, let's see now—we call ourselves the Balladeers." The Balladeers. That's a lot of what we did, lot of old time ballads and stuff.

Thus the Goose Island Ramblers, fittingly associated with its leader's Anglo-Norwegian musical roots and WLS-inspired aspirations, ceased to exist until revived in the early 1960s, when Windy joined forces with George Gilbertsen and Bruce Bollerud.

For the next 18 years, playing steadily with Vern Minor, Windy hunkered down in Madison as a mainstay in the Balladeers and, later, the Hoedowners. During that juncture, Whitford and Minor were joined by a varied succession of musicians. Some were locals, like polkabilly accordionist Donna Lunderberg, whose Norwegian-American father ran a store in Cottage Grove. World War II, however, prompted the expansion of Madison's Truax Field where members of the air force from all over the country served. Some found brides in Wisconsin and settled down. Among them: Hank Grover, a banjoist and old time singer from Virginia, and Charlie Adams, a Mississippi-born guitarist and fiddler, both of whom fused their southern sounds with the Upper Midwestern repertoire of Whitford and Minor. Then there was Paul Prestopino, a physics student at the University of Wisconsin captivated by the folk music revival that influential performers like Pete Seeger had launched on college campuses in the 1950s. Eventually, Prestopino joined the Chad Mitchell Trio, a clean-cut folk revival aggregation patterned after the Kingston Trio, which would also include singer-songwriter John Denver, to record albums for such labels as Mercury and Vanguard (Malone 2001: 37).

While Paul Prestopino's national career was taking off, Windy Whitford's more than 30-year local stint as an old time musician appeared to be ending: "I kept on going till about '62. Then I figured, well I just about had it. Going on 50 years old. I'd had a lot of fun, played a lot of music, met a lot of people."

The road, the big time, fame, and money might have tempted him, but Windy Whitford was fundamentally a family man whose music, despite its connections to distant mountaineers and cowboys, was rooted in home and community. During our extensive 1990 interview, he reflected on his mood in the early 1960s.

> When I look back on it, I wouldn't trade anything for my wife and the seven kids that we have. All of my kids play. We all get together. . . . So I said, "Where could I be any happier than . . . to be with my family and to be with the people that like our kind of music?" It seems so rewarding.

Imagining his public musical career as over, Windy began compiling a written legacy for his children that might become as treasured as the notebook with song lyrics set down by his mother in the 1890s. The songs that Windy organized, however, were his own compositions.

"My Blue Eyes Have Gone"

In 1962, while in the hospital for a checkup, Windy Whitford reflected on his Albion boyhood in a series of verses wed to the tune of the Carter Family's "Wildwood Flower." As he told me years later:

> Imagination is funny; it makes a cloudy day sunny. But this is an imaginary visit back to my home. . . .

> Well I walked down the road where I'd walked years before.
> I stood by a signboard all weathered and wore.
> The word that I made out, the name of a town
> Where I'd lived when a boy 'ere I traveled around.

Figure 2.5. The Hoedowners demonstrating the novelty of playing parts of their own and one another's instruments, Madison, Wisconsin, mid-1950s. (*Left to right*): Windy Whitford, Donna Jean Lunderberg, Vern Minor. Goose Island Rambler Collection, Wisconsin Historical Society (image 32834).

That was the start of it, see.

As I stood there looking, fond memories returned.
Thoughts of my old home made my heart yearn.
Made my feet turn down the road by the sign
For a long wanted visit to that old home of mine.

Now this is my imagination, see. Okay. So:

I walked in the driveway I'd walked years before.
Unknown were the faces I saw at the door.
They thought me a stranger, but how could they know
That the house where they lived was my home long ago.

And you know, one time we were walking by there, my oldest daughter and I, and she says, "Let's stop in." And there were the faces at the door, unknown. And the fellow says, I told him, "I used to live there, that was my old home." "Well come on in," he says, and he took us all through the house, just like it was when I was a kid. I lived there from 8 years to 17. And that place held the, whatever feelings of home that you desire most, held those feelings for me. . . .

I thought of the kitchen, the stove where it stood,
A box right behind it I kept filled with wood.
Friday night past sundown, the old house shook with noise,
With bath time and wash tubs for six happy boys.

If you don't think that was a catastrophe [Laughs], time you got done the water was all over the floor. I guess Ma had to have a lot of [Words failed him], well, anyway, that went on.

Cast as a loose narrative, sentimental, nostalgic, bound up with home, hindsight, love, loss, small details, and deep personal meaning, Windy Whitford's "Hometown" epitomizes the main thrust of his songwriting, while, not surprisingly, echoing the themes and aesthetics that captivated his parents and grandparents.

The older he grew, the more often Windy pondered the many ways in which his youthful experiences had influenced his life and art.

I never told anybody, but the house where I was born, down to Albion, burned down. Not while I was living there, but after. Maybe when I was six, seven years old. So really never had—the house was gone. Then, plus, a kind of hankering for home has always been strong in me. I don't know why. More or less, maybe more because, maybe, living with my Grandma and Grandpa—see my grandmother was a nurse and she'd be gone out taking care of patients having babies. . . . And then Grandpa would be alone. So then I thought, well they must've wanted me to go down and keep Grandpa company. So that worked out good. 'Cause I wonder, if I'd never associated with him, would I ever play the fiddle? Would I ever [have sung] those old songs?

His first song, "I'm Longing for You Tonight," was written in 1931 when, as a teenager spurned by his first love, he imagined himself alone and aging, his love still steadfast as he continued to hope his long-gone sweetheart would "hop a train and come" back home.[11] Lost love, the passage of years, and the conjoining of heart with hearth similarly occupy Whitford's "I Miss You but What Can I Do," "I Miss You since You've Gone Away," "Tarry Alone," and "When I Hear the Whippoorwill"—all of which might easily have flourished as nineteenth-century songs of unrequited love.

The loss and remembrance of home and loved ones as a result of age, distance, death, or wrongdoing compelled Windy even more. Like "Hometown," "Going Back to the Hills" conjured Albion in Windy's mind, particularly its rolling countryside and bygone musicians.

"I'm going back where the hills are calling me." That's to my old home down around Albion. To those hills. They're not hills like the Smokey Mountains or nothing, but they're hills to me. And

I want to wander through the clover fields again.
I want to see the fields of golden yellow grain.

I want to hear the banjo ring,
I want to hear the fiddle sing,
When I get back where the hills are calling me.

I think of Reierson . . . when I sing that. (CD, tracks 37–38)

Windy's similarly titled "Goin' Back to Old Virginny" both invoke his mother's plantation melodies and his Virginian friend and fellow musician Hank Grover. Two more songs of home are tributes to musical heroes: "Oklahoma Home," written for Gene Autry, and "Kentucky Mountain Home," honoring bluegrass innovator Bill Monroe. "Brother," a memorial to Windy's brother Winston, is especially poignant (CD, track 8).

In '35 I lost a brother to a hit-and-run driver. And that evening, as I sat in Grandma's old home—Grandma was sobbing and crying—but these words came to me and I wrote out the poem "Brother." And later my mother said, one day, "I miss him more and more each day." I didn't change it, I just added a little more to it. Like

All's there's left is a mound 'neath the pine trees,
Holding memories dearer each day.
Cherished love and the hopes of our lifetime
Come to rest in the grave where you lay.

But I didn't put that on any recording or anything, but I played it for a lot of people that have lost brothers and loved ones. . . . In fact I thought about making a framework where the picture would be in the insert and then across it would be a verse. Like it starts out

There's sorrow tonight in the old home
And it won't be the same any more,
For the master above has called brother
To the folds of that evergreen shore.

That would be just kind of nice, don't you think? I've thought about that for 50 years.

"Dreams of Youth," "Lonesome Road of Life," and "One Trail for Me" are also meditations inspired by his brother's death, while "Save the Bell" mourns the demolition of Albion Academy's chapel in 1941. Then there is a trio of songs—full of admonition and dismay—provoked respectively by broken marriages, child abuse, and prison terms served by once "content and happy" farmboys gone bad: "Broken Heart, Broken Homes," "God, Can It Be," and "Tempted to Do Wrong." Each prescribes the antidote of love, home, and family.

The chief departures from Windy Whitford's familiar themes—themes beloved by his ancestors, themes rooted in nineteenth-century sensibilities— are a pair of songs derived from the "Wabash Cannonball," a hobo paean to a legendary Midwestern train.[12] In 1937, during his second year working on the Oscar Mayer loading dock, Windy began wondering about the source of livestock shipped by rail to the big meat-packing plant (Whitford 2000: 9, 57). The result was "Oscar's Cannonball," invoking the company's founder and incorporating local place names (Baraboo, Elroy, Lodi, Mauston, Merrimac, Portage, Poynette, Waunakee) to praise the superiority of a cattle-hauling freight:

> She's the fastest train that ever pulled a stock car down the line.
> She can catch up with the Soo Road, and leave her far behind.
> Chicago and Northwestern, Milwaukee and St. Paul
> Could never hold a candle to Old Oscar's Cannonball. (CD, track 29)

While "Oscar's Cannonball" lauds an actual train, Windy's other take-off on the "Wabash Cannonball" imagines a metaphorical iron horse. In late December 1941, shortly after the Japanese attack on Pearl Harbor, Windy composed "Victory Cannonball," commencing with

> There's a cannonball of victory that's rolling through this land,
> From Maine to California, along the Rio Grande,
> From northern Minnesota, including one and all.
> We're all bound for glory on the Victory Cannonball.

The five subsequent verses encourage defense-plant workers, farmers, and soldiers, while urging folks at home to support the troops and offering reassurance that Jesus will embrace "our cause." A recurring chorus casts Uncle Sam as the engineer, while promoting the purchase of war bonds (Whitford 2000: 9, 67).

Like the bulk of Windy Whitford's compositions, his "Cannonball" variations are aligned with the rhetoric, themes, poetic structures, and motives common within old time country music. Besides pondering livestock marketing, "Oscar's Cannonball" frankly sought company sponsorship for a show on Madison's WIBA. Just as, in the early twenty-first century, Garrison Keillor's long-running public radio program "A Prairie Home Companion" harks back to WLS, the "Prairie Farmer Station," while musically extolling the virtues of fictitious Powder Milk Biscuits, numerous hillbilly radio performers of Windy's youthful era touted actual products through songs about the "light crust flour of Burrus Mills," Martha White Flour, and such laxatives as Black Draught, Crazy Water Crystals, Man-O-Ree, and Prunella. So why not meat packing, especially in an agrarian region where Chicago claimed to be "hog butcher of the world" and the Green Bay Packers had won football championships?

Wars similarly inspire numerous songs, and World War II was no exception. In the early 1940s, scores of country musicians composed and performed anthems of patriotic defiance, as well as sympathetic meditations on the tragedy of war. Several, like Elton Britt's rendition of "There's a Star Spangled Banner Waving Somewhere" and Red Foley's recording of "Smoke on the Water," were national hits (Malone 2002a: 194–194, 515).

And while Windy Whitford ultimately composed and performed the music that moved him most, he also hoped that his songs might both be heard and help him to earn a living.

As we have already seen, the Oscar Mayer company proved indifferent to jingles sung by the would-be Butcher Boys.[13] The song "Victory Cannonball," however, attracted considerable interest, especially from Red Foley, whom Windy had come to know through his WLS experiences. In early 1942, Foley played in Madison and Windy went to see him: "'You want to listen to this song, Red?' He was up to the Strand Theater. 'Oh, that makes the goosebumps just run up and down my backbone,' he says. 'Boy, we're going to really do something with that song.'" The pair tinkered a bit with the chorus, and soon after both Foley and Karl and Harty were singing "Victory Cannonball" on Chicago's WLS and WJJD stations. Red Foley wanted to record the song, but he also wanted Windy to sign away all of his rights for $25. Windy demurred: "I says, 'Jeez, I don't want to sell it to you, Red. I want something with my name on it that I done this. Maybe Windy Whitford can get another song, later on.' So I didn't give it to him. . . . that kind of took me down."[14]

A few years later, he tried to pitch another song. Red Foley had also liked his "My Blue Eyes Have Gone," even singing it with an attribution to "Wendell Whitford" on a WLS broadcast in the late 1930s. Unlike the "Cannonball" songs, with their commercial and political bent, this was vintage Whitford, fraught with bittersweet, highly personal remembrance. Notes set down years later in his songbook even assume a similar familiarity from his audience:

Many of you around the Edgerton, Wisconsin, area will remember the two main people of this song. One was Amy Truax, the other Laurence Wilemen, her boyfriend. They were always together, a happy twosome— where one was the other was sure to be—until Amy was stricken with appendicitis and like a flower she faded and was gone at a very young age. . . . I put myself in his place and imagined his loss as though it were my own. (Whitford 2000: 8)

Although Red Foley found it "a pretty song," Windy Whitford eventually decided to see if "My Blue Eyes Have Gone" might interest his old friend Gene Autry.

Based in Hollywood since the mid-1930s, Autry continued to tour periodically through his old Upper Midwestern stomping grounds. In 1946, he entertained troops at Madison's Truax airfield. As Windy told me:

I called him up to the hotel. I says, "Gene, would you want to listen to some of my homemade songs?" "Sure," he says, "come on up." I went up and sang some for him. And that one song, he just wanted, that was it. He says, "I'm sure we can make a go with that." He says, "Get a record of it made before I leave town and I'll take it back to Hollywood with me." . . . And so I took the record up and my wife was sitting in the lobby with me and had it on her lap. They called: "Gene Autry will see you now, Windy." Jumped. And the record fell on the floor. They were glass in the middle of them, with a little black something over 'em. And it busted. I says, "Well, no he ain't s'posed to have that. Let's just go home and forget about it." Now why didn't I say, "Gene, here I am. I busted that darn record, but I'll make another one. I'll send it to you out to California." No, I never thought of that. . . . that was a sign I guess. (CD tracks 22–23, 26)

Rather than fret ever after about broken dreams, Windy found peace in what he felt was meant to be. He often told this experience as a parable concerning the importance of home and family. As Bruce Bollerud, his friend and fellow musician put it: "It's the way Windy is, I think. It's nice in a way, because he can sort of accept things. . . . Windy felt that this was fate, that it wasn't to be at this point. . . . He always had his family. He always considered that strongly."

Had that record never shattered, had Windy Whitford "made it" with his songs, radio programs, and barnstorming tours, he might have spent the balance of his life in pursuit of national hits and trends, bowing toward Nashville, ending his career far from family and musical roots, and entering the historical record as just one more small-town Midwestern kid charmed by the evolving country music juggernaut. Fortuitously, by turning homeward and looking backward, he found another, perhaps a greater, destiny. In the early 1960s, as his musical career seemed to be over, Windy happened into an alliance with George Gilbertsen and Bruce Bollerud. Together, they revived the Goose Island Ramblers' Anglo-Norwegian name to forge a thoroughgoing polkabilly sound, a sound that interwove the most varied and venerable strands of their individual folk music repertoires into a sonic fabric that epitomized the cultural ferment of America's Upper Midwest.

3

"Smokey George" Gilbertsen

"I Can Still Remember That"

> I can remember the first live music I ever heard, and I can't tell you how
> little I was. I was standing on the back of a screen[ed] porch up on
> Buckeye Road at the top of the hill. It was Spaanem's Dairy . . . named
> after that farm family, they had a dairy there. . . . Art Spaanem and
> another fellow was setting in the kitchen playing banjo and guitar. That's
> the first live song I ever heard. I was looking through the screen door,
> and they were playing "Red Wing." I can still remember that.[1]

George Karsten Gilbertsen was born at home, September 28, 1925, in a
tarpaper shack on Blossom Lane off Buckeye Road in the town of Blooming Grove. Dependent upon and eventually surrounded by Madison, the
rustic, working-class neighborhood of George Gilbertsen's childhood was
peopled by folks of French-Canadian and Norwegian but mostly German
and Irish descent. Although a few were immigrants, most hailed from
Upper Midwestern farm families and were seeking work in the city. After
a stint with the navy during World War II, George married Helen Sennett
in 1948, raised four children in the shadow of the foundries on Madison's
east side, and worked successively as a "food trucker and maintenance
janitor" for the University of Wisconsin's Memorial Union, a milk deliverer
on a route for Bancroft Dairy, and a parking-meter repairman for the city
of Madison. Retiring from these labors at the end of 1987, he continued to
play old time music, a vocation that beckoned in the late 1920s with the
strains of "Red Wing" through a screen door.

George's mother, Martha Roeben, born in 1890 and the eldest of 11 children, grew up in Garnavillo, Iowa, a German farming community just west
of the Mississippi River and opposite Grant County, Wisconsin. Her mother
died when she was about 16, and for a time Martha had a rough life. George
recalled his mother telling him that her widowed father could not manage
with 11 kids at home, so the county intervened: "They were all split up into
different homes . . . put out and raised by different families. That's the reason that I had aunts and uncles everywhere from Kansas to Montana to
Minnesota. . . . eventually they all found out where each other was."

Martha married at "about 16, probably shotgun" to a fellow named Shaw. She gave birth to several daughters who died very young and to a trio of sons: Harold (b. 1911), Marvin (b. 1913), and James (b. 1915). Soon, however, she was abandoned by her husband. Never a good provider, he was rumored subsequently to have drowned in the Mississippi River. Seeking a better life and drawing upon her hard-won skills as a German farm cook, in 1920 Martha Roeben Shaw took her three sons 100 miles northeast to Madison, where she found work running a boardinghouse on Division Street nearby such foundries as Cooper's, Kipp's, and Madison Brassworks.

Congress had imposed Prohibition in 1919, and drinking was therefore banned in the boardinghouse. But one night in the early 1920s, Martha Roeben Shaw surprised a new boarder attempting to lift a pail of home-brewed beer into his window with a rope. The culprit was a cheerful Norwegian, Karsten "Charles" Gilbertsen, whom she would marry in 1923.

Born in Oslo (then Christiana), Norway, in 1884, Karsten Gilbertsen had left his homeland at 16 to sail the world on freighters, including five trips from Europe to the port of New York City. By his mid-30s, wanderlust sated, he looked to settle down and thought of a sister, Gina Helman, who had emigrated to Wisconsin and was living on Third Street amid Madison's working-class east side. Adopting the American name of Charles, he made his way to Lake Forest, Illinois, where he trimmed trees for a time, before hiring on with the building crew erecting what became the plush Loraine Hotel in Madison. In 1925, the year his son, George Karsten, was born, Charles Gilbertsen began work with the city of Madison's water department: "He worked there for 26 years, then he was retired for 26 years. So he was 93 years old when he passed away."

Neither of George's parents were musicians, nor had they come from musical families. Still, Charles and Martha Gilbertsen loved music and encouraged their children's interests. George characterized his mother as "one of these down-to-earth people" who worked hard and played hard. As for his dad, "he just loved music. He loved to dance." At a local house party or in a tavern featuring old time music,

> My dad used to get out there and jig a little bit. . . . It was awful close to what you see, this buck-dancing down south. [Leary: Flatfoot more?] Yeah, sure. He had something in between an Irish jig and buck-dancing. I don't know where he learned it. But like I say, he didn't play music but he loved to dance. [Leary: Sailors are known to dance.] Yeah.

The family also "had the old 78 crank-up Victrola at home." George especially liked the "Heel and Toe Polka" and "Jenny Lind," perhaps Henry Ford's Old Time Dance Orchestra's 1926 version of this tune, which has been widely played on both sides of the Atlantic since the international polka craze of the 1840s (Meade, Spottswood, and Meade 2002: 803). "I was real little when I used to listen to that, because I'd crank that thing up, and I could almost imagine there was little people in there playing that music."

In 1932, seven-year-old George Gilbertsen began to play an instrument. Two of his half brothers had already tried, without much success. Harold Shaw, the eldest, "was taking violin lessons, but then he had three fingers cut off in a punch press. So that ended the violin." Jim Shaw, the youngest, "had bought a $5 Maxwell guitar from Sears and Roebuck and wasn't doing much with it. And I started learning a few tunes on it, so he give it to me." It was a cheap, awkward instrument, "one of those meat grinders, you know, that put raspberries on the end of your fingers." But George persisted. His brother Jim also "played harmonica a little," and soon George "got going on that too . . . playing it with a holder along with the guitar."

Like Windy Whitford, who about that time was performing just down the road as the Lonesome Cowboy, the Shaw brothers and George Gilbertsen were captivated by singing cowboys encountered through radio, magazines, and song folios.

> My brother [Jim] used to have these old western magazines. And I'd hear him singing some of these songs back then. I don't know what they cost . . . a nickel or ten cents. They were old western novel magazines. And then in the back of them they'd always have about eight, ten songs back in there. . . . then he started buying these songbooks. Like WLS songbooks, Gene Autry songbooks, some of these. And that's where I started picking up some of this stuff. And then, of course, hearing it on the radio then. That's WLS and the "Suppertime Frolic" . . . [and] the big Saturday night "Barn Dance" then. And then I remember picking up from Del Rio, Texas, that always got through somehow. . . . There was some program down there too . . . [on WWL in New Orleans]: the Pickard Family.

With Obed Pickard switching on fiddle, guitar, banjo, harmonica, and Jew's harp; his wife, Leila May, on piano; sons Bubb and Charlie on guitar; and daughter Ruth on accordion, the Pickards' mixture of traditional and vaudeville songs was particularly appealing (Pickard Family 2004 M). But there was also other music swirling about, much of it, like the screened-porch picking of Art Spaanem and his pal, was at home, next door, right across the street, just down the road, as much a part of life as food and drink, light and air.

"It Was Just Like a Big Open Party"

Wisconsin's state capital and home to its leading public university, Madison has long boasted a modest but remarkably cosmopolitan citizenry. Yet the city's working-class east side—with its venerable complement of foundries, Gisholt Machinery, the Rayovac battery plant, the sprawling Oscar Mayer meat-packing complex, small houses on small lots, mom-and-pop taverns, and non-Anglo Europeans of peasant stock—has often been forgotten or pushed aside like a poor relation or a black sheep. Early twenty-first-century Madisonians are rightly thrilled by the opportunity to regularly hear live music that is otherwise unavailable in the region outside of such major metropolitan areas as Chicago, Milwaukee, and Minneapolis. In June 2004, as I wrote this chapter, Madisonians had the opportunity to visit more than 50 venues and to hear performers working in a myriad of roots musical styles. Among them: jazz and rock in all varieties, bluegrass, cowboy yodeling, honky tonk, singing guitarists in a folk revival vein, blues, funk, reggae, hip hop, Afro-Cuban jazz, Puerto Rican salsa, Cajun, zydeco, Irish pub rock, Slovenian polka, and a good deal more. Few if any of these performers and their audiences, however, have an inkling of the vibrant, varied, equally rootsy, and decidedly homemade musical scene that flourished decades before on Madison's eastern edge and in the town of Blooming Grove, where small farmsteads and a working-class neighborhood overlapped.

In 1932, the same year George Gilbertsen took up the guitar, his dad finished building a new house for the family on the lot occupied by their cramped tarpaper shack. Like a newborn child, an untried ship, or a building just completed, the Gilbertsen house—fashioned as it was by a father, a sailor, and a construction worker—had to be christened with a party. To do otherwise was to invite bad luck. So, to their kids' delight, Charles and Martha Gilbertsen threw their doors open to the neighborhood, inviting Erv and Eva Hewitt in particular. "The front room was all hard oak floor. No rugs. Boy, they just opened right up, and they had a dance." Erv Hewitt was an old time fiddler and a laborer like his friends. He worked for Rayovac making batteries. "Little short guy. His wife played the tenor guitar. . . . he'd have Genske" as a second guitarist. The trio mostly favored Anglo-Celtic square-dance tunes intermingled with old German waltzes: a sound that, with a few Norwegian incursions, was the signature of Madison's east side, where Germans, Irish, and Norwegians did the work not done by lawmakers and professors.

Nor did live music cease in the wake of the Gilbertsens' house party. Right next door, Roy and Mary Brandt "had a big apple orchard and a strawberry patch" where a kid might wander conveniently when fruit was ripe. Mary was a Dempsey from Ireland, and on summer evenings her jigs and reels rode the warm breezes.

> She had a little concertina, and she was pretty crippled up with arthritis, but she could still play that some. . . . She would kind of rock it too as she played it. Little, short, stout lady. Talked with a real brogue. She'd say [with a twinkle], "That Roy is the meanest man God ever put breath into."

Invented by Charles Wheatstone, an Englishman, in the 1830s, the diminutive, octagonal English concertina spread to Ireland by the late nineteenth century, entering the port cities first before extending into the hinterlands where its players included many women. Highly portable, with a crisp, penetrating sound, the concertina mimicked the uilleann pipes' reedy voice, and a skilled player might squeeze out melody, harmony, and rhythm while otherwise unaccompanied or mesh easily with a fiddle (*Traditional Music from Clare and Beyond* 1996 M:1–2).

As it happened, Mary Dempsey Brandt's son Al played fiddle, with young George Gilbertsen sometimes chording rhythm:

> I'd take my old guitar and drag it over there in the evening, after they'd had supper, you know. 'Course they would invite [me] for a bite to eat too. Then after supper they'd clear up. Al would get that violin out, start rosining the bow. Kind of a tall, well-put-together guy. Almost like a professor. He'd do a few like "Old Zip Coon" and a few of them old tunes. And then his mother would play "Devil's Dream" on that concertina. And I'd strum this guitar. . . . That's how I kind of got a little bit of the Irish there.

There were also the "Pittsleys across the road. Her name was Annie O'Kane from Boscobel, so she was Irish." She came by her affection for Irish music honestly. Indeed the O'Kanes, who had immigrated from Cork in the mid-nineteenth century to settle north of the lower Wisconsin River on Crawford County farmland, were a noted musical family in southwest Wisconsin for many decades. Old time fiddlers like Hank O'Kane called for dances into the 1920s, mingling Irish and German tunes; in the meantime, Charles Bannen, whose mother was an O'Kane, lilted German fiddle tunes as he played a pump organ through the 1970s, while also singing a repertoire of old time ballads—"Barney McCoy," "Miss Fogarty's Christmas Cake," "Pat Malone," "Streets of Laredo," and some 50 more—that rivaled Windy Whitford's in number and antiquity (Bohlman 1980: 171, 181, 184).[2]

Practicing incessantly, picking up tunes and tips from family and neighbors, George Gilbertsen commenced seven decades as an entertainer in 1934 at the age of nine. Sporting a harmonica rack and a thumb pick, his finger blisters hardened into calluses, George

> started playing little house parties—harmonica, guitar. In other words, I had my little one-man band that way. Sang some numbers and they would pass the hat, you know. Sometimes I'd go home feeling I was pretty rich. . . . Boy I know that silver looked awful good to me when I'd get home and dump it out.

Some of the parties were in the neighborhood, while others were in farm houses a few miles distant. Whatever the locale, the atmosphere was much the same: "Usually they had beer. I can remember that. People would be drinking beer and dancing. It was just like a big open party. They'd be in and out and dancing. Certainly no—it wouldn't be anything like today where everything's organized. They just had a good time." The dancing particularly compelled George's attention.

On most occasions, he was not the sole musician present; rather, he backed up or spelled a fiddler and, perhaps, an accordionist from time to time. The favored repertoire was a typical southern Wisconsin polkabilly mix of contra, square, and round dances, the latter mostly German waltzes and schottisches. Some pieces had shifting tunes that might alternate polka and waltz tempos in two-part or *zweifacher* fashion, while others—especially waltz quadrilles and circle two-steps—were "mixers" with callers instructing dancers to change partners frequently. Most compelling, however, were the varied, highly individualistic ways in which dancers executed common steps.

> People did know how to really express themselves when it come to dancing, because they—that's the way they did it. The square dancing today is all organized. Then, it wasn't. They just danced it the way they learned it. And it was open—you probably saw some of that down in Kentucky—this open square dancing where the caller just shouts it out. And the people just go right on through it and into it and there's a—it was altogether different. Your waltz quadrilles and your circle two-steps, the schottische, the Rye Waltz, Herr Schmidt, and all those different dances. I can remember playing and seeing all of those danced by the old timers, which was really interesting because I don't know where you'd see that today. Even the square dancing don't look like it did then.

In addition to house parties, young George Gilbertsen played for fundraisers and community events in local one-room schools, just as Windy Whitford had done a decade prior. Teaming with a pair of neighbor kids, he entertained "for Pumpkin Hollow School and Estes School and the Ellis School—that's where I went to school . . . the Frank Ellis School." His fellow musicians were "a sister and her brother . . . Mary and Bob Chittendon." Their mother, a French Canadian, would take the youthful trio around. Sometimes George did solo numbers.

> I would come out and do a little ditty on my own with the guitar and harmonica. And I'd do like the "Little Brown Jug" or "Buffalo Gals" or some of those old tunes. Ham it up a little bit. I can remember I had a cowboy suit. They always used to kid me. They said they thought it was made out of dog fur. Had big furry chaps. . . . when I'd do "Little Brown Jug," when I'd get to that [Sings] "Ah-ha-ha, you and me," I'd kick my legs out. I had a regular little dance along with it. So I had almost a vaudeville act there. So I guess it's really in you right from the start. You feel it.

The Chittendons were both fledgling Hawaiian guitar players, and the rest of the time, as George recalled, "they wanted me for the standard [guitar], for the rhythm."

The presence of Hawaiian guitar on the eastern margins of Madison in the mid-1930s was hardly surprising. By the early decades of the twentieth century, the Hawaiian steel guitar had swept much of mainland America. Portuguese sailors and Mexican cattle ranchers brought various guitars to

Hawaii's big island as early as the 1830s. In 1894, just as Hawaii became part of the American empire, Joseph Kekuku, a student at the Kamehameha Boys' School, began a series of experiments that resulted in the development of the Hawaiian guitar: steel strings replaced gut strings; the bridge was raised slightly above the frets; the guitar was played flat, balanced on the lap; and while one's right hand, armed with thumb and finger picks, articulated the melody, fretting was accomplished with a metal bar, which could also be slid along the neck to create eerie sustained tones. Soon Kekuku and other virtuoso performers, like Frank Ferera, began touring the United States, making numerous sound recordings, and influencing thousands of musicians in the bargain.[3] Hawaiian musicians entertained not only in such Upper Midwestern cities as Madison, but also in the hinterlands, winning numerous converts with their performances on vaudeville and, especially, tent Chautauqua circuits (Harrison 1958; MacLaren 1938; Tapia 1997). In 1925, for example, Bell's Famous Hawaiian Review barnstormed through northern Wisconsin, charming the locals with "singers, dancers, instrumentalists." That same year in Ashland, a northern Wisconsin port on Lake Superior sometimes jokingly dubbed "the Riviera of the Arctic Circle," 66 young women formed the Ashland Girls' Hawaiian Club. Eight years later, Otto and Iva Rindlisbacher, erstwhile Swiss musicians from Rice Lake, teamed with a pair of traveling Hawaiian musicians to perform in area opera houses and over WCCO radio in Minneapolis (Leary 1983: 223, 225).

George Gilbertsen too was affected. Inspired by the Chittendons, he tried his hand at Hawaiian guitar—thanks to Lawrence K. Valley, a French Canadian, and his wife, "who looked like a Hawaiianer." The Valleys operated what George described as "one of these deals where they went all through the country here signing kids up, and taking lessons, and then they'd get a free guitar at the end of the lessons." Both fine players, they emphasized learning by doing, augmenting lessons with a tablature system relying on numbers instead of notes. George was a quick study, acquiring such classic pieces as "Maui" and "Maui Chimes" by Palakiko and Paaluhi (1930) and "On the Beach of Waikiki" by Kalama's Quartet (late 1920s). Although he modestly reckoned he "slaughtered" the tunes, he performed well enough to be selected by the Valleys as one of their four top pupils. He never got a free guitar, however, but eventually purchased a dobro. Invented in 1928 by the Dopyera Brothers, the dobro—a steel-stringed, wood-bodied acoustic Hawaiian guitar with conical resonators to boost its sound—has been a mainstay in old time country and bluegrass music since its beginning (Malone 2002a: 127–128; see also Wilson 1990: 8).

"I Got to Play with My First Band"

George Gilbertsen's early musical career coincided not only with the proliferation of cowboy songs and Hawaiian guitars, but also with the election of Franklin D. Roosevelt and the demise of Prohibition. In 1934, as the Volstead Act was overturned, small mom-and-pop taverns sprang up on Madison's working-class east side. Typically housing a family's living quarters in a back room or upstairs apartment, supplementing a family's farm or factory earnings rather than providing the sole source of income, often nominally associated with its proprietors, and catering to a local clientele of friends and coworkers, these places were much like the inns and pubs of Old World peasant villages: regarded as extensions of the neighborhood, social clubs for working folks, family-oriented institutions open to men, women, and children alike (Leary 1998: 377–385). Before the imposition of cabaret taxes on live performances, Madison's east side tavern dances resembled the house parties that had preceded and paralleled their existence.

It was hardly surprising, then, when Erv and Eva Hewitt offered to include young George Gilbertsen on a few jobs.

> They were friends of my folks, so he says, "Well, we'll take him along, give him a little experience." So I got to play with my first band that way. He'd say, "I've got to take a little break." He'd call me, they'd call me "Karsten," that was my middle name. I went by that till I was in high school. "I got to take a little break, Karsten." So he'd take off. He played fiddle, and he'd take off. I'd be there blowing my harmonica and guitar, you know. So that was my first band experience.

The settings were akin to living rooms: Rafferty's Tavern and the Lake Edge Bar, also known as Jack's Tavern, "a very small place. There couldn't have been too many people dancing, [but] it looked like a crowd to me." Francis McMahan, a musician likewise raised on Madison's east side, tagged along with an uncle and aunt to Mike Griffin's Bar and Chris Readon's Tavern, where the Hewitt Trio entertained. In McMahan's memory, Erv Hewitt was an animated fiddler who played while simultaneously standing up and leaning backward: "He'd rub his hind end against the wall and wear out his pants" (McMahan 1988 I).

The Hewitts' crowds had no interest in foxtrots and the popular dances of the era, preferring the venerable steps enjoyed at the house parties. As George recalled, they favored

> just old time dancing. Lots of waltzes. They used to play lots of waltzes and schottische was very—you always played those at the dances. Not as heavy on the polkas as they are down around the Milwaukee area. It was more—I think it was probably because this area through here was more your German and Scandinavian. They liked their two-steps and waltzes, schottisches. That's the ones I remember mostly. And then like the waltz quadrille and the circle two-step and that.

Francis McMahan's characterization was much the same. Besides jigs, he reckoned, "These little bands played dance music: waltzes, two-steps in ⁶⁄₈ time, polkas" (McMahan 1988 I). It was on these early tavern jobs that

George acquired such old German standards as *"Du Du Liegst Mir im Herzen"* and *"Lauterbach"* (Where Has My Little Dog Gone?).

By 1939, George Gilbertsen, more than competent on standard and Hawaiian steel guitar, began to experiment with the former—commencing a series of stringed-instrument innovations that, as we shall see, would lead to his performing on electric toilet plunger and eight-stringed fiddle with the second coming of the Goose Island Ramblers.

> I would put a capo on the neck and then it'd sound like a tenor and a standard guitar together, because you'd get this real high ringing sound on one guitar. Which was a really nice combination. . . . And how we ever come up with that when we were kids, I don't know, but we did it: for sound effects, I guess, and it really worked nice.

George matched his standard, Hawaiian, and tenor-like guitar with the six-string guitar of a schoolmate, Marlin Angus, and the two entertained for house parties.

At one of them, "this big, burly construction worker . . . all I remember is his name was Jack" informed the teenagers: "I'm going to get you guys a job. I got a friend." Soon after, George Gilbertsen and Marlin Angus accompanied Jack to Spanish Village, an east side roadhouse near Oscar Mayer's meat-packing plant run by a Ukrainian immigrant, Mike Miker (CD, track 32).

> [Jack] says, "Here's the two guys I was telling you about." Well this Mike, you know, he leans over the bar and looks down at us and he says, "How old are dey?" And Jack says, "[They're] 21 and 22." "Good, I'll hire 'em," he says. [Laughs] We were 14 and 15. "Good," he says, "I'll hire 'em." So we started playing there, and it was one night a week. Saturday night, I think it was, from nine till one. His wife would set there. She was sort of the critic, I guess. She'd set there and watch us. Very stern . . . they were paying money for this. But she'd watch and she'd smile and clap a little bit. So I'd tell Marlin, "Gee, I think she liked that kind. Let's play another one like that." So we'd play another one like that and then we'd get done and she'd say, "Can't you play something else?" [Laughs] So we'd go into something else, you know. Played till one o'clock, then haul[ed] our guitars and that from Oscar Mayer clear up by the Gisholt. Walk.

The two youngsters played Spanish Village for three months, entertaining a working-class crowd of factory hands. They never managed to think up a name for themselves, although they considered themselves budding professionals playing their "first commercial job." Four hours of entertaining earned each "a dollar and a half a night," enough to buy a pair of "blue satin shirts" that "were the rage at the time," but not enough to hire a cab to go home. So they walked, sometimes attracting the attention of police officers curious about two teens wandering the streets with guitar cases after curfew.

One night, the fledgling musicians got a special thrill when a pair of local stars, Windy Whitford and Salty Hougan of the original Goose Island Ramblers, dropped into Spanish Village.

> They were wearing their orange satin shirts and cowboy hats. I don't know if they were going to play somewhere, but anyhow in they come. Set in. Windy done "Oscar Mayer's Cannonball." . . . I'd seen him playing at festivals and that, because they were a little bit older at the time. We were just teenagers, and they were up in the 20s then.

In 1939, George hardly suspected that 24 years later his musical path would converge with that of Windy Whitford and Bruce Bollerud, but even then, like "Uncle Windy," he was committed to going wherever his music might take him.

"I Liked That Old Time Music"

Over the next seven years—as a Madison teenager, a sailor during World War II, and a mustered-out veteran—George Gilbertsen played with a succession of old time bands, expanded his repertoire, learned to fiddle, developed his talents as an entertainer, traveled widely, and concluded that there was no place like home.

Besides forming a duo with Marlin Angus in the late 1930s, George had begun to play with Donnie Cook, another teen just a few years older. The two met in 1938 as competitors in the weekly Manchester's Amateur Hour, a talent contest for kids sponsored by an exclusive clothing store on Madison's capitol square. George played guitar and rack-mounted harmonica, while Donnie fiddled and used a similar harmonica rig. After 13-year-old George won "Boy of the Week" honors, with a feature and photo in the local newspaper, he and Donnie matched their strings and reeds to jam informally and play for an occasional house party.

Meanwhile, Harry Edwards—with whom George would play intermittently for the next 20 years—came south to Madison in 1939 from the sand country around Pardeeville, famous nowadays for its annual watermelon seed–spitting contest. Edwards was a string bass player who had been performing with the Fox River Valley Boys, a Pardeeville band run by his dad, Phil Edwards. Like Windy Whitford and many a southern Wisconsin country kid come to the region's big city, Harry Edwards found work on Madison's east side, specifically at the Select Candy Company, where he toiled with George Gilbertsen's older brother, Marvin Shaw. When Marvin "told him that us kids played a lot of music. He looked us up and he organized us into a little group."

The Bearcat Mountain Boys featured Edwards on string bass, George Gilbertsen on Hawaiian steel guitar, and Donnie Cook on fiddle. They emphasized hot picking and jumped-up hillbilly tunes, a style that did not sit well with George's Hawaiian guitar teacher, Lawrence K. Valley, who insisted that Hawaiian guitars ought only to be used for an "authentic" island sound: "He got awful mad. . . . And he says, 'Nothing but corn.' He was so mad. I never seen the guy again. That ended my Hawaiian career with him."

Joining the Bearcat Mountain Boys, however, marked the beginning of another musical apprenticeship for George Gilbertsen. Soon he was performing for audiences beyond Madison, for "little outdoor picnics and fairs up around Pardeeville." Although only 40–50 miles away, this was another musical world, where the tunes and styles differed considerably from both Madison's bedrock east side Irish-Germanic-Norwegian fusion and the radio- and record-driven cowboy/hillbilly sounds sweeping the country.

George fully entered that world at 16 in 1941 when Donnie Cook, wanting to spend more time with his girlfriend, left the Bearcat Mountain Boys. George and Harry soon teamed up with the latter's dad, Phil Edwards, and the Fox River Valley Boys.

They were playing up around North Freedom, Baraboo, Pardeeville, in that area. . . . they were just a bunch of old timers out on a Saturday night for playing little jobs. Good old time dance music. They had a fiddle. Harry played the bass; his dad played the guitar. They had drums and saxophone and piano. Six-piece old time dance band. Really good old time music. Little bit of Bob Wills, like "San Antonio Rose." Then they played some oldies that you hardly ever hear now. Like "Down in the Valley," not [Sings] "Down in the valley, the valley so low"—it was "Down in the Valley Waltz." And they done some of the old English military two-steps.

Back home, George was accustomed to two-steps and to circle two-steps with called figures, but these were altogether different. Related to the galop, using the step-close-step footwork of the basic waltz, although not in ¾ time but in either ²⁄₄ or ⁶⁄₈ signatures, the two-step originated in Germany in the early nineteenth century and—like the waltz, polka, schottische, and other couple dances—was acquired variously from the mid-nineteenth century on by rural and working-class people in continental Europe and the Americas (Sachs 1937: 432–433; Shaw 1949: 299–302). In the latter half of the nineteenth century, the "military two-step," which might be executed to a march or a polka, emerged in England, and it persists as part of British country and Celtic *ceilidh* dance scenes in Australia, England, Ireland, and Scotland.[4] Not surprisingly, George Gilbertsen discovered that "Harry and his dad and his grandpa and all them were English."

Established in the mid-nineteenth century as a mill town on the Fox River, Pardeeville and the surrounding Columbia County hinterlands were settled by Yankees and Yorkers of English stock, as well as by significant numbers of English and Scottish immigrants, with a scattering of Germans and Irish (Anonymous 1880: 863, 1070–1081; Jones 1914: 276–280).

So here they knew these old English two-steps, military two-steps. And that's the reason they were playing some of these, I s'pose, where orchestras around here [Madison] weren't playing 'em. Just 45 miles apart, and how different it could be. We found that out, 'cause Harry and I came to Madison later on with a dance band, and we played a military two-step, and nobody knew what to do. Just 45 miles from here they were dancing them. [Leary: How do you dance them?] Well, they were just a different tempo. Like our two-steps would be [Sings] "My little girl, da-da, da-da" for a circle two-step or something like that. Where these were those with that heavy accent, that

doot-da, deedle-da, doot-doot-doot,
da, da-da-da-da, da-dum,
da, doot-doot-dootle, de-do.

They had that bounce to 'em. The people up there, well everybody danced to 'em. . . . They'd do the old shuffle, regular old two-step shuffle [a side-by-side promenade]. It's just that it had a little different accent.

During his days with the Fox River Valley Boys, George Gilbertsen also enjoyed listening to dance callers, who seemed to proliferate, particularly to the west of Pardeeville in Sauk County where Yankees, Yorkers, English, Irish, and numerous Germans mingled. In 1963, Gustave Telschow described such old time square dances in the Baraboo River valley around 1910:

I always admired the callers as they rattled off their lingoes. . . . I could never completely memorize any one of them, but these snatches constantly keep coming to my mind: "All join hands and promenade around the hall. . . . Back to your places. . . . Swing your partners every one. . . . First lady lead to the right, swing that guy and hug him tight. . . . Lead to the next, don't bump your toes. . . . Swing that man with the pump-handle nose. . . . Swing the next guy loafing there, don't take time to comb his hair. . . . Gents bow now and ladies know how." (Telschow 1963: 124)

While his memories of particular calls 30 years later were less precise, teenage George Gilbertsen was equally enthusiastic about each caller's dedication and verve.

Whatever dance hall you were playing at, usually there was somebody there that was the regular, that always would come as the caller. They weren't hired. They'd just get up there and call it. They were known for being a caller. And I know we'd play, like over here at North Freedom, west of Baraboo there. . . . Seemed like every town, somebody'd always get up and call. It didn't matter what tune you played. . . . The caller used to just shout it out. Lot of them didn't even have microphones.

The opportunities to play with older musicians, to experience overlapping but distinctive dance and tune repertoires, and to ponder and appreciate the complexities of apparently simple Upper Midwestern old time musical scenes compelled George to recognize what he had previously intuited but never fully acknowledged: "All of a sudden I realized I liked that old time music."

Conversant with an array of old time sounds and styles, already adept at harmonica, standard guitar, and lap steel or Hawaiian guitar, George tried mandolin and fiddle in 1942 at 17. By then the United States had entered World War II, and a year later George was drafted following his 18th birthday. "So I just took my fiddle along with me. I figured I don't know much on it, so I better take it along. I was kind of glad I did." Uniting draftees and enlisted men from all over the country, the U.S. military inevitably conjoined musicians from many regions, who traded styles and licks. In the war's aftermath, as commercial media companies sought to capitalize on America's invigorated sense of shared nationhood, both "polka" and "country" music industries burgeoned (Greene 1992: chs. 10–11; Malone 2002a: ch. 7). Upper Midwestern polkabillies were no less affected.

During a two-and-a-half-year stint in the navy, George Gilbertsen met other fiddlers, played frequently, and immersed himself in the western swing style. Popularized especially by Texan Bob Wills in the 1930s, western swing was a deft fusion of Anglo-American hoedown fiddling, Mexican-American and Central European couple dance tunes, and an improvisatory African-American attack that in many ways paralleled and overlapped with the musical syntheses occurring in the Upper Midwest (Townsend 1976: 2–5, 28, 38). The Fox River Valley Boys had already been attracted to Wills's sound and had included some of his pieces in their dance jobs. Fortuitously, George "met a fiddler in Boston that had played with Bob Wills. I was stationed with him for just about three months, and I got to pick up quite a few things from him."[5] Discharged from the service in 1946, George returned to Madison accomplished on the fiddle and full of new musical ideas. He found work immediately, playing with Jack Penewell at "the Paradise Isle Bar on West Main Street."

"Good Old Madison"

Born in Stoughton, Wisconsin, and a Madison resident since 1917, John Bernard "Jack" Penewell (1897–1973) was, as George put it, "the old legend on the steel guitar, or just the Hawaiian guitar, from the vaudeville days." As a teenager, Penewell taught himself to play Hawaiian guitar, won a contest sponsored by the Madison Boy Scouts in 1917, and landed a tour on the Keith-Orpheum Junior Vaudeville Circuit. By the mid-1920s, he had performed all over the country, including radio appearances in Atlanta (WSB), Pittsburgh (KDKA), St. Louis (KMOX), Chicago (WEBH), and Madison (WIBA). Perhaps less prolific and innovative than the Milwaukee area's younger, more-celebrated guitarist and studio wizard Les Paul (born Lester Polfuss in 1915), Jack Penewell was nonetheless billed as "the world's greatest guitarist" during his vaudeville days. He was also a distinguished recording artist and inventor, making 78rpm recordings of Hawaiian, old time country, blues, and popular tunes on the Apex, Autograph, Broadway, Paramount, and Puritan labels, while patenting guitars and related accouterments that included the "Jack Penewell Twin-Six," a double-necked, twelve-string steel guitar manufactured by the Gibson company of Kalamazoo, Michigan, from 1922 through the 1930s; an unwieldy but imaginative four-necked steel guitar in 1924 that allowed a performer to play in various tunings on a single piece; an early electric guitar in 1930; and a volume control device in 1956 for electric Hawaiian guitars.[6]

In 1946, amid the contrived "South Seas" atmosphere of Madison's Paradise Isle, Jack Penewell remained a technically formidable and adventurous guitarist whose considerable experience and poise were complemented by a suave appearance. George Gilbertsen watched, listened, and learned—regarding Penewell with a mixture of awe and amusement as both "the old maestro" and "that sonofagun, when he was young, boy if he didn't look like Tyrone Power: he was the best lookin' sonofagun with that dark hair. He was a womankiller too." But Jack Penewell was nearly 50 to George Gilbertsen's 21 and, when Harry Edwards returned to Madison, George exchanged his house-band apprenticeship with "the old maestro" for a shifting series of dance-hall jobs with his youthful pal.

From the late 1940s through the early 1960s, George Gilbertsen played with a succession of polkabilly bands, overtly western in their cowboy togs, but decidedly Upper Midwestern in their accordion/string band synthesis and their mixed Anglo-European dance repertoire. Combining frequently with Harry Edwards, George also joined forces with his younger brother Leroy Gilbertsen (b. 1932), Alvin "Salty" Hougan of the original Goose Island Ramblers, and fiddling "Tex" Falkenstein in such groups as the WIBA Rangers, the Badger Ramblers, the Midwest Drovers, the Rhythm Rascals, and the Midwesterners.

The Midwesterners, the most sustained aggregation, was a dance band featuring classic post–World War II polkabilly instrumentation.

> That was Johnny Severson on guitar. Harry Edwards on [string] bass, he was the leader. Chuck Holmes was the drummer, which he later became a minister. Tex Falkenstein and I were on fiddles, and then I doubled on steel guitar. . . . Rollie Phillips was the accordion player. So we had a six-piece group.

The Midwesterners mostly "played around the Madison area" at service clubs—the American Legion, the Eagles, the Veterans of Foreign Wars—as well as in outlying Dane County communities: south to Edwards Park in the Norwegian stronghold of McFarland, north to Smitty's Hall in Waunakee where Germans and Irish mingled, and northeast to heavily German Roxbury. They also played farther afield, in Sauk County villages like North Freedom, where George and Harry had entertained with the Fox

Figure 3.1. Jack Penewell's Hawaiian group at Paradise Isle, Madison, Wisconsin, 1946. (*Left to right*): Marlin Angus, Al Flansberg, Jack Penewell, and George Gilbertsen. Both Penewell and Gilbertsen are playing amplified Hawaiian lap steel guitars. Goose Island Ramblers Collection, Wisconsin Historical Society (image 32844).

River Valley Boys. The dancers in these "little dance halls" varied in temperament from place to place.

> It was kind of interesting because each place you sort of knew the people and their habits. Like Roxbury was a place where you always knew the first 30 minutes they were just going to sit and look at you. And then all of a sudden after about 30 minutes one couple might get out, and then all of a sudden they'd all get out there. . . . Some places they'd just get right out there. North Freedom, when Harry's dad played there, oh mercy you'd—the minute that first tune come out, they'd hit that floor and they were going.

Yet the audiences' preferences for dance tunes were much the same: "The waltz quadrille, circle two-step, two-steps, a lot of waltzes and schottisches." The Midwesterners, like Phil Edwards's Fox River Valley Boys, sometimes looked beyond their region to cover Bob Wills's "San Antonio Rose," while adding Wills's "Spanish Two-Step" to their playlist. Importing variations of familiar two-steps was one thing, but incorporating such blues and hokum pieces as Wills's "Brain Cloudy Blues" and "What's the Matter with the

Figure 3.2. Harry Edwards and the Midwesterners, performers of old time music, Madison, Wisconsin, early 1950s. (*Left to right*): Tex Falkenstein, Johnny Severson, Harry Edwards, George Gilbertsen, and Rollie Phillips. Goose Island Ramblers Collection, Wisconsin Historical Society (image 32850).

Mill" required too great a leap: "Never got into that type of stuff. We never did. I think mainly because the dances were that way, that people were used to dancing a certain kind. Probably. You didn't want to pull nothin' new on them because they wouldn't get out there."

Indeed, the western-togged Midwesterners played the same venues and attracted many of the same followers as the era's local polka bands, including those led by Madisonians Francis McMahan, Tony Salerno, and Joey Tantillo (Leary and March 1996: 118). As George put it, "We all played the

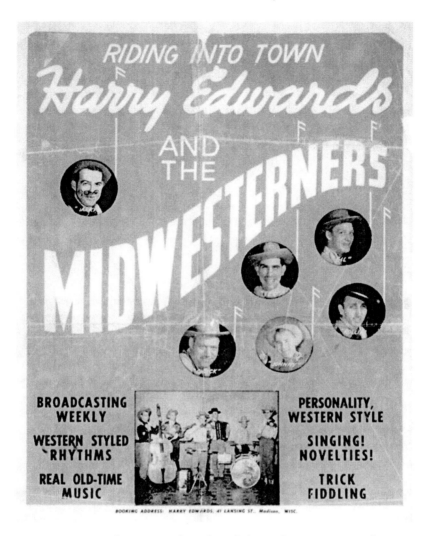

Figure 3.3. Poster for Harry Edwards and the Midwesterners, Madison, Wisconsin, early 1950s. George Gilbertsen, situated in the upper right and known as "Gil" with this band, was adept at singing novelties and, especially, trick fiddling. Goose Island Ramblers Collection, Wisconsin Historical Society (image 32838).

same places." Hip, youthful, urban dancers in downtown Madison might favor the modern foxtrots that took hold in the 1920s or the energetic jitterbug and lindy hop steps corresponding with the swinging big bands of ensuing decades, but the rural and working-class followers of the Midwesterners and kindred polka bands, spanning several generations, maintained a decidedly old time orientation toward musical and dance styles.

Besides playing with a six-piece band for regular weekend dances, George frequently performed in smaller combos on local radio stations: WIBA and

WKOW in Madison, WIBU in Poynette. The radio programs, 15–30 minutes in duration, relied on a format that had become standard all over the country since the 1920s.

> The regular routine was we'd get up there every morning and make out our program before we went on the air. We'd just get up there and decide what we—you know, you could only get in four or five numbers. So you'd have to line up what you were going to do, like a vocal, a fiddle number, a couple of instrumentals, trios, because commercials are going to fill in most of it anyhow.

George had "a lot of fun" not only playing fast and loose within the time constraints that live radio required, but also extending the medium into the realm of imagination. "There was all these little things that your audience out there—they could hear it, they knew something was going—but they never could see what was going on."

Indeed, while bands and announcers worked hard to produce a smooth, professional show, they also unraveled order through unrehearsed banter and an occasional prank. A heavy smoker in his younger days, with a puckish sense of humor, "Smokey George" earned his nickname by combining unexpected special effects with his usual fiery fiddling.

> Funny little incident. This radio announcer for WIBA back then, Al Beaumont his name was. A very well-poised guy and done these commercials. Well, I took my fiddle one time, while he was doing a commercial, and I was in back there. I blew cigarette smoke into it. You know how you blow smoke into a glass? You could pour it? I'd fill it. While he's talking I got this fiddle all filled up with cigarette smoke. Well then I got up there to do a hoe-down. I started playing, and this smoke started curling out of there. And he looked, and he got laughing. He couldn't get back into the commercial. He couldn't get over that. He looked just almost shocked, you know.

Listeners responded to the mixture of distilled virtuosity and rollicking spontaneity with appreciative letters and special requests. George and cohorts responded in kind. "Gee whiz, they'd write in to you . . . local people. You were still kind of a star to them even though it was just local. . . . I had postcards with my picture on it, with [the] WKOW microphone. I'd send 'em out to people."

Many of George's radio gigs were unpaid. Stations typically expected performers either to secure a sponsor to underwrite their air time, or to play simply for the opportunity to reach a broad audience.

> WIBU. My young brother and I, and Salty Hougan, and Wanda Starr . . . we played WIBU when we called ourselves the Badger Ramblers. We used to play variety shows and banquets. We were on WIBU on Sat-

urdays. We'd go up there. That was non-pay. That was more or less for publicity, for our own bookings.

The situation was a little better on WIBA: "The WIBA Rangers. That was Smilin' Jim McCloskey and Harry Edwards and I. And we had two morning shows there, five days a week. That was pay, of course. One was a 15-minute program, and the other was a 30-minute program."

The group was also expected to play an occasional Farm Field Day show on their sponsor's behalf. George had his best radio stint in 1948, the year he was married, when, after an audition, Madison's WKOW hired him as a staff musician. Fiddling for a variety of performers—the Campbell Sisters (Betty and Eve), Ray Carson's Dairylanders, and Helen Diller—George earned $45 a week, decent pay for the era. "At that time, I would've accepted that for life." But "then it all died out" as the station, unable to attract enough advertising revenue, laid off numerous musicians, including George Gilbertsen.

Soon after, George began working for the University of Wisconsin's Memorial Union, but for several more years he sought opportunities for fame and fortune, for the chance to make his living solely as a musician. Years before, while stationed in Portsmouth, New Hampshire, during his navy days, George and "a guitar player there were picked out of an amateur program, and they were going to send us to play in Boston on the Blue Network" (NBC). But when they arrived in Boston, "it was on the wrong day, so we never did get on the Blue Network." In 1948, however, George won Wisconsin's Centennial Fiddlers Contest with his rendition of the "Beaumont Rag." He soon parlayed victory into an appearance on the "Ted Mack Original Amateur Hour," a nationally syndicated television program featuring performers from around the country.

I got to go to New York. I think I was maybe one of the first ones on television in Madison, because that's back when they didn't even have it in the home. It was just the snowy sets in the bars. . . . I went to New York and Syracuse. I played a show in Denver. The Union was always good; they'd give me time off to go and do this stuff.

As had been the case with Windy Whitford, George Gilbertsen also played alongside WLS stars and other touring performers at local events like the Madison area's Farm Field Days.

One such group was the Dakota Roundup, led by Jimmy Wells from Aberdeen, South Dakota. Wells was a fiddler and his wife sang, as did guitarist Curly Waldsmith. Like the barnstorming movie cowboy Lash Larue, Waldsmith would also "do a whip act. . . . They had a regular variety show. It was almost like a medicine show." The group was sponsored by International Harvester, a Chicago-based farm equipment corporation that booked the Dakota Roundup "all over the country" wherever imple-

Figure 3.4. The WIBA Rangers, also known as the Quaker Melody Boys, Madison, Wisconsin, early 1950s. (*Left to right*): announcer Al Beaumont, George Gilbertsen, "Smilin' Jim" McCloskey, Harry Edwards. Goose Island Ramblers Collection, Wisconsin Historical Society (image 32841).

ments were sold. As George recalled in 1990, "When they came to Madison, I heard 'em play and I got talking to 'em. He [Jimmy Wells] asked if I'd be willing to go with 'em, and I said, well, I'd try it." Soon, George Gilbertsen was heading south to entertain around Nashville, Tennessee, and Hopkinsville, Kentucky. But three weeks on the road was enough.

> I didn't particularly like that life. I thought it was too rough. Eating in little restaurants and banging the roads. Lots of driving in cars. I guess I never quite had that killer instinct for music to that extent where I wanted to go out and sell the farm and go out and hit the road. It was there. The opportunity was there, but I just guess I preferred good old Madison. I'd been in the service and seen a lot of places, and I decided Madison was as good as they come.

Just as Windy Whitford interpreted a smashed 78 as signifying his destiny as a family man first, and then a musician, George Gilbertsen found revelation in his road time: "I liked music, it has always been quite a part of my life, but not a big enough part that I wanted to make a living out of it. So I came back home and went back to the dance band."

Figure 3.5. Norwegian dialect comedian and accordionist Mike "Tex" Holley and guitarist Ray Carson (the stage name of Ray Gensch), with whom George Gilbertsen played in 1948, are seen here as members of the Rangers, also including fiddler Larry Brudahl, bassist Lum Haskins, and drummer Earl "Cousin Fuzzy" McNellis. One of the two radio announcers is likely Hal Woods, while "Uncle Louie," leader of the comic Town Hall Players, is at the far right. WIBU Radio, Poynette, Wisconsin, 1941. Mills Music Library Collection, University of Wisconsin.

"This Novelty Stuff"

Far from stifling George Gilbertsen's creative spirit, staying at home proved stimulating. The road can prompt new songs and flashy musicianship, yet the path to national prominence can also narrow one's stylistic possibilities. A German waltz, an Irish reel, a Norwegian hoppwaltz, or an English military two-step might appeal to Upper Midwestern audiences, but how would they be received in Kentucky or Tennessee? Being back home in "good old Madison," George might still wear western clothing and play a smattering of cowboy, steel guitar, and western swing tunes, but his repertoire ranged wider and dug deeper, spanning and delving into the broad possibilities of his surrounding region. Indeed throughout the 1950s, George Gilbertsen continued to expand his skills as a versatile, virtuoso performer on fiddle, guitar, dobro, mandolin, and harmonica; to learn and even compose new tunes in the various folk traditions swirling about Madison's ethnically diverse east side; and, in the manner of an earlier generation of Midwesterners, to hone his talents as a novelty performer at a time when such musical tricks were becoming anachronisms.

In the late 1950s and very early 1960s, just before joining Bruce Bollerud to form what would become the second incarnation of the Goose Island Ramblers, George Gilbertsen teamed with a four-string banjoist, Leo Aberle, who ran the Senate Bar on East Main Street in Madison: "He was tall, slim . . . and really serious about his music. He played it good. He did have a nice little line there. One guy said to him, 'Leo, you are really good.' He said, 'I can't understand that. If I'm so darn good, how come I've been so poor all my life?'"

Possessing what George called "an altogether different style of banjo," Aberle combined lead melody lines with harmony. "He wasn't the fast razzle-dazzle type. He was more for the real touch. He had long fingers and he'd stretch them things out." Leo Aberle was particularly adept at wrapping his fingers around minor-key Polish mazurkas and Russian balalaika tunes.

> Then he had a couple cute little novelty tunes where he'd string playing cards through the strings of a banjo, which would leave him just certain strings to play on and the others would be like a snare drum, mute. And then he'd do like "Dixie" and "Yankee Doodle," and while he was playing it'd sound like a snare drum in the background. A real nice little novelty.

George absorbed Aberle's Slavic tunes, rendering mazurkas on the fiddle, while conjuring the balalaika with his mandolin. He never learned the old banjoist's card trick, but he complemented Aberle with novelty numbers of his own.

As the beaming kid in "dog fur" chaps kicking out his legs on "Buffalo Gals," or the teenaged Bearcat Mountain Boy artfully "slaughtering" Hawaiian tunes to the extent that his erstwhile teacher hollered "Nothing but corn!" George Gilbertsen had been inclined all of his performing life toward melding zany antics with stellar musicianship, toward undergirding a goofball hick exterior with a sophisticate's competence. During his stint with Harry Edwards and the Midwesterners, when George was known as "Gil," the band's poster emphasized "TRICK FIDDLING" and NOVELTIES!" Figuring "this novelty stuff" to be "pretty good stuff," George honed this part of his act sufficiently to feign a frequent musician's disaster.

> I used to use this one [fiddle] where—already I had my bow undone, but they didn't know it—and I'd be holding the frog and I'd be playing and, all of a sudden, the bow would fly apart. "Awww," they'd say, "he broke his bow." And then I'd throw the strings over, bring the bow under and the strings over, and I'd play it four string with the hair coming over and the bow underneath.

Another trick, one that Windy Whitford also used with the Hoedowners, resembled the party game "Twister" as musicians entangled in midtune to play their own and another's instrument without dropping a beat or mangling a note.

> Right in the middle of "Pop Goes the Weasel," I'd flick the fiddle around. One would start bowing the fiddle, and I'd finger it, and I'd be strumming the guitar and the other one would be picking the bass—three of us would get all twisted up. We'd have about three different variations, all in one song too. It was pretty nice stuff to do.

Novelty numbers served George particularly well in contest situations. In the 1948 Wisconsin Centennial Fiddlers Contest, George was up against several noted fiddlers, including such pals and mentors of Windy Whitford as Harv Cox and Swede Moseby, as well as Emil Simpson, leader of a popular old time band, the Nite Hawks.

> You could pick your own tunes and it was two numbers usually. The one advantage I had at the time was I was plenty young, and I had these novelty tunes worked up. The "Beaumont Rag" I used to play and that's where I used to step over and through the fiddle and back and out in front and all that. So that was a little advantage for me—I had a pretty darn good novelty number worked up. . . . But by far I wouldn't have rated myself as the top fiddler back then. Except the novelty stuff is what paid off at that time.

The "novelty stuff" contributed to George's brief stint on the "Ted Mack Original Amateur Hour." And in the early 1950s, when WKOW radio established a television station with the same call letters, Big John Schermerhorn, the announcer for an old time music program, "Dairyland Jubilee," thought of George: "He'd get me to come out for some of these shows he was putting on just to do that trick fiddle number."

Besides Leo Aberle, Red Blanchard was an early inspiration. Blanchard, a guitar-playing rural comedian from Pittsville, Wisconsin, was a regular on Chicago's WLS radio, and George eventually performed with him in variety shows in such Wisconsin farm communities as Boaz and Richland Center. "He had a guitar too that, while he was playing it, the neck would come unhinged and come apart. The neck would fly right apart on it. . . . People loved it." Combining strong musicianship with tricks and a comic flair, Red Blanchard and George Gilbertsen were participants in a larger tradition that, while hardly exclusive to the Upper Midwest, was especially strong in the region.

In the post–World War I era that witnessed both the emergence of urban "modern" bands and the self-designation of rural "old time" musicians, some of the latter performers consciously exaggerated their rustic, archaic pedigree through a combination of names (Fruit Jar Drinkers, Possum Hunters, Bogtrotters, Rubes), appearance (barnyard overalls, ill-fitting and outmoded Sunday suits, clodhopper boots, straw hats, fake beards), and skits (complete with whiskey jugs, outhouses, cow costumes, and dialect).[7]

While many such bands—whether southern, eastern, or midwestern—favored an old time instrumentation and repertoire, others combined old time elements with a playfully reckless interpretation of modern music. Typically, they might perform a hot pop number flawlessly but with unconventional instruments or parodic lyrics, perhaps combined with tricky movements or silly facial expressions and physical contortions. They might also render a song or tune expertly the first or, maybe, the last time through, thereby establishing their musical competence, before willfully destroying the piece with extraneous noises, dissonant notes, interruptions, quotations from other melodies, and the like. Whereas in the early 1960s bop saxophonist John Coltrane constructed then disassembled Rodgers and Hammerstein's "My Favorite Things" in a serious, meditative manner, the rube performers flourishing in the 1920s and 1930s assumed a decidedly comic, slapstick approach.

In the 1920s, Ezra Buzzington's All Rube Band was exemplary. Hailing from rural, central Indiana, the Buzzington band, attired in ill-fitting rustic clothing, toured the Midwest playing county fairs as well as theaters on the vaudeville circuit. On the surface they featured an old time European-American wind band instrumentation—trumpets, trombone, saxophone, clarinets, tuba—augmented by the African-American Dixieland modifications of banjo and both wood and metal percussion. The banjo, however, was a hefty bass version wielded with comic effect by Buzzington, while other members of the band might double on "a huge array of freak musical instruments," including "slide whistle, washboard, and a stunning array of bells, whistles, and horns."[8] After the Buzzington band broke up in 1929, four of its members went on to form the Hoosier Hot Shots: Paul "Hezzie" Trietsch, Ken "Rudy" Trietsch, Otto "Gabe" Ward, and Frank Kettering. In contrast to the Buzzingtons' barnyard garb, the Hot Shots assumed the personas of farmboys ineptly attempting a dapper, urbane look through sport coats, slacks, and bow ties, topped off variously by straw boaters, fedoras, or golfers' tams. Their intentionally ripped and rumpled duds, loud colors, and mismatched patterns, however, signaled rubes beneath the would-be sophisticates' veneer. Featuring Hezzie's goofy slide-whistle, a wild yet stellar musical attack, and silly songs like "I Like Bananas (Because They Have No Bones)" and "From the Indies to the Andes in His Undies," the Hot Shots became fixtures on the "National Barn Dance" of Chicago's WLS radio from 1932 to 1950, recording numerous 78s on the Columbia label (*Hoosier Hot Shots* 1992 M; Young 1994: 56).

Hailed by chroniclers and critics for their playful synthesis of rural and urban Anglo- and African-American music, reissued by Columbia as part of its Country Classics series (along with Bob Wills, Gene Autry, Bill Monroe, and Johnny Cash), and credited justly for their influence on such subsequent popular novelty bands as Spike Jones and His City Slickers, the Hoosier Hot Shots—and the earlier Buzzington aggregation—also paralleled, drew upon, and affected German and Scandinavian traditions prevalent in the Midwest.

Ezra Buzzington, to begin with, was actually Mark Schaefer who, like the Trietsch brothers who played with him before forming the core of the Hoosier Hot Shots, was a German-American farm kid from central Indiana. The Germans who immigrated in enormous numbers to the Midwest throughout the nineteenth century, and earlier to the Middle Atlantic states, brought a strong wind band tradition, as well as a penchant for comic performances by "little German bands," German-dominated "clown bands," and intentionally disheveled Dutchman bands. Adopting "Dutch," the Anglo-American rendition of Deutsch, as their nickname, Dutchman bands from the late nineteenth century through the 1930s—including Wisconsin's Famous Boscobel Dutch Band, Minnesota's Whoopee John's Orchestra, and dozens more—often donned ill-fitting, out-of-style clothing, glued on fake chin whiskers, and called attention to sometimes padded potbellies, thus embodying Yankee stereotypes of beer-swilling, sausage-chomping, impossibly outmoded foreigners (Coggeshall 1986; Leary 2004b; Leary and March 1991). Likely both Schaefer and the Trietsches were at least familiar with Dutchman musical traditions and comic stereotypes, particularly since both are sustained to the present in such Indiana communities as Fort Wayne and Evansville (Burdette 2002). Certainly, apart from the addition of the German or Chemnitzer concertina, the basic instrumentation of quintessential Dutchman groups, like that led by Hans Wilfahrt (Whoopee John) from the 1920s on, has consisted of the same wind band plus banjo and percussion instrumentation preferred by Schaefer/Buzzington. Moreover, the washboards affixed with bells and horns that Buzzington and the Hot Shots used resembled the "boomba" (aka "boombah" or "boombas"), a noisemaker combining bladder horns with percussion that has figured in Central European and Nordic pre-Lenten festivities since medieval times and continues to figure in informal music making throughout German, Scandinavian, and Slavic communities in the Middle Atlantic and Midwestern regions (Abrantes 2002; Leary and Teske 1991: 68–69). Could it be that Mark Schaefer grafted the rustic Yankee name of Ezra Buzzington onto at least some elements of a comic Dutchman tradition? Whether the answer is yes or no, just this sort of fusion happened elsewhere during the era.

In western New York state in 1927, Milo, Zeke, Otto, and George Kouf of Ithaca, old time country musicians of German-American descent, formed Ott's Woodchoppers, a band of self-described "hillbilly rubes" that affixed classic cartoons of Dutchman figures to their promotional business card (Bronner 1987: 68–70). Similarly, Woodhull's Old Tyme Masters, formed in Elmira in 1928, "began dressing up in old farmer's clothes when they appeared at the dance halls," including "fake beards, large glasses, and floppy hats." In addition to Herb Woodhull's jug blowing and his brother Floyd's bell ringing, Fred Woodhull "played a novelty percussion instrument called a 'boom-bah'" (Bronner 1987: 66).

The Upper Midwestern German-American connection to rural novelty bands is clearly evident in the case of Ferdinand Frederick Fisher. Born in

1904 in the tiny German farming community of Lourdes, in northeastern Iowa 20 miles south of the Minnesota border, "Freddie" Fisher learned to play clarinet as a youngster, performing in local bands (Edstrom 2002). In the early 1930s, just as the Hoosier Hot Shots were forming, Fisher organized the Schnickelfritz Band, drawing upon a traditional German nickname for a mischievous, foolish youngster. "His key sidemen were Nels Laakso on cornet, trumpet and slide whistle, and Stanley Fritts, who played trombone, jug, and a more elaborate version of Trietsch's washboard. Fisher himself played washboard, ocarina, slide whistle and flute, in addition to clarinet" (Young 1994: 58).

The Schnickelfritzers entertained Upper Midwestern audiences, particularly during long-standing jobs in Winona and St. Paul, Minnesota, with a repertoire of "Dixieland jazz and polkas," as well as waltzes like "The Schnickelfritz Waltz," the specialty dance "Herr Schmidt," the circle two-step "My Little Girl," and such comic Euro-American agrarian dialect songs as "Hilda Was a Darned Good Cook":

> Although her hips were wider
> Than a barrel full of cider,
> Hilda was a darned good cook.

In 1939, shortly after Fisher's band located in Hollywood, Stan Fritts and several other members left to form their own group. After considering calling themselves the Original Schnickelfritzers, they settled on the Korn Kobblers, continuing the use of "the washboard, tuned auto horns, cowbells, frying pans, and funny hats," including the felt alpine hats favored by Dutchman bands (Young 1994: 58–59).

Upper Midwestern Scandinavian bands likewise contributed to the region's mixture of rustic novelty bands. Throughout the 1920s and 1930s, Hjalmar Peterson, a Swedish immigrant to Minneapolis, led a raggedly garbed Hobo Band that entertained Scandinavian communities with performances combining strong musicianship with rustic comedy. A veteran of the Swedish *bondkomiker*, or peasant comedian tradition, Peterson assumed the stage name Olle i Skratthult (Ole from Laughtersville) to sing funny songs and deliver monologues concerning the travails of an immigrant from the backwoods. Peterson's "Olle" also artfully affected the look of a foolish Swedish bumpkin newly come to urban America through a pudding-bowl haircut, artificially blackened tooth, goofy grin, soiled frock coat, homespun woolen neck scarf, knee britches, and scuffed boots. Meanwhile, his band mingled brass, reed, and stringed instruments with a raucous percussive variation on the boomba to play polkas, waltzes, schottisches, and an occasional jazzy number (Greene 1992: 94–97, 280–281; Harvey and Hulan 1982). In addition to Hjalmar Peterson's decidedly Scandinavian parallel to the semi-German cum Anglo-American pop stylings of the Schnickelfritz Band, Ezra Buzzington, and the Hoosier Hot Shots, several Nordic bands bent the Hot Shots' name and sound in an Upper Midwestern Scandinavian direction. The Norwegian-American comic dialect singer Stan

Boreson, for example, composed and performed "Scandinavian Hot Shot," concerning an immigrant rube on the frigid shores of Lake Superior who nonetheless imagines himself a hot mambo dancer:

> I'm a Scandinavian Hot Shot,
> I'm a Hot Shot from Dulut'.
> I'm a killer-diller with a Latin rhythm,
> For a polka I don't give a hoot.

Meanwhile a pair of Finnish-American polka bands, Johnny's Hot Shots from Cloquet, Minnesota, and the Oulu Hot Shots from Oulu, Wisconsin, have paid nominal homage to the Hoosiers.[9]

For his part, George Gilbertsen enjoyed hearing the Hoosier Hot Shots over WLS, especially their slide whistle and the washboard with bells and whistles. He "dressed up a little goofy" in frumpy overalls a few times while playing with Harry Edwards in the Bearcat Mountain Boys and, in later years, appreciated Edwards's washboard playing with the Midwesterners. While at WKOW, he sometimes backed up Ray Carson and Tex Holley during the period when Holley assumed a stage Norwegian accent to perform as "Ole" (Kirschke 2002: 8). But apart from these experiences, George's participation in the novelty tradition was confined to trick fiddling. He was familiar but not actively involved with other aspects of the Upper Midwest's rustic, occasionally ethnic musical comedy. All that began to change, however, in 1962 when George fell in with Bruce Bollerud and, eventually, Windy Whitford.

As a member of the Goose Island Ramblers, George Gilbertsen continued to draw upon the dance tune repertoire that had served him well since his house party and tavern days on Madison's working-class east side; to pay homage to western swing; to play with speed and heart on guitar, harmonica, dobro, mandolin, and fiddle; and to dazzle audiences with musical tricks. But he also began to blossom as a comic, novelty entertainer in a distinctly rustic, ethnic, regional vein: ringing cowbells, blowing goose calls, plucking amplified toilet plungers, wearing both Viking horns and the braided wig of a blonde Nordic temptress, singing in a peculiar mixture of Hawaiian and Norwegian, and assisting a pseudo-drunken Dutchman through botched choruses of "Ach du Lieber Augustine."

4

Bruce Bollerud
The Hollandale Wildcat

"We Used to Have House Parties"

> I can remember down on the farm, we used to have house parties all the
> time. And when I was very young, you know like four or five years
> old . . . I'd be at these parties and I'd watch the musicians play and tap
> my foot. And I really liked what they were doing, I really enjoyed that.
> And, we had a piano there and I'd watch other people play the piano and
> say, "How do they do that?" They'd be chording along with the fiddle and
> guitar. . . . And after the party was over and they were gone, I'd try to get
> up there and copy what they did, as much as I could remember of it.[1]

Bruce Bollerud was born on October 8, 1934, and grew up near the village
of Hollandale in southwestern Wisconsin's Iowa County. His parents,
Orville Bollerud and Selma Venden Bollerud, both descendants of Norwegian immigrants, ran a large dairy farm boasting "the longest barn in Iowa
County." As a kid, Bruce did his share of chores in the family's fields and
barn. While in high school and after graduation in 1952, he also toiled on
neighboring farms and in cheese factories and drove a truck. But "all the
bright lights in Hollandale were in three blocks," so like many others from
rural southern Wisconsin, Bruce headed to Madison in 1955. He spent a
year installing window displays for Manchester's department store; then,
after a stint in the air force from January 1956 through May 1958, Bruce
worked a succession of jobs in the Madison area: on Max Crow's construction crew, where the boss taught him the trick of breaking concrete
while wielding a sledge hammer one-handed; in the Rayovac battery plant
that daily left him "blacker than a coal miner" from the graphite; as a truck
driver for Fauerbach Brewery; and in the plant and office of Carns, a company that made ventilating equipment. He married Gloria Disch in 1961, and
the couple raised two children. Eventually, with support from the G.I. Bill,
he earned bachelor's and master's degrees from the University of Wisconsin in 1971 and 1973, resulting in a career as a special education teacher
in the Madison area from 1972 until his retirement in 1997. Throughout
all these years, Bruce Bollerud played in a succession of bands, including

a nearly 40-year span with the Goose Island Ramblers. A decade younger than George Gilbertsen, Windy Whitford's junior by 22 years, Bruce Bollerud was nonetheless steeped as much, perhaps more so, in the Upper Midwest's old time polkabilly music—a happy consequence of his family's house parties and Hollandale environs.

Despite its name, Hollandale was very much a Norwegian farming community, with a sprinkling of English, Irish, and Swiss. Its founder, Ben Holland, who platted the village in 1887, was a Norwegian immigrant, Bjarne Haaland, with an Anglicized name. Holland had sailed with his parents and siblings from Bergen to New York City in 1846, continuing up the Hudson River to Albany and thence, via the Erie Canal and Great Lakes, to Milwaukee. The family first settled on a farm in northeastern Walworth County, Wisconsin, but soon moved to Iowa County's burgeoning Norwegian settlement (Crawford and Crawford 1913: 280–281; Lauper and Thompson 1987: 5). Holland attended Albion Academy and likely knew Windy Whitford's musical ancestors.

Certainly he knew Joen Hansen Bollerud, Bruce Bollerud's great-grandfather, who left Norway in 1853 at 23 to settle in Iowa County's town of Moscow on a farm near what would become Hollandale (Anonymous 1881: 965). Soon changing his first name and patronymic to John Hanson, Bruce's great-grandfather retained what had been a farm name in the old country. *Bolle* (fire) and *rud* (place) refer to slash-and-burn land-clearing methods in rocky, timbered regions. Berte "Betsy" Hanson Ensrud, whom John married in 1854, was also born in Norway and the couple raised eight children—including Bruce's grandfather Hans "Henry" Bollerud, who served as a town clerk and chairman in the late nineteenth and early twentieth centuries (Crawford and Crawford 1913: 282–283).[2]

While the Bolleruds settled in Wisconsin prior to the Civil War, the Vendens, Bruce's maternal relations, were late nineteenth-century arrivals. Their fellow Norwegian Americans, well established and occupying the best farmland, sometimes referred to them condescendingly as "newcomers" and "greenhorns." As Bruce put it, the Vendens "were just poor immigrant farmers . . . but they had a lot of fun." His grandfather Ben Venden, born in Valders in 1884, emigrated at 12 to work as a hired hand for an aunt and uncle. Ben Venden eventually farmed on his own, but mostly as a tenant on a succession of Iowa County farms. Indeed, the region's first wave of Norwegians often moved to town in the late nineteenth century and, ironically emulating the wealthy landholders they had fled, rented out their old farms to newcomers, who became landless peasants of a sort once again. Years later, Bruce drove his mother and an uncle around to "all the different places they had lived when they were growing up." Some remained, but others were "just little sort[s] of depressions in the hillside where there'd been a house at one time."

Besides farming, Ben Venden helped to support his family as a stonemason, laying the foundations of many local houses and barns. Bruce recalled him fondly: "a big rugged man" with "a great big handlebar mustache" who was hard-working and powerful even in old age.

I can remember him working for my dad when he was about 65 years old or more. . . . he and I were up in the hay mow, mowing hay. And I was probably about 14 or 15 and thought I was pretty strong . . . but Grandpa was really strong. He moved a lot more hay than I did, I'll tell you that.

At the same time, "if he wanted to take a day off and go play cards with the boys, he'd do that too, or go fishing," often with Bruce in tow. Sometimes young Bruce Bollerud would while away an afternoon at his grandparents' home. "You always felt really welcome at his house. . . . And [of] course Grandma [Sophia Venden] took care of the coffee and cookies. . . . She was the same way." From his grandparents, Bruce learned about "the old days" in Norway, "a little Norwegian," and a good deal more about life: "He never really accumulated a lot of money or material things, but he was always happy."

Sometimes, Ben Venden would "sing some of these old tunes," like *"Paul paa Haugen"* (Paul on the Hill), a comic ditty about a chicken farmer. Using his jackknife in the late spring, he delighted young Bruce by carving willow flutes of the sort made in rural Norway (Nupen 1999: 84–85). And every once in a while, he would pick up a fiddle to saw out some old Norwegian tune, like *"Stegen Vals"* (Stepladder Waltz), learned while growing up. His style was "pretty rough. . . . those hands of his from lifting rock and everything were pretty thick and pretty heavy. But he really enjoyed it."

The Vendens were known locally as a musical family. When chores were done, "in the evening, in the summertime, they'd all go out on the porch and play music." There were nine kids, two boys and seven girls, "and they all played the fiddle or the mandolin or the guitar or the pump organ or something like that." Two of Bruce's uncles, Lawrence and Chris, were especially accomplished on fiddle and four-string banjo, respectively. They often performed for house parties in a trio with Henry Hansen on bandonion. Sadly, Bruce never heard them play. When Chris Venden died young in 1940:

Lawrence was so shook up by that, so devastated, that he just put the fiddle away. And hardly ever touched it again, which I thought was a real shame. I guess every time he played, he'd hear that banjo, and it wasn't there, you know. He was a very sentimental man. He just couldn't do that. He did play for me once, out at the farm. We got together for Thanksgiving or Christmas or something. And he took his fiddle out, and I played the piano. And he played "Bye, Bye Blackbird." I would've expected something Norwegian, but that's what he played. He played it really smooth and really clean and really accurate. Not fancy, but just with the kind of a touch that you knew this guy had been good at one time. And he talked about the tunes he had played. He mentioned "Leather Britches" and "Back Up and Push" and then some Norwegian things.

Only six when his Uncle Chris died, Bruce sometimes reckoned he "was born about 20 or 30 years too late, 'cause the real big thing was a little earlier."

Not as stellar as her brothers, Bruce's mother, Selma Venden Bollerud, was nonetheless a solid backup musician, adept at chording on pump organ or piano. And she was an especially good dancer, as were all of the Vendens: "they all could waltz and schottische and polka and do some kind of a foxtrot probably or two-step." When Selma Venden was growing up in the early twentieth century, "house parties were real common at different farmers' places." And they were still thriving when Bruce was a youngster: "They'd have 'em one week at this guy's farm and then the next time at that guy's, and you know it'd sort of move around the neighborhood. Probably never got out of the neighborhood a lot, but there was still a lot of parties and a lot of fiddle music, lot of dancing." Part of a system of mutual support that also involved communal cooperation for labor-intensive tasks like threshing and silo filling, house parties were common throughout the rural Upper Midwest (Garthwaite 1990; Martin 1994: 43–62).

In the Hollandale area, they often took on a decidedly Norwegian character. Pre–Civil War settlers and newcomers alike hailed from rural areas of western Norway, where agrarian neighborhoods sustained patterns of work and festivity for centuries (Frimannslund 1956: 62–81; Gjerde 1985: 51–52). In both Old and New Worlds, folks who helped one another make hay, cut wood, and fill granaries celebrated weddings, harvests, and the Christmas season together. Norwegian "Christmas fooling," or *julebukking,* for example, was well entrenched in Hollandale's hinterlands. Similar to the wassailing of Cornish immigrants just up the road in Mineral Point, *julebukking* occurred from December 26 through January 6 as neighbors donned disguises at night to visit one another unannounced. Barging into homes to demand food and drink, they challenged their hosts' attempts to guess who they were. Musicians' homes were favorite targets, as visitors eventually dropped their masks, moved the furniture against the walls, and danced into the wee hours (Leary 1998: 346–351; Stokker 2000: 144–146, 189–191, 220–238).

Small wonder that Bruce's parents, Orville Bollerud and Selma Venden, began their courtship on the improvised dance floor of a farmhouse. Like his wife, Orville Bollerud "loved to dance." Strong, hard-working, "a farmer all his life," he was a bachelor until his mid-30s, enjoying regular visits to Hollandale watering holes like Joe's Tavern. When jukeboxes arrived in the late 1930s, Orville spent many a nickel: "he'd play waltzes and polkas and schottisches, that's what he liked." Several tunes by the Nordic Rhythm Boys were particular favorites. Once another taverngoer objected:

My dad says, "I'm going to play that jukebox; I want to hear this tune."
So he went down and he played this jukebox, and this guy went and
hit him right in the mouth. And my dad was a pretty big guy. He could
be pretty rough if he wanted to be. He got up and he whacked this guy
and knocked him right down again. I thought, that's really fighting for
what you like, for your music. The tune played.

While some other tavern regulars were just as feisty as Orville Bollerud, most were fellow "old farmers" who shared his musical taste and fondness for dancing.

Small-town, rural, and neighborhood taverns in Wisconsin and throughout the Upper Midwest—although periodically assailed by pietistic Lutheran ministers and temperance-minded Yankees—have been more generally regarded by the region's citizens as family places, extensions of Old World inns and rural and working-class social clubs (Leary 1998: 377–385). As a kid, Bruce often tagged along with his dad during down times when farmers might combine a visit to the store or the feed mill with a stop in the tavern for conversation, a drink, a bite to eat, a card game, and music. Occasionally, on a weekend evening, "if my mother was along or one of her sisters or some other lady, sometimes, you know, these old farmers would dance with the ladies."

The lack of female partners, however, did not restrain Orville Bollerud and his male companions. Like lumber-camp denizens of a prior generation, they danced with one another. Bruce fondly recalled "seeing these guys in their rubber boots and farmer overalls . . . dancing around very gracefully on a waltz." Eventually, Bruce joined in: "When I was about, I suppose, 10 or 11, somewhere in there, my dad says, 'Well, you better learn how to dance a waltz.' And then he got me out there and led me around. He was a very good dancer; he was very graceful for a big man. So I learned to waltz from my dad."

A nimble dancer and music lover, Orville Bollerud, unlike the Vendens, could neither play an instrument nor carry a tune. Every once in a while, however, "just to be funny," he launched into an off-kilter version of "The Drunkard's Lone Child," a sentimental nineteenth-century song recorded by hillbilly crooners like Vernon Dalhart in the 1920s (Meade, Spottswood, and Meade 2002: 261). A lone verse lodged in Bruce's memory:

> Out in the stormy night, sadly I roam.
> No one to love me, no friends or no home.
> Tired and hungry, I've wandered all day,
> Looking for work, but I'm too young they say.

Similar to the Ole in the Song

Unlike the sorrowful, abandoned child in his father's song, Bruce Bollerud was raised in a cheerful, tight-knit extended family amid an interdependent agrarian community. And unlike Orville Bollerud, Bruce could carry a tune. He was a featured singer in Hollandale High School's glee club, but long before he had listened well to both the singing Vendens and a succession of musical hired hands on his parents' dairy farm. Their songs, drawn mostly from oral tradition, were delivered in Norwegian, English, and the peculiar Anglo-Norsky patois that characterized everyday speech in Hollandale.

Bruce's grandparents on both sides were fluent Norwegian speakers with an appreciation of various old country dialects, as well as a rough yet serviceable command of English. Like many Upper Midwestern Norwegian Americans of her generation, Bruce's grandmother Sophia Venden mixed and shifted Old and New World languages, sprinkling her Norwegian with Anglo-American loan-words and infusing her English with notably Scandihoovian pronunciation: *j* became *y; o* was the Nordic *ø*, rendered with round mouth and puckered lips; *w* became *v; s* took on a sibilant "sszz"; the proper noun "I" was delivered more as "eh"; and *th* came out as *t* or *d*. Whereas the fall chore of cutting firewood might prompt "I was just so busy working in the woods" from a standard American English speaker, Sophia Venden's exclamation would have been closer to "Eh vas yust sø busszzy vørking in da vøødsszz" (Haugen 1969). Indeed, Bruce and his wife, Gloria, recalled that, late in her life, Sophia Venden invariably called their son "Yack" rather than "Jack."

Well aware of the comic potential of his "broken English," Ben Venden, an immigrant, unlike his American-born wife, Sophia, largely succeeded in Anglicizing his pronunciation. Yet he appreciated dialect humor and even told Bruce self-deprecating stories regarding his linguistic blunders as a teenaged immigrant.

> When he got over here, the hired man—his uncle's hired man was Norwegian of course and was quite a kidder, a joker—and he was teaching my grandfather English. But he taught him some very special words, some swear words, and my grandfather's aunt was quite a religious lady, and she was just shocked out of her mind to hear this little Norwegian boy swearing, 'cause he didn't know what he was saying at all, you know. But uh, I thought that was kind of funny.

From 1918 to 1935, Peter Rosendahl (1878–1942) made similarly comic rural doings and mangled speech the subject of some 700 "Han Ola og Han Per" comic strips published in the *Decorah-Posten,* a Norwegian-American newspaper out of Iowa that appealed to fellow Upper Midwestern Norskies. Many of the strips were gathered, beginning in 1921, into eight books by the Amundsen Publishing Company (Haugen and Buckley, 1984, 1988; Rosendahl, 1980). Ben Venden was a devoted Rosendahl fan who savored the characters' goofy rustic antics and perpetual shifting from Hadeland, Hallingdal, Dano-Norwegian, and Americanized Norwegian dialects, each laden with Norwegian English. He often read and translated the cartoons for Bruce.

Although Bruce's parents spoke English at home, his mother "grew up talking Norwegian and English—'course they talked Norwegian in the home, and they were confirmed in Norwegian." His dad's parents also spoke Norwegian at home, although not as much as the Vendens. Still, Orville Bollerud understood the language "very well," and several of his siblings could read and write in Norwegian. During Bruce's childhood in the 1930s and 1940s, the Bolleruds "milked 50 cows," an enormous number in a hand-milking era when neighboring dairy farms typically milked no more than a dozen. The family regularly employed two to three hired men who lived on the farm for stretches ranging from a few months to several years. "Some of them were what we called 'newcomers.' They'd come from Norway, originally. They still had thick accents, of course. And they spoke Norwegian a lot" (CD, track 59). Young Bruce learned smatterings of Norwegian from the talk swirling constantly around home and neighborhood and acquired the ability to shift easily from standard to Scandihoovian English: "it seemed real natural to do. It wasn't hard for me to pick up that dialect . . . 'cause so many people used to talk that way."

Bert Vinje was an especially memorable hired man. "He was from Norway, had a real thick accent," which he sometimes applied to "Nobody's Darling but Mine," a ditty better known in the 1930s through hillbilly and singing cowboy renderings by Jimmie Davis, Gene Autry, and the Prairie Ramblers (Meade, Spottswood, and Meade 2002: 226). More important, it was from Vinje that Bruce first heard "Ole Olson, the Hobo from Norway."

> Chorus:
> Ole Olson, yah they all call me Ole
> I don't know how they found out my name.
> I never told none of them fellers,
> But they all call me Ole yust the same.
>
> My name is Ole Olson.
> I yust come over from Norvay.
> I vent to New York and I can't find no vork,
> So I tink I head vest right away.
>
> Ole Olson in the city of St. Paula,
> He yust had one dollar fifty cents.
> He bought him a pint of alcohola,
> And on a hell of a bender he vent.
>
> Ole Olson met a cop with brass buttons.
> He said, "Ole you yust come with me."
> He hit me, he slammed me, he banged me,
> Locked me up with a big brass key.
>
> "Ole Olson, you hobo from Norvay,
> You got drunk and you went on a spree.
> I fine you ten days and ten dollars,
> And I hope you remember the day." (CD, tracks 60–61)

Circulating in oral tradition since at least the late 1880s, when the second wave of Norwegian newcomers arrived in the Upper Midwest, "Ole Olson" is a classic dialect song. Its Scandihoovian English verses blithely chronicle an immigrant's misadventures, while its chorus provides our earliest evidence that the name "Ole" was—like "Pat" for the Irish and "Tony" for Italians—applied generically by Americans to any Scandinavian male in their midst.[3]

Even in the twenty-first century, the stock comic characters Ole and his consort, Lena, figure in an immense, continuously evolving cycle of jokes relished throughout the Upper Midwest since the 1890s. Although set increasingly in a contemporary world of computers, terrorism, Viagra, and Sun Belt retirement homes, Ole and Lena jokes are rooted in the real experiences of newcomers (like Bert Vinje and Ben and Sophia Venden) who started life in America as hired hands in fields and barns, as cooks and maids in kitchens and parlors. In the 1970s and 1980s, while recording raconteurs born in the late nineteenth and early twentieth centuries, I encountered a spate of venerable Ole and Lena jokes commencing with: "You know, way back when, we used to have a lot of newcomers coming into this area. They'd work pretty cheap for the farmers around here." Or "You see, they're both newcomers. Lena had been here a little longer than Ole, and she worked with a farm family over there." Or "Lena got a job as a maid with a rich family tied up with one of the sawmills." Oljanna Venden Cunneen (1923–1988), Bruce's cousin, was especially adept at drawing upon her extended family's actual experiences to fashion a score of loosely related Ole and Lena jokes into a full-blown comic immigrant saga.[4]

Bruce's appreciation of Oljanna's jokes and Bert Vinje's song was heightened further by correlations between fiction and reality on the Bollerud farm. Perhaps 25–30 hired men, "a lot of them old bachelors," worked there during Bruce's childhood.

> The hired man on a farm was something like . . . the cowboy out in the west. . . . They were usually single guys. And a lot of times they wouldn't have any relatives close by. They'd work real hard and then when they got paid, they might go on a big drunk. And they might be out of commission for three, four days, or a week. So it's kind of similar to the Ole in the song there. It's really not that different. (CD, track 62)

After Bert Vinje died, Bruce Bollerud sought out Roy Anderson, another hired man who also sang "Ole Olson, the Hobo from Norway": "he remembered more of it than I did."

Comic dialect songs, like Ole and Lena jokes, were widely savored by Upper Midwestern Norwegians and Swedes alike, including folks around Hollandale. "My family and all the Scandinavian people around there always got a big kick out of that dialect stuff." Bruce kept his ears open for similar songs. His Venden cousins "had heard '*Nikolina*' and they liked that a lot." Eventually, Bruce "worked that up and sang that." In cities like Chicago, Eau Claire, Fargo, Marquette, and Minneapolis, immigrants and their descendants not only sang such songs themselves but also supported their performance by professional entertainers. Hjalmar Peterson (Olle i Skratthult) was an immigrant to Minneapolis from Värmland, Sweden, who first recorded "Nikolina" in 1917. A darkly comic ballad concerning a hapless lover whacked with a cane by his sweetheart's father, "Nikolina" addressed familiar tensions between modernizing youngsters and tradition-bound parents. Reportedly selling an unprecedented 100,000 copies

Figure 4.1. The brothers Clarence (*left*) and Ernest (*right*) Iverson, "The Vagabond Kid" and "Slim Jim," Minneapolis, late 1930s. Author's collection.

in a tiny ethnic niche market, "Nikolina" was commercially recorded six times by Skratthult and other Swedish- and Norwegian-American performers from 1917 to 1936.[5] Sometime in the 1930s, the brothers Ernest and Clarence Iverson, better known as Slim Jim and the Vagabond Kid, translated "Nikolina" into Scandihoovian English. In the 1930s and 1940s, the Iversons—raised in the rural, Norwegian-speaking community of Binford, North Dakota—had a popular Minneapolis-based radio program on WDGY and made regular forays to halls throughout the surrounding hinterlands. In 1937, they drew as many as 1,000 fan letters a week requesting favorites from a mix of German and Norwegian songs, an occasional polka, cowboy ballads, sentimental recitations about mother and home, hymns, and such comic dialect pieces as "Scandinavian Hot Shot," "I Been a Swede from Nort' Dakota" (aka "Ay Ban a Svede from Nort' Dakota"), and "Nikolina" (Greene 1992: 151–152). Their dialect version quickly entered regional oral tradition, extending well beyond the Iversons' broadcast and touring range— all the way to Hollandale. Bruce learned "Nikolina" well before Slim Jim got around to recording it commercially in the 1950s. When he finally heard that disk, Bruce found Ernest "Slim Jim" Iverson's dialect "genuine," reminiscent of so many voices from his childhood: "I have a notion that he might talk pretty close to the way he sings."

Closer to home, Guy Stinsrud had what Bruce called "an Ole act" in the early 1950s. Stocky, wearing a loud polka-dot shirt and a tousled reddish-blond wig, Stinsrud fiddled tunes like "Starlight Schottische," told dialect jokes, and cut up generally for appreciative audiences at the Green and Iowa county fairs in the early 1950s. He also relied on his Norsky brogue and "Ole Olson" persona to work as a disc jockey for Monroe's WEKZ radio.

While Norwegian and Scandihoovian English were commonly spoken and sung while Bruce was growing up, other tongues and tunes were also present: "There were Swiss and Irish and all kinds of other people around there too. Not everyone was a Norwegian, and we picked up a lot of other tunes from each other, I'm sure."

Irish settled in what would become Hollandale as early as 1846. A century later, Bruce Bollerud played and went to school with many kids of Irish descent, including a best friend, Ronnie Doran, and assorted Fitzsimmons, McCarraghers, McDermotts, McGinnitys, and McMahans. "The Irish Washerwoman" was a house-party standard.

Swiss immigrants settled New Glarus, 20 miles to the southeast, in 1846, where they immediately established a vibrant musical culture that included yodeling and couple dancing to the push-pull of a button accordion. The late nineteenth-century rise of the dairy industry in Wisconsin attracted a new wave of Swiss, who quickly established cheese factories in rural Hollandale and throughout Iowa County. Paul Fuchs, a Swiss immigrant cheese maker, and Adolph Marty, a dairy farmer, were Bollerud neighbors and button accordionists. They and other local "Schweitzers" were welcome participants in house parties, sometimes hosting such affairs in their spacious split-level cheese factories. Throughout the 1930s, touring musicians from Switzerland—including the Moser Brothers, whose virtuoso fiddling, accordion playing, and yodeling were captured on 32 78rpm recordings made from 1925 to 1927 for Victor—also played periodically for area dances (Leary 1991a: 29–30; Spottswood 1990: 203–204).

Swiss yodeling particularly dazzled Roy Anderson, a Norwegian hired man on the Bollerud farm. When Bruce was five or six, Anderson's yodeling while he did chores had a similar effect.

> I says, "Roy, how do you yodel, can you teach me how to yodel?" And he says, "Well," he says, "If you want to yodel," he said, "You got to eat grass." So my mother was wondering what I was doing out in the yard eating grass! But actually, it worked. I can yodel a little bit. (CD, track 35)

Eventually, Bruce would combine his own yodeling with melodic fragments from a Moser Brothers recording (CD, track 36). Roy Anderson also played button accordion, squeezing out Norwegian dance tunes, backing himself on "Ole Olson, the Hobo from Norway," and attempting a Swiss ländler. When Anderson died, Bruce told me, "his family gave me one of his three-row button accordions. I was very touched by that."

Another hired man, known as Fred Fogarty, made a musical impression on young Bruce Bollerud. Originally from Long Island, New York, "Fogarty" changed his name to find Depression-era work.

> He'd come out on a road gang, building a highway out here, and he'd gotten off when he got to Wisconsin. Or maybe the road was done.

Whatever it was, he stopped and stayed in Wisconsin. His name was actually Fred Hubner, which is a German name, but [the] road gang was run by a man by the name of Ryan. Somebody told him that if you wanted a job with Ryan, you'd better be Irish. So he told the guy his name was Fred Fogarty. And everybody called him Fogarty. In fact, I don't think very many people really knew what his real name was. They always called him Fogarty. But his name was Hubner. He was 75 years old, I suppose, and he liked to sing "Bill Bailey" and "Daisy, Daisy" ["A Bicycle Built for Two"]. Of course, he had a drinking problem like a lot of these old single hired men out there. And he'd get drunk and he'd sing and he'd be happy. And then he'd sing "Daisy" and then he'd start to cry, 'cause he'd think about his wife who—I guess she had died and then he'd gotten on the road gang and came out. He said he had five kids back there in New York someplace, but he didn't stay in contact with them, or didn't try to contact them, for 20 years or so and then, when he did try, they were all gone. He couldn't find 'em. So that was kind of sad.

As a teenager, Bruce would sometimes play piano while Fogarty sang, emulating in his own way the sentimental Irish tenor John McCormack, who also sang of lost loves and distant homes.

By roughly 1950, do-it-yourself recording studios—akin to self-serve photo booths—proliferated in dime stores across the country. There was one in the village of Mount Horeb, 15 miles away, "that cut a real soft 78 kind of record, cut it right on the spot while you were singing. You'd see that stuff peeling out from the cutter." Bruce's dad, with his fondness for tavern jukeboxes, insisted, "'You guys ought to make a record.' So we went down there. I played the piano and Fred Fogarty sang 'Bill Bailey.'" Fogarty died soon after, in 1951, but voice and memory persist.

When I play that [record], I can see him. I can just see him. He had kind of a bad leg and he limped a little bit and was a little bit lopsided. He was a short, short man. When he'd get a few under his belt, why he'd kinda cock his hat up kinda cocky and kinda strut down the street. I can just see him doing that yet. A funny old guy.

"A Real Sweet Sound"

There was a flip side to that cheaply made acetate 78rpm recording. Like young Elvis Presley who, in 1953, paid the Memphis Recording Service $4 to cut the Inkspots' "My Happiness" and "That's When Your Heartaches Begin" as a birthday present for his mother, Bruce Bollerud played two of his dad's favorites on the record's B-side. One was an old time, pan-Scandinavian waltz, "Life in the Finnish Woods" (*Livet i Finnskogarna*); the other was "Soldier's Joy," a reel dating back to late eighteenth-century Britain that had spread to Scandinavia by the nineteenth century (Bayard 1945:

no. 21). Bruce played both on the bandonion, a squeezebox of German origin that his mother especially favored.

When Selma Venden Bollerud was growing up, her brother Chris plucked banjo in a little band featuring Henry Hansen. Known as "Step-and-a-Half" for his slight limp, Hansen had a small 20-acre farm near Blanchardville and was legendary for his willingness to play in all seasons. After their marriage but before Bruce was born, Selma and Orville Bollerud hired Hansen for a house party.

> They had a party and it was in the wintertime and . . . they had a train down in Hollandale at that time. It came out from Madison, it went to Dodgeville, and then they had a spur that came down through Hollandale and Blanchardville. . . . So Henry Hansen and the other musician walked to Blanchardville, which was about a mile from where he lived, got on the train, and . . . rode the train to Hollandale, got off at Hollandale, walked the two and a half miles out to our farm. You know, to play this job in the middle of the winter, and it was like, God, that's really wanting to play pretty bad. I've been crazy to play all my life, but that beats me a little bit.

Walking miles to a dance over unplowed roads on a dark winter's night was not so unusual in the 1930s, nor was carrying a fiddle in a sack slung over your shoulder, but Hansen was lugging a bandonion—a boxy, weighty squeezebox that perhaps contributed to his limping gait.

Best known as a central component of Argentinean tango orchestras, the bandonion, named for instrument-maker Heinrich Band, is closely related to the German or Chemnitzer concertina. Both were developed in Saxony in the 1830s, an era that also spawned the button accordion and the hexagonal English concertina. Both have square reed chambers, controlled by buttons and conjoined by a bellows: bass reeds on the left, treble on the right, with each button yielding one note on the push and another on the pull. The bandonion, however, has a greater tonal range and a distinctive sound (Román 1988: 39–47; Wagner 2001: 79–81, 93–100).

In the mid-1940s, when Bruce told his mother he was serious about playing, "She said, 'Well, why don't you see if you can get a bandonion. I really like the sound of them.' She thought it had a real sweet sound." The idea appealed to Bruce as well, so they visited Henry Hansen in hopes of buying a cast-off instrument. Hansen's spare was "pretty well shot," but the old-timer talked at length about the bandonion and played a few tunes.

> A short time after that, there was a store in Blanchardville, kind of a general store owned by a man by the name of Tony Arneson. And I went down there, and he had a bandonion in there, a secondhand one, for sale. He wanted $25 for it, which seemed like a huge sum of money at that time. But I went down to talk to my dad. He said, "Well, all right, let's get it." And I think I was about 10, 10 or 11, at that time. So

we got that bandonion and brought it home. And I had a couple sheets of music from Henry Hansen. They have a number system on them, you know. If you know the tune at least, you can figure it out pretty handily.

Soon Bruce "was playing a couple tunes," among them his dad's favorite, "Life in the Finnish Woods."

Such sheet music was especially useful since the bandonion's reeds are not organized sequentially as tonal steps in a musical scale but scattered about like a typewriter's keys in accordance with frequency of use. Each button, consequently, is numbered. Hansen's specialized "sheets of music" very likely came from Chicago. By the closing decades of the nineteenth century, bandonion and Chemnitzer concertina players and clubs proliferated not only throughout German-speaking Central Europe, but also across the Upper Midwest wherever Germanic peoples and their Old World neighbors settled. In the 1880s, Saxon immigrant Otto Georgi—a player, teacher, importer, publisher, and promoter—was the first to establish a concertina and bandonion shop in Chicago. Other exponents followed, like Bavarian-born Henry Silberhorn (1868–1962), who arrived in Chicago in 1885 and went on to organize concertina and bandonion clubs and to teach, arrange, and produce instruction booklets (Leary 2002: 195–203; Wagner 2001: 88–92).

Besides Henry Hansen, the bandonion players active in the house parties and halls of southwestern Wisconsin included several more Norwegians—"a man by the name of Olson between Blanchardville and New Glarus" and "a Bruflat up around by Blue Mounds"—but most were Swiss Germans. As Bruce put it, "The Norwegians, I think, heard the Swiss playing it and liked that sound and picked it up." He was particularly captivated by a fellow with a "big long Swiss name," Eichelkraut, who farmed north of New Glarus. "A big heavyset man," he "bounced around a lot and jounced around a lot" while push-pulling one of several "big bandonions." The animated Eichelkraut's drumming son was rail thin and reserved. "The contrast between the two was very funny." The duo sometimes entertained at Puempel's Tavern in New Glarus or in local amateur contests, but they were also part of the Swiss Harmonica Orchestra led by Roland Luchsinger of Verona. From 1929 to 1945, that band played for dances in community halls throughout Wisconsin's rural Dane, Green, and Iowa counties, as well as for house parties and in cheese factories. Although Schweitzers formed the core of their audience, they attracted plenty of Irish, Scots, Italians, Germans, Swedes, and Norwegians (Luchsinger 1991: 6).

In 1946, at 12, Bruce teamed with a local fiddler, Herman Erickson, to begin four years of "playing out" for dancers. Erickson, who hailed from the Norwegian stronghold of South Wayne, had bought a small farm outside of Hollandale and "did electrical work on the side." A long-time acquaintance of Orville Bollerud, he was a welcome participant in the family's house parties. Bruce stayed mostly in the background, but when the

Figure 4.2. Part of Bruce Bollerud's body and the top of his bandonion are visible on the left, adjacent to fiddler Herman Erickson and tenor banjoist Paul Hughes in this Hollandale area tavern, c. 1950. Courtesy of Bruce Bollerud.

musicians took a break, he was bold enough to bring out his bandonion. "Maybe I'd play a couple tunes. That's all I knew at that time, but I'd play those." Soon after, Herman Erickson suggested, "'Let's go out and play a job.' So we did."

World War II had just ended, and beer joints throughout the Upper Midwest hired old time bands to lure thirsty weekend dancers. While a handful of spacious ballrooms might attract 7- to 10-piece barnstorming groups like Lawrence Duchow and His Red Ravens, Skipper Berg and the Viking Accordion Band, or Whoopee John's Orchestra, even the most cramped mom-and-pop tavern could wedge in a two-piece combo at one end of a "dance floor" filling the narrow gap between booths and barstools. With his parents as willing chaperones, underage Bruce Bollerud and Herman Erickson played as far afield as Warren, Illinois, just across the state line, but mostly in nearby Blanchardville, Darlington, and New Glarus.

Their repertoire was typical for the era and locale. Although they attempted an occasional modern foxtrot, like "Oh Johnny," the emphasis was on "all the old time Norwegian things. And a few hoedowns, but not very many. Mostly it was waltzes and polkas and schottisches." And perhaps a Swiss ländler in places like New Glarus.

In 1853, an Irish woman in Green County, Wisconsin, wrote in her diary that her family debated where to spend the Fourth of July. Should they stay in "Irish Hollow," visit the French settlement at Belleville, "take a look

Figure 4.3. Hans "Whoopee John" Wilfahrt, in Bavarian attire and brandishing his concertina, broadcasts with his band over Minneapolis radio, late 1930s. Author's collection.

at the nearby Dutch" (Germans), or travel to New Glarus where "we can look at the Swiss, if we can't understand them"? Deciding on the Swiss, they were soon charmed by a reenactment of Wilhelm Tell shooting an apple from his son's head, "Swiss wrestlers," as well as "Swiss dances in the dining room of the hotel." The dancers were especially compelling: "Round and round the couples would glide, while at certain intervals in the music the men would stamp their feet and emit wild whoops" (Neff and Zarrilli 1987: 5). Little had changed nearly a century later, when Bollerud and Erickson entertained: "I can remember we were playing over at New Glarus. It was really going good. And the people were dancing and whooping it up. All of a sudden, I didn't hear any sound from the fiddle while we were playing away."

When Bruce looked over at Herman, "a real thin man" who would "sit with his legs curled around," the fiddler "had pulled the bow back for a really powerful stroke at the strings, and his bow had dropped off the strings" and slid underneath them. Transfixed by the crowd, their exuberant hoots reverberating in his ears, Herman simply played until the tune's end. "It was really funny."

However much Bruce's music-crazy parents delighted in their son's playing, Herman Erickson's wife was not to be outdone.

She thought her husband was just the finest fiddle player there was. He was pretty good. He wasn't the finest, but he was good. And she would kind of circulate through the crowd and see what people were saying. If they said something good, she would report that back. And sometimes she'd go to the other bars, 'cause lot of the bars had music in those days—they'd hire one or two guys to play—and then she'd come back and she'd say, "Oh that band up at the next bar, they're not very good. They're not as good as you guys. They sound real tinny," she said. She'd always say that. Everybody else was tinny except us.

Although Bruce may have found her praise excessive, he developed a deep affection for bandonion and fiddle duets.

The bandonion, and also the concertina, were commonly paired with the fiddle in mid-nineteenth-century Europe. That combination flourished a century later in America's Upper Midwest.

When they built the bandonion, especially the big concert models, they were thinking of the violin. Because the low note was G, as it is on the fiddle. And of course the fiddle has a really long range. The bandonion, the big ones, had a three-octave range or better. So they got up to real high notes. They also have a kind of a tart sound, kind of bittersweet. It's sort of a raspy sound. It grabs you a bit. It works really well with the fiddle.

In the late 1940s, Bruce also teamed with Johnny Homme, another Norwegian neighbor who fiddled and farmed, to play for house parties and at a Blue Mounds cheese factory. Homme knew some pretty old time Norwegian waltzes and "some nice hoppwaltzes or polkas too."

By 1950, however, Bruce was ready for a change. In Hollandale High School, he learned to read music, played trombone in the school band, and took piano lessons.

I began to realize that the bandonion, for me at that time, seemed kind of limited. It was hard to play in the flat keys. The machine was built in the key of A. And it is chromatic, so you can play in any key, but it's tougher in some keys. You've really got to know what you're doing. And I wasn't really quite that good at that point. So anyway, I got ahold of a piano accordion and began to play that.

As a portable chromatic squeezebox with a keyboard akin to a piano, the piano accordion enabled Bruce to learn new tunes more quickly. Here too was a contemporary yet Old World, old-timey instrument that had become an essential component of several evolving polka and western swing styles, fusing nostalgia with modernity. "I began to kind of shift over to accordion at that point." Over the next five years, Bruce Bollerud played with a succession of larger, more-ambitious ensembles featuring piano accordion leads. And although he never played that instrument in any of them, he practiced faithfully on the side, acquiring valuable experience and an expanded musical repertoire that grafted contemporary, postwar, and regional mutations onto venerable, local, house-party roots.

"That Really Seemed Like the Big Time"

About the same time, on Chicago's South Side, 200 miles to the southwest, McKinley Morganfield, better known as bluesman Muddy Waters, traded his old acoustic guitar for an electric model, teamed up with a small ensemble anchored by drums and bass, and forged a paradoxical sound drenched in down-home experience that nonetheless resonated in urban ghettos. Likewise along the Windy City's Division Street, Walter Jagiello, better known as Li'l Wally, revolutionized Polish polka music with a driving, stripped-down, heartfelt sound that at once conjured old country villages and the experiences of America's working-class "Hunkies."[6] The musical changes occurring in rural southwestern Wisconsin may be less well known, but they were, for those who lived them, just as historic and dramatic.

Prior to World War II, and especially in the war's aftermath, Hollandale's local mixture of Norwegian dance pieces and dialect songs—sprinkled since the late nineteenth century with Anglo-American, Irish, and Swiss songs and tunes—was increasingly affected by recordings, radio broadcasts, and touring performers from afar. Whereas George Gilbertsen and Windy Whitford, living 50 miles to the east in Madison, were influenced strongly by hillbillies, singing cowboys, Hawaiian guitars, and western swing, rural Iowa County musicians like Bruce were inspired by tent-show performers, by Minnesota's Dutchman and Scandinavian crossover bands, and by the Slovenian-American sound of Cleveland's Frankie Yankovic.

As country music historian Bill C. Malone observed, "Tent-repertoire units, working out of cities in the Midwest and South, carried homemade dramas and variety entertainment into towns and villages" on a regular basis until the "onslaught of the Great Depression," experiencing their heyday in "the years between 1917 and 1930" (2002b: 190). A handful of companies carried on even longer, particularly in rustic areas where they had built a loyal following and where they were able to adapt their mixture of musical variety and skits featuring lovable bumpkins to the increasingly modernized experiences of their audiences. The Tri-State Maniacs and Tilton's Comedians both made their way to Bruce Bollerud's Hollandale hometown in the late 1940s and early 1950s. In newspaper accounts from the era, the Tilton troupe, billed as "Iowa's Finest Tent Show," featured Dick Ellis in the stock role of "Toby," a good-natured but dim country boy with freckles and unruly red hair, whom Bruce recalled as "a real rube, but with some wisdom." The Comedians' shows also included musical interludes, such plays as the temperance chestnut *Ten Nights in a Barroom,* and a pair of comedies embodying the aspirations of many a small-town youth: *From Rags to Riches* and *From Here to Hollywood.*[7] Humble though they were, Tilton's Comedians were experienced professional entertainers, with a flair and polish seldom seen in house parties or country taverns. Teenaged Bruce Bollerud was captivated by their painted truck, big tent, elevated stage, use of sets, and especially the deft way that Mr. Tilton on trombone, his wife on piano, a sax player, and a drummer not only warmed up a crowd of strangers but held them through an evening's antics.

Hans Anthony Wilfahrt (1893–1961), better known as Whoopee John for his exuberant alpine hooting, made an even stronger impression. A bandleader who played the German concertina, Wilfahrt forged a modern Dutchman polka style in the 1930s. Wilfahrt's family emigrated from "Bohemia," where Germans lived amid Czechs in what is nowadays the southwestern part of the Czech Republic. They settled with other working-class, Catholic, German-Bohemians in the rustic *Gansviertel* (Goosetown) district of New Ulm, Minnesota. There, Hans Wilfahrt grew up amid house parties where small squeezebox-dominated combos prevailed, but he was also surrounded by horn players who formed larger bands for weddings, parades, and summer picnics. In the 1920s, Wilfahrt synthesized house-party and horn ensembles, added drums and banjo, and began performing on records and radio. His nascent Dutchman sound drew heavily on a German-Bohemian repertoire of polkas, schottisches, mazurkas, ländlers, and waltzes but was also infused with elements of the era's African-American jazz: syncopation, dynamic alternation between tight arrangements and improvised solos, and a trademark romping bass horn or tuba. By the late 1930s, Whoopee John's working repertoire expanded to include Anglo-American old time standards like minstrelsy's "O Dem Golden Slippers" and especially Scandinavian tunes: *"Hasselby Steppen," "Lordagsvalsen," "Kalle Pe,"* "Lingonberry Schottische," and *"Borghild Rheinlander."* Somewhat in the manner of Anglo-American Toby, but more like "Hans Wurst," the sausage-brained stock figure in Old World German comedy, Hans "Whoopee John" Wilfahrt also charmed his mixed audiences by playing a decidedly ethnic yet broadly recognizable rustic fool who yodeled exuberantly to punctuate his horn section's surges, rolled his eyeballs crazily, stretched the bellows of his concertina to its limit, and wore frumpy lederhosen that clashed with the spiffy suits of his bandmates. By the late 1940s, his band was performing more than 300 jobs a year, spanning every corner of the Upper Midwest and winning ardent fans in Hollandale.[8]

Besides Whoopee John, such Upper Midwestern bands as Skipper Berg and the Viking Accordion Band, the Blue Denim Boys, Ray Stolzenberg and the Northern Playboys, and Fezz Fritsche and His Goosetown Band fused Germanic, Slavic, Nordic, and Anglo-American repertoires, sprinkled with comedy, in live performances, on commercial recordings, and on radio broadcasts. The Viking Accordion Band even played in Hollandale a few times, while the records of all of these groups compelled Orville Bollerud to feed the jukebox at Joe's Tavern. And at night the Bolleruds and folks throughout the western Wisconsin hinterlands tuned in "the best of Bohemian, Scandinavian, and German songs and instrumentals" on WNAX of Yankton, South Dakota; WOI of Ames, Iowa; KWNO from Winona, Minnesota; and such Wisconsin stations as WKBH in LaCrosse, Madison's WKOW, and Milwaukee's WTMJ (Corenthal 1986: 137).

Just before World War II, Gilbert Prestbroten, a Norwegian immigrant living "three miles over the hill" from the Bolleruds, formed the Rhythm

Ramblers. Like Whoopee John's Orchestra—and unlike the typical two- and three-piece combos that played semiformally around Hollandale for house parties and small tavern jobs—here was a larger band with a name, a look, bookings, and aspirations: "These were just a bunch of farmers. . . . there was five or six of them. They had a trumpet and a clarinet and a bass and drums and accordion and a guitar. About six guys. And they played 40 jobs in a row, 40 nights in a row at one time. They got a lot of work."

Demands wrought by success, combined with personnel shifts as members were drafted or started families, moved Prestbroten to suspend the Rhythm Ramblers by 1948. Two years later, however, the emergence of local youngsters like Bruce Bollerud and his high school pal Ronnie Doran prompted the band's resurgence. In 1950, while 16-year-old Bruce was occupied with barn chores, Gilbert Prestbroten came calling.

> I was sitting there behind a cow, milking her, and we talked a while. Seems like it always takes Norwegians a while to get to the point. So we talked about the weather and this and that. Finally, he got to the point. . . . he was going to start out again, and he asked if I would like to play with him. Well, I was really excited about that. That really seemed like the big time to me.

Bruce joined the musicians' union, put down his bandonion, bid Herman Erickson farewell, and began a short stint with the Rhythm Ramblers: "I sort of left the old fiddle player behind. Kind of felt like I was moving up to something bigger."

Because Gilbert Prestbroten played piano accordion, Bruce doubled on piano and trombone. His classmate Ronnie Doran blew bass notes on the tuba, and the other musicians were Rhythm Ramblers veterans: Bobby Wenger on drums, Charlie Sigg on trumpet, and Herbert Swingen switching off on trumpet and clarinet.

> We played kind of a Dutch style of old time. We did quite a few Scandinavian pieces too, but in the Dutch style. . . . The schottisches tended to be Norwegian or Scandinavian. And, of course, we always did "Life in the Finnish Woods" and "Saturday Night Waltz" (*Lordagsvalsen*) and "*Ny Fiskar Vals*" (New Fisherman's Waltz). And we would do some of the foxtrots. "Angry" and "Five Foot Two" and things like that.

Recognizably in the Whoopee John vein, the Rhythm Ramblers nonetheless shifted their inspiration's regional sound in a local, decidedly Norwegian direction. "We probably played more Scandinavian [tunes] than a lot of Dutch style bands would." And whereas Hans Wilfahrt occasionally squeezed distinctly German-Bohemian solos from his Chemnitzer concertina, the Norwegian-born Prestbroten "played a pretty Scandinavian style of accordion, with a lot of triplets and trills and embellishments around the melody notes," a style that—despite being rendered on piano accordion, surrounded by Dutchman instrumentation, and applied to a creolized repertoire—derived from, as Bruce put it, "the fiddle versions" of seemingly outmoded old timers like Herman Erickson.

Just as Bruce began to appreciate the echoes of old time Norwegian fiddling, however masked and modernized, in the Prestbroten band, several Upper Midwestern fiddlers formed eclectic bands in the 1950s that both sustained and transformed venerable Scandinavian traditions. Ralph Herman, half-German and half-Norwegian, grew up on a Wisconsin dairy farm 150 miles north of Hollandale, near Pleasantville in Trempealeau County. His paternal uncles, Fred and George Herman, played accordion and banjo, while his mother's brother, Christian Iverson, was an old time Norwegian fiddler. By 1952, when Ralph was 14, he was playing piano accordion with a guitar-picking cousin, Don Maug, and an older Norwegian fiddler, Orville Dahl. A few years later, they acquired a drummer, Al Zastrow, and a name, the Rhythm Playboys. Their repertoire was classic polkabilly—"hillbilly . . . the good waltzes, or the slow two steps, or the polkas, or the circle two steps" and a few schottisches—with a decided Norsky feel, especially on tunes like "Lordagsvalsen" (Herman 2000 I).

Closer to home for Bruce, fiddling Emil Simpson of Beloit had a popular band that played every weekend in the early 1950s in an area that encompassed and exceeded the Rhythm Ramblers' range. When guitarist Sammy Eggum not only left Simpson to form his own group but also lured away the accordion, trumpet, and trombone players, Bruce Bollerud and Herbert Swingen saw an opportunity.

> Emil was looking for musicians to keep his band going. . . . Herbert and I played trumpet and trombone. . . . Then, of course, I could double on the bandonion. And Herbert could double on clarinet and guitar and a lot of other things. He was very versatile. And we went down to meet him. Herbert was playing the guitar. And Emil said, "Now I want to get the old time tone." And he grabbed the guitar and played a G chord with one finger and one thumb. And that's the sound he wanted. We had to concentrate on getting an old time sound. But I think he knew what he was doing, because the crowd that he was appealing to liked that kind of a sound. Kind of the old house-party sound, just a little bit extended maybe. So that worked out pretty nicely.

Besides Bruce, Herbert Swingen, and fiddling Emil Simpson, the Nite Hawks included drummer Irv Hale; Simpson's wife, Tina, on piano; and "Little Joe" Weum, a 6′4″ 300-pound piano accordionist who had been a member of Mickey's Ranchhands in the mid-1930s with Windy Whitford.

Like Prestbroten's Rhythm Ramblers, the Nite Hawks performed "the German and Czech things, . . . some foxtrots," and "some of the old Norwegian tunes again," including "a couple nice schottisches" and waltzes. Yet there were differences. Emil Simpson's band performed several Polish tunes in deference to the roots of their broader working-class audience, while his chosen instrument, the fiddle, contributed to a filled-out dance-hall sound that nonetheless harked back to duos entertaining in cramped

Figure 4.4. Emil Simpson's Nite Hawks at the Wigwam in Beloit, Wisconsin, 1953. (*Left to right*): Bruce Bollerud, trombone; Herbert Swingen, trumpet; Irv Hale, drums (obscured); Emil Simpson, fiddle; "Little Joe" Weum, accordion; Tina Simpson, piano. Courtesy of Bruce Bollerud.

house parties. "Silo Filler's Waltz," evoking "kitchen sweats" following communal labor, was a particular favorite. Its tonal range and similarity to tunes that Bruce had played with Herman Erickson and Johnny Homme prompted him to work the bandonion into Nite Hawks dance jobs.

> I think it's a traditional tune. I don't think Emil wrote it. In fact, I think he mentioned some old fiddler that he had learned it from. And I've heard another man play it, this Sally Oren, Selmer Oren. . . . He calls it something else, though. But it's, it's a really excellent piece . . . that type of thing that the old Norwegian fiddlers played in this country. The music I hear from Norway doesn't sound like that so much; this is an American-Norwegian thing. . . . It's got that sidle-deedle, you know, that kind of a swing that the Norwegian stuff does and it, it has a tremendous range on it. It would be difficult to do it on a trumpet, for example, where the range is a little more limited. In fact, it runs from close to my highest note on the bandonion to the very bottom note, which would be the bottom string on the fiddle again. It's a nice piece. It's a good tune.[9]

After roughly four years with the Nite Hawks, Bruce tried his hand with a pair of bands, led by Roger Bright and by Verne Meisner, that emphasized the piano accordion while kicking yet another folk musical tradition into overdrive.

In the late 1930s, just as Minnesotan Whoopee John was drawing upon arrangements influenced by African-American jazz to meld his German-Bohemian legacy with Scandinavian and Anglo-American tunes, Frankie Yankovic was experimenting with an updated Slovenian-American polka sound that would sweep the nation a decade later. Born in 1915 and raised in Cleveland's working-class Collinwood neighborhood, Yankovic grew up immersed in Slovenian immigrant culture and began playing traditional tunes on the button accordion at 9. At 16, he switched to the more-versatile piano accordion and sought a pan-ethnic audience through a sound and repertoire that crossed cultural lines and emphasized a common American experience. Influenced partly by the Hoyer Trio—Cleveland Slovenes, who combined percussive four-string banjo with dual accordions embroidering a straight melody with staccato runs—Yankovic added string bass, piano, and eventually an oozing electronic solovox. The result was a full sound that cut through crowded dance halls, emphasized flashy solos, and injected polkas and waltzes with a swinging and sweet jazz feel. Proud of his Slovenian roots, Yankovic nonetheless sang mostly in English and drew from diverse sources. In 1948, his sprightly recording of "Just Because," originally a hillbilly number by the Shelton Brothers, was a million seller on the Columbia label. A year later, Yankovic's "Blue Skirt Waltz," an even bigger hit, was a makeover of the Czech "*Sukynka (Cervena)*/Red Skirt Waltz" with vocals by the Marlin Sisters, erstwhile Yiddish songsters.[10] Touring vigorously from the late 1940s until his death five decades later, Yankovic filled dance halls in Midwestern cities and small towns alike, mixing freely with farmers and factory hands, dazzling them with a compelling amalgam of pan-ethnic and pop tunes rendered in a fevered, amplified, decidedly contemporary style nonetheless grounded in Old World weddings and harvest dances.

Revered in Cleveland, Yankovic was arguably appreciated even more in Milwaukee and the surrounding Wisconsin hinterlands. Milwaukee had a small but thriving Slovenian working-class settlement that included stellar musicians like Louie Bashell, dubbed "The Silk Umbrella Man" for his signature tune, "*Zidana Marela*/Silk Umbrella Polka" (Leary and March 1996: 108). More important, however, it was a city dominated by Germanic and Slavic peoples, where neighborhood taverns flourished, polkas and waltzes were the dances of choice, and the piano accordion ruled.

In the late 1940s, about 8,000 students were enrolled in Milwaukee's accordion schools, a figure cited by the major trade journal (*Accordion World*) as making the Wisconsin metropolis "the best accordion city in the whole country" (Greene 1992: 230). On June 9, 1948, as "Just Because" resounded from Midwestern jukeboxes, Frankie Yankovic and His Yanks won a national "polka king" competition convened at Milwaukee's City Auditorium by electrifying the crowd with hot twin accordions.

Just as Elvis Presley, oft-celebrated as the king of rock 'n' roll, ignited a rockabilly movement with swiveling hips, holy roller abandon, African-

Figure 4.5. Bruce sits in with Feller's Swiss Band, Madison, late 1950s. (*Left to right*): Herman Feller II, piano accordion; Herman Feller, string bass; Bob Feller, clarinet; yodeler Betty K. Vetterli with alp horn; Bruce Bollerud, piano accordion. Courtesy of Bruce Bollerud.

American rhythms, and jumped-up guitars, the charismatic Yankovic inspired a generation of rural and working-class Midwestern piano accordionists, whose derivative rapid-fire fingering asserted the polka king's vision of a contemporary, pan-ethnic, regional yet thoroughly American musical identity underlain by the bedrock traditions of immigrant parents and grandparents. Thrilled by "Just Because" and "The Blue Skirt Waltz," 11-year-old Verne Meisner persuaded his Austrian-German folks to buy him a piano accordion in 1949. An immediate prodigy, he formed Verne Meisner and His Polka Boys in 1950 and by 1953, at 15, was touring regionally from a base in Whitewater, Wisconsin (Leary and March 1996: 112). Meanwhile, in New Glarus, a hotbed of Swiss music since the 1840s, more than a few were struck by similarities between the reedy sound, brisk tempos, and deft musicianship of Yankovic's Slovenian style and that of the Moser Brothers. A trio of Swiss immigrants who, joined by Rudy Burkhalter, entertained cheese-making Schweitzers in Wisconsin communities from the late 1920s into the early 1940s, the Mosers anticipated Yankovic with virtuoso playing, an emphasis on solos, the occasional fusion of Swiss and jazz idioms, and the reedy interplay of twin button accordions and clarinet over a plucked string bass.

By the mid-1950s, accordionist Roger Bright, from nearby Argyle, formed a band in the Yankovic vein. Tossing in a handful of Swiss tunes for variety, he entertained fondue diners and dancers at the New Glarus Hotel through the 1990s (Leary 1991: 29–30, 34, 42–46).

An aspiring piano accordionist, Bruce Bollerud understandably fell under Yankovic's spell. What's more, New Glarus, Roger Bright's musical turf, was only a stone's throw from Hollandale and a place where Bruce had often played. Likewise, Verne Meisner's touring range overlapped with that of Emil Simpson's Nite Hawks. And both Bright and Meisner were, like Bruce, ambitious youngsters bent on making musical marks. Small wonder that Bruce played first with Bright, then with Meisner, in 1954 and 1955, "mostly chording and laying out some good rhythm" on piano, but immersing himself in Yankovic's Slovenian-American polka idiom just the same. "They were great musicians. It was a good experience working with them."

How the Glen and Ann Thing Started

In 1956, when 22-year-old Bruce Bollerud joined the air force, he took his piano accordion along and, like fiddle-toting George Gilbertsen before him, fell in with diverse musical companions. Stationed in Little Rock, Arkansas, Bruce joined a band featuring his piano accordion; Roger Lepine, a fellow enlisted man from Rhode Island, on guitar; an occasional sax player likewise in the military; and two local musicians on bass and drums. They "played at the officers' club," a high-toned venue demanding "more foxtrots." The drummer, however, worked at a Little Rock music store and, perhaps surprisingly for the capital of a mid-South state, was part of a local Polish enclave known for its bars and rowdy, protracted Polish weddings: "Just a mob of people, and they were dancing and playing. Concertina players! And it was just very wild. . . . I spent almost every weekend out in that area. . . . There were some bars around there where we played."

Since the other Little Rock local, a string-bass-playing schoolteacher named Jim Carpenter, was originally from Wisconsin and had played tuba with the legendary Manitowoc-Bohemian bandleader Romy Gosz, the band favored "pretty much polkas" tempered by "a little country" that harked back to Bruce's house-party days where Norwegian and Anglo-American fiddle tunes mingled.

That particular combination was revived and expanded with a vengeance shortly after Bruce was discharged from the air force in May 1958. Settling in Madison, an economic and musical magnet for country boys from southern Wisconsin, he teamed quickly with an old friend from back home, Dick Peterson. Adept with several string instruments, Peterson, like Bruce, hailed from an Iowa County extended family of musical Norwegians. The two even had a cousin in common, guitarist Norman Johnsrud. "We'd get together and play. And lot of times we played for nothing just to be playing. Finally it started to gel a little bit."

From the mid- to late 1950s, with the establishment of commercial television in the Madison market, live radio featuring local musicians steadily diminished, supplanted for roughly the next decade by live television programs featuring local musicians performing on rustic sets while dancers

Figure 4.6. Bruce plays bandonion with old bandmates Dick Peterson (aka Dick Sherwood) on fiddle, Herbert Swingen on bass, and Dick's son, Mark Peterson, on guitar. Community homecoming celebration, Hollandale, Wisconsin, 2000. Courtesy of Bruce Bollerud.

whirled. Dick Peterson saw an opportunity. Mindful that media personalities often assumed Anglo-American names masking their supposedly "foreign" heritage, he dropped the name Peterson for the "more smooth and sellable" Sherwood, found a feed company sponsor, and launched a television program featuring the Dick Sherwood Band: Dick on fiddle, guitar, and banjo; his wife, Goldie, on guitar and bass; Mike Lopez, a steel guitarist from Janesville; drummer Gene Manthy from Marshall, who "played nice trumpet and nice bass too"; and Bruce trading off on piano and accordion.

Their working repertoire drew in part on the Norwegian fiddle/squeezebox duets of Iowa County house parties as Bruce played "accordion on the old time, the polkas and waltzes," Dick fiddled, and the rest of the band added polkabilly rhythm and twang: "'Lokkarin Waltz.' . . . It's very repetitious and has a sort of circular . . . motion to it because of that repeating figure that goes over and over. We did that. We did the 'Stegen Waltz' and we did the 'Johnny Homme Waltz.'" The band also "played a lot of country western," with Bruce shifting to piano. Beyond core musicians, the Sherwood band included the Johnson Brothers, a pair of singer-guitarists whose tight harmonies and hot picking added sentiment and style.

Just as military service transported Bruce Bollerud and, earlier, George Gilbertsen to distant musical milieus, it also brought performers from afar to southern Wisconsin. Madison's Truax Field became an air force base during World War II and, from the 1940s until the early 1960s, a succession of mostly southern musicians mingled with Upper Midwesterners. The Johnson Brothers, Chuck Johnston and Cliff Brizendine, "weren't really brothers, but they had played together a lot in the service." Their vocal style mimicked western Kentucky's Everly Brothers, quasi-rockabilly stars of the era whose sound drew squarely on old time country "brother duets" like the Bailes Brothers, the Monroe Brothers, and the Blue Sky Boys, Bill and Earl Bolick. Chuck also emulated the complex finger-style guitar of Don and Phil Everly's father, Ike, and his disciple Merle Travis, innovative soloists whose flying fingers picked out simultaneous rhythm and melody (Malone 2002: 115, 252)

Hard-working Dick Sherwood and his cohorts soon established a modest musical empire. His Madison-based television show was syndicated on Wisconsin stations in LaCrosse, Eau Claire, and Green Bay. His band was active; he ran a music store that offered lessons; and he even "built a trailer type deal for a mobile type of a store where he would take it out to small towns and give lessons." Bruce was involved in every phase:

> I worked in the music store . . . gave lessons. We rehearsed every week for the show. And of course we'd go out and play dance jobs. So we worked every Friday and Saturday night for sure. And usually there'd be a Sunday or a Wednesday or a Thursday. About four nights a week, probably, playing. And then the TV show. . . . So it was a full-time job. And I can remember really feeling good about that because I was playing music—which is what I really enjoy probably more than anything—and doing it full time. And I think I was making $100 a week, which was pretty good money at the time.

Good times, however, were short-lived. By 1961, Dick Sherwood was overextended; television sponsors were hard to keep; and the music store's financial obligations spiraled.

Meanwhile, a local label, Cuca Records, and a local group, the Fendermen, had combined to produce a 45rpm recording that sold a million copies and peaked at number 5 on the Billboard chart in May 1960. Based in Sauk City, a heavily German community on the Wisconsin River 20 miles northwest of Madison, Cuca Records was founded in 1959 by Jim Kirchstein, a Korean War veteran with a degree in acoustic engineering from the University of Wisconsin. During a dozen years of intense production, Cuca became Wisconsin's leading old time polka label, but also issued recordings in jazz, gospel, blues, country, and rock idioms (Leary and March 1996: 170). The Fendermen, led by Jim Sundquist and Phil Humphrey on Fender guitars, scored a big hit with a rockabilly take on "Muleskinner Blues." Originally composed and recorded with leisurely solo guitar as "Blue Yodel #8" in 1930 by Jimmie Rodgers, the song was given a driving string-band arrangement and an intense falsetto vocal lead by Bill Monroe and His Bluegrass Boys, who recorded the first of several versions in 1940. Clearly inspired by Monroe, the Fendermen's reverb-laden rendition, country boogie guitar, and exaggerated hiccuping vocals also bowed to Memphis and to Sun Records.[11]

In an era when, with a good song and a lot of luck, regional bands on tiny labels occasionally won national air play and sales, the Fendermen were one-hit wonders. After a year of touring, they disbanded in 1961, but not before inspiring the Johnson Brothers plus Bruce Bollerud to spin off from the Dick Sherwood Band. In January 1961, the Johnson Brothers recorded two songs, "Like Rachel" and "Julie Dear," that were released as a 45rpm disk (Cuca 1024; Myers 1994: 113).

Chuck and Cliff and I had been fooling around musically. They had written some songs, which were sort of rockabilly types of things. And soft rock kinds of things from that period. And we had made a record up at Cuca. It was doing pretty well in Philadelphia or Pittsburgh, someplace in Pennsylvania. Well it looked like, at the time, that we might have some kind of hit on our hands. Not necessarily a nationwide hit, but big enough that you'd want to take advantage of it. So the other band being a little rocky, and this looking like an opportunity, we decided that we would quit Dick and go on our own with this record thing. So the three of us then became [the] Johnson Brothers. We played a few local jobs, waiting for this record to take off and our ship to come in. 'Course what happened was the record started out pretty good and then, like a lot [of] them do, it peaked and fell. So we didn't go on the road after all.

It was just as well. Bruce was newly married and about to start a family. That spring, he took a day job teaching accordion, guitar, and trumpet for Forbes-Meagher Music Center. In the evenings, possessing his own sound system, he landed a contract and brought in the Johnson Brothers to form a house band at Glen and Ann's, a Madison tavern. It was to be Bruce Bollerud's musical home for the next nine years.

In many ways, Glen and Ann's was a typical mom-and-pop tavern of the sort that emerged with Prohibition's end all over Wisconsin: family owned and family run, catering to a working-class clientele, offering home-cooked food and old time music. What's more, it was a familiar place.

How the Glen and Ann thing started. . . . Dick and I and Goldie played there six months, maybe a year before the TV thing. We were there two to three nights a week too. I used to play bass at that time too. We did a lot of doubling around. I'd play accordion or bass, the upright string bass. So that was always kind of fun too.

His year-long stretch with the Johnson Brothers, however, was often fractious.

Chuck and Cliff were real good friends, but they were very competitive with one another. Sometimes, they would just get into squabbles about how you should do this or how you should do that. And it just wasn't working out sometimes. And then . . . Chuck and I got into a dispute about something or other. I think I wanted him to sing one night and

Figure 4.7. Bruce Bollerud on piano accordion with drummer "Wild Bill" Timmons and guitarist Cliff Brizendine of the Johnson Brothers at Glen and Ann's, Madison, 1960. Courtesy of Bruce Bollerud.

he didn't want to sing. He just wanted to play, 'cause he was real serious about playing the guitar. And we got into a squabble, so he left.

Meanwhile, Glen and Ann, fretting that their teenage daughter was smitten with Cliff, insisted that he leave. Distressing at the time, the Johnson Brothers' demise in 1962 could not have come at a better moment for Bruce Bollerud.

Although Glen and Ann's resembled bars scattered about Madison's rural fringes and blue-collar neighborhoods, its particular location was on University Avenue in the shadow of the University of Wisconsin. College kids with small-town or working-class Wisconsin roots wandered in easily to hear performances reminiscent of hometown musical scenes. Meanwhile, urban out-of-state students, steeped by the early 1960s in the folk revival, encountered an Upper Midwestern sound both familiar and exotic. As country music historian Bill C. Malone later observed: "A group of students . . . mostly from New York or other Northeastern states, brought to the campus an interest in folk music that had been honed at Washington Square gatherings and similar scenes" (Malone 2001: 37). One was Paul Prestopino, a lab technician in the Physics Department who played with Vern Minor and Windy Whitford in the Hoedowners before a national career with the Chad Mitchell Trio and as a backup musician with Peter, Paul, and Mary. In Bruce's words, "There was almost a parade of guys coming through."

On Thursdays and Sundays, he matched his versatile accordion in openended jams with a mostly bluegrass-oriented student crowd.

Phil Buss. He did flatpicking guitar . . . finger picking, Travis style. Played banjo, mandolin. He was a good musician. He liked to do blues really, but he did play well on bluegrass kinds of things too. Don Gale was a real tremendous banjo player. He was really fast. He put out a record of his own later on, the Bluegrass Hoppers [*The Country's Come to Town,* Cuca K-1160].

Then there was Jerry Wicentowski, another eventual Bluegrass Hopper, "a fella that played guitar and sang, beautiful voice." Besides twice-a-week jams with Bruce, these musicians often sat in on Wednesdays, Fridays, and Saturdays with the trio Bruce was building in the wake of the Johnson Brothers' departure.

For about a year, Bruce and his cohorts steered toward western tunes, with accordion, fiddle, guitar, and yodels suggestive of singing cowboys Gene Autry and the Sons of the Pioneers. Besides Bruce, the new band featured a three-neck stand-up steel guitar player with the stage name Eddie Rivers. Christened Orville Anschutz, Rivers was a farmboy from a German community near Green Bay. He played hot instrumentals like "Steel Guitar Rag" interspersed with pretty chime tones; sang "Streets of Laredo," "Strawberry Roan," and "a whole bunch of tunes you don't hear much any more"; yodeled with the best; and could sing "in two octaves, with lots of power on the bass and all kinds of power in the high part too."

Despite talent and rural Wisconsin roots, Orville "Eddie Rivers" Anschutz had been on the road in other states for too many years. A veteran performer who "had worked every rough club from here to South Dakota and back," he was accustomed to places filled with whiskey-swigging macho men and a few loose women, a far cry from the beer drinkers in Wisconsin's homey family bars. He had a stock of "dirty songs" he sometimes sang at the wrong time. One likened a woman's breasts to cherry-topped cupcakes.

And he did one called "The Ice Man," and there really aren't any dirty words in the song . . . but it sets up an analogy between ice in an icebox and a sexual situation. Ice melting and being hard, and this lady getting ice every day, and on and on . . . a double entendre type of thing. And for the average adult crowd in a bar, it's fine. Every now and then, though, there would be people who would bring some of their kids in. And then it made me uncomfortable, I know that. 'Cause you don't know how much the kid knows or should know, and what are the parents going to [do], how are they going to respond to that.

Eddie also drank too much too often, "and finally he had a car accident." One night in 1963, he ran into a railroad signal, lurched violently, and nearly bit off his tongue. "He couldn't sing for a long time. . . . He went out west and I don't know what become of him after that."

When Eddie Rivers was hurt, Bruce needed a guitar-playing singer in a hurry and asked local legend Windy Whitford to come out of retirement on a temporary basis. Fortuitously, the band's third member, who had signed on just before the ill-fated Rivers, was string wizard George Gilbertsen. Each born around a decade apart, each with his own peculiar musical experiences, Bruce Bollerud, George Gilbertsen, and Windy Whitford soon discovered that, despite opportunities to hit the road in search of musical fame, they were all family men who held day jobs and shared a deep affinity for their home territory. What's more, they all had house-party roots and the broadest imaginable familiarity with the local and external folk musical traditions contending and commingling in the Upper Midwest: Norwegian- and Anglo-American fiddle tunes and ballads, Scandihoovian and Dutchman dialect comedy, German and Slavic couple dances, Hawaiian guitars, rural novelty numbers, cowboy and hillbilly songs, bluegrass, rockabilly, and more. Soon to become the second incarnation of the Goose Island Ramblers, the trio combined these strains effortlessly and, in the bargain, made polkabilly music for the next 40 years.

5

Glen and Ann's

"More of an Old Time Sound"

Bruce and I had a little bit going. . . . When we got Windy in . . . he gave us altogether different songs . . . early ballads. . . . Then I started getting back into the acoustic, like mandolin and fiddle and dobro. So we started developing into more of an old time sound. (George Gilbertsen)

Windy Whitford, George Gilbertsen, and Bruce Bollerud—the second incarnation of the Goose Island Ramblers—hardly rambled at all during their heyday, from 1963 through 1975. They worked day jobs, helped raise families, and performed three nights a week as the house band for two Madison taverns: Glen and Ann's and then Johnny's Packer Inn. Yet by staying put, by resisting allegiance to any single popular musical genre, by valuing domesticity and community more than wanderlust and stardom, by asserting their deep and varied folk roots, the Goose Island Ramblers traversed and conjured a vast, varied, venerable cultural region. More than any barnstorming band, they epitomized the Upper Midwest's musical ferment, its creative interplay of diverse ethnic strains, its penchant for zany rustic performers, its ongoing dialectic between local traditions and national trends, and its distinctive old time sound: polkabilly.

But not immediately.

As Bruce recalled: "It certainly wasn't a full-blown idea. . . . It just sort of evolved." Raised with Norwegian and Swiss house-party tunes, master of comic dialect songs, veteran of Dutchman and Slovenian polka bands, accordionist Bruce Bollerud temporarily favored an extraregional mixture of western swing, rockabilly, honky tonk, and singing cowboy genres while playing at Glen and Ann's in the early 1960s with the Johnson Brothers and then Eddie Rivers.

When George Gilbertsen joined the band, however, the balance slowly but inexorably began to shift. Attracted to cowboy songs since childhood, adept on Hawaiian guitar and mandolin, a trick fiddler whose swinging "Beaumont Rag" had won Wisconsin's centennial fiddling championship in 1948, an old hand on the road and radio in a succession of overtly western bands, George had nonetheless been raised on Madison's working-class east side, where German, Irish, and Norwegian tunes prevailed. He had performed with Ray Carson and Tex Holley, who assumed the Norwegian comic persona of "Ole" over WKOW radio. In the late 1950s and early 1960s, matching his fiddle with the accordion of Irish immigrant Tommy McDermott, George played occasional sessions—promoted by a Father Doherty from Limerick—in small Wisconsin Irish communities, including Boscobel, Mount Hope, and Woodman, all in Grant County. And he had just finished a stint at the Senate Bar, acquiring from banjoist Leo Aberle some novelty tricks, along with a handful of minor-key Eastern European mazurkas and polkas. Stepping in with Bruce and Eddie Rivers at Glen and Ann's, George was familiar with the prevailing western repertoire, but positively beguiled by Bruce's versatile accordion playing and vocals, by the fragments of folk musical bedrock he squeezed out and sang: "Norwegian numbers and polkas," some waltzes, an occasional schottische, and comic dialect songs.

Windy Whitford added another dimension. An active performer for more than 30 years, he was convinced that his musical tastes were anachronistic, his performing career over. What's more, although he had crossed paths before with George Gilbertsen, he didn't know Bruce at all.

> In '63 Bruce Bollerud come into my life. He says, "No, you're not done yet, Windy. You come down here and play with me now. . . . If I can't find somebody I can rely on, I'm going to quit this playing here. So why don't you come down?" Well, really, I hadn't heard of Bruce. And just by some magic impulse or something he called me. (CD, track 30)

Reluctant to make too much of a commitment, Windy Whitford agreed to play for a few weeks until Bruce could find a more permanent bandmate. But something remarkable happened that first night. As Windy recalled in 1990: "This fellow stepped up. He says, 'Do you do "The Letter Edged in Black"?' Bruce says, 'No, we don't do that.' I whispered, 'This is the way it goes, Bruce.' I hummed a little bit of it. That's all it took. George was the same way." Composed in 1897, oft-recorded by hillbilly bands in the 1920s (Meade, Spottswood, and Meade 2002: 290), this sentimental parlor song was one that Windy's mother had set down in her notebook, then sang on the porch at twilight time in Albion. Decades later in a tavern on the fringe of the University of Wisconsin, Windy was surprised by the request, delighted that Bruce and George honored it, and amazed at how ably they followed his lead.

> "Boy," I says, "I never seen any people that could play like they could play." George was such a driver. . . . "He ain't going to be that the next time. Just having a good night tonight. Just chomping away." But next night would be the same thing. And it didn't make any difference if he was playing the fiddle or the mandolin or the electric guitar, . . . he just seemed to excel on whatever he was playing. . . . And Bruce was such

a congenial fellow that everybody liked him. . . . that kind of tied us together. He's kind of the kingpin, held us together, coordinated us. It just seemed like we were meant to be. (CD, track 30)

Certainly, Bruce thought so. Raised with older relatives and hired farmhands, many of whom sang, Bruce Bollerud had an affection and musical feel for old time songs and the peculiarities of singers, qualities that Windy Whitford had seldom encountered in younger performers. Hence, Bruce quickly adapted to Windy's phrasing:

Windy used to like to do a thing that I've heard a lot of the older singers do. They'll, you know, there's a standard number of bars in a song ordinarily, 32 or so forth or 16 in a phrase. Well, some of these older singers would take the turnaround spot, where there's a kind of a little break, and they'd hold it out a little bit longer. Like "Maple on the Hill," that kind of thing, where they'd hold it for quite a while. So you had to be watching for that, so that when he'd come back into the phrase, to the singing part—because then the chord changes—you had to be there.

Besides old songs, Whitford, like Bollerud, knew Norwegian fiddle tunes aplenty, bowing the basic melody while fiddling George Gilbertsen tossed off stunning harmony and fills.

Several tunes came from Clarence Reierson, including one Windy had called the "Dickeyville Waltz" since the mid-1940s.

When I played on WIBA in '44 and '45, then I had to write down every tune that we had played and put if it was BMI or ASCAP or if it was public domain. So I had to have a name for these old time Norwegian waltzes that Reierson played and the old time fiddlers played, but nobody ever knew what to call 'em. So I called this one "The Dickeyville Waltz."

Bruce, whose Hollandale home was not far from Dickeyville, immediately recognized the waltz's pedigree, while pointing out the contradictions of Whitford's improvised title.

I said, "Wendy, that's some kind of a Norwegian waltz." I said, "How can it be the 'Dickeyville Waltz'? There's no Norwegians in Dickeyville." Because I assumed there weren't any down there. It's a lead-mining area and the people down there are Cornish and Welsh and so forth. So we kind of laughed about that and started just joking around with the thing.

Eventually, the two cobbled a comic dialect song, "No Norwegians in Dickeyville," complete with esoteric references to Dickeyville's lack of *rullepølse*, a rolled-meat Norwegian delicacy, and its citizens' unfamiliarity with *Finnskogen*, the "Finnish woods" of the Norwegian-Swedish borderland celebrated in the old tune *"Livet i Finnskogen"* (Life in the Finnish Woods). One verse referred subtly to a pair of Scandinavian-American dialect songs, "My Name Is Yon Yonson" and "Ole Olson, the Hobo from Norway," while further evoking the transatlantic Norsky favorite *"Paul Paa Haugen"* (Paul on the Hill).

> There's no Yonny Yonson in Dickeyville,
> No Ole Olson or Paul on the hill,
> There's no Peter Swenson living down by the mill,
> 'Cause there's no Norwegians in Dickeyville.

Given their common, creative understanding of their region's complex musical culture, small wonder that after "two or three weeks went by," Windy recalled Bruce saying, "I'm not looking for anybody else. . . . You're just going to stay with us."

Still, Windy Whitford fretted about his age. Although Glen and Ann's was very much a mom-and-pop Wisconsin tavern with a multigenerational, working-class core clientele, its location abutted the University of Wisconsin and there was a drinking age of 18 to attract students. While a few who strayed in soon left for strictly collegiate haunts, more stayed, attracted by an old time acoustic sound that reminded some of the era's folk revival and others, especially those from the Upper Midwestern hinterlands, of hometown weddings and dance halls. As Bruce put it: "Students [began] to come in and recognize some of the old songs, either from the bluegrass area or from the folk area. And it began to be kind of cool." It took Windy a while to realize just what was happening: "'Oh,' I says, 'I'm too old to be playing down here with these young kids. They're all just like grandchildren to me. I feel so out of place, I feel so much older than them.'"

Indeed, at 50, Windy was three decades older than most college students, Bruce's senior by 21 years, and George's elder by a dozen. George even joked that the band ought to call itself "Decades" since they spanned so many. But in Bruce's estimation: "Age didn't make any difference when you were playing music . . . if you have a group that works together." In the end, the youngsters in the crowd convinced Whitford: "The kids would say, 'Oh boy, that's good, Uncle Windy.' Then I got more relaxed."

An affectionately regarded elder rather than a politely tolerated relic, the newly avuncular Whitford was not the only one with a nickname. Bars were smoky places then and "Smokey George" Gilbertsen, evoking a fiddling devil's brimstone, exhaled slyly into his instrument before particularly hot solos. Billows rose as if the strings were scorched.

> Then I had another little gimmick. . . . at that time I was smoking. I rolled my own homemade cigarettes. I had a big machine from Sears and Roebuck and I would roll a cigarette this long [about 18 inches]. . . . Bruce would come out and say I was going to play a tune with a violin bow shorter than a cigarette—and, of course, I had a small violin bow made . . . shorter than this long cigarette I made. I'd get the bow

out and somebody'd say, "Wait a minute, thought you said it was smaller than a cigarette?" I'd say, "Yeah. And, by the way, I've gotta have a puff here." And I'd haul out one of these and light it. [Laughs] And it was shorter than a cigarette. It was just this crazy stuff like that we used to do.

What Bruce similarly termed "some of this funny stuff that we did" resulted in his inevitable sobriquet. But not before the new trio chose an old name for itself.

Windy Whitford urged Bruce, in his leader's role, to make the decision:

After I knew I was going to stay with 'em, I says, "When I was young I had a band, but we had a name for our band." "What was that?" "That was the Goose Island Ramblers." "Now," I says, "you should have a name for your band." "Well, there's a place called Rumpus Ridge, and I always thought that would've been a good name." This is Bruce talking now. "I thought of calling ourselves Rumpus Ridgerunners." That sounded good. Then one day he come back. "I've been thinking it over," he says. "You had a band called the Goose Island Ramblers. Couldn't we use that name?" I says, "I'm sure we could because nobody else knew about Goose Island, only me, and that was on my dad's old farm back down at Albion and the stories that Clarence Reierson had told me about."

Bruce's inclination toward Goose Island was clearly a younger musician's tribute to a revered veteran, which Windy gratefully savored:

I was glad that Bruce said what he did. Well not that Rumpus Ridgerunners—that would've been fine . . . we were kind of a rumpus. Every time that we played, we'd be so hilarious, you know, especially with George and Bruce. George would upset everybody. And Bruce—with "Mrs. Johnson, Turn Me Loose"—and everybody just seemed to be up on their toes. But still down after all it seemed to me, I was happy that Bruce decided that himself—and not me persuading him—to call ourselves the Goose Island Ramblers. We hadn't been the Goose Island Ramblers—from '44 to '64—that'd been 20 years.

The name, two-thirds comical English mangling of the Norwegian *gud land,* resonated likewise with the band's emerging Anglo-Norwegian musical fusion.

Besides quickly warming to an array of Clarence Reierson's old Norsky dance tunes, the Goose Island Ramblers reborn made "Mrs. Johnson, Turn Me Loose" a showpiece performance (CD, tracks 63–64). The song was composed and originally recorded by Harry Edward Stewart (1908–1956). His parents, Hans and Elise Skarbo, were Norwegian immigrants to Tacoma where, after his mother's death in 1910, Harry was put up for adoption and raised by the Stewart family. He began working with Tacoma radio station

KVI in 1927, then in 1931 moved to Los Angeles, where he dreamed up an improbable Scandinavian-swami character, Yogi Yorgesson. Relying on an exaggerated Scandihoovian dialect, Stewart/Yorgesson had an extended career on radio, television, and records prior to his death in an auto accident. His classic "I Yust Go Nuts at Christmas" on Capitol sold more than a million copies in 1948 and was a holiday standard on Upper Midwestern radio and jukeboxes for decades thereafter.[1]

Although Yorgesson, in Bruce's estimation, lacked the authentic Upper Midwestern Norsky dialect that Slim Jim Iverson had applied to "Nikolina," the lyrics of his "Mrs. Johnson" told a comparably fine mock-tragic story of a meek Scandinavian bachelor relentlessly pursued by a cigar-smoking widow who has loved four husbands to death. But what began, for Bruce, as an appealing comic dialect song soon became, thanks to the antics of George Gilbertsen, a zany skit. Donning braided blonde wig and floppy bonnet, Gilbertsen-as-Viking-dominatrix cozied alongside the reluctant Bollerud, who recalled:

> George had a very expressive face and was a very good comedian on stage. . . . He would act out all these things as I was singing along. There was a place where it goes, "She smiles and says 'Howdy-do.'" And he would wave his hand in a real exaggerated kind of motion. His eyes were, y'know, he could kind of bug his eyes out. He would do that. There was another place where it would go, "Mrs. Yonson, when she sees me she yust pants constantly." He would grab the mike and really make a strong inhaling noise on there. It'd just crack, you know, it was just really wild. (CD, track 63)

Bruce compounded the hilarity, assuming a look of timid horror and investing the recurring chorus "Mrs. Johnson, Turn Me Loose" with plaintive Milquetoast tones. In the manner of Freddie "Schnickelfritz" Fisher, the Hoosier Hot Shots, and Spike Jones, Gilbertsen punctuated the close of this and other songs by clanging a cowbell or, in keeping with the band's name, honking on a goose call.

And so, through a peculiar but perfectly understandable alchemy, Bruce Bollerud emerged as "Loose Bruce the Goose." The rhyming "loose" fit the Stewart song and the genial Bollerud's ability to "hang loose," while the poetic addition of "goose" conjured both the apt proverbial phrase "loose as a goose" and the band's new name. But George Gilbertsen was not content with so brief a title. Having learned about Bruce's rough-and-ready rural heritage, George invariably found an appropriate moment or two each evening to thunder in his best barker's voice: "Ladies and Gentlemen, Loose Bruce the Goose, the Hollandale Wildcat, the Scourge of Iowa County," even adding with a cowbell's shake, "His dad had the longest barn in Iowa County."

The establishment of the trio's individual and aggregate names—collective rustic allusions to earth, wind, and fire—coincided with the development of a no less elemental folk instrumentation and repertoire. In the course of an evening, Bruce Bollerud held forth mostly on an Italian piano accordion, but every once in a while hauled out the German bandonion for an old Norwegian dance tune harking back to Iowa County house parties. A former slide trombone player, he even adeptly seized a jug to blow a raucous African-American bass line on boozy numbers like the Irish paean to whisky, "Mountain Dew" (CD, tracks 42–44). George Gilbertsen fiddled roughly half the time in sometimes Anglo-Southern, sometimes Eastern European fashion, switching intermittently to Italian mandolin or Hawaiian-derived dobro for short sets of two or three tunes, while seizing the idiosyncratic "eight banger," or eight-string fiddle, and the electric toilet plunger for novelty renditions of "Streets of Laredo" and "Black Mountain Rag" (CD, track 65). On occasional tunes, like "Wreck of the Old 97," George wrapped solos on harmonica and Jew's harp around Bruce's hot accordion runs. And he was the most frequent cowbell clanger, goose caller, and train whistle tooter. Windy Whitford provided steady rhythm on acoustic guitar, except on old Norwegian tunes or such western swing standards as "Maiden's Prayer," where he took up the fiddle in tandem with George.

The Ramblers' selection of songs and tunes was equally varied. Early on, the group settled on pieces that began and ended the evening, as well as those that signaled breaks. And almost from the beginning, the audience demanded certain favorites, like "Mrs. Johnson, Turn Me Loose" (CD, track 64) or the "Milwaukee Waltz" (CD, tracks 45–47), a celebration of Beer City revelry that combined Bruce's put-on drunken Dutchman vocals with the intentionally mangled rendering of such German-American standards as "*Ach du Lieber Augustine*" and "*Du, Du Liegst Mir im Herzen.*" In between, what might emerge was anybody's guess.

> There were certain tunes that you had to play. Once we were really rolling and getting a following, there were certain tunes that you always did. We always did the "Milwaukee Waltz," we always did "Oscar's Cannonball," we always did "Methodist Pie," what else? A lot of the novelty tunes you had to do, always. I think where the turnover, the variety came in was . . . Windy's got a lot of serious numbers. Oh, he wrote a tune about his brother that got killed by a hit-and-run driver. It's called "Brother." It's a serious, sad song in the old style. It just said things plainly. If you were grieving, you just said it. You didn't beat around the bush and come up with a lot of euphemisms and fancy ways to say it. You just said that you felt bad and you missed somebody and that kind of thing—which I think is really refreshing. Those, you know, weren't necessarily done all the time. So there'd be a lot of turnover there. Windy would pull old tunes out from the Delmore Brothers or Bradley Kincaid, things like that, and do them.

The trio never rehearsed and, until asked to do concerts in their later years, never worked out a formal set list. Rather, they fielded requests, improvised on the spot, or individually imagined something they'd like to do and pitched it to the band during the performance. As Windy put it:

Something clicked with us. . . . I think we felt it from the beginning. . . . I would say to Bruce or George, "Let's try this one here. Now this goes like this here." See, we were playing Wednesday and Friday and Saturday nights. Then, when I was working at Oscar Mayer's, I'd be thinking about, hey I'm going to try this song with 'em, and I'm going to try this one, and this one. Kind of plan ahead. And it was kind of something that made me really brighten up and look forward to every time we played. Because I could spring this on them, and they would come right back and back me up just 100 percent.

Bruce echoed these sentiments: "We never rehearsed, of course, ever. So everything that we did was done on the stage." George called it "on-the-job training."

The group never kept play lists for a given evening's show, but fans recalled the wild amalgam; a few even lugged bulky reel-to-reel tape recorders into the barroom and, like latterday Deadheads, propped a microphone in some sweet spot in the crowd's center. Dix Bruce, a Madison native who headed west, eventually working for Arhoolie Records in California's Bay Area, was inspired by George Gilbertsen's mandolin mastery around 1970 after wandering in on a typical evening.

All sorts of people: long hairs, short hairs, men, women, working people, business people, farmers, Oscar Mayer workers, you name it, an incredibly diverse crowd. The dance floor was jammed and (gasp!) The Goose Island Ramblers were playing a polka! Then they did a schottische, then a two-step, then some country, then a rock 'n' roll tune. They played a little bit of everything from the area, a lot from the Norwegian and German traditions. (Bruce 1991: 37–38)

A 1974 tape recording conveys that "little bit of everything," that polkabilly fusion, more precisely. Eighteen numbers preceded the first break. The opener, "Going to the Packer Inn," was an up-tempo, atmosphere-inducing original with a line lifted from the 1890s song "A Hot Time in the Old Town Tonight":

> Going to the Packer Inn to have a beer or two,
> Going to the Packer Inn tonight.
> Going to the Packer Inn to have a beer or two,
> We'll have a hot time in the Packer Inn tonight.

The brief ditty ended with simulated hiccups, as George extended the anticipated "beer or two" to "three or four," then struck bow to string for the driving French-Canadian fiddle tune, "St. Anne's Reel." Windy swung the exuberant convivial mood toward maudlin sentimentality, singing "Sinful to Flirt" or "Willie Down by the Pond": clutching a rose from his fickle lover's hair, Willie drowns himself in the mill pond. Bruce raised the dead with an unnamed Norwegian polka from Iowa County. Then, inspired by the Prairie Ramblers' 1940 version, the group did "Sugar Hill," celebrating

Figure 5.1. Bruce blows the jug while playing bass chords with his left hand as George fiddles and Windy strums rhythm guitar at Glen and Ann's, Madison, c. 1965. Goose Island Ramblers Collection, Wisconsin Historical Society (image 32836).

southern moonshining in three-part harmony. An unnamed hoedown followed, then the nostalgic "Sunny Southern Shore," before a comic compass shift to the Nordic "Nikolina." "Durham's Bull" invoked a playful barnyard stud, just prior to a Jimmie Rodgers blue yodel medley of misery and death: "My Good Gal's Gone Blues" and "TB Blues." Themes of parting continued with "I Will Miss You Little Darling," attributed to WLS "Barn Dance" mainstays Lulu Belle and Scotty (Myrtle Cooper and Scott Wiseman). The 12th song offered breezy relief via "Owee Chimes," with George on dobro: a bent version of Jack Penewell's rendition of "Maui Chimes," recorded originally in 1930 by the Hawaiian duet Palakiko and Paaluhi. The tongue-in-cheeky country boy and beast complaint "You Gotta Quit Kickin' My Dog Around" segued into Hank Williams's honky tonk wail, "I'm So Lonesome I Could Cry." A succession of cheery polkas provided a spiritual alternative, as well as the chance to dance vigorously: the Slovenian "E-I-O Polka," with its loopy antiphonal chorus, and the venerable jukebox anthem "Beer Barrel Polka," guaranteed to get "the blues on the run." But not for long, since the funereal "Will the Circle Be Unbroken" nearly closed out the set. Perhaps still pondering eternity, the Ramblers launched into the Zen-like non sequiturs of their "Break Song": "Oh the cat had a chicken and the chicken had a guppy / Hi old lady, is your rhubarb uppy?" (CD, track 48). As they left the bandstand, Bruce could be heard saying, "It's time to take a short pause for a good cause," with George concurring: "We'll be back in a flush."

Beers, tears, laughter, and variety persisted well into the night. Hillbilly classics about death, trains, excess, and devotion: "Soldier's Last Letter," "Orange Blossom Special," "Cigarettes and Whisky," "Sweetheart I Love You"; Arctic-Pacific dobro numbers: "Norwegian War Chant" (CD, track 40), "On the Beach at Waunakee" (CD, tracks 33–34); Nordic love songs: "Anna Marie"; and Slavic and Mediterranean polkas and waltzes. All were performed with equal doses of heart and humor.

"Definitely the Crowd and Us"

A creative melange of each member's eclectic musical experiences, the Goose Island Ramblers' polkabilly performances likewise drew incalculably on the extraordinarily active participation of the equally diverse audience that quickly emerged at Glen and Ann's. As Bruce put it:

> The college kids begin to come in. And Windy, of course, knew lots of people through the area, since he'd played for many years before. And they begin to come in. And they were, of course, working-class people. So you had these two groups, which is kind of neat in a way because they pretty well mingled and mixed. Sometimes, you know, you think of them as pretty disparate groups but, for the most part, I think they worked pretty well together.

A house band with regular gigs over a prolonged period, the Goose Island Ramblers were not compelled to charm strangers in new settings night after night; neither had they honed some act in prolonged rehearsal hoping it might dazzle from a lofty stage. Reliant on vaudeville and tent show professionalism, yet radiating the relaxed intimacy of jamming amateurs, their "act," in Bruce's words "just started to happen." Their stage was little more than a slightly raised platform, their crowd familiar faces seated roundabout in a sort of public living room only slightly smokier and more spacious than the house-party scenes of the Ramblers' respective youths. As a quintessential mom-and-pop Wisconsin tavern, family-owned and family-run, Glen and Ann's, in George's assessment, not only featured "good home cooking" but was a consummate "homey place. . . . Glen and Ann were kind of a people that—you were all like family. . . . the band was just like family to them. It wasn't like somebody they just hired to come in there."

The taverngoers, irrespective of age, class, ethnicity, political allegiance, or gender, felt similarly at home, as if participants in some recurring family reunion where they had license to take part and be themselves. The Ramblers' shows became their shows too, collective expressions of Upper Midwestern cultural identity. In the words of Smokey George, "it was definitely the crowd and us" (CD, track 39).

Packing the place, whooping and clapping, dancing, buying beer for the band, the Ramblers' crowd made requests, brought in props, fashioned novelty instruments, and frequently performed. George recalled a typical night:

> You're already set up, because we were playing there like three nights a week, sometimes four nights. So your stuff was always there. It was just a set engagement, you just walk in, tune up, start in. And it was a different era. Today, you don't promote drinkin' and drivin'. And at that time it was a pretty loose atmosphere. We wouldn't even get started hardly and they'd send up three pitchers of beer, one for each of us. And I mean pitchers. You didn't start with a glass. But the thing is, we always played so doggone hard and steady that I think we kept it wore off to where we never got in trouble with it. . . . But we'd get going, we'd just set up. It was just automatically. You could sense it. Everybody was all ready, they were rarin' to go. Just as if the show's going to start. We'd catch that from the crowd and they'd send us up some drinks. And within about 15 minutes we'd start to really get into it. And then up would come the requests, 'cause you never knew what you were going to do so much as you just played it by ear. You might play a tune you want to play, but then if the requests are coming up, you'd just keep on playing the requests. (CD, track 39)

As was the case with "The Letter Edged in Black," Windy especially savored the chance to sing some sentimental chestnut that had captivated his mother.

One night, "a guy stepped up and he says, 'Could you sing a song about Milwaukee?'" Windy immediately recalled "Milwaukee Fire" (CD, tracks 6–7):

> I didn't know the tune. I just made up my own tune to fit it. And I sang that for him. And I said, just for the heck of it, "If you ever get time, why don't you go down and see if that was a reality or what it was—if you can." "Yeah," he says, "I don't live too far from the [*Milwaukee*] *Journal*." So about three months later, he come in. He brought in a Xerox copy of the old newspaper.

Sixty-four perished on a cold January night in 1883 as the Newhall House burned (Laws 1964: 219). A disaster ballad, with images of a terrified servant girl and a desperate mother clutching her babe, circulated widely soon after. Gertrude Bell Smith Whitford had set down the verses in her late nineteenth-century notebook, and Windy read them over and over until they lodged in his memory.

More often, requests were for boisterous and comic pieces, songs cum skits like "Mrs. Johnson" or the "Milwaukee Waltz," and frenetic medleys demanding energetic dancing. George recalled:

> We used to do this one tune, we'd take our tour around the world. We'd play maybe a Russian number and then a Norwegian number; we'd go

right from one end to the other. We had a regular sort of medley. And then we'd get into this [Hums] Can-Can business, the French. And sometimes some gal'd get up on the table and start doing the can-can. We'd have quite a party. And then the students would get out and have a competition on the Russian tunes. They'd get out and try to do that Cossack dance, you know, where they'd get down, try and kick their legs out. And, boy, you should've seen some of the funniest doggone shows. Some of 'em were pretty good, others would go flying backwards. But it was really, the whole doggone night, half the show was the crowd, and the other half was the band. Everybody was passing it back and forth.

George's notion of "the show" went well beyond the tunes, songs, and dancing to include costumes, props, and novelty instruments—fundamental yet declining elements of schoolhouse skits, barn dances, mock weddings, "home talent" nights, vaudeville, and tent shows common throughout the region since the late nineteenth century.[2] Occasionally imagined or planned by the band, most such additions were provided spontaneously, unexpectedly by the crowd. Given the era and each member's tenure in western bands, the trio often wore cowboy hats and shirts as ordinary attire, but soon after George mugged the part of Mrs. Johnson, while Bruce emulated her hapless quarry, some wag brought in a blonde wig and floppy sunbonnet. George was in partial drag for every future performance of the song. Indeed the crowd soon hollered in anticipation whenever he bugged his eyes out, then clapped on wig and bonnet. Bruce switched headgear as well: "A guy brought in a whole uniform—that worked for a railroad—it was an old worn-out one. So when we did 'Oscar's Cannonball' or 'Wreck of the Old 97,' I'd put on the train hat."

He sometimes wore a feathered felt jaeger's hat for the "Milwaukee Waltz," a Mexican sombrero for the "Hat Dance" or a Tex-Mex polka, and a rube's slouch hat for "Mountain Dew." "We had a clothesline behind the stage" to hang them on. Likewise, at the height of Bruce's mock-tipsy rendition of "Milwaukee Waltz," "We had a hook hanging from the ceiling. And I'd be staggering around." In Three Stooges fashion, George offered stability by affixing "the back of my collar in that hook. And I could just sort of slouch down a little more. That was really funny" (CD, track 46).

George Gilbertsen's Hawaiian dobro performances, typically offered in a set of three or four comically mangled tunes, were especially theatrical. "Somebody brought in a grass skirt," George recalled, and later on "that bucket of horns. . . . somebody had a bucket made up and they put them [cow] horns on it." Rigged out in a hula dress and pseudo-Viking helmet, George might begin the set with fairly straight and highly accomplished versions of a Hawaiian march—the "March of the Little Tin Dobro" nominally altered to "The Little Tin Dodo"—and "Maui Chimes," dubbed with a wink as "Owee Chimes." Foolishness entered full swing with "On the Beach at Waunakee," both a reference to the Kalama Quartet's original "On the Beach of Waikiki" and a landlocked village north of Madison. After creditably intoning the original's Hawaiian-English chorus about romance between a mainland tourist and an island woman, George switched to an extended small-town Wisconsin monologue about a smooching couple chased by Waunakee's chief of police. Along the way, they cut through Smitty's Hall, a well-known dance spot for old time music, nearly get "picked off" by Oscar's Cannonball as it hauls cattle to Madison, dash through Hanson's Tavern to trip over a bucket of bullheads by the back door, then dart to Pheasant Branch, shaking the chief for good on County M (CD, track 34). Having conflated Hawaii with the Upper Midwest through helmet, song, and skirt, George concluded the set by parodying the already slightly facetious "Hawaiian War Chant," a piece previously warped by Spike Jones and the klezmer comedian Mickey Katz.[3] The Ramblers' erstwhile Norsky repertoire and Gilbertsen's Viking headgear resulted in "Bruce or somebody hollering, We're going to play 'Norwegian War Chant.'" Finger picks flashing in his right hand, breakneck sliding tones rippling from the bar in his left, red-faced, hopping, and bellowing some inchoate war cry while his grass skirt shook, George resembled Hagar the Horrible lost in the South Seas: a musical version of Ole and Lena on vacation (CD, track 40). As George put it, "they used to say that hearing us was only part of it—you had to see us. It was a regular novelty show."

Drawing on his amateur hour, fiddlers contest, and vaudeville experience, George did a bit of trick fiddling with the Ramblers. As Bruce put it: "He'd step through the fiddle and play it behind his back and behind his head and hold it out this way and play it like that, like a bass fiddle. He just had a whole routine worked out."

George's playful yet virtuoso and versatile musicianship inspired one audience regular, Harry Gillingham, to craft a pair of unique instruments that figured prominently in the Ramblers' shows: the electric toilet plunger and the eight banger. A musician himself, Gillingham repaired instruments for the Madison violin builder Lawrence LeMay. His electric toilet plunger was a regular "plumber's friend," fitted out with "a wooden plug down in the end of it so it was firm—so that I could get a good grip on it. Then the cord around there [tacked at both ends for a strap]. Then he had a little wooden nut on the end and then these two strings with a bridge." The strings were steel and affixed to a pickup for amplification. Outfitted with finger picks, George played the plunger like a dobro. "I used to do the 'Hawaiian March' on it and then I used to do 'Black Mountain Rag'" (CD, track 65). The latter, coaxing a lot of music from a limited instrument, brought appreciative grins from finger-picked-guitar aficionados in the audience familiar with the 1964 version recorded by North Carolinian Doc Watson.[4] Grins soon became guffaws. "I'd get done and I'd be so enthused with it that I give it a big kiss," George recalled, then he'd make a disgusted face, sputter, mutter "Ouuggh!" and wipe his mouth clean. "And people would laugh. But the thing is, it was brand new."

Arguably as creative as fellow Wisconsin innovators Jack Penewell and Les Paul, whose double-necked steel guitar and solid-body electric guitar were manufactured by Gibson in 1922 and 1952 respectively, Harry Gillingham was content to make one-of-a-kind instruments, more interested in mischief than marketing. As Bruce Bollerud put it, Gillingham's

> eight banger was something else. It was really a mandolin neck on there. It was an eight-string fiddle, but with pairs of strings like a mandolin has. . . . It was a hard instrument to build because the pressure on the instrument was double from having twice as many strings. When Harry put that together, it took some real engineering. . . . But it had a powerful sound. It was a wild, wailing sound. It just, I don't know, it made me think of the wild Irish, out on the moors or something, with the wind screaming.

George elaborated:

> It had eight strings going over the bridge, not like a Norwegian Hardanger [with four strings above the bridge and four or five sympathetic strings below]; this had eight strings actually going over the bridge. He took a mandolin neck and mounted it on a violin body. When I first started using this at Glen and Ann's, Bruce says, "Smokey's got this new instrument here," he said, "we don't have a name for it yet. It's part mandolin and part fiddle." And some gal jumped up, she didn't even give it a thought, she said, "Call it a mandofiddle." The whole place just went up in an uproar. She sat down real fast after she said that. We ended up, it was "eight banger" we called it.

The name was an agrarian inside joke. Stationary two-cylinder engines, used on Midwestern farms in pre-electrification days to power water pumps and milking machines, were known as "two bangers" because of their frequent, noisy backfiring. By extension, a cow that only gave milk from three of four teats was a "three banger" (Mitchell 1984: 158). Hence, "eight banger" neatly signaled a peculiar, cacophonous creation.

George contributed to the instrument's distinctive voice, one characterized by slightly dissonant overtones harking back to the Norwegian Hardanger fiddle:

> And that had a real weird sound because I tuned it—well, it was double sets of strings like a mandolin, but then I tuned the first two in harmony, and then the rest of them I had in octaves in unison. A thin, a high string and a thick string, so I tuned 'em in unison but in octaves apart. And that had a weird sound to it.

Playing the instrument was quite a challenge. George continued:

> To make it effective, I used to use a viola bow because it was heavier, more hair, and I could really bite in because, boy, it took some pressure to play that thing. And you had to flat finger it. You couldn't come

down with the round part of your finger because part of that, doggone, it wouldn't quite fret right because you didn't have frets on there like a mandolin. So part of your finger's ahead of your other part, if you get what I mean. You're on two strings, but one part of your finger's just ahead of the other part, so the strings wouldn't be quite accurate. So you had to flat finger it, see, to get 'em to come out true—where, with the mandolin, you come down and the fret makes it even.

Because of the instrument's complications, George typically used it for just two pieces, the fiddle tune "Old Joe Clark" and "Streets of Laredo," the tragic ballad of a dying cowboy with a low part tailor-made for what Gilbertsen dubbed the eight banger's "mournful sound."

A jug rounded out the audience contributions to the Ramblers' array of instruments. As Bruce recalled:

> There was a fellow came in and brought a jug in and he wanted to play jug. . . . Then there was another fella come in that played pretty well. He was, I think, a member of a jug band. They were kind of popular at that time. Jim Kweskin and Dave Van Ronk and some of these groups were pretty big names nationally.

Van Ronk began playing jug band music in New York City in 1958, teaming up with blues scholar Samuel Charters who, two years before, had made field recordings of Gus Cannon, an African-American musician from Memphis who led Cannon's Jug Stompers on recordings in the 1920s. By the early 1960s, Jim Kweskin & the Jug Band had begun making a succession of recordings on Vanguard with Fritz Richmond on jug. These eastern, urban folk music revivalists drew particular inspiration from both Cannon's Jug Stompers and the Memphis Jug Band, especially tunes like "Minglewood Blues" and "K. C. Moan," which had been reissued on LP as part of the avant-garde artist Harry Smith's *Anthology of American Folk Music*.[5] Having developed a good lip from his trombone-playing days in polka bands, Bruce warmed to the jug right away: "It appealed to me. So I begin to pick up the jug and experiment with that. And pretty soon I was playing the jug on 'Mountain Dew' and a few other things" (CD, tracks 42–44). His bass lines and occasional lead on the jug, partially imbued with a gravelly African-American sound, also shaded toward the romping tuba or bass horn attack of Minnesota German or Dutchman bands, especially those—led by Harold Loeffelmacher, Elmer Scheid, and Syl Liebl— that favored an exuberant, improvised, melodiously flatulent "oompah" (Leary 1990a: 2–3). Soon, the Ramblers acquired a five-gallon jug of their own, harking back in turn to the big jug blown back in the late 1930s by Alvin "Salty" Hougan of the original Goose Island Ramblers.

Besides playing with Windy Whitford, Hougan had also teamed up with George Gilbertsen to perform as the Badger Ramblers in the late 1940s and early 1950s. Some of their crowds were "pretty sparse," in George's recollection. That didn't stop Salty, whose nickname matched his forward puckish personality, from cutting up and cajoling: "He'd say, 'Don't forget, folks, the band's drinking too. Shorty Pabst and a whiskey sour.' Or he'd say, 'Don't forget, we're not a bunch of camels up here that we can go seven days without a drink.' But he was sort of this frosty type that could come out with that, see." Mostly a string bass player, he brought his bull fiddle to some of the Ramblers' early jobs at Glen and Ann's. Like his bandmates Windy and George, Bruce regarded Hougan as "quite a character. A very funny guy, a very funny guy. He and George, I think, are somewhat alike in that they both got this wild, crazy sense of humor. Salty's probably was a little more wild than George, in a way. He was a funny guy."

The trio learned Wobbly bard Joe Hill's "I Worked for a Farmer" (CD, track 21), a comic song concerning sabotage by ill-treated threshing crews, from Salty, and they saluted him on an eventual recording—*Velkommen Til Stoughton Den Syttende Mai*—by substituting "Salty Hougan" for "Paul Paa Haugen." Harv Cox, fiddling former leader of the Oklahoma Cowboys, with whom Windy had played in the 1930s, sometimes stepped in to saw out and sing "Watermelon Smilin' on the Vine," an old minstrel-show song recorded by such southern string bands as Gid Tanner and the Skillet Lickers. Likewise, Bruce's old bandmate Verne Meisner—an innovative Slovenian-style piano accordionist whose polka career extended from the 1950s until his death in 2005—would also sit in now and then while traveling through Madison.

That a jug player or two, as well as a parade of old musical sidekicks, crossed over from crowd to center stage was hardly surprising in Glen and Ann's, where both the homey atmosphere and the band's audience-oriented, anything-goes-style fostered the old time house-party experience with which all the Ramblers had grown up. As George put it:

> We'd get lot of audience participation. We'd get guys come up and sit in with us. My goodness, we'd have fiddlers, banjo players. I remember this one big old Norwegian guy'd get up and play a fiddle tune, and he had hands on him—I don't know how he could even play a fiddle— and he'd play a Norwegian tune. Had great big fingers. "Hans" I think they called him [Hans Dybevik]. And then Wild Bill Martin would get up with his five-string banjo. We'd always get harmonica players.

One was Bruce's cousin, Olaf "Ole" Venden, a heavy-equipment operator born in 1916 in the rural town of Vermont, a hilly Norwegian stronghold in western Dane County. Bruce had heard him play at many family gatherings and welcomed his Venden cousin at Glen and Ann's: "There were certain people that would come in and sit in a lot. And, of course, Ole was one of them. He'd get up and play a couple tunes. And he had sort of a unique style on the harmonica where he'd play and then kind of hit the chords in between so it was kind of a full style for one guy." Ole drew especially on his "accordion style"—so-called because it incorporated both chords and melody, as if using the left- and right-hand buttons of some squeezebox—to play old time Norwegian tunes.

Figure 5.2. Alvin "Salty" Hougan, with his jug and assorted string instruments (string bass, four-string banjo, lap steel guitar, mandolin, and guitar), Madison, c. 1940. Goose Island Ramblers Collection, Wisconsin Historical Society (image 32847).

Tommy McDermott was another regular contributor. An Irish immigrant from Elphin in County Roscommon who had joined the American air force in the 1950s, been stationed at Madison's Truax Field, and eventually married and settled in Wisconsin's capital city, McDermott was a fine accordionist who played through the 1990s in local groups like the Emerald Isle Ceili Band (Emerald Isle Ceili Band 1997 M). Invariably called upon to play the Irish-American standard "The Irish Washerwoman," McDermott held forth on jigs, reels, and hornpipes from his youthful days, several of which the Ramblers began to perform regularly.

Then there were guest singers aplenty. One was Vern Minor, the "Lake Edge Crooner," who, like Salty Hougan, had performed in the original Goose Island Ramblers and for years thereafter with Windy Whitford. Bruce recalled fondly how

> he'd come up and sing a few songs. And I always thought he had a very sweet voice. He had a really nice, nice voice. And he and Wendy really sang well together, I'd thought, because they worked together for years. And they always had these old songs that I had never heard even. "Whippoorwill." . . . They were real old country songs.

Minor's "Whippoorwill" dated to the 1860s and had been first recorded in the early 1930s by such WLS hillbilly stalwarts as Bradley Kincaid and Scott "Skyland Scotty" Wiseman (Meade, Spottswood, and Meade 2002: 225–226).

Other fans had different tastes. Bruce recalled: "Then there was this big Bob Borgrud that came in and sang 'Jealous Heart' and 'We Live in Two

Figure 5.3. Irish accordionist Tommy McDermott (*second from left*) sits in with the Goose Island Ramblers at Glen and Ann's, Madison, c. 1965. Goose Island Ramblers Collection, Wisconsin Historical Society (image 32830).

Different Worlds,' things like that. Did it very seriously. He'd usually be about half schnockered-up. He was just a big giant of a man, singing very tenderly." Using the Ramblers as one might nowadays use a karaoke system, Borgrud favored his immediate era's honky tonk hits, as did a guitarist who, inspired by recording artist Faron Young, belted out "I've Got Five Dollars and It's Saturday Night." Meanwhile, an exuberant woman named Clara, perhaps from Madison's Italian-American Greenbush neighborhood, complemented Bruce's Scandihoovian singing with her rendition of Sicilian-American Nicola Paone's comic dialect number "Show Me How (You Milk the Cow)."[6]

As a regular attendee of Ramblers' performances in the late 1960s and early 1970s, Dix Bruce recalled these and other audience members joining in:

> There's Sid White's cousin, the teenage guitar picker who'll do Doc Watson's "Black Mountain Rag" or "The Wildwood Flower." There's Dave Hoff with a manner, dress, and style straight out of the forties who jumps up and sings in his incredible vibrato voice "The Tattooed Lady." . . . There's Tom McDermott the Irish button accordion player or Dan Cook the accordion player or Bob Lotz the harmonica player. There's Frank the four string banjo player or Cousin Ole the harmonica player. Yodelers, fiddlers, singers, and even dancers come out of the woodwork from all over the country to be with the Goose Island Ramblers. (Bruce c. 1975)

The varied audience participation, along with numerous and novel instruments, costume shifts, and comic skits brought, as George put it, "more variety in the show. And that's what people come for, to see your shows."

Unlike the musical variety shows of radio and television, however, the Ramblers' evening entertainments were neither planned nor rehearsed. They emerged spontaneously as the "guest stars" simply turned up. And while a few participants, like Bob Borgrud, tilted toward Nashville and the era's country hits, most favored the old time polkabilly mixture of Anglo-American and European immigrant sounds that had interwoven in the Upper Midwest since the mid-nineteenth century.

More than 300 miles to the north, Florian Chmielewski used a similar approach in launching a television program, "Chmielewski Funtime," on Duluth's WDSM that featured an evolving polkabilly sound from 1955 through the 1990s—the longest tenure of any musical variety show on American television. The grandson of fiddling Polish immigrants, the accordion-playing Chmielewski absorbed the old time obereks, kujawiaks, and mazurkas of his parents and grandparents, but he also learned Anglo-American, Czech, Finnish, French-Canadian, German, Irish, Norwegian, Slovenian, and Swedish songs and tunes from friends, neighbors, records, and regional radio. In 1955, when his show was broadcast live, Florian was approached during a commercial by a Finnish farmer from northern Wisconsin: "He said, 'I've got two kids here who are good accordion players. Can you put them on?'" Moments later, although he'd never heard them perform, Florian introduced the Maki Twins. "I took a chance and they went over." He took similar chances ever after, eventually syndicating his show to 25 stations concentrated mostly in the Upper Midwest and northern Great Plains. Like the Goose Island Ramblers, Florian Chmielewski naturally eschewed slick, narrow, premeditated, hit-parade production for a spontaneous, egalitarian, eclectic, regionally grounded house-party format, thereby captivating a large, loyal, continuous audience. "People really love that. I think that's what makes a party" (Chmielewski 1990 I; Chmielewski 1991: 17).

"Turn That Thing On, We'll Think of Something"

Although the Goose Island Ramblers never launched a regular radio or television program, they made a remarkable series of recordings on Sauk City, Wisconsin's Cuca label in the 1960s.

Their first LP was prompted, in Windy's recollection, by students from the University of Wisconsin:

> George used to say, "Well, our music only goes to the front door, Windy." But some of the fellows asked, that first year, couldn't you—the fellows that were graduating—leave something with us that we could have to remember you by? And Bruce said his wife's cousin was this Jim Kirchstein up at Sauk.[7] We could make an album, maybe, if they'd buy one. "Would you guys buy an album if we made one?" "Oh, yes, yes." "Well maybe we better do that, then." So April 7th of '64, that's when we went up. (CD, track 27)

By the spring of 1964, Kirchstein's Cuca label was thriving, releasing a torrent of 45s and LPs by a wide array of Wisconsin bands, particularly in rock, country, polka, and polkabilly genres. Bruce had cut a 45 there three years before with the Johnson Brothers. In the meantime, many of his former musical associates—Roger Bright, Sammy Eggum, Verne Meisner, and Dick Sherwood—had all recorded at Cuca. Likewise George Gilbertsen's brother LeRoy waxed "Russian Rumble" and the "Anniversary Song" in April 1962 (Myers 1994: 113–117).

Bruce made arrangements for studio time and, packing up their instruments, the Ramblers headed northeast to Sauk City. Accustomed to the encouragement of a few beers and a raucous crowd, Bruce and his cohorts were slightly intimidated by the prospect of making music in a silent, sober studio.

> George and I said, "Well, let's stop and have a couple shots before we go in there. Get loosened up a little bit." And Windy was real nervous about that. He didn't know if we should do that or not. I think we were all kind of nervous about it, really. But we did anyway. We had a couple drinks and went down there. Of course, Jim was real easy to work with.

Confronted by a band without firm set lists, sheaves of lyrics, or arrangements, Jim Kirchstein was pleasantly startled by the Ramblers' competent informality.

> Jim says, when we come in, "Well where's your material? What're you going to do? Where's your program? Where's your numbers and your music?" Bruce says, "Turn that thing on, we'll think of something." "Windy," he says, "sing 'Oscar's Cannonball.'" As I remember, that's the first number we done. (CD, tracks 27–29)

From then on, the band played continuously, bantering and deciding between tunes, while Jim Kirchstein had the sense to let the tape roll. Rather than pausing, asking for a track to be played back, possibly doing a second take, then briefly rehearsing the next number, the Ramblers, as Bruce put, "just cut everything. I don't think we did anything twice at all. We played the tune, it was recorded, that was it—it was canned."

And because, in George's words, "We just went straight on through," Jim Kirchstein was hard pressed to isolate one track from another. His inspired decision, prompted by the ease with which the Ramblers recreated their tavern show, was to treat the studio recording as a "live" event. The resulting *A Session with the Goose Island Ramblers* (Cuca LP K-1110) is one continuous track, mixing music with playful asides and interjections. Windy was dismayed at first:

> "Oh my God, he's got all that talking on there and everything. Let's do this, or let's play this." I told Jim, I says, "Gee, what the heck did you

do that for?" He says, "I wanted to show people what kind of a band you guys were. You didn't have to rehearse and rehearse in order to do something. You just went ahead and done it." He says sometimes people come up there and they'll rehearse and rehearse and they'll come back another time before they'll even cut an album. I could say this: whatever we done was natural, anyway. It wasn't put on.

Bruce concurred: "I thought that was the neat part of the record, 'cause it was more like the way we were. When we played and everything, it was very natural. We weren't very formal at all, that's for sure." Bruce also appreciated the album's "insight into the process of the way we recorded." By simply being themselves, with a little help from Jim Kirchstein, the old timey Goose Island Ramblers' 1964 *Session* anticipated such visionary artists as Bob Dylan and the Beatles in producing an LP offering a modernist behind-the-scenes, or "contextualized," glimpse of studio goings-on.

Five months later, in September 1964, the group returned to Sauk City to record enough material for two more LPs: *From Blue Grass to Russian Gypsy* (Cuca K-1111) and *Doin' the Hurley Hop* (Cuca K-1112). They also recorded seven numbers at the request of the Chamber of Commerce in Stoughton, a heavily Norwegian community just south of Madison that spawned the American revival of Norwegian floral painting, or *rosemaling*, sponsored a folk-dance troupe decked out in traditional *bunads,* and was once the site of old time fiddlers contests where Clarence Reierson and a youthful Windy Whitford competed.[8] The LP was issued in conjunction with the celebration of May 17, Norwegian Constitution Day: *Velkommen Til Stoughton Den Syttende Mai* (Cuca K-2010).

Together, the recorded tracks offer a fair glimpse of the group's collective repertoire: the Irish emigrant ballad "Barney McCoy" (CD, track 5); the maudlin "The Letter Edged in Black" from Windy's mother's notebook; nameless Norwegian fiddle tunes acquired from Windy's dance-hall mentor Clarence "Fiddlesticks" Reierson; a pair of outlaw and disaster ballads oft-recorded and sung when Windy and George were young: "Jesse James" and "Wreck of the Old 97"; Bradley Kincaid's comic "Methodist Pie," gleaned by Windy from WLS; plus a trio of Whitford compositions: "My Blue Eyes Have Gone" (CD, tracks 23–26), coveted by Red Foley and Gene Autry; "Going Back to the Hills," celebrating Albion; and his butcher boy's salute to the cattle train, "Oscar's Cannonball" (CD, track 29). Bruce brought a wealth of Norwegian songs and tunes: *"Paul Paa Haugen"* (CD, tracks 55–58), a comic barnyard ditty that his mother used to sing; the sentimental sailor's song "Anna Marie"; and dance tunes like *"Stegen Vals"* and the schottische "Sentimental Selma." There were also "Ole Olson, the Hobo from Norway" (CD, track 61), acquired from the Bolleruds' hired men, along with the Norsky and Dutch dialect foolishness of "Nikolina," "Mrs. Johnson, Turn Me Loose" (CD, track 64), and the "Milwaukee Waltz" (CD, tracks 45–47). Then there was Bruce's rendition of the Irish moonshining song, "Mountain Dew" (CD, tracks 42–44), anchored by a raunchy oompahing jug, as well as the sprightly Polish "Francuszka Polka" (CD, tracks 51–54), augmented by macaronic vocals: "Hey, hey, *jak sie masz?* / Hey, hey, hello Stash." George contributed several breakneck instrumentals on mandolin, Fender guitar, and the eight banger: the Russian "Katinka" garnered from Leo Aberle and his own "Goose Island Stomp" and "Old Joe Clark." His dobro, talking blues, and Hawaiian-Norsky patois dominated "March of the Little Tin Dodo," "On the Beach at Waunakee" (CD, track 34), and "Norwegian War Chant" (CD, track 40). And he sang goofy novelty songs like "Shut the Door (They're Coming through the Window)."

The Ramblers' LPs sold briskly from the bandstand and modestly in local record stores. "Mrs. Johnson, Turn Me Loose" backed with "Oscar's Cannonball" (Cuca 1184), a single from their September 1964 session, reportedly sold 5,000 copies, aided by air play on Madison radio and jukebox rotation in southwestern Wisconsin taverns.[9] Rife with local references, emphasizing regional dialect, and rendered through the deft interplay of accordion, fiddle, dobro, and guitar, the Cuca 45 succinctly conveyed the band's polkabilly essence. Yet the "Hurley Hop" (CD, track 50), a collective composition, arguably reveals more about the Ramblers' sense of themselves, their audience, and the rowdy Upper Midwestern house-party atmosphere that emerged thrice weekly in a working-class mom-and-pop tavern bordering the University of Wisconsin.

Nominally chronicling the trio's jaunt to Hurley—a wide-open former mining and logging town, infamous for the taverns and whore houses crowding Silver Street—the "Hurley Hop" is really about the Ramblers' relationship with the faithful from Glen and Ann's. As Bruce recalled:

> We were driving up to Sauk City to record. Something came up about Hurley. Somebody made a joke about a Hurley hop or whatever. And I think we wrote that damn thing on the way to Sauk City. And I think I put most of it together, but George and Windy came up with a verse or a line here and there. And we recorded the thing.

The song kicked off with a driving mandolin riff that might have been made by bluegrass pioneer Bill Monroe if, during his oil refinery stint in northern Indiana, he had wandered into the wrong neighborhood to play polkas with squeezebox-toting immigrants. With George skittering along on mandolin, Windy providing steady rhythm on guitar, and his own accordion pumping out bass chords, Bruce slid into the first verse, an imaginary stroll down Hurley's Silver Street. An "awful racket" draws him into a tavern to behold "The Goose Island Ramblers, as big as they could be." The second verse reveals that the scene is actually closer to home.

> There was Smokey George on fiddle, Uncle Windy on guitar,
> But Loose Bruce the Goose, I wonder where you are?
> He's standing in the corner, a big smile on his mug,
> Playing "Good Old Mountain Dew" and blowing on the jug.
> I took a look into the crowd and there sat Glen and Ann,
> A clapping and cheering and egging on the band.

> There was Little Tex from Texas and the Swanson Brothers too,
> By gosh I think there must've been at least half of the U.

Bruce buzzed across the next bridge with his jug, crossing into a final verse celebrating the pleasant "frenzy" wrought by the swinging, singing, and dancing of the Ramblers and their crowd, including, as Bruce testified:

> a lot of the local people. . . . Little Tex from Texas was a student from Texas that went here. And he'd come in and we always had to play a Texas song for him. And we'd make some joke about a Texas longhorn or something like that, you know. He was always going like this [Using his hands to simulate horns on his head]. So he was in there. Of course, Glen and Ann were in there. The Swanson brothers. They were two [Norwegian] brothers that went to school here. . . . So there were quite a few local characters.

In subsequent live performances, the group members and their audience savored the song for its cameo of a typical evening.

Those evenings ended, however, in the late 1960s with Glen's death. Reluctant to manage the place on her own, Ann was also courted by an eager buyer, Marshall Shapiro, an urbane local sportscaster whose musical tastes did not extend to the rustic Goose Island Ramblers. The folk revival—which helped to propel collegians onto erstwhile working-class turf to hear a band graft Anglo-American old time sounds onto European ethnic dance pieces and dialect songs—had been bumped from the nation's hit parade by a youth-oriented juggernaut of soul music, blues, and rootsy rock 'n' roll. Given its location, Glen and Ann's was ripe for transformation into the Nitty Gritty, a combination college bar and hangout for well-educated hipsters. As Madison's *Isthmus*, an alternative weekly emphasizing arts and politics, proclaimed, "Marshall Shapiro took over Glen 'n' Ann's and made the Gritty one of the hottest spots in town by booking the likes of Luther Allison, Muddy Waters, Hound Dog Taylor, Bonnie Raitt, Otis Rush, Siegel-Schwall . . . Tracy Nelson, and Ben Sidran."[10]

George Gilbertsen's perspective was understandably different:

> Marsh . . . changed the whole atmosphere. So that's when we, you might say, were canned. That's when we went to Packer Inn. I think what would've been kind of nice—because, boy, we really had a crowd established there and a thing going—he could've run both. He could've really run both, and that would've been the route to go. Have a little of both. Because that way you would've got more crowd, and everybody would've been happy too. Because we didn't necessarily have to play three, four nights a week. Two nights of soul and two nights of us would've been fine, something like that.

The Ramblers' last night at Glen and Ann's was, in Bruce's estimation, "a big party," a real-life rival to the imaginary frenzy of the "Hurley Hop": "It was just a riot. The place was absolutely mobbed. And the bartenders were opening champagne behind the bar and it would spill over and go on the floor. . . . It was just wild and crazy."

In 1970, the Ramblers' faithful followed them to Johnny's Packer Inn, located on a suburban thoroughfare miles to the southeast, but the move severed ongoing connections with students, and the homey atmosphere that Glen and Ann had fostered was gone. The Packer Inn was, as George put it, "just a bar." By 1975, the band had been together for more than a dozen years. Windy was 62, ready to slow down a bit, to play occasional jobs with his seven musical children, and George yearned to travel, play a little now and then, and pursue a woodworking hobby. Bruce, on the other hand, wanted more gigs and wondered about forming a band that might fit into the region's thriving polka scene. So the Goose Island Ramblers called it quits—but only temporarily.

Catching On Again

The end of the Goose Island Ramblers' run in Madison taverns coincided fortuitously with the beginning of America's most powerful fascination with folk cultural roots since the Great Depression. The nation's 1976 bicentennial, the televising of Alex Haley's ancestral saga *Roots,* the rise of racial and ethnic identity politics, the countercultural or antimodern "back to the land" movement, and the emergence and maturation of such federal "public folklore" organizations as the Office of Folklife Programs at the Smithsonian Institution, the American Folklife Center at the Library of Congress, and the Folk Arts Program within the National Endowment for the Arts all combined to coax more than a few traditional artists out of retirement, broaden their audience, and heighten public awareness of their significance.[11] So it was for the Goose Island Ramblers.

On February 17 and November 18, 1976, 23-year-old Philip Martin interviewed Smokey George Gilbertsen about old time fiddling. In the years to come, accompanied by documentary photographer Lewis Koch, Martin would also conduct sessions with Windy Whitford and Bruce Bollerud.[12] Educated at prep schools, the son of international folk dance enthusiasts, Martin had been inspired to play fiddle tunes and seek out old time musicians through his involvement with Folklore Village Farm. Situated in the hills of Iowa County, a scant 10 miles northwest of Bruce Bollerud's Hollandale home, Folklore Village was founded by Jane Farwell (1918–1993) on what had once been her family's farm. The adventurous Farwell, recipient of a self-designed major in rural recreation from Antioch College, lived and traveled throughout Europe in the post–World War II era, accumulating a collection of regional folk costumes and a repertoire of folk dances. Returning to southwestern Wisconsin in 1967, she launched a series of folk dance gatherings that steadily attracted followers, including Martin's parents. Farwell's Nordic travels, her attraction to Scandinavian "folk schools" with their emphasis on fusing conventional education with cultural traditions, and her particular southwestern Wisconsin and Upper Midwestern roots compelled her to include Scandinavian and Scandinavian-American musicians aplenty in Folklore Village doings.[13] Young Phil Martin was especially captivated by what he heard and saw. He subsequently traveled throughout Scandinavia, encountering traditional musicians and, once back home, carried his fiddle and tape recorder into the homes of regional old time performers.

In the late 1970s, Martin established the Wisconsin Folklife Center as a documentary subsidiary of Folklore Village Farm, won folk arts grants from federal and state agencies, conducted intensive field research with traditional musicians, and set about producing slide/tape programs, sound recordings, concerts, and essays.[14] By the early 1980s, while working part time for the Wisconsin Arts Board, Martin fostered the creation of a state folk arts coordinator position (held by Richard March since its inception in 1983), helped to produce several series on Wisconsin public radio, and established the Wisconsin Folk Museum.

The Goose Island Ramblers figured in Martin's key early undertakings. Photographs from various stages of their individual careers and Whitford's reminiscences suffused *A Kingdom of Fiddlers*, a 1980 Martin/Koch slide/tape program celebrating rural house parties, lamenting modernity, and encouraging youngsters to seek out elder fiddlers to revive fading traditions. Meanwhile, Bruce Bollerud's bandonion renditions of "*Stegen Vals*" and "Johnny Homme's Waltz" were included on Martin's *Across the Fields* LP/cassette production in 1982. That same year—thanks to Martin's connections with Wisconsin public radio, where folk revival aficionado Tom Martin-Erickson had begun the still-popular "Simply Folk" weekend program in 1978—the Ramblers came out of retirement to be photographed, tape a program, and be featured in "Those Goose Island Ramblers" in the February 1982 edition of the network's magazine, *Airwaves*.

While Phil Martin was capturing the life histories and musical performances of Upper Midwestern old timers, I had begun to do the same, particularly in northern Wisconsin and the Upper Peninsula of Michigan. Along the way, I purchased commercial recordings made by regional musicians, including several Ramblers LPs. I had heard about the group already from Richard March when we were fellow graduate students in folklore at Indiana University from 1973 to 1977. A Chicago native, March had lived in Madison during the Ramblers' heyday, and his brother Bob was a banjo-playing physics professor who sometimes sat in with the band. In the fall of 1983, March arrived in Madison to become the Wisconsin Arts Board's folk arts coordinator, while I moved to the city in January 1985. For roughly the next decade, both individually and collectively, Martin, March, and I followed the separate and overlapping musical efforts of Windy, George, and Bruce, while lending occasional support. In June 1987, for example, Richard March and I recorded Bruce Bollerud for the pilot of a Wisconsin public radio series, "Down Home Dairyland." We eventually produced three half-hour programs featuring the Goose Island Ramblers.[15]

During all this time, the individual Ramblers remained musically active. All three might turn up for periodic Wisconsin old time fiddlers gatherings, while Bruce was a fixture in the area's annual Accordion Jamboree. George continued to jam informally with his immigrant Irish accordionist pal, Tommy McDermott, even playing with him in the Emerald Isle Ceili Band's St. Patrick's Day dance jobs for the Madison area's Shamrock Club. Likewise, George and Windy sometimes played for fun at one or the other's home, venturing out to entertain at a June farm breakfast or the Stoughton Senior Center. The late 1980s also found Windy leading the Goose Island Family Band that included several of his kids—Bonnie, Joyce, and Winston—with Smokey George sometimes sitting in for summer evening performances at the Sunny Side, a bar and supper club on Lake Kegonsa north of Stoughton. And all this time, Bruce fronted his Good Times Band for regular jobs at Madison's Lion's Club, the East Side Businessmen's Club, and the Essen Haus, a German-American restaurant that, like Glen and Ann's, was a student hangout.

Despite their span apart, the three continued to perform much of the Ramblers' core repertoire, with George and Windy veering toward sentimental ballads, hot fiddle and dobro numbers, and lilting Norwegian waltzes, while Bruce favored Norsky and Dutchman dialect songs, Swiss and cowboy yodels, a broader span of polka tunes, and a sprinkling of western swing standards. Not surprisingly, their old fans and many newcomers sought them out, and by the early 1990s the Ramblers' faithful demanded their reunion.

Bill Graham and others persuaded the trio to perform and be videotaped in May 1990 at Madison's Elk's Club. At the same time, Graham—a diehard "country boy" who befriended the Ramblers just as they were starting out and as he was launching what would be a highly successful office supply business—contacted the State Historical Society of Wisconsin offering to pay for the documentation of the band's career. The Elks Club performance was packed to overflowing. As George put it, the Goose Island Ramblers were "just sort of catching on again." Meanwhile, the historical society, lacking the expertise to honor Graham's request, subcontracted with the Wisconsin Folk Museum, which Martin directed and where I was affiliated as a staff folklorist. In June and July of that year, I interviewed Whitford, Gilbertsen, and Bollerud at length, then oversaw studio sessions on July 19 and 24 that resulted in a new recording, *Midwest Ramblin'*, released in the fall of 1990.

Composed of 27 tracks, *Midwest Ramblin'* included previously unrecorded mainstays from their 1963–1975 stint: the set-opening "Going to the Packer Inn" and their goofy "Break Song" (CD, track 48); "In Heaven There Is No Beer," the Beer State's unofficial anthem, with Bruce singing in English, the original German, and Norwegian; a Swiss yodel, a Norwegian schottische, a German polka, a Slovenian waltz, and a minor-key Russian fiddle tune; "Black Mountain Rag" on the toilet plunger (CD, track 65); "Streets of Laredo" on the eight banger; the "Milwaukee Fire" from Windy's mother (CD, tracks 6–7); several of Windy's own ballads, including "Brother," regarding his brother's death from a hit-and-run driver in 1935 (CD, track 8);

Figure 5.4. Bruce Bollerud and Ralph Hoff sing a duet while performing as the Good Times Band at the Speedway Bar, Madison, early 1980s. Courtesy of Bruce Bollerud.

one of Clarence Reierson's two-steps (CD, tracks 10–12); "I Worked for a Farmer" by Wobbly organizer Joe Hill (CD, track 21); the broken-English Bollerud-Whitford original "No Norwegians in Dickeyville"; and a good deal more.

Energized by their faithful and armed with a new recording, the Goose Island Ramblers played throughout the 1990s. Their pace was slower—no more thrice-weekly beer-fueled workouts—and their settings different, as platforms slightly raised above dimly lit tavern floors gave way to spotlights and concert stages. Beginning in 1992, hailed as exemplary bearers of regional tradition, they played the first of several jobs at Folklore Village. In March 1994, the Ramblers traveled to the barns of Wolf Trap to perform in the "Europe in America" segment of the Folk Masters series produced by folklorist Nick Spitzer for the Smithsonian Institution. That fall, they also entertained a packed house in Madison's Barrymore Theater, formerly the Eastwood Theater, where, as the Lonesome Cowboy, Windy had crooned western songs in 1933; and they were featured in "Polka from Cuca," a Wisconsin public television production highlighting the German, Polish, Slovenian, Swiss, and polkabilly musicians featured in the 1960s on Jim Kirchstein's Cuca label. When the Stoughton Opera House, once the site of Norwegian-dominated old time fiddlers contests, was restored in 1995, "Windy Whitford and the Goose Island Ramblers" were honored as featured artists and celebrated in a souvenir program profiling the band's accomplishments.

During their final active decade, the Ramblers and their audience—still melding an old agrarian working-class base with university-educated folkies, but swollen by the children and grandchildren of the band's original followers—grew more reflective. Modestly amazed by their longevity, increasingly aware of their place within Upper Midwestern and American folk musical history, the band's members made retrospective anecdotes an integral part of their performances. As Windy told me:

> We got some great jobs. We played at Great Hall [in the University of Wisconsin, Madison, Memorial Union], for instance. Here's three little musicians. When you think about, like me, coming from the farm when I was a little kid. "Oh, I'll never be able to do this or do that. All that was for the more talented, more educated people. No I couldn't do that." And to find things happening to you, it kind of gives you a feeling of confidence, maybe, that people liked what we do. And this old grandpa that didn't want to start to play with these fellows, when we'd be at different places—like at Great Hall or up at Green Bay or down at Racine, UW-Parkside—and people would come up to me and say: "What was music like when you were a boy?" "Gee, I'm glad you asked. I'll tell you what it was like. It was Grandpa and his fiddle when I was a little kid."

As folklorists appreciative of the Ramblers' significance, Phil Martin, Richard March, and I did our best to help with the telling. In 1997, Texan Bill C. Malone, author of the definitive history *Country Music, U.S.A.* (2002a), came to live in Madison, where he soon became both the weekly host of WORT radio's "Back to the Country" and an admirer of the Goose Island Ramblers. In his most recent book, *Don't Get above Your Raisin': Country Music and the Southern Working Class*, Malone observed: "I had to move to Madison, Wisconsin, to find a survival of the kind of stage shows that once characterized country music. . . . The Ramblers do not simply perform a concert of songs; above all, they present a program of 'entertainment.'"

Linking their repertoire to the thread of comic songs running through old time country music, while connecting their raucous costumed antics with the likes of hayseed comedians extending from nineteenth-century minstrel and tent shows to television's long-running "Hee Haw," Malone could hardly miss the divergent elements that "delighted Midwestern audiences" especially: "accordion player" Bruce Bollerud's "exaggerated German accent," marked by "slurred diction" for the mock-drunken "Milwaukee Waltz"; George Gilbertsen's "'Norwegian War Chant,' improvising guttural phrases while wearing a colander to which simulated Viking horns have been attached" (Malone 2002b: 171). In conversations, Malone frequently told me that the Goose Island Ramblers reminded him most of Louisiana's Hackberry Ramblers. Led by Luderin Darbone, born like Windy Whitford in 1913, the Hackberry Ramblers merged an old time "Cajun" sound—itself a creolized gumbo of French ballads, Afro-Caribbean blues, and Central European couple dances built around the fiddle and a modified German button accordion—with the hillbilly and western swing sounds emerging in the 1930s.[16]

In the summer of 1998, the year of Wisconsin's sesquicentennial, the Goose Island Ramblers turned down an invitation to play in hot, humid Washington, D.C., for the Smithsonian Institution's annual Festival of American Folklife. Windy Whitford was slowing down at 85, so the group performed instead that August for a Wisconsin version of the folklife festival on Madison's capitol square. Throughout the late 1990s, Smokey George had admonished audiences: "If you're planning on hearing the Goose Island Ramblers, my advice is 'Don't wait too long.'" Heeding their own words, the band crowded into Jim Kirchstein's Mount Horeb living room in the summer of 1999 for a marathon final recording session, resulting in three nostalgically titled new cassettes: *The Way It Was* (KCC-1113), *Memories for Tomorrow* (KCC-1114), and *One More Time* (KCC-1115). The sound and repertoire were vintage Ramblers: old ballads ("Lulu Walls"), fiddle tunes ("Liberty Two-Step"), minstrel songs ("Alabama Jubilee"), and comic ditties ("Durham's Bull") from Anglo-American tradition; western swing and honky tonk numbers like "Bubbles in My Beer" and "Waltz across Texas"; "Honolulu March," a Hawaiian dobro tune; the Irish "Haste to the

Figure 5.5. George Gilbertsen, wearing his pseudo-Viking "bucket of horns," launches "Norwegian War Chant" on the dobro as the Goose Island Ramblers, with Windy Whitford on guitar and Bruce Bollerud on accordion, perform on the capitol square in Madison as part of Wisconsin's sesquicentennial folklife festival, 1998. Photo by Robert E. Olsen.

Wedding" and "Tom McDermott's Hornpipe"; the Scandihoovian dialect song "John Johnson's Wedding"; a spate of German and Nordic couple dances; a Mexican polka; and plenty more.

In the fall of 1999, the Ramblers played two "farewell concerts" at familiar venues: one on September 24 at Madison's Barrymore Theater, the other on October 15 at Folklore Village in the rolling hills of Iowa County—their last hurrah. Kenneth Wendell "Uncle Windy" Whitford died on June 10, 2000. He was buried in Albion's Evergreen Cemetery, not far from the Goose Island farm where he grew up. Appropriately, his visitation was on June 13 in nearby Stoughton, that Norsky fiddling stronghold where he'd played with Clarence Reierson, while his June 14 funeral shifted to Madison's Lake Edge United Church of Christ, not far from the root beer stand where he met his long-time musical partner Vern Minor, "The Lake Edge Crooner." Mourners and music filled the church where many testified to Whitford's worth during the service and reception. Few of the tributes, however, were as eloquent as his own assessment of what it was like to be a Goose Island Rambler: "You wouldn't care if you faced the king of England. You played for anybody if you felt the way I felt with those fellows."

Windy Whitford's death and the demise of the Goose Island Ramblers, occurring as they did at the dawn of a new millennium, roughly coincided with the appearance of several lavishly produced, well-publicized, and sweeping assessments of American folk music. Curiously and distressingly, the foremost among them, *American Roots Music* (Santelli, George-Warren, and Brown 2001)—composed of a public television series, a set of documentary compact disks, and an illustrated coffeetable book—mentions neither the Goose Island Ramblers, nor any group like them, nor the Upper Midwest, nor polka music ("billy's" sometime better half). Indeed the Nordic, German, and Slavic Americans populating our nation's north-central hinterlands are ignored entirely, as if they did not exist or, worse yet, were incapable of creatively participating in the richly and rightly celebrated folk musical processes exhibited by America's British, Celtic, African, French, Hispanic, Asian, and American Indian peoples.[17] The Goose Island Ramblers deserve better. Indeed their persistence, popularity, and parallels with the experiences of so many Upper Midwestern polkabillies demand a reexamination of our notion of American folk music, a new paradigm that will adequately account for the folk music that Americans actually make.

6

⌘

Canons and Cannonballs

Conservative Theories, Consensus Ideologies

> To accept the existence of folk music in the modern world requires a reformulation of many of the conservative theories that scholars and ideologues have long used to delimit folk music as a genre. (Bohlman 1988)

Folk music is a protean and elusive concept that, in simplest terms, signifies a powerful, enduring relationship between a particular cultural group and a distinctive musical style. Bound up with environment, custom, and identity, sustained through the informal interactions of performers and audiences, creatively modifying rather than unconsciously emulating external influences, folk music is fundamentally local. Nonetheless intellectuals, activists, and entrepreneurs throughout the world have repeatedly conjoined folk music with nations (Abrahams 1992: 19–29; Bronner 2002). In geographically vast, regionally diverse, culturally complex America, the homogenizing construction of what our schools, performance venues, mass media, and record companies call American folk music commenced in the nineteenth century as a succession of influential figures elevated, venerated, and celebrated certain groups, styles, and places while minimizing or ignoring others.

In 1888, 100 years prior to Philip Bohlman's welcome call for a reformulation of entrenched conceptions of folk music internationally, the pioneering American folklorist William Wells Newell articulated the beginnings of a powerful yet restrictive national vision of America's folklore—an intellectual and ideological manifesto that, particularly with regard to widely held notions of American folk music and song, prevails in the twenty-first century. In the inaugural publication of the *Journal of American Folklore,* Newell, the journal's editor and first president of the newly founded American Folklore Society, declared that "Folk-Lore in America" consists of "a. Relics of Old English Folk-Lore (ballads, tales, superstitions, dialects, etc.); b. Lore of Negroes in the Southern States of the Union; c. Lore of the Indian Tribes of North America (myths, tales, etc.); d. Lore of French Canada, Mexico, etc." (Newell 1888: 3). Far from accidental, the sequence, rhetoric, inclusions, and omissions of Newell's inventory coincided with powerful currents of thought roiling throughout his life and times.

Of English lineage, born into one of New England's wealthiest families, educated at Harvard, Newell (1839–1907) was a Unitarian minister and schoolmaster prior to 1883, when an inheritance enabled him to pursue folklore scholarship independently (Bell 1973: 7–21). Then as now, affluent urban Anglo-Protestant easterners with Ivy League degrees wielded enormous and self-interested influence in American life. In keeping with a prevailing Darwinian *zeitgeist* favoring his social class, Newell was a firm believer in his intellectual and moral superiority, in the inevitability and ultimate virtues of modernizing forces, and in the notion that folklore did, indeed must, consist of increasingly archaic "survivals," of residual cultural fragments from savage eras to be duly noted and prized for their historic curiosity even as they faded before the welcome onslaught of progress.

Just as his era's historians gave Puritans and Pilgrims pride of place as nation builders, Newell commenced his consideration of America's folklore by invoking his own kind—albeit mostly at arm's length. As Newell went on to point out, urban children might play games of ancient origin, while "belief in witchcraft lingers . . . in the neighborhoods of eastern cities," yet the words "Old English" and "relics" and Newell's subsequent commentary indicate that, rather than including his fellow refined Bostonian grown-ups, Newell associated Anglo-American folklore with youngsters, the working class, and dwellers in such hinterlands as the "remote valleys of Virginia and Tennessee" and perhaps the wilds of Maine (1888: 4). Especially in the southern Appalachians, putative "contemporary ancestors" were both ennobled for their supposedly pure Anglo-Saxon traditions and reviled or pitied as backward folk who, however reluctant they might be, must be educated (Whisnant 1983). With Cromwellian sensitivity, Newell acknowledged the American presence of "Scotch and Irish ballad singers," not for performing decidedly Scottish and Irish folk music and song, but for preserving, "in their respective dialects, songs which were once the property of the English-speaking race" (1888: 4).

"The second division of folk-lore," Newell continued in a paragraph of elaboration, concerns "American negroes . . . a race who, for good or ill, are henceforth an indissoluble part of the body politic of the United States" (1888: 5). Curiously, Newell's outline emphasized "Negroes in the Southern States of the Union," despite the abundant presence of African Americans in Boston, Philadelphia, and New York, where he spent most of his life and where the abolition movement's debates regarding race dominated public discourse, especially in the Unitarian circles that Newell frequented. Paradoxically, Thomas Wentworth Higginson's commentary on the wedding customs of black folks in Boston appeared in the first volume of the *Journal of American Folklore* (1888: 235–236).

Why American Indians were listed third and why the adjective "old" was reserved exclusively for Anglo-Americans suggest that hierarchy and authority trumped chronology and courtesy. It also bespeaks relative proximity and significance. By the late nineteenth century, American Indians east of the Mississippi River had been largely annihilated, assimilated, or "removed," to use the official euphemism for forced migration that was adopted and enacted in the 1830s during the presidency of Andrew Jackson. Largely absent from what Newell called "the Eastern States," American Indians and their folklore would have to be studied on reservations created within "the newer States and Territories." There, "for the sake of the Indians themselves, it is necessary that they should be allowed opportunities for civilization." Meanwhile, assorted schoolmasters, missionaries, bureaucrats, and proto-anthropologists and folklorists might ameliorate the losses of native peoples by capturing shards of "their picturesque and wonderful life" before it became "absorbed and lost in the uniformity of the modern world" (1888: 5–6).

Newell's final inclusion of "French Canada" and "Mexico" looks beyond the United States to consider our non-Anglophone North American neighbors, without directly referring either to the presence of Franco-American people in Louisiana for more than a century or to the far lengthier, more numerous presence of Spanish-speaking peoples in America's Southwest. Other European Americans—whether recent immigrants or the abundant and musically influential long-time citizens of German heritage—received no direct mention at all, a telling oversight at a historical moment when New England had become more Catholic than Protestant, when—particularly in urban areas—French Canadians, Irish, Italians, Portuguese, Slavs, Jews, and people of other nationalities and ethnicities outnumbered "old stock" Americans.[1] Although "Old English Folk-Lore" merited seven vivid paragraphs of elaboration, other European Americans were granted a single terse sentence: "The fourth department of labor named consists of fields too many and various to be here particularized, every one of which offers an ample field to the investigator" (1888: 6).

To his credit, Newell addressed this oversight briefly in a note published in the last number of the *Journal of American Folklore*'s first volume: "It has been shown that French and German immigrants, in Louisiana and Pennsylvania, have not only brought with them the popular traditions of their respective countries, but preserved these in a curious and characteristic form."[2] Nonetheless, Newell's schematic of the field of American folklore clearly puts Anglo Americans first and locates them in ancestral and lower-class New England, with strong connections to the South, Appalachia in particular. African Americans constitute a powerful, ineradicable Other imaginatively confined to the South, reality notwithstanding. American Indians are way out west where, with regard to folklore, they have become ghosts, spirits of the past who occasionally haunt but do not hinder their nearly civilized descendants. Asian Americans do not exist at all. And non-Anglo European Americans are at once beyond the nation's borders and "too many and various" to deserve particular notice.

In offering this summary, I do not mean to pillory William Wells Newell, who was not only very much a product of his times but also quite a liberal thinker for his era in turning his attention to the traditional arts of common people at a time when the academy was overwhelmingly and narrowly fixed on high culture. Rather, I am arguing that notions of American folklore, and by extension American folk music and song, have been constructed at particular historical moments by particular people for particular purposes.

In the late nineteenth and early twentieth centuries, chroniclers grappling with conceptualizations of American folklore, folksong, folk music, and folk dance invariably looked to New England and thence across the Atlantic to England, even when quite different realities flourished all around them. In 1889, for example, Wardon Alan Curtis graduated from the University of Wisconsin with a degree in classics, then went on to pursue a career in journalism, eventually settling in New Hampshire. His essay "'The Light Fantastic' in the Central West: Country Dances of Many Nationalities in Wisconsin," published in *Century*, a popular national magazine, in 1907 demonstrates a clear understanding of cultural pluralism as a hallmark of life in Wisconsin and in what was then regarded as "the West" (or sometimes the "Old Northwest") but is now conceived of as the Upper Midwest:

> I am speaking of Wisconsin, because it happens to be the State where I have pursued my ethnological studies, and because it epitomizes the central West. No other Western state has such a diversity of racial elements. Illinois alone, with its queer colony of Portuguese Protestants at Jacksonville, has an element which Wisconsin has not. None but Wisconsin has Bulgarians and Flemings. It has an Indian population of over eight thousand. It is the greatest Welsh, Cornish, Norwegian, and German state. It has Icelanders with Minnesota; Bohemians with Iowa; and French, Finns, and Hollanders with Michigan. The oldest and only purely Hungarian colony in America is on its soil, and the largest colony of Swiss. It has native white elements as old as the Knickerbockers, and even English-descended families who go back one hundred and fifty years on Wisconsin soil. (Curtis 1907: 571–572; reprinted in Leary 1998: 251–258)

Curtis went on to offer vivid glimpses of musical goings-on at Irish, German, Norwegian, and Swiss dances, while briefly mentioning similar events among French, Hungarians, Poles, Menominees, Ojibwes, Czechs, and Flemish Belgians. And he even sketched a typical polkabilly affair, held by the German Adolph Baumgartner in an "ill-lighted, bare old house" with Germans, Irish, Norwegians, and Yankees in attendance:

> A violin and an accordion were scraping and wheezing away in the corner and a silent mob of young people, with serious and even strained faces, were pounding painfully through a waltz, accenting the first beat of each bar with an extra hard thump of the hard thumps they were dealing the floor. (1907: 570)

Pioneering in his focus on an American region's non-Anglo European folk musical cultures, Curtis nonetheless far exceeded Newell's benign and inadvertently condescending stance to pledge allegiance to the most chilling aspects of his era's racially informed evolutionary thought, its fascination with environmental determinism, and its faith in assimilation to a purportedly superior Yankee mainstream.

In the late nineteenth century, inspired by Charles Darwin's theories of natural selection, Anglo-American social scientists posited cultural theories contending that peoples and societies evolved from simple to complex forms. They further argued that Northern Europeans, challenged by a cold climate, had achieved the height of civilization. Therefore, Nordic or Aryan peoples—prominently represented in America by so-called Anglo Saxons—were, in their estimation, clearly superior (Fredrickson and Knobel 1980: 844–845; Higham 1955). That WASP supremacy was championed by a Wisconsin Yankee from Madison in the early twentieth century is hardly a coincidence. This was, after all, the era when the region's population swelled with immigrant Catholic and Jewish Southern Europeans and Slavs and when the Great Migration of African Americans from the mid-South to Midwestern cities was waxing.

During the early decades of the twentieth century, prominent Madison intellectuals and civic organizations embraced racist evolutionary theories in the name of progressive politics. Edward A. Ross, who left Stanford in 1907 to join the University of Wisconsin faculty as a sociology professor, drew upon his subsequent Upper Midwestern experience to publish *The Old World in the New* as a contribution to then-contemporary debates regarding notions of who was or was not a true American. Maligning Italians as mentally and morally deficient, branding Jews as having "little feeling for the particular," and fretting most about "The Alarming Prospect of Slavic Immigration" (1914: 106–119, 160, 139), Ross's work has been aptly characterized as "a scholarly counterpart to the Ku Klux Klan" (Abramson 1980: 154). Indeed, Ross's xenophobia heralded the coming of considerable Ku Klux Klan activity in Wisconsin, particularly with the onset of Prohibition and jingoism following World War I. The Klan in Madison worked in coalition with several University of Wisconsin fraternities, the Young Men's Christian Association, and prominent religious and political leaders. United in their notion that "Americanization" meant conformity to Anglo Protestantism, they contrived in particular to "clean up" the Greenbush neighborhood, a hotbed of wine-drinking polkabillies which, "along with Italians of Sicilian origin . . . was the home of most of Madison's Jews and a high proportion of its small African American population" (Messer-Kruse 1993: 29).

Wardon Alan Curtis was but one of many for whom Wisconsin's population harbored potential cultural dangers which, if left unchecked, might mongrelize and debase the American populace. Not only was the state home to various supposedly inferior Indian peoples, but its population teemed with the "lowest" Europeans: Celts, Slavs, and Finns (who were, so went the logic, not true Scandinavians because their Finno-Ugric language and customs were not "Teutonic"). Moreover, even some of the state's plurality of Germans were southern German Catholics, inferior "mentally and morally," as Curtis put it, to Protestants of northern German heritage (1907: 575).

Beyond repression—through, for example, Wisconsin Yankee legislators' attempts to outlaw the customs and languages of non-Anglo Europeans—the state and nation's concerned WASPs saw two evolutionary solutions to what they perceived as the Upper Midwest's cultural problems. First, the region's healthy natural environment might, within a generation or two, mysteriously confer salubrious benefits. And second, the proximity of various "foreigners" to upstanding Yankees might spark steady imitation leading to the assimilation of succeeding generations. Consequently, Curtis remarked with scant regret that his opportunities to "study ethnology at country dances" were nearly at an end:

> In another generation, if not sooner, it will all be American. With the cessation of immigration to Wisconsin, the link with the Old World has been broken. The old tongues are heard no more. English is fast becoming the language of the churches, last stronghold of foreignism. The paper published in a foreign tongue will soon be a curiosity. The body of the central West will be of all races, but the spirit is and will remain the Americanism of Massachusetts, of fifty years ago. The genius of the New England founders of these commonwealths is still the over-soul of the central West. (Curtis 1907: 579)

It would be 30 years before another observer even conceived of mentioning *both* the Upper Midwest's "stronghold of foreignism" and the "genius of New England founders" in connection with American folk music, dance, and song.

In 1913, John Lomax simultaneously broadened and narrowed the scope of William Wells Newell's definition of "Folk-Lore in America" in an address, "Some Types of American Folk-Song," delivered to the American Folklore Society and subsequently published in the *Journal of American Folklore* (1915: 1–17). Shifting his titular rhetoric from Newell's wide-ranging consideration of folklore that, whatever its origins, might be found within the nation, Lomax emphasized "American Folk-Song"—particular songs that were bound up with and emblematic of the American experience. Although the recipient, like Newell, of a Harvard education, John Lomax (1867–1948) was born in Mississippi and raised in Texas as part of, in his words, "the *upper* crust of the po' white trash" (Porterfield 1996: 8). As a rural southerner and westerner schooled in the East, he had a hard-won larger view of the nation's cultural composition, a special fascination with the songs of cowboys and other common folk, and a firsthand acquaintance with the performances of Anglo-American, African-American, and Mexican-American folk. For John Lomax, American folksong was embodied by

> the ballads of the miners, particularly of the days of '49; the ballads of lumbermen; the ballads of the inland sailor, dealing principally with

life on the Great Lakes; the ballads of the soldier; the ballads of the railroader; the ballads of the negro; and the ballads of the cowboy. Another type, of which I would like to give examples, includes the songs of the down-and-out classes,—the outcast girl, the dope fiend, the convict, the jailbird, and the tramp. (Lomax 1915: 3)

Going well beyond Newell's limited consideration of "relics" to include newly composed or revamped songs and recognizing the contributions of workers, country folk come to town, and the era's swelling underclass, Lomax would go on to record the songs and tunes of Cajun French in Louisiana. Such canonical expansions, however, were offset by constrictions. Unlike Newell, Lomax found no place for American Indians in his consideration of American folksongs, nor were such Asian Americans as the West's numerous Chinese included; non-Anglo Europeans, except Hispanic and French Americans, were similarly neglected.

John Lomax's limited yet vigorous and prophetic vision of American folk music as a powerful creative force—rooted in ancient traditions yet expressing the experiences of rural and working-class peoples and flourishing most visibly among Anglo and African Americans—would gain a firm hold on the nation's imagination by the 1930s. In the intervening years, most chroniclers and constructors of America's nascent folksong canon shared Lomax's Anglo- and African-American preoccupation, but with a separate and often unequal emphasis. Between 1916 and 1918, traveling throughout southern Appalachia, the English folksong collector Cecil Sharp and his assistant Maud Karpeles set down nearly 300 songs and almost 1,000 tunes from performers of mostly British heritage, thus joining the "quest" of kindred intellectuals and college faculty who ventured beyond salon and ivory tower as self-described "ballad hunters" and "song catchers."[3] Most were English professors like Louise Pound (1872–1958) of the University of Nebraska, whose ambitious overview, *American Ballads and Songs* (1922), commenced with a consideration of "English and Scottish Ballads in America," then continued with an exclusive examination of Anglo-American folksongs that implicitly championed their primacy as authentic national treasures. In his unmatched assessment of the complex ways in which folklore has been employed by architects of American culture, Simon Bronner noted subsequently that Pound "excluded black folk songs, feeling that they deserved separate consideration, and without comment, she omitted immigrant traditions of non-English speakers" (Bronner 1998: 225–226). In 1922, the same year as Pound's publication, African-American folklorist Thomas Talley authored *Negro Folk Rhymes,* which was quickly followed by a spate of related books: *The Negro and His Songs* (1925) by Howard Odum and Guy B. Johnson; Dorothy Scarborough's *On the Trail of Negro Folk Songs* (1925); and Newman Ivey White's significantly titled *American Negro Folk- Songs* (1928). No one addressed the omission of American Indians and non-Anglophone immigrants. Yet, in retrospect, it is worth commenting that before, during, and well after Louise Pound's long Nebraska-based lifetime, folk musical cultures flourished among her home state's African-American, Czech, Danish, Irish, Italian, German, Russian, Mexican, Plains Indian, and Swedish peoples (Olson 1976).

The linking by prominent academicians of Anglo-American folksongs, and secondarily the songs of African Americans, with the common experience and heritage of all Americans was accentuated, beginning in the 1920s, when Robert Winslow Gordon (1888–1961) abandoned college classrooms to toil as an emissary of the federal government. A native of Maine and a ballad scholar who, like William Wells Newell and John Lomax, had studied at Harvard, Gordon was fascinated with recording technology. Throughout the 1920s, armed with a portable cylinder recorder, Gordon traversed New England, the San Francisco Bay Area, and the mountain and coastal South, recording sea shanties, old English ballads, southern Appalachian fiddle tunes, and African-American spirituals. In 1928, when the enterprising Gordon was appointed to be the first archivist of the newly formed Archive of American Folk Song at the Library of Congress, his private collection became a public legacy, while his emphasis on Anglo-American and, to a lesser extent, African-American performances as quintessentially American folksong acquired primacy and authority within what has become the nation's foremost folk culture repository.[4]

In 1933, when John Lomax replaced Gordon as the folksong archivist at the Library of Congress, the imbalance between Anglo- and African-American emphases shifted incrementally toward parity. As Archie Green, in an essay probing the historical and ideological origins of the Archive of American Folk Song, would observe at the outset:

> [A] limiting formula stunted the archive—a nativistic view of Anglo-Saxonism. Some nineteenth century collectors had used the term primarily in philological reference, but others knew it as a shibboleth for purity of race and imperialistic policy. Some ballad scholars held an imbedded belief that Anglo-Saxon lore (curiously, also tagged *Elizabethan*) was not only quintessentially American but also an antidote to Catholic, Celtic, alien, radical, or assorted dark-skinned terrors. Many New England jingoists became active in movements to restrict immigration; some opposed the rise of institutions formed by newcomers; others retreated into a state of bitter melancholy, persuaded that their America was doomed. (1985: 66–67)[5]

Back in 1910, for example, former president Theodore Roosevelt contributed a brief preface to John Lomax's *Cowboy Songs and Other Frontier Ballads*. Perhaps best remembered nowadays for his progressive opposition to corporate "robber barons," for fostering national parks, and for inspiring the birth of the teddy bear, Roosevelt was also the "Hero of San Juan Hill," a rough-riding, big-stick-wielding, muscular Christian champion of America's imperial ambitions and a guardian of WASP ascendancy. Accordingly, he commended Lomax's collection of songs from the American West to "the people of all our country" and affirmed "the reproduction here on this new continent of essentially the conditions of ballad-growth which obtained in medieval England." The opening paragraph of John Lomax's subsequent "Collector's Notes" echoed Roosevelt in conjoining England with America: "Out in the wild far-away places of the big and still unpeopled west . . . survives the Anglo-Saxon spirit that was active in secluded districts in England and Scotland even after the coming of Tennyson and Browning" (Lomax 1910: xvii). Yet as the identifier, shortly thereafter, of the more expansively constituted "Some Types of American Folk-Song" and as a field researcher who, in 1933, would embark on an ambitious recording trip throughout the American South, "Lomax knew in his bones that black and Tejano buckaroos were neither Anglo-Saxon bards nor medieval exemplars" (Green 1985: 68).

Indeed, by the mid-1930s, John Lomax, and even more so his son Alan, had come to embrace a concept of American folksong as the expression of what the elder Lomax had characterized in 1913 as "the down-and-out classes," be they black or white. It was the height of the Great Depression and, under the administration of Franklin D. Roosevelt, an array of federally funded folklorists set about capturing the nation's traditional songs and stories, not only because these materials constituted an as yet scarcely documented grassroots cultural history, but also because a common understanding of American folklore might serve to unite the nation's citizenry at a time of economic crisis that would soon be compounded by the turmoil of World War II (Dwyer-Schick 1975; Hirsch 1988). Yet, unlike his southern agrarian father, whom Alan Lomax succeeded as the archivist for the Archive of American Folk Song from 1937 to 1942, the younger Lomax was motivated by what Archie Green aptly described as "a heady mix of liberal and radical, populist and Marxist values" (Green 1985: 68). In this regard, he shared a nation-building vision with such kindred and influential federal employees as Benjamin Botkin, director of the Joint Committee on Folk Arts of the Works Progress Administration, and the ethnomusicologist Charles Seeger, head of cultural programs within the Resettlement Administration and the WPA (Hirsch 1987; Reuss 1979).

In the late 1930s and early 1940s, by then a veteran of field recording trips throughout the American South, Alan Lomax shuttled from Washington, D.C., to New York City, producing a succession of well-publicized concerts and nationally syndicated radio programs that contributed mightily to making Huddie Ledbetter, Molly Garland Jackson, and Woodrow Wilson Guthrie into what would become widely regarded as a holy trinity of American folk music and song. The African-American Ledbetter, a former field hand and prison inmate best known as "Leadbelly," knew scores of old songs and came to epitomize the creative spirit of an oppressed yet resilient people. "Aunt Molly" Jackson was the matriarch of a blacklisted Kentucky coal-mining family who fused militant union sentiments with the high lonesome sound of southern Appalachian ballads and Baptist hymns. A guitar-strumming Anglo-American westerner, singing witty, incisive, socially conscious songs in a Will Rogers drawl, "Woody" Guthrie embodied the battered but cheerfully defiant Dust Bowl refugee.[6] Working with Woody Guthrie and Pete Seeger—the self-taught banjo-picking son of

Charles Seeger who was beginning to wed folksongs with activist involvement in labor and civil rights movements—Alan Lomax imagined an American folksong anthology, *Hard-Hitting Songs for Hard-Hit People* (1967), that would add an eloquent plea for cultural equity to his father's sympathy for the nation's beleaguered blacks and working-class WASPs. More than any other figures, whether working individually or collectively, Alan Lomax, Pete Seeger, and Woody Guthrie performed, produced, and inspired an American folksong revival that would dominate the nation's popular music from the late 1950s through the early 1960s and that persists to the present.[7]

Yet not all folk performers recorded during the New Deal era—whether by federally funded or independent field researchers—were citizens of the Deep South, the Appalachian mountains, and the Great Plains. And even in those areas, stellar non-Anglo European performers might easily be found. Indeed, given America's actual cultural composition, it should not be surprising that the folklorists laboring variously in the 1930s and early 1940s for the Archive of American Folk Song, the Farm Security Administration, the Federal Writers Project, the Resettlement Administration, and on their own encountered non-Anglo European traditional musicians aplenty. For example, besides gathering the songs of African-, Anglo-, Cajun-, and Hispanic-American cowboys, farmers, and laborers in the Lomaxes' native Texas, the seldom cited and largely forgotten William Owens recorded the Lone Star state's Czechs, Germans, Italians, and Swedes performing both old country pieces and proto-polkabilly songs and dance tunes.[8] Meanwhile, in the perpetually neglected Upper Midwest of 1937, Sidney Robertson captured the songs and tunes of French-Canadian, Finnish, Lithuanian, Norwegian, Polish, Serbian, Scots Gaelic, and Swiss performers in the Chicago area, Minnesota, and Wisconsin (Hickerson 1982: 73). But as Joseph Hickerson pointed out during a 1976 conference assessing the "neglected heritage" of "ethnic recordings in America": "On the federal level, there was some reluctance at first to publicize the recordings of foreign-language singers in the United States. Congressional philosophy was not strongly pluralistic, and the melting-pot persuasion was prevalent" (Hickerson 1982: 77).

Nor were attitudes much different among nongovernmental yet politically active champions of American folk music and song. Although pervasive right-wing attempts to harness folksong to the nativist Anglo-Saxon cause—notably Henry Ford's anti-jazz square dance campaign and the whites-only White Top Folk Festival orchestrated by the Ku Klux Klan–affiliated Virginia composer John Powell—had largely faded by the late 1930s, the Left espoused a stance very much in keeping with the American Communist party's embrace of a more mainstream Popular Front, which regarded folksong as the expression of the masses and "Communism as 20th Century Americanism."[9] With regard to folksong, however, "Americanism" might have been defined by Wardon Alan Curtis, since it was juxtaposed with "foreignism" in a national context. While singers on the Left might demonstrate international solidarity by singing in Spanish, for example, to commemorate the sacrifices of Abraham Lincoln Brigade members who fell fighting Franco's fascists, their songs concerning the conditions of American life evoked piney mountains, levee camps, and lone prairies. Highly influential groups like the Almanac Singers, formed in 1939, featured Pete Seeger, Woody Guthrie, and Alan Lomax's sister Bess, with Alan sometimes offering advice and support. Performing chiefly in northern cities to working-class folk of diverse backgrounds, "the Almanacs fused the essence and excitement of rural Southern string bands with the passion of labor song and the dry, clever wit of New York's cabarets" (Cohen and Samuelson 1996: 77). Inspiring legions of college students in the years to come, the Almanacs nonetheless, as Pete Seeger's biographer David Dunaway ironically observed, performed most often for ethnic working-class audiences in New York "that might know jazz, Yiddish, or Slovak tunes better than Appalachian ones" (Dunaway 1981: 118, 92). Dunaway might have invoked any number of other ethnic groups as well, including Finns, who at the time enjoyed the polkas, waltzes, and schottisches of Viola Turpeinen in their New York City workers' halls, while singing along to the politically charged, American-centered, mixed-language songs of Finnish-American Wobbly organizers and sympathizers T-Bone Slim (Matt Valentine Huhta), Arthur Kylander, and Hiski Salomaa.[10]

In 1997, Stephen Wade collaborated with Rounder Records and the American Folklife Center at the Library of Congress to produce a retrospective compact disk, *A Treasury of Library of Congress Field Recordings*, drawn from various annotated albums of 78rpm recordings originally released beginning in 1941 by the Archive of American Folk Song. The 30 performances included nearly equal numbers of African and Anglo Americans, supplemented by an Irish miner from Pennsylvania, two American Indians from Oklahoma (one Creek, the other Kiowa), and a Louisiana Cajun. Except for New Yorker Learned Hand, who was a Supreme Court justice based in Washington, D.C., at the time of recording, the other singers hailed from Virginia, North Carolina, Alabama, Mississippi, Tennessee, Kentucky, Arkansas, Oklahoma, and Texas. Not surprisingly, the CD's back cover offered a familiar, authoritative pronouncement:

> Since 1928, Library of Congress fieldworkers have gathered thousands of American folksongs in farmhouses, prison barracks, and schoolrooms across the nation. Researchers traveled the back roads of the Delta, the Appalachians, and the Great Plains using battery-powered disc-cutting machines as they ventured beyond the grid of rural electricity. Here are thirty of the greatest performances from the legendary Library of Congress recording series, lovingly selected, annotated, and remastered. This *Treasury* is an extraordinary collection of America's folk voices, a State of the Union circa 1941.

Once again, "the Delta, the Appalachians, and the Great Plains" constitute "the nation." Once again, "American folksongs" and "America's folk voices" do not include all of the songs, all of the voices, all of the people. Once again, conservative theories and consensus ideologies have been advanced by a well-meaning, well-positioned individual working in collaboration with a venerable public institution and a respected commercial media company.

No wonder that Bernard Johnson—an old time polkabilly fiddler from southwestern Wisconsin who mingled Anglo-Celtic, Czech, and Norwegian traditional tunes—chose these words when revealing the scope and limitations of his repertoire to me in 1989: "There's folk music. I never tried to play that."[11] I have often wondered what William Wells Newell, Robert Winslow Gordon, Louise Pound, John Lomax, Alan Lomax, and many more would have made of Bernard Johnson's innocent response to their considerable intellectual legacy, to the paradox of a thoroughgoing American folk musician's alienation from the concept of his nation's "folk music"? Knowing what I do of their lives and thoughts, I like to think that they would have abandoned their elegant, streamlined notions for a messier but truer vision of American folk music and song. Indeed, Alan Lomax almost did exactly that.

Fieldwork Forgotten: Alan Lomax Goes North

Alan Lomax, who died in 2002 at 87, was eulogized appropriately as the world's most influential chronicler of and advocate for folk musical traditions.[12] An award-winning writer, radio producer, and filmmaker, a fraction of whose astonishing field recordings from all over the world occupy more than 100 compact disks in Rounder Records' current Alan Lomax Collection series, Lomax "discovered" or popularized such icons of American roots music as Leadbelly, Jelly Roll Morton, Aunt Molly Jackson, Woody Guthrie, and Muddy Waters in the 1930s and 1940s. And in the 1950s, while in England, his broadcasts over BBC radio introduced American hillbilly and blues genres to leading exponents of England's "skiffle" movement, thus laying the groundwork for rock's British "invasion."[13]

Few if any associate Lomax even remotely with America's Upper Midwest, non-Anglo European-American performers, and creolized polkabilly sounds. Indeed for seven decades, as a prominent and prolific intellectual who never forgot his Mississippi and Texas roots, Alan Lomax wielded tremendous influence in canonizing and publicizing his home territory's folk music as quintessentially American folk music. In recent years, techno wizard Moby, guitar-slinger Rory Block, Hollywood filmmaker turned blues documentarian Martin Scorsese, and many more have sampled, covered, and dramatized Lomax's southern recordings especially. Most successfully, perhaps, Minnesota's Coen brothers opened their film *O Brother, Where Art Thou?* and its accompanying soundtrack album with a remake of "Po' Lazarus," Lomax's 1959 recording of a Mississippi chain gang (2000 M).

But as a folklorist raised amid all sorts of complicated, compelling Upper Midwestern musical traditions, I have long wondered what might have happened had Alan Lomax been raised in Ishpeming, Eau Claire, or Eveleth. In 1976, while working on the mall in Washington for the Smithsonian Institution's summer-long Bicentennial Festival of American Folklife, I gaped in outraged disbelief at an immense national map looming above the "Regional America" stage. Reproduced from Alan Lomax's classic *Folk Songs of North America* (1960), the map was shaded to indicate musical regions and festooned with place names invoked in songs. Although names abounded in the East, the South, and the West, the Upper Midwest was terra incognito. Complete voids yawned in Iowa and the Dakotas, while the only place dotting Wisconsin was, erroneously, Northfield—as if that Minnesota city, sung about in "The Bandit Cole Younger," had been heisted across the border by the bank-robbing James gang.

Soon after, poking through archival collections at the Library of Congress and the State Historical Society of Wisconsin, I was amazed to learn that Alan Lomax, woeful geography notwithstanding, actually made field recordings in the Upper Midwest. Years later, I'm convinced that, had it not been for a combination of accident and ideology masquerading as historical fact, the Upper Midwest might have occupied a significant chapter, along with the South and all other regions, in the story of American folk music. A small part of that larger story emerged in the late 1930s against the backdrop of the Roosevelt administration's efforts to end hard times, face the threat of war, and unite the nation's people.

In the fall of 1938, 23-year-old Alan Lomax—a veteran of forays in Haiti and throughout the American South—crossed into Wisconsin on a field trip for the Archive of American Folk Song. He had been on gravel back roads for more than two months in a car with bad brakes, its trunk weighed down by a massive battery-powered acetate-disk recorder. Wending his way from Detroit through lower Michigan, then across the Straits of Mackinac to the Upper Peninsula, he recorded "about a thousand songs, lumberjack, lake sailor, Irish, Southern Negro, Finnish, Serbian, Polish, Canadian French, German, Hungarian, and Croatian" (Lomax 1939: 220). He might also have mentioned Lithuanian, Slovenian, Swedish, and Ojibwe performers since they too were coaxed to perform. On October 15, short on funds, beset by pressing responsibilities elsewhere, his fragile stock of blank disks nearly exhausted, Alan Lomax confided in a postcard sent from Ironwood, Michigan, to his Washington boss, Harold Spivacke, "I'm tired as hell and ready to come home."[14]

With one last burst of energy, he crossed the border into Wisconsin, traveling an hour west to the Bad River Ojibwe Reservation. Throughout the nineteenth century, Woodland Indian peoples, affected by the fur trade and logging, had learned fiddle tunes from French and Irish immigrants, sometimes fusing them with their own performance traditions. Menogwaniosh Anakwad (1849–1911), known as George Cloud, was one such fiddler; his son, Joe, was another. Lomax penciled "(A), Joe Cloud, No. 1" on the paper sleeve of a disk. As it spun, he set the scene in the sonorous drawl that would charm national audiences on CBS a year later:

These fiddle tunes are being recorded by Joe Cloud in Odanah, Wisconsin, on October 16, 1938, for the Archive of American Folk Song in the Library of Congress. Mr. Cloud is fifty-three and has the blood of the Chippewa Indians flowing in his veins. He has played the fiddle since he was fifteen years old and learned to play from his father, who was also a fiddler. He plays entirely by ear. (Cloud 1938 M)

At once familiar and mysterious, Cloud's tunes—the well-known reel "Devil's Dream," the "Red River Jig" with its asymmetrical or "crooked" metís phrasing, a pair of Ojibwe "squaw dances" usually played on the big drum—exemplified the creative synthesis that is Upper Midwestern folk culture.[15] Nearly a half century would pass before anyone else recorded the like.

Alan Lomax's foray into unfamiliar geographical, cultural, and musical territory was prompted by Sidney Robertson, prior to her marriage to the noted composer Henry Cowell. Born in San Francisco, trained at Stanford and in Paris in Romance languages and music, Robertson (1903–1995) was part of a movement in the 1930s that combined progressive politics with an antiauthoritarian aesthetic vision embracing both folksong and the musical avant garde. In 1936, following a year as director of the Social Music Program of the Henry Street Settlement School on New York City's Lower East Side, she worked for the federal Resettlement Administration and, subsequently, the Farm Security Administration. Her boss and mentor, prominent ethnomusicologist and activist Charles Seeger, regarded the sustenance of folk music traditions as essential to the well-being of the Depression's dejected and displaced peoples. Hence, in the late 1930s, Sidney Robertson made field recordings, while assisting with folk festivals and related public programs.[16]

She was particularly active in 1937, recording Finnish kantele players and Croatian tamburitzans from Minnesota's Mesabi Iron Range, as well as lumber-camp ballad singers and fiddlers from northern Wisconsin. Her Upper Midwestern efforts resulted in collaborations with the Works Progress Administration's Wisconsin Folklore Project, based at the State Historical Society of Wisconsin, the fledgling multicultural National Folk Festival, and the Archive of American Folk Song in the person of Alan Lomax. In May 1937, with Charles and Dorothy Moulding Brown of the State Historical Society of Wisconsin's museum, Sidney Robertson helped to shape Chicago's Fourth Annual National Folk Festival. Thanks largely to Robertson and the Browns, over the next decade the National Folk Festival included numerous performers from the Upper Midwest: Finns from the Minnesota Iron Range and Scandinavian dancers from Minneapolis; Wisconsin's Winnebago (Ho-Chunk) singers and dancers, New Glarus Swiss yodelers, a French chanteuse from Oconto, Norwegian psalmodikon players from McFarland, Milwaukee's Polish dancers, and Rice Lake's Wisconsin Lumberjacks with their accordion/string band/polkabilly melding of French, Irish, metís, Norwegian, Swiss, and Yankee repertoires.[17]

Sidney Robertson's May 1937 recordings of the Rice Lake troupe particularly intrigued Alan Lomax. Influenced by a brawny, mostly-male notion of American folk music and song championed by his father, Alan was seeking broader regional coverage and a better understanding of loggers as he

Figure 6.1. The Wisconsin Lumberjacks pose prior to their participation in the National Folk Festival in Chicago. (*Back row, left to right*): Earl Schwartztrauber, snare drum; Frank "Frenchy" Uchytil, cigar box guitar; J. H. Wallis, mayor of Rice Lake. (*Front row, left to right*): Otto Rindlisbacher, Swiss button accordion; Iva Rindlisbacher, Viking cello; Ray Calkins, cigar box guitar (aka the "Paul Bunyan Harp"), Rice Lake, Wisconsin, 1937. Author's collection.

worked toward publishing *Our Singing Country* (1941). In May 1938, when the Wisconsin Lumberjacks came to Washington as part of the moveable National Folk Festival, Lomax recorded them for the Library of Congress. The Lumberjacks were led by Otto Rindlisbacher (1895–1975). Born to Swiss immigrant musicians, he played Swiss tunes on a button accordion. There were also Norwegians aplenty in Rice Lake, including newly emigrated piano accordion virtuoso Thorstein Skarning. Otto and his wife, Iva, toured with Skarning from 1911 to 1921, performing both "alpine" and Norwegian dance tunes. He eventually made and mastered the nine-string Norwegian Hardanger fiddle and, since Rice Lake was a logging town and Otto's Buckhorn Tavern a woodsmen's hangout, he naturally played four-string fiddle, favoring French-Canadian, Celtic, and "Indian" fiddle tunes of the sort Menogwaniosh Anakwad and Joe Cloud played in lumber camps (Leary and March 1996: 17–20).

By May 1938, Alan Lomax had formed plans for his own Upper Midwestern recording trip. Sidney Robertson, after returning to Washington in late 1937, had moved home to launch the WPA's California Folk Music Project. The field was open. On June 9, 1938, Harold Spivacke, chief of the Division of Music, wrote to the librarian of Congress recommending approval of Alan Lomax's request for $965 to cover the expenses of a two-month trip "to record folk songs for the Archive" in "the Lake States—Michigan, Wisconsin, and Minnesota."

Invoking Robertson, on July 1 Lomax dutifully wrote to Charles Brown, director of the State Historical Society of Wisconsin's museum:

> The Archive of American Folk Song is planning for this summer a rapid recording survey of folk music in Michigan, Wisconsin, and Minnesota. This work is to be done by a modern field recording machine, with the idea in mind of getting down in the most accurate fashion the folk tunes and the folk styles of the region, for preservation and scholarly study. (Lomax 1938)

Briefly acknowledging his acquaintance with Sidney Robertson, Brown responded 10 days later:

> I am much pleased to learn that you are planning to undertake some recordings of folk tunes and styles in Wisconsin during the present summer. . . . I have shown your letter to Mrs. Dorothy Moulding Brown, who is the folklore authority in our state and has labored in that field for some years. She thinks we have something for you in lumberjack, Norwegian, Swiss and other songs and fiddlers, key-harp, salmodikon, horn, and other players on rare and old time instruments which you will like to record. (Brown 1938)

Although a distinguished archaeologist with a long-standing enthusiasm for folktales, Charles Brown had a limited grasp of folk music traditions. Likewise, there is scant evidence that his wife, Dorothy Moulding Brown, who was then steadily publishing admirable essays on Woodland Indian legends in *Wisconsin Archeologist*, had much more to offer.

In contrast, Sidney Robertson's response was far more specific, full of helpful leads and wry, unfettered observations based on her own tireless fieldwork. On June 14, 1938, she wrote:

> Dear Alan: Hastily: Of course, go to Michigan, Wis. and Minn. with my blessing. . . . Go see Dr. Brown, U. of Wis., head of Wis. Hist. Soc. He goes in for pamphlets about Wis.'s glorious hist. for the kiddies, but by now the WPA project he sponsored, headed by Gregg Montgomery, may have unearthed some real river singers. When I was there Mrs. Montgomery promised me names of people around LaCrosse but never came across with 'em, I think because she decided to keep Wis. stuff in her own hands. However, mostly she seemed to busy herself with copying Wis. songs out of books. . . . Southwest of Madison, Wis. about 15 miles is a town containing a gent named Slam (not Sam) Anderson. He runs a clothing store filled with Norwegian chests and antiques upstairs, and can direct you to the psalmodikon singers . . . Norwegians. . . . Please do make a date ahead with Charles and Bob Walker, Crandon,

Wis. . . . old timers up there, the real stuff. . . . I'm green with envy, you must know! I love the Iron Range country in Minnesota, but Wisconsin simply has my heart. . . . Drop in on L. G. Sorden, Farm Security Administration, Rhinelander, Wis. He was to look out for singers for me, and is a peach of a guy. . . . He's the man who inquired on my third trip to Crandon whether I'd found any men living with their wives yet in that town. . . . I don't wish you any hard luck, but I can't help sort of hoping that you get so fascinated by Minnesota and Michigan that you'll sort of skip Wisconsin! (Robertson 1938)

Robertson was prophetic, but not because Wisconsin failed to fascinate. Quite the contrary. Lomax had too much good luck in Michigan, neglecting Minnesota entirely and managing but a brief border crossing from Ironwood to Hurley and Odanah, Wisconsin.

Michigan's Upper Peninsula particularly charmed Lomax. In 1946, folklorist Richard Dorson spent five months roaming what locals call "dah U.P.," straying briefly, like Lomax, into northern Wisconsin. There Dorson, the leading American folklorist of his generation, discovered what he would call "one of the richest storytelling regions in the United States." The preface to his *Bloodstoppers and Bearwalkers* exclaimed, "the abundance and diversity of the oral traditions I found still stagger me" (Dorson 1952: 1). Dorson's enthusiastic remarks echoed those made eight years earlier by Alan Lomax after his efforts in the very same area:

The Upper Peninsula of Michigan proved to be the most fertile source of material. After six weeks of recording a mass of lumberjack, Finnish, and French folk-songs, I felt that there was enough material in the region for years of work. Near Newberry, Munising, Greenland, and Ontanogan, it was comparatively easy to find lumberjack singers. Everywhere through the Copper Country and south of it, Finnish singers generously furnished me with more material than I had time to record. And in Champion and Baraga I found French ballad singers who still enjoy[ed] ballad fests that lasted all night. (Lomax 1939: 221)

While plenty of these 1938 performers actively sustained old country songs and tunes, just as many were crossing and dissolving musical borders, thereby appealing creatively to the polyglot of peoples that thronged the region's house parties and halls.

On the Bad River Ojibwe Reservation, where immigrant and indigenous loggers mingled, the aforementioned Joe Cloud accordingly fiddled crooked metís tunes, with their synthesis of Ojibwe melodies and French and Irish jigs, while bowing out women's dance pieces instead of beating the rhythm on a hand drum. In Posen and Metz, a Yankee, Irish, Polish, and north German settlement in northeastern lower Michigan, Lomax's field recordings reveal not only thoroughgoing Polish tunes, but also square-dance pieces played by Tony Strzelecki in a skittery, syncopated, improvisatory musical dialect fusing the *wiejska,* or village fiddling, of rural Poland with the string-band tradition of Anglo and Irish Americans: "The Irish Washer-woman," "Weevily Wheat," "Devil's Dream" (AFS 2312A1–3), and "Turkey in the Straw" (AFS 231B2). Alongside their old country Polish ballads, Lomax captured the Romel Brothers' version of a well-known immigrant song, "W Żelaznej Fabryce" (In a Steel Mill), with its mixed-language account of abuse from an Anglo-American foreman: "*Jak on godamuje, roboty nie rzuc'*" (Even though he "goddamns" me all the time, I'm not going to throw the job away).[18] Likewise, the Lewandowski Sisters, kin to local fiddlers Philip and Casimir "Cash" Lewandowski, sang Polish duets, but were also faithful listeners to Chicago's WLS "Barn Dance." Their dialect-inflected, tightly harmonized take on Gene Autry's cowboy-pop hit "Gold Mine in the Sky" sounded like the Girls of the Golden West by way of western Poland (AFS 2320A1).

Michigan's Upper Peninsula yielded a number of equally eclectic polka-billy sounds that cut across and combined many cultural elements in characteristic regional fashion. Such lumber-camp singers as Nils Larson and Bert Graham of Newberry treated Lomax to different versions of "Ay Ban a Svede from Nort' Dakota" (AFS 2341A1 and 2345B1), a fractured-English comic ballad known throughout the Upper Midwest, concerning an immigrant farmhand's misfortunes when he ventures to "Mannasota" to experience "da big state fair."[19] Meanwhile, the repertoires of Baraga's otherwise decidedly French performers included several hybrid as well as distinctly Anglo-Celtic songs and tunes. Among them were Edward King's French rendering of Jimmie Rodgers's "Mother the Queen of My Heart," complete with yodeling (AFS 2447A); Mose Bellaire's "As I Went Out Walking One Fine Summer Evening" (AFS 2444B1); and Exilia Bellaire's "I Went to Marquette" (AFS 2442B1). Mose Bellaire's song, known in Ireland as "Rocking the Cradle," is the lament of a father tending his child while its mother goes out "to a ball or a party." Abandoning the French-Canadian intonations marking his erstwhile speech and song, Bellaire shifted for his performance to the decidedly Irish "woods singing" then common in the region's lumber camps.[20] Exilia Bellaire's "I Went to Marquette," referring to a nearby city in the Upper Peninsula, is known as "I Went to Market" among northeastern Wisconsin's Walloon French. Alternating French and English lyrics, it chronicles the misadventures of a country child come to shop in town.[21] Similarly, Fred Foucault played fiddle tunes from diverse sources. The titles Lomax noted were "French Polka," "Rocky Road to Dublin," "French Clog," "Devil's Dream," "Scotch Tune," and "Old Mother Flanagan" (AFS 2409B–2410A3).

The Finns whom Alan Lomax recorded in the western U.P. performed unaccompanied vocals and solo instrumentals on button accordion, German concertina, harmonica, and Finnish *kantele*. Predictably, they offered dance tunes, darkly comic plaints of farmworkers, ballads concerning figures like the "Finnish Robin Hood," hymns, and other survivals of old country pedigree. Their collective repertoires, however, brimmed with remarkable instances of musical fusion of the sort Lomax encountered among the region's Ojibwes, Poles, and French. The *kantele*-plucking lay preacher Pekka Aho, for example, sang a Finnish-language version of the Anglo-Protestant gospel standard "Abide with Me" (AFS 2388A). Spurning the *kantele*'s harplike strains, Emil Maki borrowed the tune of the "Battle Hymn of the Republic" and snatches of its "Glory, glory hallelujah" chorus to conjoin bitterly opposed Lutheran "church Finns" and socialist "hall Finns" in heaven, where they all might enjoy a friendly beer as accordions played (AFS 2334B1). Frank Maki acquired tune and sentiment from cowboy balladry's "When the Work's All Done This Fall" to express the feelings of a Finnish merchant seaman from Savo far from his sweetheart (AFS 2363B). And Kusti Similä mixed Finnish and English to transform the World War I anthem "It's a Long Way to Tipperary" into a lament for his home in Eveleth on Minnesota's Iron Range, which was sung and scatted over a button accordion's push-pull (AFS 2392B2, 2393A1).

In the aftermath of his Upper Midwestern foray, Alan Lomax would publish texts and tunes of the English-language lumber-camp and Great Lakes songs he recorded, while several of these were also included on such Library of Congress recordings as *Songs of the Michigan Lumberjacks* (AAFS L56). His brief 1939 comments on Michigan's French singers, however, were his last published word on the subject, while the region's Finnish performers merited only a terse sentence in a popular essay that appeared a year later in *The American Girl*: "I remember one Finnish singer in the Middle West, from whom we were recording a song about a Finnish Robin Hood" (Lomax 1940; reprinted in Cohen 2003: 51). The Polish, Ojibwe, and other cultural groups were all but forgotten, as was the striking, pervasive presence of creolized, regional polkabilly songs and tunes.

Yet Alan Lomax can hardly be faulted for missed opportunities. Leaping from the ruts of an intellectual Chisholm Trail that he helped to establish would have required a good deal more experience, perspective, and effort. Few others were doing similar work at the time. And folk music fieldwork—whether undertaken as an independent, an academic, or a government employee—is never unaffected by the larger political economy. Once back in Washington at 1938's end, Alan Lomax was compelled by other work. The war in Europe was under way, with America increasingly involved. Amid a growing war effort, the underfunded Archive of American Folk Song required broad-based public support to survive. From 1939 to 1940, Alan Lomax wrote and directed "American Folk Songs," a popular American School of the Air radio series surveying English-language folksongs from the archives' holdings. By 1941, joining with the head of the Library of Congress's Music Division, Harold Spivacke, to contend that the Archive of American Folk Song was a defense-related institution worthy of increased funding, Lomax undertook a series of war-related folksong radio projects that would eventually bring him to the Office of War Information. Following World War II, he left government employment entirely to become, among other things, director of folk music for Decca Records. Eventually his involvement with the left-wing People's Songs and the 1948 Progressive party presidential campaign of Henry Wallace resulted in his inclusion in *Red Channels*, a handbook compiled by conservative witch-hunters bent on purging "un-American" Americans from the nation's media. Having established connections with England's BBC radio during World War II and contracted by Columbia Records to produce a multi-LP World Library of Folk and Primitive Music, Lomax left for London in 1950 (Filene 2000: 145–158, 161–163; Gregory 2002: 137–138, 163). By the time he returned, eager to do fieldwork throughout his native South, 20 years had passed since 1938. His Upper Midwestern experience must have seemed a long way off.

Furthermore, while in Europe, Lomax developed a fierce disregard for the accordion, an instrument central to the Upper Midwest's characteristic sound. His anti-squeezebox stance echoed a succession of critics who, despite erstwhile solidarity with rural and working-class peoples in Old and New Worlds, imagined a golden age of unsullied folk authenticity that had been polluted by machines and mass production. Invented in the late 1820s, widely marketed by the 1830s, the accordion had become a global instrument by the mid-nineteenth century. Portable, relatively inexpensive, loud enough to be heard above the stomp of dancers, possessing a right-hand row of buttons for articulating melody, a left-hand row for bass notes and harmonizing chords, and a familiar reedy voice, the accordion allowed a player to meld with fiddles, wind instruments, and percussion or to serve as a compelling one-man band. What's more, although real command of the instrument required special talents and considerable experience, rank novices could quickly learn to push-pull an acceptable tune or two. No wonder that the instrument was embraced by farm and factory hands throughout Europe; by sailors and city folk worldwide; by Germanic, Nordic, and Slavic immigrants from the Upper Midwest to the Pacific Northwest; and by blacks, Cajuns, and Chicanos across the South from coast to coast.[22] And no wonder that it was decried throughout Europe by ensembles of established musicians who found themselves displaced, and by romantic intellectuals whose senses rebelled at change. Declaring the accordion the "arch enemy of folk music," an early twentieth-century Finnish opponent declared: "Do not dance to the screeching, insidious accordions. Burn them."[23] In 1907, the Swedish composer Hugo Alfvén was equally shrill and emphatic. "Chop up all the accordions that come in your way, stamp them to a jelly, cut them into pieces and throw them into the pigsty, because that is where they belong!"[24] Folk musicians everywhere ignored their admonitions.

Prior to his transatlantic fieldwork, Alan Lomax had encountered button accordionists among the "black French," or Creole peoples, of southwestern Louisiana. Huddie Ledbetter too played one-row button accordion, in addition to his more-celebrated twelve-string guitar, in the years immediately after his encounters with the Lomaxes. Yet, as Jared Snyder has pointed out, Leadbelly's squeezebox "merited only a passing mention in John Lomax's biography of the singer and not one query in Alan Lomax's extensive interview for the Library of Congress. His instrument was regularly mislabeled as a concertina, the equivalent of labeling a banjo as a guitar or an organ as a piano."[25]

In 1954, assisted by the ethnomusicologist Diego Carpitella, Lomax made a series of recordings throughout Italy that resulted in a volume of Columbia's series World Library of Folk and Primitive Music. Preferring that Europeans maintain more ancient musical traditions associated with fiddles or bagpipes and referring, in accompanying album notes, to the accordion as "this pestiferous instrument," Lomax argued that "during the nineteenth century the accordion has done . . . severe damage to the old folk music of Central Europe."[26]

Perhaps the many-stranded Upper Midwestern polkabilly sounds he encountered in 1938—sounds that paralleled developments in Europe but also resonated with the exciting cross-cultural fusions that so dazzled him throughout the American South and West—were associated with dinning accordions and dismissed? Yet, were it not for the combination of historical forces, accident, and ideology, perhaps the subsequent work of Alan Lomax, the folk revival, and even our larger understanding of American folk music might have been quite different. Instead, despite having urged superiors, in a 1938 letter from Michigan's U.P., "that I be sent back to the area next summer," and despite having added extravagantly that it might be "the most interesting country I have ever traveled in," Alan Lomax never completed what he had imagined only a few months before as a "rapid recording survey of folk music in Michigan, Wisconsin, and Minnesota."[27]

Beyond the Front Door

The guitar- and banjo-maddened folk revival, the popularity of blues and bluegrass performers on college campuses, the emergence of rock 'n' roll out of the rootsy musical interplay of southern blacks and whites, and the growth of public and academic folklore programs combined throughout the 1950s and beyond to foster a broadly recognized, little-challenged consensus that Anglo- and African-American traditions truly constituted American folksong. Any curiosity that might have existed during that era about the folk music of non-Anglo Europeans in the Upper Midwest may well have been discouraged by the region's most nationally prominent musical performer, Lawrence Welk, a figure who has come to be regarded in American popular culture as the antithesis of roots music. In 1951, Welk—a German-Russian accordionist hailing from rural North Dakota, who was by then the leader of a veteran road band based in Los Angeles—launched what would endure as the nation's longest-running musical variety program, "The Lawrence Welk Show." Although ever-mindful of his polkabilly roots, Welk established a boilerplate "champagne music" sound that was a far cry from the Goose Island Ramblers' sonic shot-and-a-beer boilermaker. Like the upwardly mobile South Texas *orquesta* exponents who both prettified and rejected working-class conjunto music, Welk strayed from crossroads and neighborhood barrooms to high-tone ballrooms, favoring sweet jazz and even sweeter pop played, sung, and danced to by trim, prim, conventionally attractive, conservatively groomed, perpetually smiling performing members of the Welk "family," a sort of Mickey Mouse Club musical fantasy for adults.[28] Their occasional highly orchestrated, homogenized, and idealized representations of accordion-based polkabilly music, sprinkled amid a preponderance of hit parade standards, embraced the bland aesthetics of toothpaste commercials and smiley-face ad campaigns.

To be sure, by the 1970s especially, as civil rights and ethnic revitalization movements proliferated, many folklorists and ethnomusicologists increasingly acknowledged the sustained, inescapable presence of varied folk culture traditions within American life. Yet they were, and to a large extent continue to be, considered chiefly as discretely bounded and sometimes stagnant pools rather than as tributaries ebbing and flowing into one another and up against the nation's musical mainstream. Dissenting voices arguing for a synthetic, inclusive approach to what constitutes America's folk music and song were few and far between.

In the mid-1970s, on the occasion of America's bicentennial, Richard K. Spottswood produced Folk Music in America, a series of LP recordings each accompanied by an informative, illustrated booklet. *Dance Music: Reels, Polkas, & More* (vol. 4), *Dance Music: Ragtime, Jazz, & More* (vol. 5), and *Songs of Migration & Immigration* (vol. 6) were particularly noteworthy for selecting and interrelating a broad array of cultural traditions, including those of Scandinavians and Slavs, that are essential to a fully informed understanding of the nation's folk music.[29] Most recently, in 2002, Kip Lornell substantially revised his 1993 textbook, *Introducing American Folk Music,* and added a new subtitle, *Ethnic and Grassroots Traditions in the United States,* which partially reflected increased attention to the creolized Germanic, Scandinavian, Slavic, and Woodland Indian sounds common within and beyond the Upper Midwest.[30] Five years earlier, Lornell had heralded his expansive and revised vision of American folk music with an anthology, *Musics of Multicultural America* (1997), coedited with Anne K. Rasmussen, that considered the hybrid, evolving musical traditions of Arab, Czech, Japanese, Jewish, Hispanic, Tohono O'dham, and West Indian Americans, as well as indie feminist punk rockers, alongside the more familiar roots sounds of Anglo and African Americans.

The Lornell-Rasmussen anthology was reviewed appropriately by the prominent ethnomusicologist Bruno Nettl, who many years before had been the proverbial lone voice crying in the wilderness. Writing in *Ethnomusicology* in the fall of 1999, Nettl raised and answered a critical rhetorical question regarding accepted notions of American folk music:

Are we still at it, or have we come a long way? To both, yes. We are still trying to define American musical culture; define it as both melting pot and cultural mosaic. And we must continue. But we have here a book unlike anything we have seen in the past. In reading it, I am reminded of a day, forty years ago, when the distinguished folklorist Richard Dorson urged me to write a book about American folk music that took in more than the English-Scottish-Irish heritage. He thought it an offbeat notion, but it made sense to me; living at the time in Detroit, where the English professor Thelma James had long, to widespread scholarly astonishment, been collecting the stories and recipes and descriptions of rituals from the ethnic communities of her students at Wayne State University. So I did as bidden and published, in 1961, a very brief survey of traditions extant in the USA, with two chapters on non-Anglo immigrants (*An Introduction to Folk Music in the United States*). Despite its many mistakes and limitations it was received kindly, and yet astonished students and colleagues often asked how I could claim that the songs of Hungarians in Cleveland, the hymns of the Amish, the music of my Syrian neighbors in Detroit could be as truly American as "Barbara Allen" and "The Jam on Gerry's Rock." But the suggestion was there, and it is surprising that it should have taken forty years for it to be taken up in a more comprehensive treatment that looks at the music of [the] USA in what strikes me as a realistic way—a collection of traditions. The many syntheses and historically-oriented textbooks on American music of the last decades have continued to see a unicultural tradition with the occasional bow to African American and Native American music. (Nettl 1999: 557–558)

Perhaps matters might have been different had Nettl not adorned his cover with an accordionist during a guitar- and banjo-dominated era, but I doubt it. As Nettl went on to say:

In 1961, it was conventional to look at "folk" traditions, to emphasize the "authentic," to look for ways in which immigrants from Europe had maintained purity, had provided examples of "marginal survival." We have come a long way, as *Musics of Multicultural America*, by contrast, emphasizes traditions that interact with each other and with mainstream popular music, and shows what the American environment has done to the musical cultures that have been brought. We have on hand a work that presents a more realistic picture of what musical life in America is (and has been) like than the traditional histories of American music, or the surveys of folk music. (Nettl 1999: 558)

In alignment with Nettl, Lornell, Rasmussen, Spottswood, and a handful of others, I have tried, throughout this book, to offer a realistic picture of musical life in America's Upper Midwest, and to relate that regional part to the national whole.

Despite their status as sainted local practitioners of a widespread polkabilly sound, the Goose Island Ramblers, the genre they exemplify, and their home territory have been largely ignored within the most widely recognized considerations of American folk music. The performers of "Oscar's Cannonball" have not figured in the nation's canon. And yet they belong. Their absence, the ignoring of kindred polkabillies, and the neglect of Upper Midwesterners generally require nothing less than a reassessment of what constitutes American folk music.

Indeed, the musical lives of the Goose Island Ramblers—decidedly Upper Midwestern, multicultural, *and* inescapably American—argue for a more inclusive, fluid notion of American folk music, one that exchanges ethnic hierarchy for egalitarianism, one that stresses process over pedigree, one that emphasizes the creolized experiences that unify diverse participants in common musical scenes. Nor are the experiences of the Goose Island Ramblers and their fellow Upper Midwestern polkabillies unique within American life. They resonate with the funk and ferment of the intercultural musical exchanges that have reverberated in New York and New Orleans, in logging camps and mining locations, over airwaves and through cyberspace, in all of those places that have never been isolated bastions of monocultural purity (if such places ever existed)—thoroughgoing American places where consistently rootsy, constantly evolving, and wildly combinatory musical experiences constitute *the* American folk musical norm.

As I interviewed Windy Whitford in the final decade of his life, he wondered about the fate of the musical legacy he had created with fellow Goose Island Ramblers:

> Things have a way of happening, don't they? They twist you around and you get affiliated with people that you never dreamed that you— just like you and I sitting here talking now. What do you s'pose ever made this really materialize? [Leary: Lotta things.] Like George says, "Our music only goes to the front door." Now when I talk to people like you, our music and our reputation, or whatever it is—of playing old country songs and that—is gone on beyond the front door. It gets out in the world to you and you're going to spread it to other people, and other people are going to hear it. Now maybe it will live forever?

I hope so.

Timeline
Significant Dates Involving and Affecting
the Goose Island Ramblers

1839   Windy Whitford's maternal great-grandfather Horace Bliven settles in Wisconsin.

1849   Birth of Charles Squire Smith, Whitford's fiddling and fife-playing grandfather.

1853   Joen Hansen Bollerud and Berte Hanson Ensrud, Bruce Bollerud's great-grandparents, emigrate from Norway to settle near what would become Hollandale, Wisconsin.

1880   Birth of Gertrude Bell Smith, old time ballad singer and Windy Whitford's mother.

1888   American Folklore Society is formed. William Wells Newell's definition of "Folk-Lore in America" ignores the Upper Midwest and non-Anglo Europeans generally.

1890   The Norwegian dialect song "Ole Olson, the Hobo from Norway" is circulating in Upper Midwestern oral tradition.

1893   The German concertina and the bandonion are featured as imported musical instruments at Chicago's Columbian Exposition.

1894   Gertrude Bell Smith begins compiling a notebook of old time songs. Joseph Kekuku develops the Hawaiian guitar.

1896   Ben Venden, Bruce Bollerud's fiddling maternal grandfather, emigrates to Wisconsin from Valders, Norway.

1907   Wardon Alan Curtis describes the performance of a Wisconsin polkabilly band in the national magazine *Century*.

1913   Birth of Kenneth Wendell "Uncle Windy" Whitford on February 25 in Albion, Wisconsin. John A. Lomax's address concerning "Some Types of American Folk-Song" stresses African- and Anglo-American contributions.

1917 Hawaiian guitarist Jack Penewell of Stoughton, Wisconsin, debuts in vaudeville. The Swedish immigrant singer Hjalmar Peterson, aka Olle i Skratthult (Ole from Laughtersville), records the bestselling song "Nikolina."

1921 Windy Whitford takes up the fiddle.

1922 Louise Pound's *American Ballads and Songs* focuses exclusively on Anglo-American folksongs.

1924 Chicago's WLS radio launches its Saturday evening "Barn Dance" program. Whoopee John Wilfahrt begins broadcasting "Dutchman" music on WLAG, Minneapolis.

1925 Birth of George Karsten "Smokey George" Gilbertsen on September 28 in the town of Blooming Grove. The Moser Brothers, Swiss immigrant performers who toured throughout Wisconsin, make their first 78rpm recordings for Victor.

1926 Henry Ford–sponsored fiddle contests proliferate in the Upper Midwest. Whoopee John records his first 78s for Okeh.

1927 Whitford begins to play with Clarence "Fiddlesticks" Reierson.

1928 The Dopyera Brothers invent the dobro.

1929 Whitford tunes in Chicago's WLS "Barn Dance" and is inspired to take up guitar by the singing and playing of Bradley Kincaid.

1931 Whitford plays on Janesville's WCLO with Harv Cox's Muleskinners and on Madison's WHA with George Matson.

1932 George Gilbertsen begins to play his brother Jim's guitar and harmonica.

1933 Whitford tours northern Wisconsin with Harv Cox's Montana Cowboys; Freddie Fisher forms the Schnickelfritz Band; the Hoosier Hotshots join the WLS "Barn Dance."

1934 Birth of Bruce Bollerud on October 8 in Hollandale, Wisconsin; Whitford plays with the Lonesome Cowboys on WIBU; Gilbertsen begins playing at house parties; Prohibition ends, and tavern dances commence.

1935 Whitford begins a two-year stint with Mickey's Ranch Hands.

1937 Whitford teams with Vern Minor to found the original Goose Island Ramblers; Slim Jim and the Vagabond Kid, "Scandihoovian" radio singers, are at the height of their popularity.

1938 Alan Lomax records polkabilly musicians in Michigan and Wisconsin for the Archive of American Folksong at the Library of Congress.

1939 Whitford unsuccessfully seeks Oscar Mayer radio sponsorship; Gilbertsen takes up Hawaiian guitar, begins playing at Madison's Spanish Village tavern, joins the Bearcat Mountain Boys.

1941   Gilbertsen joins the Fox River Valley Boys.

1942   Gilbertsen takes up mandolin and fiddle.

1944   The Goose Island Ramblers become the Balladeers.

1945   Bollerud acquires a used bandonion, begins playing with fiddler Herman Erickson.

1946   Whitford's record of "My Blue Eyes Have Gone," intended for Gene Autry, is destroyed; Gilbertsen forms a duo with Hawaiian guitarist Jack Penewell.

1948   Gilbertsen joins Madison's WKOW as a staff musician, wins Wisconsin's Centennial Fiddlers Contest, plays on the "Ted Mack Original Amateur Hour," and tours with the Dakota Roundup; Slovenian polka band leader Frankie Yankovic is crowned "America's Polka King" at a Milwaukee ballroom; Yogi Yorgesson, composer of "Mrs. Johnson, Turn Me Loose," begins his recording career on Capitol.

1950   Bollerud makes a do-it-yourself 78 of "Soldier's Joy" and "Life in the Finnish Woods," joins Gilbert Prestbroten's Rhythm Ramblers, a Dutchman/Scandinavian hybrid band.

1951   Bollerud joins Emil Simpson's Nite Hawks, plays Czech, German, Norwegian, and Polish tunes. The "Lawrence Welk Show" debuts on Los Angeles television.

1954   Bollerud plays with two Yankovic-inspired Slovenian bands, first in one led by Roger Bright and then in one led by Verne Meisner.

1955   "Chmielewski Funtime," the Upper Midwest's most enduring polkabilly television program, begins its nearly half-century run on Duluth's WDSM.

1958   Bollerud joins the Dick Sherwood Band, favoring a Norwegian and country repertoire.

1959   Gilbertsen plays with four-string banjoist Leo Aberle.

1960   The Fendermen record "Muleskinner Blues" for Sauk City, Wisconsin's Cuca Records. It becomes a number 5 national hit on the Billboard charts and establishes the Cuca studio.

1961   Bollerud teams with the rockabilly-oriented Johnson Brothers, cuts a 45 on Cuca, and begins playing at Glen and Ann's tavern in Madison; Bruno Nettl publishes *An Introduction to Folk Music in the United States* with an accordionist on the cover.

1962   Gilbertsen joins Bollerud and Eddie Rivers at Glen and Ann's.

1963   Rivers departs; Whitford joins Bollerud and Gilbertsen to form the second coming of the Goose Island Ramblers.

1964 The Goose Island Ramblers record three and a half LPs for Cuca Records in Sauk City.

1970 The Goose Island Ramblers move to Johnny's Packer Inn when Glen and Ann's tavern is sold and becomes the blues- and soul-oriented Nitty Gritty.

1975 The Goose Island Ramblers temporarily call it quits.

1976 Folklorist Phil Martin and documentary photographer Lewis Koch begin field research with the Goose Island Ramblers.

1977 The American Folklife Center at the Library of Congress convenes a conference on "Ethnic Recording in America: A Neglected Heritage."

1982 The Ramblers are featured in a retrospective program produced by Madeline Uraneck for Wisconsin public radio.

1990 The Goose Island Ramblers commence a final decade of performance, while making a new recording, *Midwest Ramblin'*.

1994 The Ramblers perform in the "Europe in America" segment of the Folk Masters series produced by Smithsonian Institution folklorist Nick Spitzer at the barns of Wolf Trap just outside Washington, D.C.

1995 The Ramblers are guests of honor at the restored Stoughton Opera House, site of old time fiddlers' contests from the 1920s through the 1940s.

1997 The Goose Island Ramblers baffle a Heritage Awards panel at the National Endowment for the Arts, Washington, D.C.

1999 The Ramblers perform a series of "farewell concerts" and record three new cassettes on the Cuca label.

2000 Death of Kenneth Wendell Whitford on June 10.

2001 The public television series, coffeetable book, and multiple CD series *American Roots Music* ignores the Upper Midwest, polka musicians, and hybrid polkabilly performers.

2006 Bruce Bollerud continues to play regular jobs with the Good Times Band, while sometimes teaming up with George Gilbertsen and Herbert Swingen, formerly of the Nite Hawks, to recreate the polkabilly sounds of their youth.

Glossary

Ballad. A song that tells a distinct linear story through a series of verses. Traditional or folk ballads, existing in many versions, were widespread in Europe at the time of immigration to the Upper Midwest and flourished in the region.

Bandonion (sometimes spelled "bandoneon"). A bellows-driven instrument with square-shaped left-hand bass and right-hand treble reed chambers controlled by buttons. Invented by and named for Heinrich Band in Saxony in the 1840s, the bandonion became a major instrument in Argentinean tango music in the twentieth century. Its Upper Midwestern exponents were Germans, Swiss, and a few Norwegians.

Bass horn (aka "brass bass"). Vernacular term for the tuba, the essential bass instrument in Upper Midwestern Bohemian (Czech) and Dutchman (German) polka bands.

Bohemian polka band. Bohemia is a German term for Cechy, nowadays the Czech Republic. Czechs and ethnic Germans from Czech realms established brass and reed "wind" orchestras throughout the Upper Midwest in the mid-nineteenth century. In the 1920s, through the innovations of performers like Romy Gosz of Manitowoc, Wisconsin, Bohemian bands added drums and either a piano or piano accordion to form dance bands favoring polkas, waltzes, and ländlers.

Boomba. Also known as the "boombah," "boombas," "stump fiddle," "stumpf fiddle," and "Paul Bunyan fiddle," this mostly percussive instrument consists of a broomstick outfitted variously with a bell, pie plate, wood block, washboard, and bicycle horn. Played with a drumstick, the boomba derives from pre-Lenten noisemakers widely played throughout Central and Northern Europe since medieval times. In the Upper Midwest, they have been part of tavern revelries, polka festivals, and the kitchen bands of senior citizens.

Bull fiddle. A string bass or bass fiddle.

Button accordion. Sometimes referred to as a "button box" or simply a "box," this bellows-driven instrument has rectangular-shaped left-hand bass and right-hand treble reed chambers. Treble reeds are controlled by buttons arranged in as few as one and as many as four rows, with each row corresponding to a different key. Just as a harmonica yields one note

189

on exhalation and another on inhalation, the buttons of a button accordion produce a given note on the push, while the pull offers the next highest note of a major scale. Invented in Germany in the 1830s, button accordions were not only inexpensive, portable, and learned with relative ease, but they also allowed a single performer to combine melody, harmony, and rhythm. Not surprisingly, button accordions entered many folk and vernacular traditions in the nineteenth century and remain significant in such contemporary American styles as Cajun, zydeco, conjunto, Czech, and Slovenian.

Circle two-step. A "mixer" wherein two-step–dancing couples, circling a dance floor in counterclockwise fashion, heed a bandleader's command to "change partners." Typically, the men stay in place, while the women join with the dancer behind them; then with the call "Everybody two-step!" dancing resumes until the next call to change partners.

Czech polka band. See Bohemian polka band.

Dialect song. A comic narrative song concerning some American immigrant's misadventures, rendered in slightly exaggerated "broken English" but often sprinkled with "foreign" words. In the Upper Midwest, dialect songs circulated in oral tradition, in print, and through sound recordings concerning Finnish, German, Italian, Norwegian, Slovak, and Swedish immigrants.

Dobro. A wood-bodied, steel string guitar, outfitted with cone resonators in the sound chamber and typically played on one's lap with finger picks. Invented by and named for the Dopyera Brothers (Do-Bro) in the late 1920s, the dobro originally figured in Hawaiian bands and nowadays is found chiefly in bluegrass and old time country bands.

Dutchman polka band. As Anglicizations of Deutsch (German), "Dutch" and "Dutchman" have been common terms for Germanic Americans since the eighteenth century (e.g., "Pennsylvania Dutch"). In the 1920s, Minnesota Germans Hans Wilfahrt ("Whoopee John") and Harold Loeffelmacher founded influential dance bands featuring the rhythm of drums and a romping tuba in support of polka, waltz, schottische, and ländler melodies carried by a German concertina and a combination of trumpets, saxophones, and clarinets. When Loeffelmacher named his band the Six Fat Dutchmen in 1934, others emulated both the sound and the name. Since that time, scores of Upper Midwestern bands, building upon the style established by Wilfahrt and Loeffelmacher, have called themselves Dutchmen.

Eight banger. The invention of Madisonian Harry Gillingham, this one-of-a-kind eight-stringed instrument, played with a cello bow, was composed of a mandolin neck affixed to the body of a conventional fiddle.

Electric toilet plunger. An intentionally foolish "novelty" instrument resembling one-stringed fiddles and the African-American "diddly bow" (a wall-mounted single string), this Harry Gillingham invention involved fastening an electric pickup and a steel string to a common toilet plunger, or "plumber's friend."

English concertina. Invented by the Englishman Charles Wheatstone in the

1830s, this diminutive bellows-driven reed instrument (about the breadth of a large hand) has been popularly associated with sailors and nowadays plays a central role in the English country dance revival.

Fiddle tune. A generic term for mostly Anglo-American instrumental tunes played on the fiddle. Arising in the late eighteenth and early nineteenth centuries, these tunes—typically jigs, reels, and hornpipes—consist of two sections or strains, each of which is played twice in succession, with the performance persisting for as long as dancers and musicians prefer. English, Irish, Scottish, and French-Canadian fiddlers especially brought such fiddle tunes to the Upper Midwest's cities, rural communities, and lumber camps.

Four-string banjo. Lacking the shortened fifth "drone string" of African-derived and bluegrass-associated five-string banjos, the four-string plectrum banjo entered Upper Midwestern dance band instrumentation via late nineteenth-century ragtime, minstrel show, and parlor traditions. By the 1920s, the four-string tenor banjo especially was a common rhythm instrument in Dutchman and Slovenian polka bands, as well as in Norwegian country bands.

Galop. A dance to a fast polka tempo during which couples do not turn, but bound vigorously from one side of the floor to the other in a manner suggestive of a horse's gallop.

Gammaldans. Literally "old dance," this Norwegian term, in wide use among Norwegian Americans, refers to such old time nineteenth-century couple dance tunes and steps as the polka, the waltz, and the schottische.

German concertina. Similar in shape and construction to the bandonion, but lacking that instrument's tonal range, the German concertina—sometimes called the Chemnitzer concertina after the Saxon city where it was invented in the 1830s—was introduced to the Upper Midwest in the 1880s. In the 1920s, it became a central instrument in the region's Polish and Dutchman polka bands, and in the twenty-first century such concertinas continue to be made by small manufacturers in Illinois, Wisconsin, and Minnesota.

Hardanger fiddle. Named for Norway's Hardanger region and that nation's most revered instrument, the Hardanger fiddle, or *hardingfele,* is distinguished by four or five strings inserted beneath a raised bridge. When the four strings atop the bridge are bowed, the sympathetically tuned unbowed strings below resonate. Featuring fancifully carved lion's head scrolls and decorated with pearl inlay and floral patterns drawn with India ink, Hardanger fiddles were widely played and made by Norwegian immigrants to the Upper Midwest, where a Hardanger fiddle association remains active today.

Hoppwaltz. An old time Norwegian-American polka, with "hopp" referring to the polka's characteristic hop-step.

Jubilee songs and singers. Disdaining the sometimes racist comic hokum of minstrel shows, African-American jubilee singers were especially active on Upper Midwestern vaudeville and Chautauqua tent show circuits in the late nineteenth and early twentieth centuries, performing a mixture of "Negro spirituals" from the days of slavery and "jubilee" songs of emancipation in harmonizing quartets.

Kujawiak. A Polish couple dance in waltz time, which involves side-by-side walking steps and slow turns underneath one another's joined hands.

Ländler. This mid-nineteenth-century alpine dance is especially favored by Upper Midwesterners of Austrian, Bavarian, Bohemian, and Swiss descent. Commencing with an opening measure dominated by airy clarinets, the ländler has fancy turning moves which few dancers know. Since ländlers are fundamentally waltzes, most dancers are content executing characteristically twirling waltz steps.

Mazurka. A mid-nineteenth-century dance of Polish origin that spread throughout Europe and became particularly popular among Norwegian fiddlers in the Upper Midwest. Performed in ¾ time, at a slightly slower pace than the waltz, this dance involves sliding steps, promenades, and turns.

Metís fiddle tunes. Fiddle tunes played by European-Native (metís) peoples— typically French, Scottish, or Irish intermarried with Menominee, Ojibwe, or Potawatomi—that exhibit irregular phrasing, odd numbers of strains or sections, and extended introductions and endings resembling the melodic and rhythmic patterns of Woodland Indians' songs and drumming.

Minstrel show. A variety show composed of music, dance, songs, and skits performed initially by white male performers blackening their faces in imitation of southern blacks. In the post–Civil War era, black performers—sometimes dubbed "Ethiopian minstrels"—were also active. Minstrel shows toured throughout the Upper Midwest through roughly the 1920s, popularizing many songs and tunes throughout the region.

Norwegian country band. Although significant numbers of Norwegian immigrants and their descendants played Hardanger fiddles, far more favored four-string fiddles. By the late nineteenth century they were blending *gammaldans* repertoires and old country string band tunes with the jigs, reels, and related fiddle tunes of their English, Irish, and French neighbors. In addition, goofy dialect songs concerning rubes come to town, plaintive Norwegian songs of the homeland, and fervent Lutheran hymns all paralleled the style and sentiments of southern hillbilly performers. By the 1920s, Norwegian country bands emerged as a ubiquitous, distinctive Upper Midwestern polkabilly phenomenon.

Oberek. A Polish couple dance in ¾ time, but played at a faster tempo than the waltz.

Piano accordion. An early twentieth-century innovation, popularized chiefly by Italian Americans, the piano accordion essentially replicates a piano's keyboard, with all of the sharps and flats, allowing a squeezebox player to perform in any key. Widespread throughout the Upper Midwest as a solo instrument and as part of many local combos, the piano accordion became the major instrument in the Slovenian polka style established by Frankie Yankovic and others beginning in the late 1930s.

Polish polka band. From the mid-nineteenth century through roughly the early 1930s, Upper Midwestern Polish dance bands were typically composed of some combination of fiddles, a clarinet, and a bowed bass or cello. German concertinas entered the mix gradually, and by the late 1930s drummers and trumpet players became increasingly common. In the post–World War II era, performers like Chicagoan Walter Jagiello ("Li'l Wally") established a modern Polish polka band sound featuring a melodic concertina augmented by twin trumpets, a clarinet embroidering the melody, and a rhythm section composed of a booming electric bass and busy drumming patterns accented by rimshots.

Polka. Performed by a couple executing a hop-step close-step pattern in 2/4 time, this dance emerged around 1830 in a Germanized Czech region near the Polish border. Within a decade, the polka had claimed the allegiance of dancers in Europe and America, and it was one of several couple dances commonly known among Upper Midwestern immigrants of diverse backgrounds. In the 1920s, as European-American dance bands formed, many came to be called "polka bands," despite the fact that they played a broader repertoire of dance tunes.

Schottische. A German dance from the 1840s created in romantic emulation of Scottish dancers, the schottische features running steps, hops, and twirls by couples. It is especially popular in Upper Midwestern communities where German and Nordic peoples settled.

Slovenian polka band. Since the late 1930s, Slovenian polka bands in Milwaukee and the Lake Superior region have favored an instrumentation of twin piano accordions, an occasional tenor saxophone, string bass, and four-string tenor banjo. Typically, one accordion carries the melody, while the other plays rapid staccato improvisations, sometimes echoed by a saxophone. The string bass and banjo, played percussively with a pick, carry the rhythm for fast polkas and moderate waltzes.

Tamburitza. A lute-like stringed instrument introduced by Ottoman Turks into the Balkans. In the nineteenth century, Croats and Serbs especially formed tamburitza orchestras, which they sustained upon immigration—particularly in such urban, industrial cities as Pittsburgh, Cleveland, Gary, Chicago, and Milwaukee.

Two-step. A couple dance in 2/4 polka tempo, but with a sliding step instead of the polka's characteristic hop-step.

Waltz. A whirling couple dance in 3/4 time that originated in Austria in the early nineteenth century and, like the polka, was a basic dance well known to European immigrants upon their arrival in the Upper Midwest.

Waltz quadrille. A waltz with variations performed within quadrilles, or squares, of two couples each, with dancers alternately waltzing and joining hands to promenade at a caller's behest.

Zweifacher. German for "two forms," this couple dance typically alternates slow waltz and fast polka tempos, thus adding variety to an evening's dancing.

Recordings Issued by the Goose Island Ramblers

A Session with the Goose Island Ramblers (1964, LP, Cuca Records K-1110)

"Bird of Paradise"
"Run for the Roundhouse, Nellie"
"Jesse James"
"Bring Me Back My Blue Eyed Boy"
"Kickin' My Dog Around"
"Wreck of the Old 97"
"Beer Barrel Polka"
"My Blue Eyes Have Gone"
"Shut the Door"
"Talking Blues"

From Bluegrass to Russian Gypsy (1964, LP, Cuca Records K-1111)

"Mountain Dew"
"Oscar's Cannonball"
"Francuszka Polka"
"Milwaukee Waltz"
"Orange Blossom Special"
"The Letter Edged in Black"
"Going Back to the Hills"
"Great Speckled Bird"
"Two Guitars"
"Mrs. Johnson, Turn Me Loose"
"Goose Island Stomp"
"Crepe on the Little Cabin Door"
"Black Mountain Rag"
"Norwegian War Chant"

Doin' the Hurley Hop (1964, LP, Cuca Records K-1112)

"Hurley Hop"
"Nikolina"
"Katinka"
"Way Downtown"
"On the Beach at Waunakee"
"Methodist Pie"
"Cigarettes, Whiskey and Wild Women"
"March of the Little Tin Dodo"
"Old Joe Clark"
"Barney McCoy"

*Velkommen Til Stoughton Den Syttende Mai (1965, LP, Cuca
    Records K-2010)*

"Paul paa Haugen"
"Anna Marie"
"Ole Olson, the Hobo from Norway"
"Stegen Vals"
"Sentimental Selma"
"Nottero og Koster Vals"
"Ryerson [*sic*] Vals"

*Midwest Ramblin' (1990, cassette, Wisconsin Folk Museum;
    reissued on compact disc, 2004, Center for the Study of
    Upper Midwestern Cultures CSUMC 001)*

"Going to the Packer Inn"
"In Heaven There Is No Beer"
"Reierson's Two-Step"
"No Norwegians in Dickeyville"
"Swiss Yodel Waltz"
"Wendy's Schottische"
"Scratch Your Nose Polka"
"I Worked for a Farmer"
"Black Mountain Rag"
"Streets of Laredo"
"Brother"
"Dream of the Miner's Child"
"Abner Juve's Waltz"
"Kukavica"
"Break Song"
"Old Wampus"
"Sauerkraut Polka"
"Have Pity on Me"
"Milwaukee Fire"

"Victory Cannonball"
"Ballad of JFK"
"Chris's Waltz"
"Tobacco Setter's Waltz"
"Avoca Polka"
"Good Morning Judge"
"Auction paa Strømmen's"
"Clover Blossoms"

Best of the Goose Island Ramblers (1994, compact disc, Cuca KCD 1100)

"Hurley Hop"
"Nikolina"
"Old Joe Clark"
"Methodist Pie"
"Cigarettes, Whiskey and Wild Women"
"On the Beach at Waunakee"
"Wreck of the Old 97"
"Mrs. Johnson, Turn Me Loose"
"Mountain Dew"
"Oscar's Cannonball"
"Francuszka Polka"
"Milwaukee Waltz"
"Orange Blossom Special"
"Going Back to the Hills"

There's No Norwegians in Dickeyville (1994, cassette, Cuca KCC 1110)

"There's No Norwegians in Dickeyville"
"Ryerson [*sic*] Two-Step"
"Norwegian War Chant"
"Going Back to Old Virginia"
"Hurley Hop"
"Chinese Breakdown"
"Dear Old Southern Home"
"Spanish Two-Step"
"Francuszka Polka"
"On the Beach at Waunakee"
"Wreck of the Old 97"
"Milwaukee Waltz"
"Faded Love"
"Mrs. Johnson, Turn Me Loose"
"Oscar's Cannonball"
"Run for the Roundhouse, Nellie"
"When the Work's All Done This Fall"

"I'm Going Back to the Hills"
"Sweetheart, I'm Sorry"

The Way It Was (1999, cassette, Cuca KCC 1113)

"The Wreck of the Titanic"
"Fiddle Medley: Liberty Two-Step, Two-Step in G, Texas High-Step"
"Jambalaya"
"Willie, My Darlin' Come Back"
"I've Still Got a Crush on You"
"Rosalita"
"Sugar Hill"
"Harmonic Waltz"
"Waltz across Texas"
"Who Broke the Lock on the Hen House Door?"
"Durham's Bull"
"Behind the Swinging Doors"
"When the Stars Begin to Shine"
"Swing Fiddle Rag"
"Seasons of My Heart"
"When the Roses Bloom Again for the Bootlegger"
"George's Finnish Polka"
"Goofus"

Memories for Tomorrow (1999, cassette, Cuca KCC 1114)

"A Flower Blooming in the Wildwood"
"Old Timer's Waltz"
"Newberry Polka"
"Puttin' on the Style"
"Bubbles in My Beer/My Confession"
"John Johnson's Wedding"
"Never Take No for an Answer"
"Honolulu March"
"Alabam'"
"Blue Ridge Mountain Home"
"Sage Brush Shuffle"
"Gary's Polka"
"My Old Pal of Yesterday"
"Sakkijarven Polkka"
"Smokey's Favorite Norsk Waltz"
"Fiddle Medley: Soldier's Joy, Big Eared Mule, Turkey in the Straw"
"Wabash Blues"

One More Time (1999, cassette, Cuca KCC 1115)

"Red Rooster Two-Step"
"Beaumont Rag"

"Corrida #1"
"Who Will Walk Her Tonight in the Heather?"
"Selma's Waltz"
"Prisoner's Song"
"Wicky Wacky Wicklow"
"Right or Wrong"
"Lulu Walls"
"Tom McDermott's Hornpipe"
"Life in the Finnish Woods"
"There Is a Spot in My Heart for You"
"Alabama Jubilee"
"Styrman's Waltz"
"Clarinet Polka"
"Fiddle Medley: Maggie in the Woods, Haste to the Wedding"
"Hand Me Down My Walking Cane"

*All the Songs from the Barrymore Concert 1999 (1999, two
    compact discs, Cuca KCD 1116)*

CD 1

"Goin' to the Barrymore (Packer Inn)"
"Dream of the Miner's Child"
"Die Lustige Holzhacker Bua"
"Red Rooster Two-Step"
"When the Work's All Done This Fall"
"Mrs. Johnson, Turn Me Loose"
"Irish Medley: Irish Washerwoman, Tivoli Jig, Rakes of Kildare, Scotland the Brave"
"San Antonio Rose"
"Styrman's Waltz"
"Sauerkraut Polka"
"Sugar Hill"
"Sakkijarven Polkka"
"When the Stars Begin to Shine"
"Mauii Chimes"
"There's No Norwegians in Dickeyville"
"Reierson Two-Step"
"My Confession/Bubbles in My Beer/Rosalita"
"Picture on the Wall"
"Way Downtown"
"Fiddle Medley: Soldier's Joy, Big Eared Mule, Turkey in the Straw"
"Break Song"

CD 2

"Beaumont Rag"
"A Flower Blooming in the Wildwood"
"Hurley Hop"

"Sage Brush Shuffle"
"Jambalaya"
"George's Finnish Polka"
"I've Still Got a Crush on You"
"Wreck of the Old 97"
"Milwaukee Waltz"
"Oscar's Cannonball"
"Corrida #1"
"Who Broke the Lock on the Hen House Door?"
"Ole Olson, the Hobo from Norway"
"Norwegian War Chant"
"Maggie in the Woods/Haste to the Wedding"
"The Wreck of the Titanic"
"There Is a Spot in My Heart for You"
"Cigarettes, Whiskey and Wild Women"
"Sweetheart, I'm Sorry"
"Will the Circle Be Unbroken"

Notes

Chapter 1

1. For a succinct, informed consideration of Robert Zimmerman's self-invention as Bob Dylan, particularly in relation to constructions of American folk music prevailing in the 1950s and early 1960s, see Filene (2000: 205–232). For an imaginative, often murky, yet stimulating treatment, see Marcus (1997: ch. 4). Dylan tells his own story best (2004).

2. Alan Lomax characterized bluegrass as "folk music with overdrive" in the title of an essay published by *Esquire* (1959). Rosenberg (1985) offers the genre's most comprehensive history, with Smith (1965) serving as a pioneering short introduction and Malone (2002: 322–367, 541–550) offering the most reliable recent overview.

3. In *Escaping the Delta: Robert Johnson and the Invention of the Blues,* Elijah Wald contends that prevailing notions of African-American music in the South might also be reassessed so as, among other things, to account for musicians like the black fiddler Howard Armstrong—an eclectic musician whose experiences and repertoire are not that different from Bob Andresen's. Born in 1909, Armstrong grew up in LaFollette, Tennessee, alongside children of immigrant German, Italian, and Polish miners, from whom he learned both languages and tunes. Settling in Chicago in the 1930s, he played in black neighborhoods, but also where Irish, Italians, Germans, and Bohemians made their homes. His CD *Louie Bluie,* companion to Terry Zwigoff's eponymous film, includes not only assorted rags, stomps, drags, and blues, but also the Czech polka "Barushka" (*Baruška*) and the German "*Du Du Liechst [Liegst] Mir im Herzen*" (Armstrong 1985 M). As Wald, who spent several years as Armstrong's accompanist, points out:

> He always prided himself on being able to play whatever job came along, which meant that he mastered the whole square-dance repertoire, plus a full night's worth of Italian or Polish favorites, since his corner of eastern Tennessee had a large immigrant population from these countries. He can sing sentimental Gene Autry numbers, play an elegant guitar arrangement of "Stardust" with all the fancy jazz chords in all the right places, and toss off a handful of Hawaiian and Mexican songs. (2004: 53–54)

4. Biographical information on Bob Andresen comes from a 1994 tape-recorded interview conducted by the author and from a memorial essay by Pine and Nusbaum (1995). Andresen's voluminous musical collection is now

201

housed at the University of Wisconsin's Mills Music Library, an inventory of which is online at http://music.library.wisc.edu/Andresen/Andresen.htm.

5. While a great deal has been written about barn dances and old time music on southern radio stations (Malone 2002a: 486–487), we lack a comparably rich, systematic treatment of the eclectic sounds that flourished in the Upper Midwest. Studies of WNAX in Yankton, South Dakota (Hagerty 1975), and KSTP in St. Paul (Barfuss 1983) offer a beginning, as does a brief overview, "Early Midwestern Radio Barn Dances," which keys on WLS in Chicago and WHO in Des Moines (Patterson 1975). The Co-op Shoppers that Bob Andresen mentions featured accordion, fiddle, clarinet, and piano. In addition to playing in Fargo, they also had a show across the border in Moorhead, Minnesota, on KVOX (Barron 1987: 30). Andresen interviewed the former radio singer Famous Lashua at the latter's home in Mountain Iron, Minnesota, in 1983. For more about Don Messer, arguably the most prominent Canadian fiddler of the mid-twentieth century, whose radio and television broadcasts encompassed both Franco- and Anglo-American tunes, see Rosenberg (1990). See Greene (1992: 151–153) regarding Ernest Iverson (Slim Jim) and his brother and frequent musical partner, Clarence (aka the Vagabond Kid).

6. The Wildwoods' "foreign" or "ethnic" tunes were especially well known in the Upper Midwest and also often recorded on 78s in the early twentieth century. See their abundant presence in the discographies of Gronow (1977) and Spottswood (1990). The 1942 country song "Blue Eyes Crying in the Rain" was soon rendered into Croatian and recorded on a 78 by the Dunav Tamburitza Orchestra for the Chicago area's Balkan label (*Stare I Dobre* c. 1977 M). The tune has been widely played in the Lake Superior region for 50 years and was recorded by the Gogebic Range Tamburitzans (c. 1980 M).

7. Otto Rindlisbacher's lumber-camp tunes, recorded in 1941 for the Archive of American Folk Song at the Library of Congress, may be heard on Rounder Records' *Folk Music from Wisconsin*, a reissue of an earlier Library of Congress LP. For a sketch of Rindlisbacher's life and a sampling of his Swiss and Norwegian tunes, see Leary and March (1996: 17–20, program 4).

8. Studies of American folk music and of folk music generally have been characterized by conceptions of the music and musicians as emanating from distinct, usually ethnically or racially defined, cultural groups who have long associations with particular places. To the contrary, however, Philip V. Bohlman has argued that the forces of modernization collapse time, space, and community to form a thriving sonic "marketplace," a sort of "bazaar for the confluence of musical repertoires and the exchange of musical concepts" (Bohlman 1988: 124). Mark Slobin has similarly called for a greater understanding of the "micromusics" made by "subcultures," while emphasizing consideration of the complex ways in which individual musicians form bands to interact with each other and their often eclectic audiences (Slobin 1993: 98–108). Encouragingly, a small section of the massive volume of the *Garland Encyclopedia of World Music* devoted to "The United States and Canada" (Koskoff 2001) concerns "Border Crossings and Fusions," while including an account by Beverly Diamond of "Intercultural Traditions on the Canadian Prairies" (342–345) that comes very close indeed to describing Bob Andresen's and, as we shall see, the Goose Island Ramblers' musical experiences of frequent, varied, intercultural musical exchanges in public, ethnically neutral sites accessible to a plurality of peoples.

9. Succinct profiles of various ethnic groups nationally and within the Upper Midwest may be found in Thernstrom (1980), while Zelinsky offers a series of useful maps illustrating the region's unique concentrations of Germanic, Irish, Nordic, and Slavic peoples (1973: 30–31). For particularly useful overviews of ethnic diversity in Minnesota and Wisconsin, see Holmquist (1981) and the Wisconsin Cartographer's Guild (1998: 2–31). Current has argued that Wisconsin is a "living ethnological museum" with its various Algonquian, Iroquois, and Siouxan peoples, its status as the "most German" and most foreign-stock American state, and its growing population of black, Hispanic, and Asian peoples (1977: 56). Meanwhile, Buenker suggests that Wisconsin's "public culture" is "essentially the adaptation of European folk culture, with its emphasis on family, church, locale, hard work, food, drink, music, entertainment, and recreation" (1988: 71).

10. Regarding the doctrine of first effective settlement, see Zelinsky (1973: 13–14).

11. Jon Gjerde chronicled the often contending forces of Americanization and immigrant cultural retention in the Midwest, concluding that neither won out entirely. Rather, many communities in the region established "ethnicized patterns" that "did not illustrate an 'Americanization' or assimilation" but contributed "to a pluralist structure in American society" (Gjerde 1997: 246–247). Horace Kallen formed and articulated the concept of cultural pluralism as a significant, profoundly democratic factor in American life during his tenure at the University of Wisconsin (Kallen 1924). For rich accounts of folk cultural pluralism in the Upper Midwest and Wisconsin, respectively, see Bercovici (1925) and Holmes (1944). Archie Green links cultural pluralism to the evolving activities of the Archive of American Folk Song (1985: 69–71). For overviews of folk musical pluralism in Wisconsin and the surrounding Upper Midwest, see Leary (1987) and Leary and March (1996).

12. Examples of cognate traditions among Upper Midwesterners are legion and will be sketched below. Here, I will mention a few additional sources. Regarding late nineteenth-century song and dance among cranberry harvesters that included Czechs, Germans, Ho-Chunks, Irish, and Yankees, see Leary (1987: 50). Ojibwe and metís wintertime social dancing, including the performance of square dances and the creolized "49 Song" couple dance, is treated in Vennum (1982: 42–43). While Rickaby remarked that, in the Upper Midwest's lumber camps, "the hegemony in song belongs to the Irish" (1925: xxv), he encountered performers of diverse heritage. For accounts of French house parties and musical contributions to lumber-camp performances, see Starr (1981). The house parties of Norwegians and their various German, Irish, and Yankee neighbors are examined by Larson (1975: 18–23), Martin (1994: 43–63), and Beetham (2005: 9–11, 14). For weddings and seasonal dances of Germanic, Scandinavian, and Slavic peoples, see the various anthologized essays and commentary in Leary (1998: 252–283, 346–355, 362–370). Stokker elaborates on festivities associated with wintry nocturnal *julebukking* by Norwegians (2000: 144–146, 189–191, 220–238).

13. In his reminiscent novel, *The Mongrels* (1946), Sigurd J. Simonson characterizes the origins and speech of northern Minnesota's woods workers in 1885:

The talk was rough talk, and in many languages. The sound of broken German . . . the broken Scandinavian talk of the Danes, Swedes, and

Norwegians. There were also Russ-Poles who in common with the rest swore fluently in English, although unable to talk fluently otherwise. (10)

Simonson subsequently describes a dance where a Scandinavian fiddler, Niels Nielsen, seconds the Irishman Patrick Murphy. The pair plays waltzes, two-steps, and square dances, with a Czech, Alfred Novak, doing the calling (153–159). For reports of similar ethnic and musical mixtures in Upper Midwestern lumber camps, see Leary (1983: 221–222) and Martin (1994: 21–24).

14. Bands similar to Mon Pleasure's were active in Michigan in the late nineteenth century. Paul Gifford mentions "such prominent groups as Charles Fischer's Orchestra of Kalamazoo and Theodore Finney's Orchestra of Detroit," which combined violins and wind instruments to perform a repertoire that included quadrilles and "round dances such as waltzes, schottisches, mazurkas, and two-steps" (Gifford 1987: 192).

15. For evidence of an Anglo-European creolized folk musical repertoire in northern Minnesota and eastern North Dakota, see Andresen (1978). The Swedish-American fiddler Bertel Malm of South Dakota and Jarle, Wilbur, and Elizabeth Foss of North Dakota collaborated on a series of LPs in the 1970s and 1980s featuring various regional fiddlers in particular. Their tunes were a mixture of Swedish, Norwegian, Czech, and German polkas, waltzes, and schottisches, along with Anglo-American hornpipes, jigs, reels, rags, country gospel songs, hillbilly yodels, and honky tonk laments. A representative sampling appears on Malm (1972 M); *1976 Bicentennial Fiddlers Contest* (1976 M); *We Rode Our Horses and Played with Fiddlers from Yankton, South Dakota, to Havana, North Dakota* (1983 M); and *Fiddlers Had Fun in Yankton, SD* (1986 M). For biographical and musical portraits of Jarle and Wilbur Foss, see Beetham (2005: 158–163). For assessments of the similarly combinatory folk musical scene in northern lower Michigan and that state's Upper Peninsula, see Gifford (1987); Leary (1988); Leary and March (1996: 84–86); and the profiles of various members of the Original Michigan Fiddlers Association (1986).

16. The rural Michigan reception to a touring Bohemian band and dogs howling while Kryl plays are both found in Harrison (1958: 2, 100). For accounts of local Bohemian bands in the Upper Midwest, see Greene (1992: 19–21) and Leary (1997).

17. For distinctions among the button accordion, the piano accordion, and the German or Chemnitzer concertina—each of them quite different instruments—and their role in Upper Midwestern ensembles, see the glossary to this book, plus Leary and March (1996: 139–146); Wagner (2001); and Leary (2002).

18. For photographs and brief profiles of Berg's band, as well as of several that were similar in instrumentation, repertoire, and touring range (Big Ole, the Co-op Shoppers, Darrel Fischer and the Minnesota Lumberjacks, Clarence Zahina and His Barnstormers, Si Perkins and His Cornhuskers, Shirley Boen and His Scandinavians, Ray Stolzenberg and the Northern Playboys, and Cousin Fuzzy's Country Cousins), see Barron (1987: 14, 26, 30, 135, 179, 229, 232, 251, 255).

19. In the late 1920s, entrepreneurs promoted contests in northwestern Wisconsin's *Eau Claire Leader* for the best not only fiddlers but accordionists, harmonica players, and jig dancers. In 1926, Stoughton, Wisconsin's *Courier Hub* reported that the local old time fiddlers contest was offering

16 different prizes. Besides best all-around fiddler and best trick fiddler, they included laziest fiddler, best Norwegian selection, best left-handed fiddler, and more (Martin 1994: 100–101).

20. For considerations of *bygdedans* versus *gammaldans* in the Upper Midwest, as well as insights into the former's relationship with the Hardanger fiddle, see Larson (1975: 1–6); Martin (1979, 1980); Kvam (1986: 64–105); Hoeschen (1989); Beetham (2005: 11–13); and *Norwegian-American Music from Minnesota* (1990 M).

21. For excellent accounts of Henry Ford's sponsorship of old time fiddling and fiddlers contests, with particular attention to his ideological warp, see Bronner (1987: 33–38) and Gifford (1987: 196–197; 2001: 352–358).

22. The foregoing sketch of Ford-sponsored old time fiddling contests in Wisconsin and Minnesota is based on a 44-page typescript that the late Guthrie T. "Gus" Meade kindly sent me in 1987, after he had combed Upper Midwest newspapers and transcribed articles concerning contests in their particular locales.

23. Brian Brueggen, leader of a German-American, or Dutchman, polka band, referred to his sound—rooted in the 1920s innovations of Whoopee John Wilfahrt—as "old time music with a lot of drive" (Leary and March 1991: 21). In the 1970s and 1980s, Greg Zurawski of Stevens Point, Wisconsin, produced a radio program and weekly dance both dubbed the "Old Tyme Dance Party" (Zurawski 1988 I). During its tenure from the 1960s through the early 1990s, *Entertainment Bits,* the trade journal of the Minnesota Ballroom Operators Association, consistently used the term "old time" to categorize polka and polkabilly bands active in Minnesota, Wisconsin, Michigan, northern Illinois, Iowa, Nebraska, and the Dakotas. Around 1980, Dennis Brown published an *Old Timers Picture Album,* further described as a "collection of pictures of polka bands and the musicians that styled the brand of old time music to the liking of dancers in Southern Minnesota" (1980: i). Historian Victor Greene acknowledged the term's currency by offering *Old Time Ethnic Music in America* as the subtitle of his *A Passion for Polkas* (1992).

24. Kip Lornell offers a fine short overview of the folk revival (2002: 240–272). See also Ronald Cohen's straightforward history (2002) and Cantwell's provocative meditation (1996). Mostly southern, decidedly Anglo-American–oriented discussions of "What Is Old Time Music?" are offered by Nowell Creadick (March 1973: 19–20) and Robert E. Nobley (June 1973: 2–3) in successive issues of the *Devil's Box.* Bronner demonstrates that the phrase "old time music" was in use in the Northeast by the 1890s (1987: 189).

25. In the late 1940s, Chicago's Polish Mountaineers, featuring the lead vocals of Wladziu Zaremba, released a 78, RCA Victor 25–9207, "Piosenka Cowboy (Cowboy's Polka)" backed with "Dziura (Dooda)-Polka." From 1939 to 1949, Leonard Romanowski (1905–1991), a dairy farmer from Weyerhaeuser in rural northwestern Wisconsin, played fiddle in the Polish Barn Dance Band over WJMC radio in nearby Rice Lake (Leary 1991b: 11–12).

26. Evans (1969) offers a history of WLS with particular attention to its programming for a rural, Midwestern audience. Biggar (1971) chronicles the beginnings of the celebrated WLS "Barn Dance." The Little German Band, Ukrainian choirs, Olaf the Swede, and others may be glimpsed in photographs, profiles, and program listings scattered throughout the *WLS Family Album* published annually in the 1930s and 1940s, as well as in the *Stand By* guide to weekly programming and live performances throughout

the region. The August 17, 1936, issue of *Stand By*, for example, noted that Olaf the Swede would play at Wisconsin's Elroy Fair, for the Methodist Episcopal Church in Pawpaw, Illinois, and at the Vermilion County Fair in Cayuga, Indiana. The online database http://www.NewspaperArchive.com reveals that on Friday, September 27, 1935, Wisconsin's *Oshkosh Northwestern* described Olaf the Swede as one of several "famous radio characters" performing as part of a "WLS show" at the Winnebago County Fair. Patterson (1975) mentions "Swedish yodeler Ole Yonson" as a WLS performer in the 1930s, while pointing out that roughly half of the 32 "Barn Dance" performers active in 1932 were Midwesterners.

27. Tony Russell lists more than 40 non-Cajun accordion players in the index to performers for his *Country Music Records: A Discography, 1921–1942* (2004: 985–1011). And although there is no such omnibus discography for the decade following World War II, the presence of accordionists in "country" bands surely increased as a result of interactions among fellow soldiers who were hillbilly, polka, or polkabilly musicians, as well as a result of direct exposure to European squeezebox players (see Greene 1992: 207–208, 249–250).

28. Polkabilly sounds do not enter into either Charles Townsend's (1976) or Cary Ginell's (1993) otherwise excellent studies of western swing founders Bob Wills and Milton Brown, respectively. More recently, Bill C. Malone notes that western swing "reflected the diverse mingling of musical cultures (Cajun, Tex-Mex, German, Bohemian, black, cowboy, Anglo) that prevailed in the Southwest" (2002a: 158, 506).

Chapter 2

1. All quotations, unless otherwise indicated, are from K. Wendell Whitford and were transcribed from a tape-recorded interview conducted by the author at the Whitford home in Cottage Grove, Wisconsin, on July 12, 1990. Copies of the original reel tape recording and a full transcription are in the archives of the State Historical Society of Wisconsin.

2. Nicholas E. Tawa argues that "such songs belong in the parlor, not the minstrel category," while pointing out the abolitionist sympathies and "broad, indiscriminate awareness of brotherhood" of their composers and singers (1980: 89).

3. Sometimes also titled "No More the Moon Shines on Lorena" or "Lorena, the Slave," this song is completely different from (although often confused with) the Reverend H. D. L. Webster's "Lorena"—concerning a swain's longing for his far-off southern belle—that was a favorite of Confederate soldiers, particularly Jeb Stuart, during the Civil War. For Webster's composition, see Glass (1964: 231–233) and Wellman (1959: 25–27).

4. Regarding the twilight hour as a time for family music making, as well as the particular songs favored, it is instructive to read the reminiscence of Rose Schuster Taylor (b. 1863), who grew up on a Dane County farm not far from Albion. Her parents were German immigrants who settled first in New York state in 1848 and later traveled via the Erie Canal to settle in Wisconsin in 1855. The family would settle on their large screened porch on warm evenings:

> Here father played his horn and flute, and the family sang German songs, canal songs, Negro songs, and yodeled. Neighbors half a mile or more away, heard and enjoyed the music with us, on still evenings.

I miss the twilight of the summer evenings in Wisconsin. These hours belonged to the family alone. (Taylor 1945: 435)

5. Philip Martin, who interviewed Windy Whitford on several occasions between 1979 and 1988, published an account of Windy's experiences with "Grandpa Smith" (Martin 1994: 65–66) which includes mention of "Buffalo Gals," "Bully of the Town," "Campbells Are Coming," "Flow Gently Sweet Afton," "Golden Slippers," and "White Cockade." When I interviewed Windy in 1990, he mentioned "Bully of the Town," "Flow Gently Sweet Afton," and the other tunes cited in this section.

6. It's worth noting that the tunes played in Wisconsin by migrants from New York in the latter half of the nineteenth century correlate well with many tunes that Simon Bronner found to be mainstays among *Old-Time Music Makers of New York State*, among them "Arkansas Traveler," "Buffalo Gals," "Captain Jinks," "Darling Nellie Gray," "Devil's Dream," "Flop-Eared Mule," "Girl I Left behind Me," "Haste to the Wedding," "Irish Washerwoman," "Money Musk," "Pop Goes the Weasel," and "Yankee Doodle."

7. Phil Martin draws upon interviews and excerpts from the Stoughton *Courier-Hub* to describe the Stoughton fiddlers contests of 1926 and beyond (Martin 1994: 96–101); Ole Bull's tenure in Madison, 1872–1876, and his popularity among Dane County's fiddling Norwegians appears in Haugen and Cai (1993: 174–183, 220, 222, 224); Frank Custer's Madison *Capitol Times* "Looking Backward" column of February 1977 concerning the 1927 Stoughton contest is reprinted in Windy Whitford's self-published and unpaginated *The Way It Was* (2000); in 1987 old time music researcher Guthrie T. Meade sent me two typed manuscripts gleaned from Minnesota and Wisconsin newspaper accounts of 1926 old time fiddlers contests, including excerpts from Madison's *Capitol Times*, March 8–15.

8. Here, I am very briefly and simply sketching a much larger, more complex story. Bill C. Malone examines the role of southern Appalachian and western stereotypes and repertoires in the formation of country music (1993); see also Douglas Green, "The Singing Cowboy: An American Dream" (1978). In complementary fashion, Benjamin Filene (2000: 25, 40, 52) limns the role of folklorists and entrepreneurs in locating America's "folk" in the South and the West. I will return to this topic in the final chapter.

9. Established in 1917 by students in the University of Wisconsin's Physics Department, Wisconsin public radio, in keeping with its claim, may well be "the oldest station in the nation." It is certainly the oldest public radio station. In the 1920s, the Madison-based station featured live broadcasts by local Irish, Norwegian, and "Winnebago" (Ho-Chunk) musicians. By 1933, Grover Kingsley, the "Old Time Fiddler" had a weekly farm program at noon, while a Saturday afternoon "fiddle fest" regularly included George Matson, Arne "Swede" Moseby, and Windy Whitford (Leary and March 1996: x).

10. Issues throughout the 1930s of *Stand By*, the weekly program guide for WLS, include a section promoting "Appearances of WLS Artists in YOUR Community." Appearances were especially frequent in Illinois, Indiana, Iowa, lower Michigan, and southern Wisconsin. Reminiscences by listeners from the era extend further. Robert Peters, raised near Eagle River in Wisconsin's north woods, recalled that in the 1930s his father—a polkabilly musician who "played accordion, violin, and mandolin at taverns"—had a Sears and Roebuck Silvertone radio that operated on storage batteries. Reception from Milwaukee and Chicago stations was incon-

sistent and static-filled. Nonetheless, "every morning Dad tuned to WLS, 'The Prairie Farmer Station,' for the country music stars" (Peters 1993: 69, 51). In Toivola, a Finnish settlement in Michigan's Upper Peninsula, Jenny "Jingo" Viitala, eventually an accomplished performer of Finnish and old time country music, likewise tuned into WLS during the Depression:

> By the time I was a teenager, mountain music had swept like wildfire through our rural community. Since we didn't have any money to go anywhere, especially during the winter, we stayed up all hours of the night listening to radios that ran on car batteries . . . Patsy Montana, Skyland Scotty and Lulu Belle, Linda Parker and all the rest from WLS Chicago. (Vachon 1975: 131)

In central Wisconsin's sand country, Jerry Apps and his family's hired man likewise tuned in and emulated the "Barn Dance" (Apps 1999: 73–79).

11. In 2000, shortly before Windy Whitford's death, his children Gene and Debbie gathered 25 of the lyrics and tunes for their father's songs into a privately printed book, *The Way It Was: Original Songs by Windy Whitford*. Windy provided brief notes about the inspiration for each song on pages 7–9, and my remarks here draw from those notes and from Windy's comments during our 1990 interview session.

12. There were at least two fast Midwestern trains dubbed the "Wabash Cannonball" in the 1880s and 1890s, inspiring a song that began to circulate in many versions by the early twentieth century. From 1929 on, it was often recorded by hillbilly musicians, including Roy Acuff, whose 1936 version was especially popular (Cohen 1981: 373–381). Although the numerous recordings listed by folksong scholar Norm Cohen are overwhelmingly by southern artists on major labels, the song has also flourished in the repertoires of Upper Midwestern polkabilly musicians, including Jingo Viitala Vachon of Toivola, Michigan, who translated it into Finnish (Leary 1983: 227).

13. Despite his employer's indifference to "Oscar's Cannonball," Windy Whitford performed the song regularly for more than 60 years, recording it first in 1942 on a "home disk" (a single-copy record made in Madison) and again in 1964 with the second coming of the Goose Island Ramblers. In the mid-1980s, folklorist Archie Green reissued the 1964 version of "Oscar's Cannonball" on volume 1 of his two-LP labor song anthology, *Work's Many Voices* (JEMF 110).

14. Red Foley's undated offer-to-purchase letter on WLS stationery, the accompanying contract, and a more detailed account of the "Victory Cannonball" incident appear in Whitford (2000: 23–28).

Chapter 3

1. This and most subsequent quotations from George Gilbertsen are transcribed from an interview session we did on June 27, 1990, at George's home on Waubesa Street in Madison, Wisconsin. I also gleaned supplemental information from telephone conversations with him on June 23 and July 10, 2003.

2. The commingling of Irish and German old time music on the east side of Madison has yet to be studied in full. For a brief glimpse, see Leary and March (1996: 115–119). In 1944, Fred Holmes commented briefly on the presence of Irish players:

"Sure, I'll jig for ye, if ye come around tonight when my friend Red Jack O'Connor, is over here with his fiddle," volunteered Timothy Crimmins of Madison. "When I was young, I would have been the champeen except for a little error. I still have my old hat and fiddle that I brought over from Ireland." (Holmes 1944: 187)

Holmes also mentions Tom Croal, an Irish fiddler from Hill Point in Sauk County (p. 187). In 1926, Croal was living in Milwaukee where, on January 23, the *Milwaukee Sentinel* proclaimed, "Thomas F. Croal, Milwaukee, Wins Fiddlers Crown" (Meade 1987: 2–3). Perhaps Croal (1856–1962), whose descendants reside in Madison, also spent time there during his long life (Martin 1994: 119).

3. Here, I am telling a very short version of a far longer story. A solid introduction to Hawaiian music, including a biographical sketches of Joseph Kekuku and an overview of the dissemination of Hawaiian steel guitars, may be found in Mitchell and Kanahele (1979: 365–378); see also Lornell (2002: 187–189). Perhaps the best audio introduction to the sound is the reissue *Hawaiian Steel Guitar Classics, 1927–1938* (1993 M). Malone summarizes the influence of Hawaiian steel guitar on country music (2002: 26, 498–499); see also Wilson (1990: 8).

4. In July 2003, assorted Web sites still included the military two-step. The Headlanders Ceilidh Band observed that "the military two-step is another couples dance that appears early on in most ceilidh programmes. It's a lively, bouncy dance" (www.headlanders.freeserve.co). Another site (www.footstompin.com/music/celt) pairs the military two-step with the "Colonel Bogey March," while a third (www.scottishdance.net/ceilidh/dances.html) provides instructions on steps and suggests a "6/8 pipe march" as musical accompaniment.

5. George remembered this fiddler only by his nickname, "Whitey," and recalled that the fellow had a photograph of himself playing with Bob Wills. Nobody identified as "Whitey" turns up in either Charles Townsend's definitive biography of Wills nor in the listing of band personnel in Bob Pinson's appended discography (Townsend 1976: 339–346). Perhaps Whitey sat in with the Wills band at a dance job. Whether he was a regular with Wills or not makes little difference, however, since Whitey was steeped sufficiently in the western swing style to pass along its nuances to George Gilbertsen.

6. The Wisconsin Music Archives of the Mills Music Library at the University of Wisconsin includes 78s and test pressings of Penewell recordings, a microfilm copy of his musical scrapbook, and a file of newspaper clippings and related documents concerning Penewell's musical career and inventions.

7. The playful and sometimes combative adoption of stereotypically uncouth mannerisms by southern performers has received the most attention (Green 1965). Simon Bronner's research, however, reveals that a plethora of old time bands in New York state did much the same thing beginning in the 1920s. They included Woodhull's Old Tyme Masters, the Hornellsville Hillbillies, Ott's Woodchoppers, the Rusty Reubens, Woody Kelly's Old Timers, the Trail Blazers, Old Dan Sherman and His Family, the Lone Pine Ramblers, the Bennett Family, and the Tune Twisters (Bronner 1987: 63–75).

8. Photographs of the Buzzington band and scant background information may be found on the Hoosier Hot Shots Web site, www.hoosierhotshots

.com. The quotations offered here are by Douglas B. Green, both a country music historian and "Ranger Doug" of the singing cowboy group Riders in the Sky, and they appear in the booklet accompanying the compact disk *Hoosier Hot Shots: Rural Rhythm, 1935–1942* (1992 M).

9. In a December 15, 1943, edition of the *Minneapolis Tribune*, the journalist John R. Sherman identified and assailed the Minnesota-Wisconsin border country as the "Birthplace of Corn." Referring specifically to Freddie "Schnickelfritz" Fisher, "Whoopee John" Wilfahrt, Skipper Berg's Viking Accordion Band, the Midnight Suns (a Minneapolis band led by Olle i Skratthult veteran Ted Johnson), and Pa Trister and His Screwballs of LaCrosse, Wisconsin, Sherman lamented the "blatant, old-fashioned hokum with funny hats, costumes, horseplay and noise-making hardware" favored by such groups. His sensibilities were wounded particularly by what he described as the "untrammeled sounds [of] 6–7 piece bands that specialize in jerky-rhythmed unsophisticated music of hayseed heritage, featuring cowbells and other freak pseudo-musical noises" (cited in Greene 1992: 160–161, 299).

Chapter 4

1. This and other quotations from Bruce Bollerud in this chapter are transcribed from interviews conducted by the author at Bruce's Madison home in June 1987 and on July 16, 1990, as well as during a performance at the Wisconsin Folk Museum in Mount Horeb on June 3, 1995. Further information was gleaned through telephone conversations with Bruce on July 23 and August 21, 2003, and June 24, 2005. On February 21, 2005, Bruce also offered written additions to my manuscript, while telling me several anecdotes about which I took notes.

2. In Anglicizing their names, the Bolleruds followed patterns common among Norwegians in the Upper Midwest (Haugen 1969: 206–214).

3. Bjarne Andresen, the son of immigrants from southern Norway, was born in Minneapolis in 1906 and grew up in rural Cass County. As a kid, he heard "Ole Olson" performed regularly at house parties. His version, recorded in 1977 by his son Bob, includes three additional verses concerning a cunning newsboy's swindling of the Norsky greenhorn:

> I buy me penny ticket for St. Paul,
> Get on in an extra fine car.
> The conductor comes round and he tells me:
> "Sneak in where those immigrants are."
>
> Oh newsy, he tells me to buy book,
> He tells me to take yust one look.
> I see where the dollars stick out of a corner,
> For a dollar I buy me that book.
>
> But newsy is darn slick with money.
> He gives me the change only half.
> When I ask for the rest of that money,
> Oh newsy gives me the horse laugh.

In the 1930s, Earl C. Beck also recorded a version from John Frederickson of Frankfort, Michigan, while mentioning that the "song has been reported from Nebraska and Wyoming" (1941: 30–31). The latter reference is likely to a version with two verses and a chorus which was said by Mrs. Flo

Hastings, who could not recall the tune, to have been sung in the Medicine Bow Mountains of southeastern Wyoming since the mid-1880s (Rickaby 1925: #13, 220–221). In this case, "Ole" has "just come down from Minnesota" and has a sister who "lives in Dakota." Unlike in the Bollerud and Andresen renditions, however, the main character's real name is *not* Ole after all—a fact revealed in the chorus. The Wyoming song also includes a phrase in Norwegian about Ole's supposed survival on an exclusive diet of *lutefisk* and herring:

> And they all call me Ole and Ole,
> But Ole is not my name.
> Ole, Ole, Ole, Ole just the same.
> They say I'm a Norsk from Norway,
> *Som lever po Lutfisk [sic] ock Sil.*
> They say I'm a rat and I better go back to Norway.

In the mid-1980s, Ardis Folstad of Dunn County, Wisconsin, published a fictionalized account concerning the experiences of her grandfather Even Amundson in a lumber camp on the Red Cedar River in the mid-1870s. She includes a version of the "Ole" song very similar to the Wyoming text, also with no tune, which was supposedly used by non-Norsk woods workers to tease her grandfather (Folstad 1987?: 34–35). A sheet-music version of the song, entitled "Ola, They Call Me Ola" and further described as "A Scandinavian Dialect Song," was attributed to Hilton "Ola" Hansen, the "Scandinavian Hillbilly," and was published by Crown Publications of Racine, Wisconsin, in 1939. In 1952, Little Oscar's Gang—a Norwegian band and comedy troupe that worked in eastern Montana, the Dakotas, and Minnesota—made a 78rpm recording of "Ole" that was reissued on *Stranded in the U.S.A.* (2004 M).

4. For full texts of these and other Scandinavian-American jokes, along with photographs and biographies of performers like Oljanna Venden Cunneen, see Leary (2001c: 63–81, 210–213).

5. The best overviews of Hjalmar Peterson's musical and theatrical career are Harvey and Hulan (1982) and Harvey (1983: 503–515). While the exact sales for "Nikolina" are uncertain, claims were made for the 100,000 figure (Gronow 1977: 13; 1978). Peterson (Olle i Skratthult) first recorded the song for Victor in New York City in March 1917, and then recorded it again for Victor, but this time in Chicago, on July 7, 1929. The Norwegian singer Robert Sterling (Halfdan Meyer) recorded it twice—as "Nikoline" for Victor on July 19, 1917, just a few months after Skratthult's first recording, and as "Nicoline" for Columbia on January 1, 1918. Charles Widden, a Swedish immigrant comedian like Peterson, made a version in New York for Victor on June 6, 1921, while Ted Johnson, a Minneapolis veteran of the Peterson/Skratthult band, cut "Nikolina" for Vocalion on October 29, 1936. Two years later, on October 7, 1938, folklorist Alan Lomax made a field recording of Mary Valeer singing what he set down as "Nicolina" in Bessemer, Michigan (Spottswood 1990: 2634, 2701, 2715, 2718, 2727, 2732).

6. Muddy Waters's development of a blues sound that was simultaneously modern and old time, urban and rural, is ably chronicled by Palmer (1982: 132–169) and Filene (2000: 76–132), while Keil (1992: 46–60) traces the parallel Polish polka innovations of Waters's fellow Chicagoan Walter Jagiello. In the early 1990s, Richard March conceived of a half-hour radio program on "Wally and Muddy," which we produced as part of our "Down Home Dairyland" series on the Wisconsin public radio network.

7. The online database http://www.NewspaperArchive.com includes several dozen citations between 1933 and 1957 concerning performances by the Tilton-Guthrie players, subsequently Tilton's Comedians, in such small Iowa towns as Britt, Clarion, Cresco, Crystal Lake, Greene, Hampton, Lime Springs, Nashua, and Ruthven. Slout offers a rich treatment of tent and Toby shows alike (1972: ch. 8, plates 29–38), while Clark (1963) and Mickel (1967) focus exclusively on Toby.

8. Lavern J. Rippley (1992) offers a grand overview of Whoopee John's career, enriched by many photographs. Kip Lornell (1985) sketches Whoopee John's stylistic shift from the 1920s to the 1930s. Regarding Wilfahrt's pioneering influence on Minnesota's German musicians and the emergence of the Dutchman style, see Leary (1990) and Leary and March (1991). Victor Greene (1992: 154–156) argues for the regional and national significance of Whoopee John, while paying closer attention to subsequent New Ulm Dutchman bands led by Harold Loeffelmacher, Victor "Fezz" Fritsche, and Ellsworth "Babe" Wagner. Slout links the Anglo-American Toby figure to the sort of comic "Hanswurst" bumpkin persona embodied by Wilfahrt (1972: 85).

9. Selmer Oren, born in Stoughton in 1909, was a farmer and fiddler who remained active through the 1980s. Lewis Koch's photograph of fiddling, overall-clad Oren graces the cover of Philip Martin's *Farmhouse Fiddlers* (1994: 120, 122). After his death, the Southern Wisconsin Old Time Fiddlers Association issued a cassette with 22 of Oren's tunes, mostly Norwegian waltzes, hoppwaltzes, and schottisches, plus a few polkas, "Raggedy Ann" (aka "Ragtime Annie"), and Bob Wills's western swing classic "San Antonio Rose" (Oren 1995 M).

10. For Frankie Yankovic's account of his life and music, see Dolgan and Yankovic (1977). Richard March (1985) offers the best account of Yankovic's stylistic innovations in comparison to the "button box" basis of Slovenian traditional music, while Victor Greene provides authoritative treatment of Yankovic's ascension to "polka king" status (1992: 229–242).

11. The Fendermen's "Muleskinner Blues" was originally released as CUCA J-1003-A. It has been reissued several times, most recently in 1996 on the Classics label of Bredaryd, Sweden: *Cuca Rock 'n' Roll Story* (CD 703). For discographic information on the Fendermen and Cuca records, see Myers (1994: 77–80).

Chapter 5

1. The most complete biography of Stewart may be found online at http://www.yogiyorgesson.com. "I Yust Go Nuts at Christmas" was a 78rpm recording (Capitol 57–781). Gronow cites its million-selling status and places the recording within the context of post–World War II bilingual and dialect recordings (1982: 25). Growing up in northwestern Wisconsin in the late 1950s and early 1960s, I regularly heard this song on WCCO radio, Minneapolis, during the Christmas season; and in July 1981, I purchased a copy of the 78rpm recording at a garage sale in Washburn, Wisconsin. From the mid-1980s through the present, John Kraniak, host of the "Entertainment" program on Madison's WORT radio, has played Yorgesson on his annual Christmas special.

2. In addition to the vaudeville and tent show acts sketched in chapter 1, it is worth mentioning that costumed skits and related comic entertain-

ment by touring Upper Midwestern polkabilly bands and radio entertainers were quite common throughout the first half of the twentieth century. The singing Norwegian Olson Sisters and the aforementioned band-leading Swede Olle i Skratthult, with their bungling immigrant comic skits, held forth in the decade following World War I (Greene 1992: 93–97). In the late 1920s, Lawrence Welk toured the Dakotas as part of George T. Kelly's Peerless Entertainers, a troupe that combined dance music with skits incorporating Norwegian and Swedish bumpkins (Welk 1971: 81–87). Throughout the 1930s, Skipper Berg's Viking Accordion Band delighted audiences with a number of costumed rustic comic acts, including "The Anvil Chorus," complete with a spark-emitting electric anvil, the "Horse Act," with "two of the boys in a gunny sack stuffed horse costume," and the "Rube Act" (Berg and Berg 1992: 51–54). In the 1940s, Darrel Fischer—a former Freddie "Schnickelfritz" Fisher sideman—led the Minnesota Lumberjacks, a band that featured skits like "The Passing of the Outhouse" and "Playing the Musical Tree" (Barron 1987: 179). In 1947, Earl McNellis, raised on a Minnesota farm and a veteran of Uncle Louie and the Town Hall Players, formed the Cousin Fuzzy Band that barnstormed northeastern Wisconsin and performed on Green Bay's WBAY radio (see http://internationalpolka .com.halloffame/1985/Fuzzy.html). Several of the group's rube skits from 1952 have been reissued on compact disk (Uncle Ozzie and Cousin Fuzzy 1998 M).

3. A reissue of Spike Jones's 1946 recording "Tu-Hu-Wa-Hu-Wai (Hawaiian War Chant)" may be heard on *Novelty Songs Crazy and Obscure, 1914–1946* (2000 M). Mickey Katz, known as "The King of Klezmer Comedy," recorded a Yiddish-dominated "Mechaiye War Chant" with his Kosher-Jammers as a 78 (RCA Victor 25–5095). A 1958 rendition, with a slightly different title ("It's a Michaye in Hawaiye") has been reissued on compact disk (Katz 2000 M).

4. Arthel "Doc" Watson, born in Deep Gap, North Carolina, in 1923, grew up immersed in southern old time music. "Discovered" in 1960 by folklorist and mandolinist Ralph Rinzler, then director of the Newport Folk Festival and subsequently the director of the Smithsonian's Festival of American Folklife, Watson had a tremendous impact on collegiate fanciers of bluegrass and southern old time music. His guitar version of the fiddle tune "Black Mountain Rag," accompanied by Rinzler's liner notes, appears on *Doc Watson* (1964 M).

5. Dave Van Ronk cites his 1958 collaboration with Samuel Charters in liner notes for Dave Van Ronk and the Jug Stompers, *Rag Time Jug Stompers* (1964). Regarding Charters's recording of Gus Cannon, see Charters (1959). Jim Kweskin & His Jug Band are most easily sampled on his *Greatest Hits!* double LP (1970). Harry Smith's 1952 three-box, six-LP *Anthology of American Folk Music* was reissued in a boxed set of three CDs and two booklets by Smithsonian Folkways (1997). The booklet includes an essay, "The Old Weird America," on Smith's enormous influence on the folk revival, and Bob Dylan especially, culled from Greil Marcus (1997); for another astute assessment of the Smith anthology's impact, see "Smith's Memory Theater" in Cantwell (1996).

6. I am indebted to Bill Lagerroos (2005) for his recollections of such Ramblers' guests as Verne Meisner, the honky tonk singer whose name is forgotten, and Clara who covered Nicola Paone. Paone's comic cow song was recorded in New York City around 1950 on his own label, Etna (ET 1506); three copies of it are in the Mills Music Library at the University of

Wisconsin. For more on Paone's long career, see Greene (1992: 210–217) and Primeggia et al. (1994).

7. Although Windy referred to Jim Kirchstein as the cousin of Bruce's wife, the kinship was more distant. Jim Kirchstein's aunt Fola was married to Gloria Disch Bollerud's uncle Clarence. And so Bruce and Jim knew one another slightly from extended family doings.

8. America's largest and longest-running Syttende Mai festival, the Stoughton event is ably chronicled by Alexander (1986).

9. In a feature published in the Oscar Mayer corporate newsletter, Windy Whitford stated that the 45 sold "over 5,000 copies in the first six months" following its recording (Anonymous 1990).

10. This anonymously penned retrospective account about the Nitty Gritty's early years appeared in a mid-August 1981 edition of *Isthmus*, reprinted as a "Twenty Years After" feature on August 14, 2001. Muddy Waters (McKinley Morganfield) is, of course, the noted Mississippi bluesman first recorded by folklorist Alan Lomax on Stovall's plantation in 1941 before he moved to Chicago, where his recordings on Chess Records would climb the R&B charts and profoundly influence such "British invasion" rock musicians as the Rolling Stones. Hound Dog Taylor, Otis Rush, Luther Allison, and Siegel-Schwall were likewise "Chicago blues" exponents, the latter a white duo still active in the Madison area where Jim Schwall makes his home. Bonnie Raitt, a show tune singer's daughter charmed by the blues, has gone on to international fame as a pop singer and media commentator on blues music. Tracy Nelson, a Madison native, was the leading force in Mother Earth, a late 1960s Bay Area band, named for a tune by bluesman Memphis Slim, that fused soul, blues, and Nashville country. Jazz pianist Ben Sidran, a fixture on the Madison scene since the 1960s, played with soulful Texan rockers Steve Miller and Boz Scaggs when they were students at the University of Wisconsin.

11. Succinct essays on the "American Folklife Center," "Public Folklore" (including the Folk Arts Program of the National Endowment for the Arts), and the "Smithsonian Institution Center for Folklife and Cultural Studies" may be found in Brunvand (1996: 16–17, 602–606, 672–673). For a sketch of how these federal programs affected Wisconsin, see Leary (1998: 23–25).

12. Martin cites dates for two interviews with George Gilbertsen and six with Windy Whitford—the first on September 6, 1979, the last on October 27, 1988—in his *Farmhouse Fiddlers: Music & Dance Traditions in the Rural Midwest* (1994: 119, 121). Martin likewise interviewed Bruce Bollerud, accompanied by photographer Lewis Koch, while doing research for a booklet and a corresponding documentary sound recording, separately published but both with the same name: *Across the Fields: Traditional Norwegian-American Music from Wisconsin* (1982).

13. For a brief profile of Jane Farwell, see Casey (1981: 17–19). Further information about Farwell and Folklore Village, the organization she founded, is offered at http://folklorevillage.org.

14. Martin offers an overview of his work in "Hoppwaltzes and Homebrew" (1985: 26–34); see also the introduction to his *Farmhouse Fiddlers* (1994: 9–13). Nearly 20 years before, he wrote a pioneering essay on Edwin Johnson (1905–1984), a Swedish fiddler from Dalarna who emigrated to Minneapolis in 1924 and had a summer cabin in Hayward, Wisconsin (1976: 10–11). Johnson joined with his son Bruce and grandson Paul Dahlin, both fiddlers, to form the American Spelmans Trio, a celebrated Swedish-American group featured in the Smithsonian Institution's 1976

Festival of American Folklife and captured on a widely distributed Rounder Records LP: *Old Country Folk Fiddling by Edwin Johnson, Bruce Johnson & Paul Dahlin* (Rounder 6004, 1976). Martin's research on the Upper Midwest's Norwegian Hardanger fiddlers also resulted in a pair of groundbreaking essays (1979: 10–11; 1980: 10–11).

15. "Humorous Scandinavian Dialect Songs" aired in 1988, with "The Goose Island Ramblers" and "Windy Whitford: The Soul of Wisconsin's Country Music" following in 1990. All three programs have been reissued on cassette and compact disk as part of the *Down Home Dairyland* book/recording package (Leary and March 1996). The "Windy Whitford" show occupies tracks 1–26 on the CD accompanying this book, while "The Goose Island Ramblers" show appears on tracks 27–54. Tracks 55–64 are taken from "Humorous Scandinavian Dialect Songs." Track 65 comes from the Goose Island Ramblers recording *Midwest Ramblin'* (1990).

16. *"Jolie Blonde"* (Arhoolie CD-399), including Chris Stachwitz's booklet and 26 performances issued in 1993 on the occasion of the Hackberry Ramblers' 60th anniversary, provides a fine introduction to the group's sound and significance.

17. The same fundamental assessment might be made of Richard Crawford's otherwise extraordinarily thorough *America's Musical Life: A History* (2001), with its apt commitment to "American diversity" and attempt to "illuminate parallels and intertwinings that give this country's music making its distinctive character" (2001: ix). To his credit, Crawford relies upon immigration historian Rudolph Vecoli to recognize the presence of Germans, Scandinavians, and Slavs in the Midwest and to acknowledge that they have continued to make music (783–784). Yet no mention is made in nearly 1,000 pages of what that music might be. Likewise, the question of ethnicity vis-à-vis America's musical life is cast in terms of "acculturation (the melting pot) and resistance to it (cultural pluralism)," without considering the sort of creolization that inevitably occurs when diverse participants in a given region interact musically with one another as well as with the cultural mainstream (783).

Chapter 6

1. Chinese Americans were likewise notably neglected, despite their inescapable, crucial participation in railroad construction and mining throughout the West and the emergence of "China towns" in urban centers along the Pacific Coast and in New York City. An anonymously written essay on "The Funeral Ceremonies of the Chinese in America" did, however, appear in the first volume of the *Journal of American Folklore* (1888: 239–240). For a succinct evaluation of Newell's inclusions and omissions, see Bronner (2002: 15–16).

2. Newell (1889: 1–2). Bronner offers astute commentary on Newell's evolutionary thinking, while reprinting both his opening salvo regarding "Folk-Lore in America" and his subsequent note in *Folk Nation: Folklore in the Creation of American Tradition* (2002: 79–86).

3. In 1917, Olive Dame Campbell, a wealthy educational missionary from New England to the southern Appalachians, joined with Cecil Sharp to publish the first edition of *English Folk-Songs from the Southern Appalachians*. The last of several editions, *English Folk Songs from the Southern Appalachians* (1932), attributed solely to Sharp, was published eight years after his death through the efforts of his assistant, Maud Karpeles.

Wilgus (1959: ch. 3) chronicles the academic seekers pursuing Anglo-American ballads preceding and in the wake of Sharp's efforts. Among them, W. Roy Mackenzie invoked Knights of the Round Table through *The Quest of the Ballad* (1928); John Lomax favored romance via *Adventures of a Ballad Hunter* (1947); and Dorothy Scarborough conjured big game hunters or, at the least, butterfly collectors with *A Song Catcher in the Southern Mountains* (1937)—thus suggesting a title for the 2000 film *Songcatcher*, regarding the quests and adventures of an imaginary ballad-seeking precursor of Cecil Sharp.

4. Gordon's life and times are ably presented by Debora Kodish (1986). In 2004, Rounder Records, in cooperation with the Archive of Folk Culture at the Library of Congress, reissued in CD format an LP and booklet originally produced by Kodish and Neil V. Rosenberg, *"Folk-Songs of America": The Robert Winslow Gordon Collection, 1922–1938* (1978 M).

5. For the larger context of nativism and Anglo Saxonism in relation to immigrants, see Higham (1955). Tawa (1982) and especially Greene (2004) consider the music and songs of immigrant and ethnic groups, particularly as they comment on life in America. In *Romancing the Folk: Public Memory and American Roots Music,* Benjamin Filene echoes Archie Green in noting that many early folksong collectors feared both the effects of industrialization on "old-time culture" and the "racial degeneration" brought about by the increasing presence of black people and Eastern European immigrants in their midst. Accordingly, song collectors who were "mostly white Anglo-Saxon Protestants . . . established *their* heritage as the true American culture" (2000: 25–26). See also Regina Bendix regarding the ethnocentrism of America's late nineteenth- and early twentieth-century folksong scholars, *In Search of Authenticity: The Formation of Folklore Studies* (1997: 90): "The privileging of the [English and Scottish] ethnic heritage embodied in the Child ballads also represents an intellectual flight from the multicultural realities of post–Civil War New England."

6. Alan Lomax's friendships with Leadbelly, Woody Guthrie, and Aunt Molly Jackson and his pivotal role in bringing each to a national audience are ably chronicled in a trio of biographies: Wolfe and Lornell on Leadbelly (1992: 221–222, 236); Klein on Guthrie (1980: 142–146, 148–158); and Romalis on Jackson (1998: 104, 159). For a larger consideration of Alan Lomax's relationship to all three vis-à-vis constructing notions of American folksong, see Filene (2002: 64–70).

7. For well-documented straightforward accounts, see Cohen (2002) and Lornell (2002: 240–246, 249–261).

8. Chapters on assorted non-Anglo European singers and musicians in Texas during the 1930s are offered in Owens (1983: 193–234). In his introduction, William Owens acknowledges the critical encouragement of an old friend and confidant of John Lomax, Roy Bedichek:

> He thought I could do for other songs what Lomax had done for the cowboy. He talked of introducing me to Lomax, but I had met him several years before in Dallas. As he seemed less interested in me as a collector, more interested in my giving him what I had collected, I declined. (1983: 10–11)

9. David Whisnant examines the role of Anglo-Saxon nativist composer John Powell in Virginia's White Top Folk Festival, 1931–1939, an enterprise that Charles Seeger characterized as "reactionary to the core" and "really sinister" (1983: 181–252). Regarding the relationship between the

American Left and its embrace of mainstream conceptions of folk music and song, see Denisoff (1971: 50–54); Lieberman (1989: 33–34); and Cohen and Samuelson (1996).

10. Regarding the relationship between dance musician Viola Turpeinen and her working-class immigrant audience, see Leary (1990b). Juha Niemela profiles Arthur Kylander and Hiski Salomaa, with reference to their I.W.W. associations (1997: 107–112). For a full text of Kylander's Wobbly song *"Lumber Jäkki"* (Lumberjack), see Leary and March (1993: 268–271). T-Bone Slim was the pen name of Wobbly songwriter and Hudson River barge captain Matt Valentine Huhta (Kornbluh 1988: 84–85).

11. Born in Richland County, Wisconsin, in 1910, Bernard Johnson farmed in the Bloom City area. His ancestors were Ohio Valley settlers of English heritage who migrated to southwestern Wisconsin where their neighbors included Czechs and Norwegians. I recorded Bernard's personal ethnomusicological observations during an old time fiddlers contest at Blue Mounds, Wisconsin, on July 1, 1989.

12. This section on Alan Lomax draws from a pair of my prior essays (Leary 2001b and 2004a).

13. Lomax's life and extensive folk music collections may be glimpsed on the Web sites of the Alan Lomax Archive (http://www.alan-lomax.com) and the American Folklife Center at the Library of Congress, recipient of the Alan Lomax Collection (http://www.loc.gov/folklife/lomax). For a rich sampling of Lomax's writings, accompanied by critical introductions assessing his life and work, see Cohen (2003).The current state of Rounder Records' ongoing Alan Lomax Collection of compact disks and accompanying booklets may be discovered on the label's Web site, http://www.rounder.com. Filene chronicles the circumstances surrounding Lomax's leaving America for England (2000: 161–163). For an account of Lomax's work with the BBC, including attention to his influence on the skiffle movement, see Gregory (2002: 136–169).

14. Alan Lomax's letter to Harold Spivacke, his field recordings, and additional correspondence from the fall of 1938, some of it quoted below, are held by the Archive of Folk Culture that forms part of the American Folklife Center in the Library of Congress, Washington, D.C.

15. Joe Cloud's tunes and Alan Lomax's on-disk commentary constitute Archive of Folk Song (AFS) recordings 2469–2470.

16. Regarding Sidney Robertson Cowell's background and her 1937 folk music fieldwork in Minnesota and Wisconsin, see Topping (1980); Hickerson (1982: 73); Kerst (1999); and Leary (2001a: 479–486). Nicole Saylor's Web site focuses on Sidney Robertson Cowell's fieldwork in Wisconsin, http://csumc.wisc.edu/src.

17. Correspondence involving the Browns, Sidney Robertson, and Sarah Gertrude Knott, director of the National Folk Festival, forms a special collection in the archives of the Wisconsin Historical Society: "Correspondence and Records of the Works Progress Administration, Wisconsin Folklore Project." For further discussion of the Browns and Robertson vis-à-vis the National Folk Festival, see Leary (1998: 26–27; 2001a: 479–480).

18. For another version, along with a full bilingual text of this song (AFS 2320A3), see Leary and March (1993: 276–278).

19. Perhaps the best-known comic Swedish immigrant dialect song, the variously titled "Swede from North Dakota" was well known by the early twentieth century from the Upper Peninsula of Michigan to North Dakota, as well as in the Pacific Northwest, where many Swedes worked seasonally

as both loggers and farmhands. George Milburn first published a version in his anthology of hobo and Wobbly songs, *The Hobo's Hornbook* (1930: 139). For a representative text and tune, along with an expanded discussion of the song's provenance, see Leary and March (1993: 260–262).

20. Rickaby noted the strong Irish influence on the style of woods singers in Minnesota, Wisconsin, and Michigan (1926: xxv). Emery DeNoyer, arguably Wisconsin's finest lumber-camp singer, was born near Saginaw, Michigan, of French-Canadian parents and lived most of his life in northern Wisconsin. His tenor voice, loud volume, slow delivery, free rhythm, and restrained yet present ornamentation (featured on *Folk Music from Wisconsin* 1950s M) align with Mose Bellaire's delivery and exhibit the Irish-derived "woods style" observed by Edward D. Ives in Maine and the Canadian Maritimes (Ives 1978: 385).

21. The Wisconsin version was recorded in the late 1970s by researchers working for Belgian radio and subsequently issued on an LP accompanied by bilingual notes; *Anthologie du Folklore Wallon: Les Wallons d'Amerique (Wisconsin)* (1981 M).

22. The most recent and best account of the accordion's emergence and global cultural significance is Christoph Wagner's *Das Akkordeon: Oder die Erfindung der populären Musik* (2001). Wagner also produced a companion CD, *Global Accordion: Early Recordings, 1927–1948* (2001 M).

23. Ilkka Kolehmainen of the Finnish Folk Music Institute chronicled an early twentieth-century Finnish anti-accordion coalition of folklorists, churchmen, educators, and nationalists (1989: 29).

24. Hugo Alfvén's rant is quoted by Birgit Kjellström in her essay on the accordion (1975). Sverker Hylten-Cavallius kindly brought this quote to my attention and provided a translation.

25. Snyder (1997: 38–39). Snyder's comments regarding Alan Lomax's interview with Leadbelly draw from Wolfe and Lornell (1992: 179, 309, 313, 314). For a full consideration of Leadbelly's accordion playing, see Snyder (1994). The equally prominent African-American folk musician Muddy Waters, who made his first recordings in 1941 for Alan Lomax, acquired an old button accordion from a neighbor lady as his first instrument (Palmer 1982: 100). Elsewhere, Elijah Wald points out that commercial record companies likewise limited their conception of southern black music: "the fact that so few black banjo players—or fiddlers, or accordionists—were recorded had less to do with what was available than with the perceptions of 'record men'" (2004: 52). Indeed, Wald points out that folklorist Harry Hyatt even reported on a black accordionist who, like the legendary guitarist Robert Johnson and many others, supposedly went to the crossroads seeking musical powers from the devil (Hyatt 1970–1978: vol. 1, 108; Wald 2004: 266).

26. Lomax's quote about the "pestiferous" accordion appears in the booklet accompanying a compact disk reissue of his 1950s Columbia release, *Italie: Chants & Danses/Songs and Dances of Italy* (1989 M). In a 1988 conversation with Jared Snyder, Lomax reiterated his notion that the accordion homogenized traditional European dance music by usurping the former role of bagpipes and fiddle (Snyder 1997: 39).

27. Alan Lomax did, however, make one more recording trip to the Upper Midwest. In 1943, working with CBS and the BBC on the wartime series "Trans-Atlantic Call," Lomax interviewed "dozens of Duluthians." On Sunday, June 20, he gathered "an ore dock puncher, a lake captain, a typical lumberjack, representatives of foreign born American groups, and the

Normanna chorus" in the studios of KDAL to produce a program on "the importance of the Duluth-Superior harbor as an iron ore shipping port" (Anonymous 1943: 6). I am indebted to Arne Alanen for this information.

28. The regional and ethnic origins and subsequent wholesale and wholesome nationally oriented pop-music trajectory of Lawrence Welk's career are vividly conveyed in his autobiography (1971). For a discussion of genteel Texan-Mexican *orquesta* music as it departs from working-class conjunto music, see Peña (1985). Despite Welk's prevailing abandonment of his polkabilly origins, most Upper Midwestern exponents of the genre persist in considering him an honorable musical veteran. Perhaps ironically, Welk also attracted ardent followers among African and Mexican Americans in the South. Elijah Wald reminds us:

> [I]n the early 1960s Chris Strachwitz was horrified to find that most of the rural musicians he recorded for his Arhoolie roots label, from blues singers to Tex-Mex bands and Louisiana zydeco outfits, were enthusiastic fans of Lawrence Welk. (Welk had a strong enough following among black listeners to reach the R&B top ten in 1961, with the harpsichord-led "Calcutta." The world is not a simple place). (Wald 2004: 97)

29. The Folk Music in America series was part of the Library of Congress's American Revolution Bicentennial Project, funded by the National Endowment for the Arts and issued from 1976 to 1977. These long out-of-print LPs and booklets are currently being revised for CD reissue by Richard K. Spottswood. On January 24–26, 1977, the American Folklife Center at the Library of Congress convened an appropriately subtitled conference, "Ethnic Recordings in America: A Neglected Heritage," subsequently published as a book with the same title (American Folklife Center 1982).

30. See especially chapter 8, "Ethnic and Native American Traditions," in Lornell (2002: 170–213). Easily the most sophisticated single-volume overview of American folk music, Lornell's work is somewhat constrained by the fact that his accompanying CD is limited to recordings in the Smithsonian/Folkways catalog. By way of compensation, he offers a commendable listing of relevant readings, recordings, and films.

Sources

Books, Essays, and Unpublished Manuscripts

Abrahams, Roger D. 1992. "The Public, the Folklorist, and Public Folklore." In *Public Folklore,* ed. Robert Baron and Nicholas R. Spitzer. Washington, D.C.: Smithsonian Institution Press. Pp. 19–29.

Abramson, Harold J. 1980. "Assimilation and Pluralism." In *Harvard Encyclopedia of American Ethnic Groups,* ed. Stephan Thernstrom. Cambridge, Mass.: Harvard University Press. Pp. 150–160.

Abrantes, Wendy. 2002. "Folk Instrument: American Boom Bah." Paper for a folklore class, University of Pennsylvania, Harrisburg.

Adolphson, Svea M. 1976. *A History of Albion Academy 1853–1918.* Beloit, Wis.: Rock County Rehabilitation Services.

Alexander, Martha. 1986. "Stoughton, Wisconsin's Syttende Mai Celebration: The Dynamic of a Small-Town American Festival." Ph.D. diss., Indiana University, Bloomington.

American Folklife Center. 1982. *Ethnic Recordings in America: A Neglected Heritage.* Washington, D.C.: American Folklife Center, Library of Congress.

Anderson, Rasmus B. 1895. *The First Chapter of Norwegian Immigration (1821–1840): Its Causes and Results.* Madison, Wis.: Author.

Andresen, Robert F. 1978. "Traditional Music: The Real Story of Ethnic Music and How It Evolved in Minnesota and Wisconsin," *Minnesota Monthly* 107 (October). Pp. 9–13.

Anonymous. 1877. *Madison, Dane County, and Surrounding Towns, Being a History and Guide.* Madison, Wis.: William J. Park.

———. 1880. *The History of Columbia County, Wisconsin.* Chicago: Western Historical Society.

———. 1881. *History of Iowa County, Wisconsin.* Chicago: Western Historical Company.

———. 1888. "The Funeral Ceremonies of the Chinese in America," *Journal of American Folklore* 1:3. Pp. 239–240.

———. 1906. *History of Dane County, Biographical and Genealogical.* Madison, Wis.: Western Historical Association.

———. 1915. "Ole Pleased a Large House," *Grand Rapids Tribune.* May 19, p. 1.

———. 1917. "Accordeon Concert Pleases," *Capital Times.* December 20.

———. 1918. "A Notable Concert," *Grand Rapids Tribune.* January 17.

———. 1943. "Broadcast Tells Story of Duluth," *Duluth News-Tribune.* June 17, p. 6.

————. 1948. *Sons of Norway Songbook*. Minneapolis, Minn.: Supreme Lodge of the Sons of Norway.

————. 1990. "Oscar Mayer Brings Celebrity Status to Country Singer," *Oscar Mayer Report* (August).

————. 1999. "The Leader of the Band," *Hospice Care*, insert in Madison, Wisconsin, *Capital Times*, November 17. Pp. 1–2.

————. 2001. "Twenty Years Ago," *Isthmus*. August 10.

Apps, Jerry. 1999. *When Chores Were Done*. Amherst, Wis.: Amherst Press.

Barfuss, Gerald. 1983. *David Stone in Sunset Valley: The Story of the KSTP Barn Dance*. Minneapolis, Minn.: James D. Thueson.

Barnouw, Victor. 1977. *Wisconsin Chippewa Myths and Tales*. Madison: University of Wisconsin Press.

Baron, Robert, and Nicholas R. Spitzer. 1992. *Public Folklore*. Washington, D.C.: Smithsonian Institution Press.

Baron, Robert, and Anna C. Cara. 2003. "Creolization and Folklore—Cultural Creativity in Process," *Journal of American Folklore* 116:459. Pp. 4–8.

Barron, Lee. 1987. *Odyssey of the Mid-Nite Flyer: A History of Midwest Bands*. Omaha, Nebr.: El Roy V. Lee.

Bayard, Samuel Preston. 1945. *Hill Country Tunes: Instrumental Folk Music of Southwestern Pennsylvania*. Philadelphia: American Folklore Society.

————. 1982. *Dance to the Fiddle, March to the Fife: Instrumental Folk Tunes in Pennsylvania*. University Park and London: Pennsylvania State University Press.

Beck, Earl C. 1941. *Songs of the Michigan Lumberjacks*. Ann Arbor: University of Michigan Press.

Beckwith, Martha Warren. 1931. *Folklore in America: Its Scope and Method*. Poughkeepsie, N.Y.: Vassar College, the Folklore Foundation.

Beetham, Julane. 2005. "Norwegian-American Old-Time Fiddling in the Heartland: Interpretation of a Creolized Tradition." M.A. thesis, Institutt for Folkekultur, Høgskolen Telemark, Norway.

Bell, Michael J. 1973. "William Wells Newell and the Foundation of American Folklore Scholarship," *Journal of American Folklore* 10:1–2. Pp. 7–21.

Bendix, Regina. 1997. *In Search of Authenticity: The Formation of Folklore Studies*. Madison: University of Wisconsin Press.

Bercovici, Konrad. 1925. *On New Shores*. New York and London: Century.

Berg, Leighton A., and Valborg Berg. 1992. *Viking Accordion Band Reflects Colorful History*. Lake Mills, Iowa: Stoyles Graphic Services.

Berget, Derek. 2001. "Peterson's Folklore." Paper for American folklore class, University of Wisconsin.

Biggar, George. 1971. "The WLS National Barn Dance Story: The Early Years," *JEMF Quarterly* 7:23. Pp. 105–112.

Blaustein, Richard. 1975. "Traditional Music and Social Change: The Old-Time Fiddlers Association Movement in the United States." Ph.D. diss., Indiana University.

Bohlman, Philip. V. 1980. "The Folksongs of Charles Bannen: The Interaction of Music and History in Southwestern Wisconsin," *Wisconsin Academy of Sciences, Arts, and Letters* 68. Pp. 167–186.

————. 1988. *The Study of Folk Music in the Modern World*. Bloomington: Indiana University Press.

Bronner, Simon J. 1987. *Old-Time Music Makers of New York State*. Syracuse, N.Y.: Syracuse University Press.

———. 1998. *Following Tradition: Folklore in the Discourse of American Culture*. Logan: Utah State University Press.

———. 2002. *Folk Nation: Folklore in the Creation of American Tradition*. Wilmington, Del.: Scholarly Resources.

Brown, Charles. 1938. Letter to Alan Lomax, July 11. Alan Lomax Correspondence, 1938. Archive of Folk Culture, Library of Congress.

Brown, Dennis. 1980. *Old Timers Picture Album*. Lakefield, Minn.: Dennis Brown.

Browner, Tara. 2002. *Heartbeat of the People: Music and Dance of the Northern Pow-wow*. Urbana: University of Illinois Press.

Bruce, Dix. c. 1975. "The Goose Island Ramblers." Paper for a course at the University of Wisconsin.

———. 1991. "On Wisconsin," *Fretted Instrument Guild of America* 35:5. Pp. 37–39.

Brunvand, Jan H., ed. 1996. *American Folklore: An Encyclopedia*. New York: Garland.

Buenker, John D. 1988. "Wisconsin as Maverick, Model, and Microcosm." In *Heartland: Comparative Histories of the Midwestern States*, ed. James H. Madison. Bloomington: Indiana University Press. Pp. 59–85.

Burdette, Alan R. 2002. "'Ein Prosit der Gemütlichkeit': The Traditionalization Process in a German-American Singing Society." In *Land without Nightingales: Music in the Making of German-America*, ed. Philip V. Bohlman and Otto Holzapfel. Madison, Wis.: Max Kade Institute for German American Studies. Pp. 191–220.

Butterfield, C. W. 1880. *History of Dane County, Wisconsin*. Chicago: Western Historical Company.

Campbell, Olive Dame, and Cecil J. Sharp. 1917. *English Folk-Songs from the Southern Appalachians*. New York and London: Putnam.

Cantwell, Robert. 1996. *When We Were Good: The Folk Revival*. Chapel Hill: University of North Carolina Press.

Casey, Betty. 1981. *International Folk Dancing U.S.A.* Garden City, N.Y.: Doubleday.

Cassidy, Frederic G. 1947. *The Place-Names of Dane County, Wisconsin*. Greensboro, N.C.: American Dialect Society.

———. 1985. *Dictionary of American Regional English*, vol. 1, introduction, A–C. Cambridge, Mass.: Harvard University Press.

Cassidy, Frederic G., and Joan Houston Hall. 1991. *Dictionary of American Regional English*, vol. 2, D–H. Cambridge, Mass.: Harvard University Press.

Charters, Samuel. 1959. *The Country Blues*. New York: Oak.

Chmielewski, Florian. 1991. *Florian Chmielewski: Mixing Polkas with Politics*. Sturgeon Lake, Minn.: Author.

Clark, Larry Dale. 1963. "Toby Shows: A Form of American Popular Theatre." Ph.D. diss., University of Illinois.

Coggeshall, John M. 1986. "'One of those Intangibles': The Manifestation of Ethnic Identity in Southwestern Illinois," *Journal of American Folklore* 99:392. Pp. 177–207.

Cohen, Norm. 1981. *Long Steel Rail: The Railroad in American Folksong*. Urbana: University of Illinois Press.

Cohen, Ronald D. 2002. *Rainbow Quest: The Folk Music Revival and American Society, 1940- 1970*. Amherst and Boston: University of Massachusetts Press.

———. 2003. *Alan Lomax: Selected Writings, 1934–1997*. New York and London: Routledge.

Cohen, Ronald D., and Dave Samuelson. 1996. *Songs for Political Action: Folkmusic, Topical Songs and the American Left, 1926–1953.* Hamburg, Germany: Bear Family Records.

Corenthal, Michael G. 1986. *The Iconography of Recorded Sound 1886–1986: A Hundred Years of Commercial Entertainment and Collecting Opportunity.* Milwaukee, Wis.: Yesterday's Memories.

———. 1991. *The Illustrated History of Wisconsin Music, 1840–1990.* Milwaukee: Yesterday's Memories.

Crawford, George, and Robert M. Crawford. 1913. *Memoirs of Iowa County, Wisconsin: From the Earliest Historical Times Down to the Present.* Chicago: Northwestern Historical Association.

Crawford, Richard. 2001. *America's Musical Life: A History.* New York: Norton.

Creadick, Nowell. 1973. "What Is Old Time Music?" *Devil's Box* 20 (March). Pp. 2–3.

Current, Richard N. 1977. *Wisconsin: A Bicentennial History.* New York: W. W. Norton.

Curtis, Wardon Alan. 1907. "'The Light Fantastic' in the Central West: Country Dances of Many Nationalities in Wisconsin," *Century* 73. Pp. 570–579.

Daniel, Wayne. 1983. "George Daniell's Hill Billies: The Band That Named the Music?" *JEMF Quarterly* 19:70. Pp. 81–84.

Degh, Linda. 1966. "Approaches to Folklore Research among Immigrant Groups," *Journal of American Folklore* 79:314. Pp. 551–556.

Denisoff, R. Serge. 1971. *Great Day Coming.* Urbana: University of Illinois Press.

Dessureau, Robert M. 1922. *History of Langlade County Wisconsin: From U.S. Government Survey to Present Time, with Biographical Sketches.* Antigo, Wis.: Berner Brothers.

Dolgan, Robert, and Frank Yankovic. 1977. *The Polka King: The Life of Frankie Yankovic.* Cleveland, Ohio: Dillon and Liederbach.

Dorson, Richard M. 1952. *Bloodstoppers and Bearwalkers: Folk Tales of Canadians, Lumberjacks, & Indians.* Cambridge, Mass.: Harvard University Press.

Dunaway, David King. 1981. *How Can I Keep from Singing: Pete Seeger.* New York: McGraw-Hill.

Dwyer-Schick, Susan. 1975. "The Development of Folklore and Folklife Research in the Federal Writer's Project, 1935–1943," *Keystone Folklore Quarterly* 20. Pp. 5–31.

Dylan, Bob. 2004. *Chronicles, Volume One.* New York: Simon and Schuster.

Edstrom, Frances. 2002. "Rediscovering Schnickelfritz," *Winona Post* Web site, www.winonapost.com/11800/schnickelfritz.html.

Erickson, Alfred O. 1949. "Scandinavia, Wisconsin." *Norwegian American Studies and Records* 15. Pp. 185–209.

Evans, James F. 1969. *Prairie Farmer and WLS: The Burridge D. Butler Years.* Urbana: University of Illinois Press.

Filene, Benjamin. 2000. *Romancing the Folk: Public Memory and American Roots Music.* Chapel Hill: University of North Carolina Press.

Flom, George T. 1909. *A History of Norwegian Immigration to the United States.* Iowa City: n.p.

Folstad, Ardis. 1987? *Vi Hadde Det Godt Her* (We Had It Good Here). Dunn County, Wis.?

Fredrickson, George M., and Dale T. Knobel. 1980. "History of Prejudice and Discrimination." In *Harvard Encyclopedia of American Ethnic Groups,* ed. Stephan Thernstrom. Cambridge, Mass.: Harvard University Press. Pp. 829–847.

Frimannslund, Rigmor. 1956. "The Old Norwegian Peasant Community: Farm Community and Neighborhood Community," *Scandinavian Economic History Review* 4. Pp. 62–81.

Garland, Hamlin. 1891. *Main-Travelled Roads*. Boston: Arena Publishing Company.

———. 1917. *A Son of the Middle Border*. New York: Macmillan.

Garthwaite, Chester. 1990. *Threshing Days: The Farm Paintings of Lavern Kammerude*. Mount Horeb: Wisconsin Folk Museum.

Gifford, Paul. 1987. "Fiddling and Instrumental Folk Music in Michigan." In *Michigan Folklife Reader*, ed. C. Kurt Dewhurst and Yvonne Lockwood. East Lansing: Michigan State University Press. Pp. 187–204.

———. 2001. *The Hammered Dulcimer: A History*. Lanham, Md.: Scarecrow.

Gillett, P. T. 1932. "Fiddlers We Have Known." Music folder, Wisconsin Room, Antigo Public Library, Antigo, Wisconsin.

Ginell, Cary. 1993. *Milton Brown and the Founding of Western Swing*. Urbana: University of Illinois Press.

Gjerde, Jon. 1985. *From Peasants to Farmers: The Migration from Balestand, Norway, to the Upper Middle West*. Cambridge: Cambridge University Press.

———. 1997. *The Minds of the West: Ethnocultural Evolution in the Rural Middle West 1830–1917*. Chapel Hill: University of North Carolina Press.

Glass, Paul. 1964. *Singing Soldiers: A History of the Civil War in Song*. New York: Grosset & Dunlap.

Green, Archie. 1965. "Hillbilly Music: Source and Symbol," *Journal of American Folklore* 78:309. Pp. 204–228.

———. 1983. "Farewell Tony," *JEMF Quarterly* 19:72. Pp. 231–240.

———. 1985. "The Archives Shores," *Folklife Annual* 1:1. Pp. 61–73.

Green, Douglas B. 1978. "The Singing Cowboy: An American Dream," *Journal of Country Music* 7:2. Pp. 4–62.

Greene, Victor R. 1992. *A Passion for Polkas: Ethnic Old Time Music in America, 1880–1960*. Berkeley: University of California Press.

———. 2004. *A Singing Ambivalence: American Immigrants between Old World and New, 1830–1930*. Kent, Ohio: Kent State University Press.

Gregory, E. David. 2002. "Lomax in London: Alan Lomax, the BBC and the Folk-Song Revival in England, 1950–1958," *Folk Music Journal* 8:2. Pp. 136–169.

Gronow, Pekka. 1977. *Studies in Scandinavian-American Discography*, 2 vols. Helsinki: Finnish Institute of Recorded Sound.

———. 1978. "Recording for the Foreign Series," *JEMF Quarterly* 12:41. Pp. 15–20.

———. 1982. "Ethnic Recordings: An Introduction." In *Ethnic Recordings in America: A Neglected Heritage*. Washington, D.C.: American Folklife Center, Library of Congress. Pp. 1–49.

Hagerty, Bernard C. 1975. "WNAX: Country Music on a Rural Radio Station, 1927–1955," *JEMF Quarterly* 11; reprinted in *Exploring Music Roots: Twenty Years of the JEMF Quarterly*, ed. Nolan Porterfield. Lanham, Md.: Scarecrow, 2004. Pp. 118–126.

Hall, Wade. 1996. *Hell Bent for Music: The Life of Pee Wee King*. Lexington: University Press of Kentucky.

Hamm, Charles. 1983. *Yesterdays: Popular Song in America*. New York: W. W. Norton.

Handy, W. C. 1941. *Father of the Blues.* New York: Macmillan.

Harkins, Anthony. 2004. *Hillbilly: A Cultural History of an American Icon.* New York: Oxford University Press.

Harrison, Harry P. 1958. *Culture under Canvas: The Story of Tent Chautauqua.* New York: Hastings House.

Harvey, Anne-Charlotte Hanes. 1983. "Swedish-American Theater." In *Ethnic Theater in the U.S.,* ed. Maxine S. Seller. Westport, Conn.: Greenwood. Pp. 491–524.

Harvey, Anne-Charlotte, and Richard Hulan. 1982. *Teater, Visoften och Bal: A National Tour of Theater, Music and Dance Traditions of Swedish Americans.* Washington, D.C.: National Council for the Traditional Arts.

Haugen, Einar. 1969. *The Norwegian Language in America: A Study in Bilingual Behavior.* Bloomington: Indiana University Press.

Haugen, Einar, and Joan N. Buckley. 1984. *Han Ola og Han Per.* Oslo: Universitetsforlaget.

———. 1988. *More Han Ola og Han Per.* Iowa City: University of Iowa Press.

Haugen, Einar, and Camilla Cai. 1993. *Ole Bull: Norway's Romantic Musician and Cosmopolitan Patriot.* Madison: University of Wisconsin Press.

Helgeson, Thor. 1985. *From the Indian Land,* translated and annotated by Malcolm Rosholt from volumes originally published in 1915 and 1917. Iola, Wis.: Krause.

Hickerson, Joseph C. 1982. "Early Field Recordings of Ethnic Music." In *Ethnic Recordings in America: A Neglected Heritage.* Washington, D.C.: U.S. Government Printing Office. Pp. 67–83.

Higginson, Thomas Wentworth. 1888. "Brides Dancing Barefoot," *Journal of American Folklore* 1:3. Pp. 235–236.

Higham, John. 1955. *Strangers in the Land: Patterns of American Nativism, 1860–1925.* New Brunswick, N.J.: Rutgers University Press.

Hirsch, Jerrold. 1987. "Folklore in the Making: B. A. Botkin," *Journal of American Folklore* 100:3. Pp. 3–38.

———. 1988. "Cultural Pluralism and Applied Folklore: The New Deal Precedent." In *The Conservation of Culture: Folklorists and the Public Sector,* ed. Burt Feintuch. Lexington: University Press of Kentucky. Pp. 46–67.

Hoeschen, Kevin. 1989. "The Hardanger Violin in the Upper Midwest: Documentation and Interpretation of an Immigrant Tradition." M.A. thesis, University of Minnesota.

Holmes, Fred L. 1944. *Old World Wisconsin: Around Europe in the Badger State.* Eau Claire, Wis.: Hale.

Holmquist, June. 1981. *They Chose Minnesota: A Survey of the State's Ethnic Groups.* St. Paul: Minnesota Historical Society.

Houghton, Barbara Coan. 1999. "The Goose Island Ramblers: Heartland Harmonizers," *Mature Lifestyles* 13:11. Pp. 1–2.

Hyatt, Harry M. 1970–1978. *Hoodoo-Conjuration-Witchcraft-Rootwork: Beliefs Accepted by Many Negroes and White Persons These Being Orally Recorded among Blacks and Whites.* 5 vols. Quincy, Ill., and New York: Memoirs of the Alma Egan Hyatt Foundation.

Ives, Edward D. 1978. *Joe Scott: The Woodsman-Songmaker.* Urbana: University of Illinois Press.

Jabbour, Alan. 1996. "Fiddle Music." In *American Folklore: An Encyclopedia,* ed. Jan H. Brunvand. New York: Garland. Pp. 253–256.

Jones, J. E. 1914. *A History of Columbia County, Wisconsin.* Chicago and New York: Lewis.

Kallen, Horace. 1924. *Culture and Democracy in the United States.* New York: Boni and Liveright.

Keesing, Felix. 1939. Reprint, 1971. *The Menomini Indians of Wisconsin.* New York: Johnson Reprint.

Keil, Charles. 1992. *Polka Happiness.* Philadelphia: Temple University Press.

Kempf, Barbara. 1974. "Meet Doc Williams: Country Music Star, Country Music Legend," *JEMF Quarterly* 10:1. Pp. 1–13.

Kerst, Catherine Hiebert. 1999. "Lady on Wheels: Sidney Robertson Cowell's Folk Music Collecting Practice." Paper delivered at the American Folklore Society annual meeting, Memphis, Tenn.

Kirschke, Amy M. 2002. "Songs to Remember: Grandpa Carson in His Crooning Days." Paper for folklore of Wisconsin class, University of Wisconsin.

Kjellström, Birgit. 1975. "Dragspel," *Sohlmans Musiklexikon* 2. Pp. 329–335.

Klein, Joe. 1980. *Woody Guthrie: A Life.* New York: Knopf.

Klymasz, Robert. 1972. "'Sounds You've Never Heard Before': Ukrainian Country Music in Western Canada," *Ethnomusicology* 16:3. Pp. 381–396.

Kodish, Debora. 1986. *Good Friends and Bad Enemies: Robert W. Gordon and the Study of American Folksong.* Urbana: University of Illinois Press.

Kolehmainen, Ilkka. 1989. "'Do Not Dance to the Screeching, Insidious Accordions: Burn Them': The Accordion in Finnish Folk Music," *Finnish Musical Quarterly* 2. Pp. 29–31.

Koretzky, Henry. 1992. Review of the Goose Island Ramblers' *Midwest Ramblin', Old Time Country* 8:3. Page 27.

Kornbluh, Joyce. 1988. *Rebel Voices: An I.W.W. Anthology.* Chicago: Kerr.

Koskoff, Ellen, ed. 2001. *The United States and Canada,* vol. 3, *Garland Encyclopedia of World Music.* New York: Garland.

Kvam, Janet Ann. 1986. "Norwegian-American Dance Music in Minnesota and Its Roots in Norway: A Comparative Study." Ph.D. diss., University of Missouri, Kansas City.

Lagerroos, Bill. 2005. E-mail correspondence with the author, June 14.

Larson, LeRoy W. 1975. "Scandinavian-American Folk Dance Music of the Norwegians in Minnesota." Ph.D. diss., University of Minnesota.

Larson, Ron. 1991. *McFarland's Norwegian Heritage.* McFarland, Wis.: McFarland Historical Society.

Lauper, Lucile, and Ethelyn Thompson. 1987. *The Hollandale Review: The History of the Village of Hollandale From 1887 to 1987.* Blanchardville, Wis.: Ski Printers.

Laws, G. Malcolm. 1964. *Native American Balladry: A Descriptive Study and Bibliographical Syllabus.* Philadelphia: American Folklore Society.

Leary, James P. 1983. "Ethnic Country Music along Superior's South Shore," *JEMF Quarterly* 19:72. Pp. 219–230.

———. 1984. "Old Time Music in Northern Wisconsin," *American Music* 2:1. Pp. 71–87.

———. 1987. *The Wisconsin Patchwork: A Commentary on Recordings from the Helene Stratman-Thomas Collection of Wisconsin Folk Music.* Madison: University of Wisconsin, Department of Continuing Education in the Arts.

———. 1988. "Czech- and German-American 'Polka' Music," *Journal of American Folklore* 101:401. Pp. 339–345.

———. 1990a. *Minnesota Polka: Dance Music from Four Traditions.* St. Paul: Minnesota Historical Society.

———. 1990b. "The Legacy of Viola Turpeinen," *Finnish Americana* 8. Pp. 6–11.

———. 1991a. *Yodeling in Dairyland: A History of Swiss Music in Wisconsin.* Mount Horeb: Wisconsin Folk Museum.

———. 1991b. "Folk Arts of Eastern Europeans in the Chippewa Valley, 1890–1925." Eau Claire, Wis.: Chippewa Valley Museum.

———. 1992. "Sawdust and Devils: Indian Fiddling in the Western Great Lakes Region." In *Medicine Fiddle,* ed. James P. Leary. Bismarck: North Dakota Humanities Council. Pp. 30–35.

———. 1996. "Polka." In *American Folklore: An Encyclopedia,* ed. Jan H. Brunvand. New York: Garland. Pp. 574–576.

———. 1997. "Czech Polka Music in Wisconsin." In *Musics of Multicultural America,* ed. Kip Lornell and Anne Rasmussen. New York: Schirmer. Pp. 25–48.

———. 1998. *Wisconsin Folklore.* Madison: University of Wisconsin Press.

———. 2001a. "The Discovery of Finnish American Folk Music," *Scandinavian Studies* 73:3. Pp. 475–492.

———. 2001b. "Fieldwork Forgotten; or, Alan Lomax Goes North," *Midwestern Folklore* 27:2. Pp. 5–20.

———. 2001c. *So Ole Says to Lena: Folk Humor of the Upper Midwest.* Madison: University of Wisconsin Press.

———. 2002. "The German Concertina in the Upper Midwest." In *Land without Nightengales: Music in the Making of German-America,* ed. Philip V. Bohlman and Otto Holzapfel. Madison, Wis.: Max Kade Institute for German American Studies. Pp. 191–232.

———. 2004a. "O Cheesehead, Where Art Thou? Alan Lomax and Wisconsin's Folk Music," *Wisconsin Academy Review* 50:4. Pp. 23–29.

———. 2004b. "Dialect Songs among the Dutch," *Midwestern Folklore* 30:1. Pp. 15–35.

Leary, James P., and Richard March. 1991. "Dutchman Bands: Genre, Ethnicity, and Pluralism." In *Creative Ethnicity: Symbols and Strategies of Contemporary Ethnic Life,* ed. Stephen Stern and John Allan Cicala. Logan: Utah State University Press. Pp. 21–43.

———. 1993. "Farm, Forest, and Factory: Songs of Midwestern Labor." In *Songs about Work: Essays in Occupational Culture,* ed. Archie Green. Bloomington: Folklore Institute, Indiana University. Pp. 253–286.

———. 1996. *Down Home Dairyland: A Listener's Guide.* Madison: University of Wisconsin Extension.

Leary, James P., and Robert T. Teske. 1991. *In Tune with Tradition: Wisconsin Folk Musical Instruments.* Cedarburg, Wis.: Cedarburg Cultural Center.

Lieberman, Robbie. 1989. *My Song Is My Weapon.* Urbana: University of Illinois Press.

Lomax, Alan. 1938. Letter to Charles Brown, July 1. Alan Lomax Correspondence, 1938, Archive of Folk Culture, Library of Congress.

———. 1939. "Archive of American Folksong: Report of the Assistant in Charge," *Annual Report of the Librarian of Congress.* Washington, D.C.: U.S. Government Printing Office.

———. 1940. "Music in Your Own Back Yard," *American Girl.* Pp. 5–7, 46, 49.

———. 1959. "Bluegrass Background: Folk Music with Overdrive," *Esquire* 52. P. 108.

———. 1960. *The Folk Songs of North America.* New York: Doubleday.

Lomax, Alan, with Woody Guthrie and Pete Seeger. 1967. *Hard-Hitting Songs for Hard-Hit People.* New York: Oak.

Lomax, Alan, and John A. Lomax. 1941. *Our Singing Country.* New York: Macmillan.

Lomax, John A. 1910. *Cowboy Songs and Other Frontier Ballads.* New York: Sturgis and Walton.

———. 1915. "Some Types of American Folk-Song," *Journal of American Folklore* 28:107. Pp. 1–17.

———. 1947. *Adventures of a Ballad Hunter.* New York: Macmillan.

Lornell, Kip. 1985. "The Early Career of Whoopee John Wilfahrt," *John Edwards Memorial Foundation Quarterly* 21:5–6. Pp. 51–53.

———. 2002. *Introducing American Folk Music: Ethnic and Grassroots Traditions in the United States,* 2d ed. Boston: McGraw-Hill.

Lornell, Kip, and Anne K. Rasmussen. 1997. *Musics of Multicultural America.* New York: Schirmer Books.

Luchsinger, Tim. 1991. "Swiss Music." Paper for folklore of Wisconsin class, University of Wisconsin.

Lukas, Martha. 1983. "A History of Dance Bands and Dance Music in Langlade County from 1878 to the 1980s." Music folder, Wisconsin Room, Antigo Public Library, Antigo, Wisconsin.

Lyon, George W. 1999. *Community Music in Alberta: Some Good Schoolhouse Stuff!* Calgary, Alberta: University of Calgary Press.

Machann, Clinton. 1983. "Country-Western Music and the 'Now' Sound in Texas-Czech Polka Music," *JEMF Quarterly* 19:69. Pp. 3–7.

Machann, Clinton, and James Mendl. 1983. *Krásna Amerika.* Austin, Tex.: Eakin.

Mackenzie, W. Roy. 1928. *The Quest of the Ballad.* Princeton, N.J.: Princeton University Press.

MacLaren, Gay. 1938. *Morally We Roll Along.* Boston: Little, Brown.

Malone, Bill C. 1993. *Singing Cowboys and Musical Mountaineers: Southern Culture and the Roots of Country Music.* Athens: University of Georgia Press.

———. 2001. "Bluegrass Wisconsin," *Wisconsin Academy Review* 47:2. Pp. 34–39.

———. 2002a. *Country Music, U.S.A.,* 2d rev. ed. Austin: University of Texas Press.

———. 2002b. *Don't Get above Your Raisin': Country Music and the Southern Working Class.* Urbana: University of Illinois Press.

March, Richard. 1983. "The Tamburitza Tradition." Ph.D. diss., Indiana University.

———. 1985. "Slovenian Polka Music: Tradition and Transition," *JEMF Quarterly* 21:75/76. Pp. 47–50.

Marcus, Greil. 1997. *Invisible Republic: Bob Dylan's Basement Tapes.* New York: Holt.

Martin, Philip. 1976. "Ed Johnson: Heavenly Sounds from the Devil's Instrument," *Wisconsin Trails* 17:4. Pp. 10–11.

———. 1979. "The Hardanger Fiddle in Wisconsin," *Ocooch Mountain News* 5 (August). Pp. 10–11.

———. 1980. "Hardanger Fiddlers," *Ocooch Mountain News* 6 (January–February). Pp. 148–149, 161.

———. 1985. "Hoppwaltzes and Homebrew," *Sing Out!* 31:3. Pp. 26–34.

———. 1994. *Farmhouse Fiddlers: Music & Dance Traditions in the Rural Midwest.* Mount Horeb, Wis.: Midwest Traditions.

Mattson, Joy. 2002. "Walking Along, Singing a Song: William August Homann." Paper for American folk and vernacular music class, University of Wisconsin.

Meade, Guthrie T. 1987. "Minnesota and Wisconsin Old Time Fiddle Contests in 1926 Newspapers." Typescript in the author's possession.

Meade, Guthrie T., with Dick Spottswood and Douglas S. Meade. 2002. *Country Music Sources: A Biblio-Discography of Commercially Recorded Traditional Music.* Chapel Hill: Southern Folklife Collection, University of North Carolina at Chapel Hill Libraries.

Messer-Kruse, Timothy. 1993. "The Campus Klan of the University of Wisconsin: Tacit and Active Support for the Ku Klux Klan in a Culture of Intolerance," *Wisconsin Magazine of History* 77:1. Pp. 3–38.

Mickel, Jere C. 1967. "The Genesis of Toby: A Folk Hero of the American Theater," *Journal of American Folklore* 80:318. Pp. 334–340.

Milburn, George. 1930. *The Hobo's Hornbook.* New York: Ives Washburn.

Milnes, Gerry. 1999. *Play of a Fiddle: Traditional Music, Dance, and Folklore in West Virginia.* Lexington: University Press of Kentucky.

Mitchell, Donald D. Kilolani, and George S. Kanahele. 1979. "Steel Guitar." In *Hawaiian Music and Musicians: An Illustrated History,* ed. George S. Kanahele. Honolulu: University of Hawaii Press. Pp. 365–378.

Mitchell, Roger E. 1984. *From Fathers to Sons: A Wisconsin Family Farm,* a special issue of *Midwestern Journal of Language and Folklore* 10:1–2.

Mon Pleasure, Charles W. 1910–1911. "Adventures of a Violinist," *Platteville Witness and Mining Times,* December 28–May 17.

Morrison, Craig. 1996. *Go Cat Go! Rockabilly Music and Its Makers.* Urbana: University of Illinois Press.

Murphy, W. W. 1993. *Benton, New Diggings and the Irish Immigration into Lafayette County.* Darlington, Wis.: Lafayette County Historical Society.

Myers, Gary E. 1994. *Do You Hear That Beat: Wisconsin Pop/Rock in the 50s and 60s.* Downey, Calif.: Hummingbird Publishing.

Nathan, Hans. 1946. "The Tyrolese Family Rainer, and the Vogue of Singing Mountain-Troupes in Europe and America," *Musical Quarterly* 32:1. Pp. 63–79.

Neff, Deborah, and Phillip Zarrilli. 1987. *Wilhelm Tell in America's "Little Switzerland."* New Glarus, Wis.: Wilhelm Tell Community Guild.

Nettl, Bruno. 1962. *An Introduction to Folk Music in the United States,* rev. ed. Detroit: Wayne State University Press.

———. 1978. "Some Aspects of the History of World Music in the Twentieth Century: Questions, Problems, and Concepts," *Ethnomusicology* 12. Pp. 123–136.

———. 1999. Review of *Musics of Multicultural America, Ethnomusicology* 43:3. Pp. 557–559.

Nettl, Paul. 1952. *National Anthems.* New York: Ungar.

Newell, William Wells. 1888. "On the Field and Work of a Journal of American Folk-Lore," *Journal of American Folklore* 1:1. Pp. 3–7.

———. 1889. "Editor's Note," *Journal of American Folklore* 2:4. Pp. 1–2.

Niemela, Juha. 1997. "Cultural Reflections in Finnish American Songs," *Journal of Finnish Studies* 1:3. Pp. 100–116.

Nobley, Robert E. 1973. "What Is Old Time Music?" *Devil's Box* 21 (June). Pp. 19–20.

Nupen, Dagfinn. 1999. *Eldre Folkemusikkinstrument: LÆring på gamlemåten.* Ørsta/Høydalsneset, Norway: Dagfinn Nupen.

Nusbaum, Philip. 1989. *Norwegian-American Music from Minnesota: Old-Time and Traditional Favorites.* St. Paul: Minnesota Historical Society Press.

O'Donnell, Brian. 2003. "Leizime Brusoe: Wisconsin Northwoods Fiddler," *Old-Time Herald* 9:1. Pp. 14–17.

Odum, Howard W., and Guy B. Johnson. 1925. *The Negro and His Songs.* Chapel Hill: University of North Carolina Press.

Olson, Paul. 1976. *Broken Hoops and Plains People: A Catalogue of Ethnic Resources in the Humanities.* Lincoln: University of Nebraska Press.

Original Michigan Fiddlers Association. 1986. *Old Time Music & Dances of Yester-year.* N.p.: Original Michigan Fiddlers Association.

Owens, William. 1983. *Tell Me a Story, Sing Me a Song.* Austin: University of Texas Press.

Palmer, Robert. 1982. *Deep Blues.* New York: Viking Penguin.

Pankake, Jon, and Marcia Pankake. 1994. Review of the Goose Island Ramblers' *Midwest Ramblin', Old-Time Herald.* Spring. Pp. 47–48.

Patterson, Timothy A. 1975. "Country Music among the Flatlanders: Early Midwestern Radio Barn Dances," *Journal of Country Music* 6:1. Pp. 12–18.

Peña, Manuel. 1985. *The Texas-Mexican Conjunto: History of a Working-Class Music.* Austin: University of Texas Press.

Penewell, Jack. File folder of newspaper clippings, Wisconsin Music Archives, Mills Music Library, University of Wisconsin.

Peters, Robert. 1993. *Crunching Gravel.* Madison: University of Wisconsin Press.

Petersen, William J. 1959. "New Year's Day in Iowa," *Palimpsest* 11:1. Pp. 1–32.

Pine, Howard, and Philip Nusbaum. 1995. "In Memoriam: Robert F. Andresen, 1937–1995," *Inside Bluegrass* 21:7. Pp. 22–23.

Plantenga, Bart. 2004. *Yodel-Ay-Ee-Oooo: The Secret History of Yodeling around the World.* New York: Routledge.

Porter, James. 1978. "The Traditional Music of Europeans in America." In *Selected Reports in Ethnomusicology,* 3, ed. James Porter. Pp. 1–23.

Porterfield, Nolan. 1979. *Jimmie Rodgers: The Life and Times of America's Blue Yodeler.* Urbana: University of Illinois Press.

———. 1996. *Last Cavalier: The Life and Times of John Lomax.* Urbana: University of Illinois Press.

Pound, Louise. 1922. *American Ballads and Songs.* New York: Scribner's.

Primeggia, Pamela R., Salvatore Primeggia, and Joseph J. Bentivegna. 1994. "Nicola Paone, Narrator of the Italian American Experience." In *Italian Americans in a Multicultural Society,* ed. Jerome Krase and Judith N. DeSena. Stony Brook, N.Y.: Forum Italicum. Pp. 89–105.

Reiman, Lewis C. 1981. *Between the Iron and the Pine.* AuTrain, Mich.: Avery Color Studios.

Reuss, Richard. 1979. "Folk Music and Social Conscience: The Musical Odyssey of Charles Seeger," *Western Folklore* 38. Pp. 221–238.

Rickaby, Franz. 1925. *Ballads and Songs of the Shanty-Boy.* Cambridge, Mass.: Harvard University Press.

Rippley, Lavern J. 1992. *The Whoopee John Wilfahrt Dance Band.* Northfield, Minn.: St. Olaf College.

Robertson, Sidney. 1938. Letter to Alan Lomax, June 14. Sidney Robertson Cowell Correspondence, Archive of Folk Culture, Library of Congress.

Romalis, Shelly. 1998. *Pistol Packin' Mama: Aunt Molly Jackson and the Politics of Folksong.* Urbana: University of Illinois Press.

Román, Manuel. 1988. "Notes on the History of the Bandonion." In *The Bandonion: A Tango History,* ed. Javier Garciá Mendéz and Arturo Penón. London, Ontario: Nightwood. Pp. 39–47.

Rosenberg, Neil V. 1985. *Bluegrass: A History.* Urbana: University of Illinois Press.

———. 1990. "Whose Music Is Canadian Country Music? A Precis." In *CanMus Documents 5: Ethnomusicology in Canada*, ed. Bob Witmer and Beverly Diamond. Toronto: Institute for Canadian Studies. Pp. 236–238.

Rosendahl, Peter. 1980. *Selections from Han Ola og Han Per.* Spring Grove, Minn.: Ye Olde Opera House.

Ross, Edward. 1914. *The Old World in the New.* New York: Century.

Russell, Tony. 2004. *Country Music Records: A Discography, 1921–1942.* Oxford and New York: Oxford University Press.

Sachs, Curt. 1937. *World History of the Dance.* New York: Norton.

Samuelson, Dave. n.d. "The Prairie Ramblers: The WLS Swinging String Band," reprinted from an unknown source in Whitford, *The Way It Was.* 2000. Pp. 72–73.

Santelli, Robert, Holly George-Warren, and Jim Brown. 2001. *American Roots Music.* New York: Ginger Group Productions and Rolling Stone Press.

Scarborough, Dorothy. 1925. *On the Trail of Negro Folk-Songs.* Cambridge, Mass.: Harvard University Press.

———. 1937. *A Song Catcher in the Southern Mountains.* New York: Columbia University Press.

Schoolcraft, Henry Rowe. 1839. *Algic Resources.* New York: Harper.

Scott, Frank. 2003. Review of *Slow Music, Roots and Rhythm Newsletter* 127 (February–March). P. 29.

Sharp, Cecil J. 1932. *English Folk Songs from the Southern Appalachians,* 2 vols. Oxford: Oxford University Press.

Shaw, Lloyd. 1949. *The Round Dance Book.* Caldwell, Idaho: Caxton.

Simonson, Sigurd J. 1946. *The Mongrels.* New York: Diana.

Slobin, Mark. 1993. *Subcultural Sounds: Micromusics of the West.* Hanover, N.H.: Wesleyan University Press/University Press of New England.

Slout, W. L. 1972. *Theatre in a Tent: The Development of a Provincial Entertainment.* Bowling Green, Ohio: Bowling Green University Popular Press.

Smith, L. Mayne. 1965. "An Introduction to Bluegrass," *Journal of American Folklore* 78:309. Pp. 245–256.

Snyder, Jared M. 1994. "Leadbelly and His Windjammer: Examining the African American Button Accordion Tradition," *American Music* 12:2. Pp. 148–166.

———. 1997. "Squeezebox: The Legacy of Afro-Mississippi Accordionists," *Black Music Research Journal* 17:1. Pp. 38–39.

Spottswood, Richard K. 1990. *Ethnic Music on Records: A Discography of Ethnic Recordings Produced in the United States, 1893–1942,* 7 vols. Urbana: University of Illinois Press.

Starr, Mary Agnes. 1981. *Pea Soup and Johnny Cake.* Madison, Wis.: Red Mountain.

Stokker, Kathleen. 2000. *Keeping Christmas: Yuletide Traditions in Norway and the New Land.* St. Paul: Minnesota Historical Society Press.

Talley, Thomas. 1922. *Negro Folk Rhymes (Wise or Otherwise).* New York: Macmillan.

Tapia, John E. 1997. *Circuit Chautauqua: From Rural Education to Popular Entertainment in Early Twentieth Century America.* Jefferson, N.C.: McFarland.

Tawa, Nicholas. 1980. *Sweet Songs for Gentle Americans: The Parlor Song in America, 1790–1860.* Bowling Green, Ohio: Popular Press.

———. 1982. *A Sound of Strangers: Musical Culture, Acculturation, and the Post–Civil War Ethnic American.* Metuchen, N.J.: Scarecrow.

Taylor, Rose Schuster. 1945. "Peter Schuster: Dane County Farmer (II)," *Wisconsin Magazine of History* 28:4. Pp. 431–454.

Telschow, Gustave. 1963. *Those Dear Hills of Home.* North Lake, Wis.: Keystone.

Thernstrom, Stephan, ed. 1980. *Harvard Encyclopedia of American Ethnic Groups.* Cambridge, Mass.: Harvard University Press.

Titon, Jeff Todd. 1977. *Early Downhome Blues: A Musical and Cultural Analysis.* Urbana: University of Illinois Press.

Topping, Brett. 1980. "The Sidney Robertson Cowell Collection," *Folklife Center News* 3:3. Pp. 4–5, 8.

Townsend, Charles R. 1976. *San Antonio Rose: The Life and Music of Bob Wills.* Urbana: University of Illinois Press.

Tribe, Ivan. 1984. *Mountaineer Jamboree: Country Music in Western Virginia.* Lexington: University Press of Kentucky.

Vachon, Jingo Viitala. 1975. *Sagas from Sisula.* L'Anse, Mich.: L'Anse Sentinel.

Vennum, Thomas, Jr. 1982. *The Ojibwe Dance Drum: Its History and Construction.* Smithsonian Folklife Studies, No. 2. Washington, D.C.: Smithsonian Institution Press.

Wagner, Christoph. 2001. *Das Akkordeon: Oder die Erfindung der populären Musik.* Mainz: Schott Musik International.

———. 2002. "Old World Hillbillies: Swiss Music Entertainers on Tour through the United States during the 1920s." Madison, Wis.: Max Kade Institute for German American Studies. Electronic publication, http:// mki.wisc.edu. Pp. 1–9.

Wald, Elijah. 2004. *Escaping the Delta: Robert Johnson and the Invention of the Blues.* New York: HarperCollins.

Welk, Lawrence. 1971. *Wunnerful, Wunnerful! The Autobiography of Lawrence Welk.* New York: Bantam.

Wellman, Manly Wade. 1959. *The Rebel Songster: Songs the Confederates Sang.* Charlotte, N.C.: Heritage House.

Whisnant, David. 1983. *All That Is Native and Fine: The Politics of Culture in an American Region.* Chapel Hill: University of North Carolina Press.

White, Newman I. 1928. *American Negro Folk-Songs.* Cambridge, Mass.: Harvard University Press.

White, Richard. 1991. *The Middle Ground: Indians, Empires, and Republics in the Great Lakes Region, 1650–1815.* Cambridge: Cambridge University Press.

Whitford, Kenneth W. 2000. *The Way It Was: Original Songs by Windy Whitford.* Madison: n.p.

Wiff, P. M. 1986. "Just Fiddlin' Around." In *And All Our Yesterdays . . . Book Five,* Spring Valley chapter of the Pierce County Historical Society. Pp. 35–60.

Wilgus, D. K. 1959. *Anglo-American Folksong Scholarship since 1898.* New Brunswick, N.J.: Rutgers University Press.

———. 1975. "Bradley Kincaid." In *Stars of Country Music,* ed. Bill C. Malone and Judith McCulloh. Urbana: University of Illinois Press. Pp. 86–94.

Wilson, Joe. 1990. *Masters of the Steel String Guitar: A National Tour of American Guitar Styles.* Washington, D.C.: National Council for the Traditional Arts.

Wisconsin Cartographer's Guild. 1998. *Wisconsin's Past and Present: A Historical Atlas.* Madison: University of Wisconsin Press.

Wittke, Carl. 1952. "The Immigrant Theme on the American Stage," *Mississippi Valley Historical Review* 39. Pp. 211–232.

Wolfe, Charles K. 1982. *Kentucky Country*. Lexington: University Press of Kentucky.

Wolfe, Charles K., and Kip Lornell. 1992. *The Life and Legend of Leadbelly*. New York: HarperCollins.

Young, Jordan R. 1994. *Spike Jones off the Record: The Man Who Murdered Music*. Beverly Hills, Calif.: Past Times.

Zelinsky, Wilbur. 1973. *The Cultural Geography of the United States*. Englewood Cliffs, N.J.: Prentice-Hall.

Media Productions (M)

Across the Fields: Traditional Norwegian-American Music from Wisconsin, produced by Philip Martin. 1982. LP. Folklore Village Farm/Wisconsin Folklife Center FVF 201.

American Fiddle Tunes, ed. Alan Jabbour. 2000. Compact disc and booklet. Library of Congress Archive of Folk Culture and Rounder Records RNR 18964–1518–2.

American Spelmans Trio. 1976. *Old Country Folk Fiddling by Edwin Johnson, Bruce Johnson, and Paul Dahlin*. LP. Rounder 6004.

American Yodeling, 1911–1946, ed. Christoph Wagner. 1998. Compact disc and booklet. Trikont US-02462–2.

Andresen Guitar Group, *Jack Pine Style,* vols. 1 and 2. 1993. Cassette. Jack Pine JP-101, JP- 102.

———. *Guitar Hymns.* 1994. Cassette. Jack Pine JP-103.

"Andresen Show," *Down Home Dairyland,* produced by James P. Leary and Richard March. 1994. Radio program. Wisconsin Public Radio.

Anthologie du Folklore Wallon: Les Wallons d'Amerique (Wisconsin), ed. Francoise Lempereur. 1981. LP and booklet. Namur, Belgium: Centre D'Action Culturelle de la Commonaute D'Expression Francaise FM33010.

Anthology of American Folk Music, ed. Harry Smith. 1952. Six LPs and booklet. Folkways Records 02951.

Armstrong, Howard. 1985. *Louie Bluie*. CD and booklet. Arhoolie CD 470.

Cloud, Joe. 1938. Field recordings by Alan Lomax for the Library of Congress, Archive of Folksong. AFS 2469–2470.

Doc Watson. 1964. Liner notes by Ralph Rinzler. LP. Vanguard VSD-79152.

Dylan, Bob. 1963. "With God on Our Side," *The Times They Are A-Changin'.* LP. Columbia CS 8905.

Emerald Isle Ceili Band. 1997. *The Moon behind the Mill*. Cassette. Emerald Isle Ceili Band CT 1001.

Fiddlers Had Fun in Yankton, SD. 1986. LP. Westmark Records 21738.

Finseth, Leonard. 1979. *Scandinavian Old Time*. LP. Banjar Records BR 1834.

———. 1981. *The Hills of Old Wisconsin*. LP. CMS Recordings.

Folk Music from Wisconsin, ed. Helene Stratman-Thomas. 1960. LP and booklet. Library of Congress AFS L55. Reissued 2001 on compact disc with additional photographs, Rounder Records RNR 18964–1521.

"Folk-Songs of America": The Robert Winslow Gordon Collection, 1922–1932, ed. Neil V. Rosenberg and Debora G. Kodish. 1978. LP and booklet. Archive of Folk Song, Library of Congress AFS L68.

Global Accordion: Early Recordings, 1927–1948, ed. Christoph Wagner. 2001. Compact disc and booklet. Wergo Weltmusik SM 1623 2.

Gogebic Range Tamburitzans. c. 1980. LP. Gogebic Range Tamburitzans.

Hawaiian Steel Guitar Classics, 1927–1938, ed. Bob Brozman and Chris Strachwitz. 1993. Compact disc and booklet. Arhoolie/Folklyric CD 7027.

Hofner, Adolph. 1980. *South Texas Swing.* Compact disc and booklet. Arhoolie/Folklyric CD 7029.

Honor the Earth Powwow, ed. Thomas Vennum, Jr. 1991. Compact disc and booklet. Rykodisc RACS 0199.

Hoosier Hot Shots: Rural Rhythm, 1935–1942, ed. Douglas B. Green. 1992. Compact disc and booklet. Columbia/Legacy CD 52735.

Italie: Chants & Danses/Songs and Dances of Italy, ed. Alan Lomax. 1989. Compact disc and booklet. Arion FN 62083.

Kalama's Quartet: Early Hawaiian Classics, 1927–1932, ed. Bob Brozman and Chris Strachwitz. 1993. Compact disc and booklet. Arhoolie/Folklyric CD 7028.

Katz, Mickey. 2000. *Greatest Shticks,* ed. Steven Lederman. Compact disc and booklet. Koch Records KOC-CD-8059.

Kessinger, Clark. 1972. *Old-Time Music with Fiddle and Guitar.* LP and booklet. Rounder Records 0004.

Kivela, Johnny and Einar Kivela. c. 1960. *Johnny's Hot Shots.* LP. Sound Recording Company SRC-5088.

Malm, Bertel. 1972. *The Fiddling Swede.* LP. Mark Records 21542.

Massey, Louise, and the Westerners. 2000. *Ridin' Down That Old Texas Trail,* ed. Wayne W. Daniel. Compact disc and booklet. Cattle CCD235.

1976 Bicentennial Fiddlers Contest: Yankton, South Dakota. 1976. LP. Al Opland Recording MC6210.

Northland Hoedown, produced by Bob Andresen. 1984. Cassette. Inland Sea Recordings. Initially broadcast on KUMD radio, Duluth, Minn.

Norwegian-American Music from Minnesota: Old-Time and Traditional Favorites, ed. Philip Nusbaum. 1990. LP and booklet. Minnesota Historical Society 55101.

Novelty Songs Crazy and Obscure, 1914–1946, ed. Keith Chandler. 2000. Compact disc and booklet. Trikont US-0276.

O Brother, Where Art Thou? 2000. Compact disc and booklet. Lost Highway.

Oren, Selmer. 1995. *Hall of Fame Fiddler.* Cassette. Southern Wisconsin Old Time Fiddlers Association.

Pickard Family. 2004. *Walking in the Parlour: Old Time Playing and Singing.* Compact disc and booklet. British Archive of Country Music B.A.C.M. 084.

Slow Music: Texas Bohemia II, ed. Thomas Meinecke. 1996. Compact disc and booklet. Trikont US-0222.

Songcatcher, directed by Maggie Greenwald. 2000. Film. Ergo Arts.

Songs of Migration & Immigration, Folk Music in America series, vol. 6, ed. Richard K. Spottswood. 1977. LP and booklet. Library of Congress LBC 6.

Sons of the Pioneers. 1973. *The Sons of the Pioneers,* ed. Ken Griffis, notes by Norm Cohen. LP. John Edwards Memorial Foundation JEMF 102.

Stare I Dobre (Oldies but Goodies). c. 1977. LP. Balkan Records BLP 5013.

Stranded in the U.S.A.: Early Songs of Emigration, ed. Christoph Wagner. 2004. Compact disc and two booklets. Trikont US-0326.

Texas Bohemia, ed. Thomas Meinecke. 1994. Compact disc and booklet. Trikont US-0201.

Texas-Czech, Bohemian, & Moravian Bands, 1929–1959, ed. Chris Stachwitz. 1993. Compact disc and booklet. Arhoolie/Folklyric CD 7026.

Traditional Music from Clare and Beyond, ed. Gearoid O'Hallmhurain. 1996. Compact disc and booklet. Celtic Crossings OWR-0046–2.

A Treasury of Library of Congress Field Recordings, ed. Stephen Wade. 1997. Compact disc and booklet. Rounder Records CD 1500.

Uncle Ozzie and Cousin Fuzzy. 1998. *Memory Sounds.* Compact disc. Cuca Records KCG- 1000.

We Rode Our Horses and Played with Fiddlers from Yankton, South Dakota, to Havana, North Dakota. 1983. LP. Westmark Custom Records 21716.

The Wildwoods. c. 1980. Cassette. Privately produced by Tim Andresen and Gary Andresen.

Work's Many Voices, Vol. 1, ed. Archie Green. 1986. LP and insert. John Edward Memorial Foundation JEMF 110.

Yodel: Straight from the Soul. 1996. Video. Good Earth Productions.

Interviews (I)

Andresen, Robert F. 1994. Tape-recorded interview conducted by James P. Leary. Duluth, Minnesota, January 16. Interviewer's collection.

Bollerud, Bruce. 1987. Tape-recorded interview conducted by James P. Leary and Richard March. Madison, Wis., June. Down Home Dairyland Collection, Wisconsin Music Archives, University of Wisconsin.

———. 1990. Tape-recorded interview conducted by James P. Leary. Madison, Wisconsin, July 16. Goose Island Ramblers Collection, State Historical Society of Wisconsin.

———. 1995. Tape-recorded interview conducted by James P. Leary. Wisconsin Folk Museum, Mount Horeb, Wis., June 3. Interviewer's collection.

———. 2003. Telephone conversations with James P. Leary. July 23 and August 21.

———. 2005. Telephone conversation with James P. Leary. June 24.

Chmielewski, Florian. 1990. Tape-recorded interview conducted by James P. Leary. Sturgeon Lake, Minnesota, February 8. Minnesota Polka Collection, Minnesota Historical Society.

Dorschner, Ray. 1988. Tape-recorded interview conducted by James P. Leary and Richard March. Evansville, Wisconsin, May 1. Down Home Dairyland Collection, Wisconsin Music Archives, University of Wisconsin.

Finseth, Leonard. 1988. Tape-recorded interview conducted by James P. Leary. Mondovi, Wis., May 23. Down Home Dairyland Collection, Wisconsin Music Archives, University of Wisconsin.

Gilbertsen, George. 1990. Tape-recorded interview conducted by James P. Leary. Madison, Wisconsin, June 27. Goose Island Ramblers Collection, State Historical Society of Wisconsin.

———. 2003. Telephone conversations with James P. Leary. June 23 and July 10.

Herman, Ralph. 2000. Tape-recorded interview conducted by James P. Leary. Pleasantville, Wis., July 19. Chippewa Valley Museum.

Johnson, Bernard. 1989. Tape-recorded interview conducted by James P. Leary. Blue Mounds, Wisconsin, July 1. Down Home Dairyland Collection, Wisconsin Music Archives, University of Wisconsin.

Maki, Reino. 1981. Tape-recorded interview conducted by James P. Leary and Matthew Gallman. Washburn, Wisconsin, March 11. Northland College Collection, Wisconsin Music Archives, University of Wisconsin.

McMahan, Francis. 1988. Tape-recorded interview conducted by James P. Leary and Richard March. Madison, Wisconsin, May 9. Down Home Dairyland Collection, Wisconsin Music Archives, University of Wisconsin.

Retka, Gene. 2004. Telephone conversation with James P. Leary. Little Falls, Minnesota, June 13.

Synkula, Bruno. 1981. Tape recorded interview conducted by James P. Leary. Ashland, Wisconsin, February 23. Northland College Collection, Wisconsin Music Archives, University of Wisconsin.

Waupoose, Everett "Butch." 1989. Tape-recorded interview conducted by James P. Leary. Neopit, Menominee Nation, May 13. Interviewer's collection.

Whitford, Kenneth Wendell. 1990. Tape-recorded interview conducted by James P. Leary. Cottage Grove, Wisconsin, July 12. Goose Island Ramblers Collection, State Historical Society of Wisconsin.

Woodford, Fred. 1994. Tape-recorded interview conducted by James P. Leary. Eau Claire, Wisconsin, August 10. Chippewa Valley Museum.

Zurawski, Greg. 1988. Tape-recorded interview conducted by James P. Leary. Custer, Wisconsin, February 26. Down Home Dairyland Collection, Wisconsin Music Archives, University of Wisconsin.

Companion Website Track Listing
www.oup.com/us/polkabilly

Track	Code	Description	Length
1	I	Comments on Charles Squire Smith: The music teacher	0:33
2	C	Intro	0:20
3	M	Goose Island Ramblers: "Windy's Schottische"	0:18
4	C/I	Intro to and interview of Kenneth Wendell "Windy" Whitford	1:13
5	M	Goose Island Ramblers: "Barney McCoy"	2:32
6	C	Transition and intro to "Milwaukee Fire"	0:43
7	M	Robert Walker: "Milwaukee Fire," followed by the Goose Island Ramblers: "Milwaukee Fire"	1:49
8	M	Goose Island Ramblers: "Brother"	4:41
9	C	Whitford's repertoire	0:33
10	M	Goose Island Ramblers: "Reierson's Two-Step" (begins)	0:17
11	I	Interview with Whitford	0:44
12	M	Goose Island Ramblers: "Reierson's Two-Step" (continues)	1:14
13	M	Goose Island Ramblers: *Auction pa* [sic] *Strømmen's* (begins)	0:25
14	C/I	Comments on Whitford and Norwegian fiddlers; Whitford comments	0:48
15	M	Goose Island Ramblers: *Auction pa* [sic] *Strømmen's* (continues)	0:24
16	C/I	Origins of the name of the Goose Island Ramblers; Whitford comments	1:28
17	M	Prairie Ramblers: "Shady Grove"	1:22
18	C	Outro on Prairie Ramblers; Transition	0:19
19	C/I	Intro to Salty Hougan; Whitford comments	1:46
20	C	Intro to "I Worked for a Farmer"	0:13
21	M	Goose Island Ramblers: "I Worked for a Farmer"	2:23
22	C/I	Whitford's near-national fame; Whitford comments	1:12

Key for Letter Codes
 I = Interview or comments from performers/consultants
M = Musical selection
C = Comments from hosts Jim Leary or Rick March

Track	Code	Description	Length
23	M	Goose Island Ramblers: "My Blue Eyes Have Gone" (begins)	1:10
24	C	End and rebirth of the Goose Island Ramblers	0:17
25	C	Outro and credits	0:31
26	M	Goose Island Ramblers: "My Blue Eyes Have Gone" (continues)	1:52
27	I	Windy Whitford interview	0:35
28	C	Intro	0:13
29	M	Goose Island Ramblers: "Oscar's Cannonball"	3:11
30	C/I	Rebirth of the Goose Island Ramblers; Whitford comments	1:19
31	C	Choosing a name for the new group	0:24
32	C/I	Intro to George Gilbertsen; Gilbertsen interview	1:05
33	C	Intro to "On the Beach at Waunakee"	0:14
34	M	Goose Island Ramblers: "On the Beach at Waunakee"	3:11
35	C/I	Intro to Bruce Bollerud; Bollerud interview on Roy Anderson	1:02
36	M	Goose Island Ramblers: "Swiss Yodel Waltz"	2:44
37	C/I	Intro to Whitford; Whitford comments on his style	0:56
38	M	Goose Island Ramblers: "Going Back to the Hills"	2:20
39	C/I	Playing at Glen and Ann's bar; interview of George Gilbertsen	1:05
40	M	Goose Island Ramblers: "Norwegian War Chant"	0:35
41	C	Goose Island Ramblers' props	0:28
42	M	Goose Island Ramblers: "Mountain Dew" (begins)	0:45
43	I	Interview of Gilbertsen: Theft of the jug	0:58
44	M	Goose Island Ramblers: "Mountain Dew" (continues)	0:33
45	M	Goose Island Ramblers: "Milwaukee Waltz" (begins)	1:18
46	I	Interview of Bruce Bollerud: Comments on George Gilbertsen	0:20
47	M	Goose Island Ramblers: "Milwaukee Waltz" (continues)	0:51
48	M	Goose Island Ramblers: "Break Song"	0:31
49	C	Intro to "Hurley Hop"	0:28
50	M	Goose Island Ramblers: "Hurley Hop"	2:22
51	M	Goose Island Ramblers: "Francuszka Polka" (begins)	0:12
52	C	Final comments on Goose Island Ramblers	0:13
53	C	Outro and credits	0:27
54	M	Goose Island Ramblers: "Francuszka Polka" (continues)	1:05
55	M	Goose Island Ramblers, *"Paul paa Haugen"* (begins)	0:15
56	C	Intro	0:15
57	C	Intro to Bruce Bollerud	0:20
58	M	Goose Island Ramblers, *"Paul paa Haugen"* (continues)	1:10
59	I	Bruce Bollerud interview: Growing up on a Norwegian farm in Wisconsin	0:28
60	C/I	Learning "Ole" song; Bollerud comments	0:40

Key for Letter Codes
 I = Interview or comments from performers/consultants
 M = Musical selection
 C = Comments from hosts Jim Leary or Rick March

Track	Code	Description	Length
61	M	Goose Island Ramblers: "Ole Olson, the Hobo from Norway"	4:09
62	C/I	More on the Goose Island Ramblers; Bollerud interview	1:00
63	C/I	Intro to "Mrs. Johnson"; Bollerud comments	1:12
64	M	Goose Island Ramblers: "Mrs. Johnson, Turn Me Loose"	3:40
65	M	Goose Island Ramblers: "Black Mountain Rag"	1:29

Key for Letter Codes

I = Interview or comments from performers/consultants

M = Musical selection

C = Comments from hosts Jim Leary or Rick March

Index

Note: All place names (except major cities) are in Wisconsin unless otherwise indicated.

"Mother the Queen of My Heart," 178
"Mountain Dew," 137, 142, 145, 151
Mount Hope, 132
Mount Horeb, 21, 111, 159
"Mrs. Johnson, Turn Me Loose," 135–136, 137, 140, 142, 151, 152
Muddy Waters, 117
"Muleskinner Blues," 126
Muleskinners, the, 58
Munising, Michigan, 177
"My Blue Eyes Have Gone," 65, 70–71, 151
"My Fatherland," 22
"My Good Gal's Gone Blues," 139
"My Happiness," 111
"My Little Girl," 98
"My Name Is Yon Yonson," 134
"My Old Kentucky Home," 42, 43
"My Pretty Quadroon," 42, 43

National Folk Festival, 174, 175
Natvig, Trace, 53
"Near the Cross," 7
Neighbor Ike, 58
Nelson, Red, 58
Nelson, Tracy, 153, 214n10
Nettl, Bruno, 182–183
Newberry, Michigan, 177, 178
Newell, William Wells, 161–164, 166–168, 172
New Glarus, as a site for Swiss musical performers, 21, 115, 174; in the experiences of the Goose Island Ramblers, 110, 113, 114, 123. See also Swiss American music
New Lost City Ramblers, 30
Newport Folk Festival, 30
"New Roswell Schottische," 34
New Ulm, Minnesota, 118
"Nikolina," 24, 108–109, 136, 139, 151, 211n5
"Nobody's Darling but Mine," 60, 107
"No Norwegians in Dickeyville," 133–134, 157
Nordic Rhythm Boys, 104
Northfield, Minnesota, 173
North Freedom, 83, 84, 86, 87
Norwegian American music, in the Upper Midwest, 6–9, 13, 15, 17, 19, 21, 24, 25, 29, 32, 36, 98, 99, 120, 149, 164, 170, 174, 175, 176, 210–211n3, 213n2; in the repertoire of the Goose Island Ramblers, 38, 49–54, 62, 64, 76, 83, 93, 103, 105–111, 114, 116, 119, 120, 121, 125, 130, 131, 132, 133–134, 135–136, 138, 140, 141, 143, 146, 151, 152, 156, 160
Norwegian Hill Billies, the, 33–34
"Norwegian War Chant," 140, 143, 152, 158, 159
novelty musical performances, 28, 66, 93–99, 134–135, 143–145, 210n9
"Ny Fiskar Vals" (New Fisherman's Waltz), 119

O'Connor, Ralph, 64
O'Connor, "Red Jack," 209n2
Oconto, 174
Odanah, 173
"O Dem Golden Slippers." See "Golden Slippers"
Oja, Harold, 7
Oja, Niilo, 7
Ojibwe music, 7, 173, 178. See also metís fiddle music
O'Kane, Hank, 77
"Oklahoma Home," 68
Olaf the Swede, 33
"Old Joe Clark," 145, 152
"Old Mother Flanagan," 178
"Old Rose Waltz," 34
"Old Time Mazurka," 7
old time music, as a term, 26–31, 85, 97, 205n23, 209n7
Ole and Lena, 99, 107–108, 109–110, 132, 143
"Ole Olson, the Hobo from Norway," 6, 107–108, 110, 134, 151, 210–211n3
Ollie i Skratthult. See Peterson, Hjalmar
Olson Sisters, the, 213n2
Omro, 29
O'Neil, Dennis, 18, 19
"One Trail for Me," 68
Ontanogan, Michigan, 177
"On the Beach of Waikiki," 79, 142
"On the Beach at Waunakee," 140, 142–143, 152
"Orange Blossom Special," 140

Wicentowski, Jerry, 129
Wickboldt, Helen, 39, 63
Widden, Charles, 7, 211n5
"Wildwood Flower," 65, 148
Wildwoods, the, 7–8, 202n6
Wileman, Laurence, 69
Wilfahrt, Hans "Whoopee John."
  See Whoopee John's Orchestra
Williams, Doc, 35
Williams, Hank, 139
Williams, Jim, 20
Williams, Milo "Cy," 35
Williams, Roger, 40
"Willie Down by the Pond," 138
Willmer, Minnesota, 29
Wills, Bob, 4, 64, 83, 85, 87, 96,
  209n5
"Will the Circle Be Unbroken," 139
"Will You Love Me When I'm Old?"
  45
Winona, Minnesota, 98
Wisconsin Arts Board, 155
Wisconsin Folklife Center, 155
Wisconsin Folk Museum, 155, 156
Wisconsin Historical Society.
  See State Historical Society of
  Wisconsin
Wisconsin Lumberjacks, the, 175
Wisconsin sesquicentennial folklife
  festival, 159
Wiseman, Scott "Skyland Scotty,"
  147. See also Lulu Belle and
  Scotty
Wolowic, Stan, 34
Woodford, Elmer, 16
Woodford, Fred, 15–16, 27, 35
Woodford, Glen, 16
Woodford, Guy (aka Guy Wood),
  16, 27–28
Woodhull's Old Tyme Masters, 97,
  209n7

Woodchoppers, the, 7
Woodhull's Old Tyme Masters, 97
Woodman, 132
Woods, Hal, 93
"Wreck of the Old 97," 56, 137,
  142
"W Żelaznej Fabryce" (In a Steel
  Mill), 178

"Yankee Doodle," 48, 94, , 207n6
Yankovic, Frankie, 7, 117,
  122–123, 124
Yankton, South Dakota, 60
"Ye Olde Rye Waltz," 34. See also
  "Rye Waltz"
Yiddish songs and tunes. See
  Jewish American music
yodeling, in the Upper Midwest,
  6, 20–21, 27, 34, 54, 57, 206n4;
  in the repertoire of the Goose
  Island Ramblers, 38, 64, 110,
  129, 148, 156. See also Rodgers,
  Jimmie
Yogi Yorgesson, 135–136, 212n1
"You Gotta Quit Kickin' My Dog
  Around," 139
Young, Faron, 148

Zabel, Tony, 58
Zamphir, 7
Zastrow, Al, 120
"Zidana Marela/Silk Umbrella
  Polka," 122
Zimmerman, Robert. See Dylan,
  Bob
"Zip Coon," 77
Zittau, 15
"Zum Lauterbach Hab Ich Mein
  Strumpf Gelorn," 29, 35, 81
Zvonimir Orchestra, the, 23
Zwigoff, Terry, 201n3

LaVergne, TN USA
25 October 2010

202115LV00001B/2/P